THE CAMBRIDGE COMPANION TO
# MALEBRANCHE

Each volume of this series of companions to major philosophers contains specially commissioned essays by an international team of scholars, together with a substantial bibliography, and will serve as a reference work for students and
nonspecialists. One aim of the series is to dispel the intimi-
dation such readers often feel when faced with the work of a
difficult and challenging thinker.

The French philosopher and theologian Nicholas Malebranche (1638–1715) was one of the most important figures
of the early modern period. A bold and unorthodox thinker,
he tried to synthesize the new philosophy of Descartes with
the religious Platonism of St. Augustine. This is the first
collection of essays to address Malebranche's thought com-
prehensively and systematically. There are chapters devoted
to Malebranche's metaphysics, his doctrine of the soul, his
epistemology, the celebrated debate with Arnauld, his philosophical method, his occasionalism and theory of causality,
his philosophical theology, his account of freedom, his moral
philosophy, and his intellectual legacy.

New readers will find this the most convenient and accessible guide to Malebranche currently available. Advanced
students and specialists will find a conspectus of recent developments in the interpretation of Malebranche.

*The Cambridge Companion to*
# MALEBRANCHE

Edited by

Steven Nadler
*University of Wisconsin, Madison*

PUBLISHED BY THE PRESS SYNDICATE OF THE UNIVERSITY OF CAMBRIDGE
The Pitt Building, Trumpington Street, Cambridge, United Kingdom

CAMBRIDGE UNIVERSITY PRESS
The Edinburgh Building, Cambridge CB2 2RU, UK    http://www.cup.cam.ac.uk
40 West 20th Street, New York, NY 10011-4211, USA    http://www.cup.org
10 Stamford Road, Oakleigh, Melbourne 3166, Australia
Ruiz de Alarcón 13, 28014 Madrid, Spain

© Cambridge University Press 2000

First published 2000

Printed in the United States of America

*Typeface* Trump Medieval 10/13 pt.    *System* LATEX 2$_\varepsilon$   [TB]

*A catalog record for this book is available from the British Library.*

*Library of Congress Cataloging in Publication Data*
The Cambridge companion to Malebranche / edited by Steven Nadler.
     p.  cm.
     Includes bibliographical references.
     ISBN 0-521-62212-3 (hardcover) – ISBN 0-521-62729-X (pbk.)
     1. Malebranche, Nicolas, 1638–1715.  I. Nadler, Steven M., 1958–
     B1897.C36 2000
     194 – dc21

                                                  00-022060


ISBN 0 521 62212 3   hardback
ISBN 0 521 62729 X   paperback

# CONTENTS

vii

     Human Justice
     PATRICK RILEY                                          220

10   The Critical Reception of Malebranche, from His Own
     Time to the End of the Eighteenth Century
     STUART BROWN                                           262

11   Malebranche's Life and Legacy
     ANDRÉ ROBINET                                          288

     Bibliography                                           305

     Index                                                  317

# CONTRIBUTORS

JEAN-CHRISTOPHE BARDOUT is Maître de conférences at the Université de Brest. He is the author of *Malebranche et la métaphysique* (Presses Universitaires de France, 1999).

STUART BROWN is Professor of Philosophy at the (British) Open University. He has written extensively on seventeenth- and eighteenth-century philosophy, especially on Leibniz. He has a particular interest in the critical reception of Malebranche, and was editor of and contributor to *Nicolas Malebranche: His Philosophical Critics and Successors* (Van Gorcum, 1991).

NICHOLAS JOLLEY is Professor of Philosophy at Syracuse University. He is the author of *Leibniz and Locke: A Study of the New Essays on Human Understanding* (Oxford, 1984), *The Light of the Soul: Theories of Ideas in Leibniz, Malebranche and Descartes* (Oxford, 1990), and *Locke: His Philosophical Thought* (Oxford, 1999). He is the editor of *The Cambridge Companion to Leibniz* (Cambridge, 1995) and (with translator David Scott) *Nicholas Malebranche, Dialogues on Metaphysics and on Religion* (Cambridge, 1997).

ELMAR J. KREMER is Professor of Philosophy at the University of Toronto. His recent publications include a translation, with introduction, of Antoine Arnauld, *On True and False Ideas, New Objections to Descartes's Meditations, and Descartes's Replies* (Edwin Mellon Press, 1990), and articles on Arnauld in *The Great Arnauld and Some of His Philosophical Correspondents* (University of Toronto Press, 1994) and *Interpreting Arnauld* (University of Toronto Press, 1996), both of which he also edited; *Chroniques de Port-Royal* (44: 1995), and *Logic and the Workings of the Mind*, edited by Patricia A. Easton (1997).

THOMAS M. LENNON is Professor of Philosophy at the University of Western Ontario. He is the author of *The Battle of the Gods and Giants* (Princeton, 1993) and *Reading Bayle* (Toronto, 1999).

DENIS MOREAU is Maître de conférences at the Université de Nantes. He is the author of *Deux cartésiens: La polémique entre Antoine Arnauld et Nicolas Malebranche* (Paris: J. Vrin, 1999). He is also the editor of *Lettre-préface des Principes de la Philosophie de Descartes* (Paris: Garnier-Flammarion, 1996), and *Livre IV de la Somme contre les Gentils de Thomas d'Aquin* (Garnier-Flammarion, 1999).

STEVEN NADLER is Professor of Philosophy at the University of Wisconsin, Madison. He is the author of *Arnauld and the Cartesian Philosophy of Ideas* (Princeton, 1989), *Malebranche and Ideas* (Oxford, 1992), and *Spinoza: A Life* (Cambridge, 1999). He is the editor of *Malebranche: Philosophical Selections* (Hackett, 1992), *Causation in Early Modern Philosophy* (Penn State Press, 1993), and *A Companion to Early Modern Philosophy* (Blackwell, forthcoming).

PATRICK RILEY is Professor of Political Science at the University of Wisconsin, Madison. He is the author of numerous works in the history of philosophy, including *The General Will Before Rousseau* (Princeton, 1986) and, most recently, *Leibniz's Universal Jurisprudence: Justice as the Charity of the Wise* (Cambridge, 1996). He has also edited Kant's political writings and Leibniz's political writings.

ANDRÉ ROBINET is Professor at the Université Libre de Bruxelles and Director of Research at the Centre Nationale de la Recherche Scientifique (CNRS), Paris. He is the author of numerous editions and studies on modern and contemporary philosophy.

DONALD RUTHERFORD is Associate Professor of Philosophy at the University of California, San Diego. He is the author of *Leibniz and the Rational Order of Nature* (Cambridge, 1995) and articles on a variety of topics in early modern philosophy.

TAD SCHMALTZ is Associate Professor of Philosophy at Duke University. He is the author of *Malebranche's Theory of the Soul* (Oxford, 1996), and of various essays on the history of early modern philosophy.

# ABBREVIATIONS

The following abbreviations are used for references to Malebranche's writings. All other works cited by author and year of publication are found, with full reference information, in the bibliography.

| | |
|---|---|
| *OC* | *Oeuvres complètes de Malebranche* |
| *Search* | *De la recherche de la vérité* |
| *LO* | *The Search After Truth*, translated by Thomas M. Lennon and Paul J. Olscamp |
| *Dialogues* | *Entretiens sur la métaphysique* |
| *JS* | *Dialogues on Metaphysics*, translated by Nicholas Jolley and David Scott |
| *TNG* | *Traité de la nature et de la grace* |
| *R* | *Treatise on Nature and Grace*, translated by Patrick Riley |

The following abbreviations are used for writings by other philosophers.

| | |
|---|---|
| AT | *Oeuvres de Descartes*, edited by Charles Adam and Paul Tannery |
| CSM | *The Philosophical Writings of Descartes*, translated by John Cottingham, Robert Stoothoff, and Dugald Murdoch |
| VFI | Antoine Arnauld, *Des vraies et des fausses idées* |
| OA | *Oeuvres de Messire Antoine Arnauld* |
| K | Arnauld, *On True and False Ideas*, translated by E. J. Kremer |

STEVEN NADLER

# Introduction

When the great philosopher, scientist and mathematician René
Descartes died in 1650, some of his most vehement opponents –
and there were many – must have hoped that would be the end of his
philosophy as well. Little did they suspect that Cartesianism would
be the dominant philosophical paradigm for the rest of the century.
In France, the most important Cartesian – perhaps, in fact, the most
important philosopher – of this period was a Catholic priest from a
prominent and well-connected family in Paris. Nicolas Malebranche
was widely recognized by his philosophical and theological contemporaries across seventeenth-century Europe as an intellectual force to
be reckoned with, a bold and unorthodox synthesizer of the thought
of St. Augustine and Descartes and a systematic thinker of the first
rank.

Thus, it is surprising that Malebranche is only now finding his
rightful place in the pantheon of early modern figures – along with
Descartes, Spinoza, Leibniz, and the others – deemed worthy of study
by contemporary philosophers in the Anglo-American tradition. (The
French, of course, have recognized his importance all along.) While
Malebranche's thought is deeply rooted in his theological agenda
and, more broadly, in the particular intellectual and religious environment of early modern France, much of it is of perennial philosophical value, and plenty of his ideas and arguments continue to
be of interest to philosophers today. Malebranche is most famous –
or, as some would prefer to say, infamous – for his doctrine of occasionalism, an often ridiculed theory in which God is the only true
and active causal agent in the universe. However, this doctrine is
grounded both in a sophisticated analysis of the nature of causal relations and in a clear perception of the metaphysical problems facing

I

a substance ontology. His equally theocentric theory of knowledge, the so-called "doctrine of the vision in God," while soundly rejected for its "enthusiasm" by such a thinker as John Locke, nonetheless rests on an important and influential critique of Cartesian episte-mology and an analysis of truth and representation.

This is not to say that one should ignore much of what Male-branche himself deemed crucial in his system (the theological frame-work) in order to get at a few "analytical" gems. The beauty of any philosophical system lies in its organic unity and economy, in the way a few basic and simple principles are used to resolve a variety of problems. As the essays in this volume show, the interest and importance of Malebranche's philosophy lies not just in some of the particular arguments or theses he offered to resolve one conundrum or another, but also in the way all the parts of his system fit together into a coherent whole. For example, when looked at in its proper context – as an answer to some pressing philosophical and scientific problems facing the new mechanistic physics of the seventeenth cen-tury to which Malebranche was committed – occasionalism starts to shed some of its prima-facie absurdity. A divine being may not be the sole efficacious agent in nature, but in its time the theory made good sense as a way to resolve some of the tensions within Cartesian nat-ural philosophy. Some of the considerations offered in its behalf are, as many philosophers have seen, still compelling.

Hume, perhaps the most important philosopher ever on the prob-lem of causation, recognized the role Malebranche played in rais-ing the crucial questions about our knowledge of necessary connec-tions in nature. Leibniz's solution to the problem of evil owes much to Malebranche's theodicy. Further, Locke credited Malebranche for at least seeing the difficulties inherent in the traditional Cartesian account of mental representations. However, the full impact of Malebranche's *oeuvre* comes only when one sees the larger picture and recognizes how the metaphysics, the epistemology, the philo-sophical theology, the moral philosophy, and the science all fit to-gether to produce one of the most creative and original philosophical systems of the early modern period.

Nicolas Malebranche was born in Paris on August 6, 1638, one of the many children of Nicolas Malebranche, a royal secretary, and his wife, Catherine de Lauzon. Because of a malformation of the spine – a painful condition that would affect him for the rest of his life – he was kept at home for his education, under the direction of his intelligent and pious mother, until the age of sixteen. In 1654, he entered the Collège de la Marche, from which he graduated two years later as Maître ès Arts. The education he received there, heavily laden with Aristotelianism, left Malebranche highly dissatisfied. After studying theology for three years at the Sorbonne – a Scholastic curriculum with which he was equally discontent – and rejecting the offer of a canonry at Notre-Dame de Paris, Malebranche entered the Oratory in 1660. He was ordained on September 14, 1664.

His four years in the Oratory proved to be of great intellectual consequence for Malebranche, particularly with respect to his philosophical and theological development. The order had been founded in 1611 by Cardinal Bérulle, who had a deep veneration for St. Augustine and who was also a good friend of Descartes (although the Oratory was, on the whole, firmly anti-Cartesian in its sentiments). While studying Biblical criticism, ecclesiastical history, and Hebrew, Malebranche, like the other Oratorians, immersed himself in the writings of Augustine. He also certainly knew of the doctrines of Descartes through those professors of the order who considered themselves adherents of this new philosophy. He did not actually read any of Descartes' works, however, until 1664, when, strolling down the rue St. Jacques, he happened upon a copy of Descartes' *Treatise on Man* (*L'Homme*) in a bookstall. The event was life-changing: Malebranche's early biographer, Father Yves André, tells us that the joy of becoming acquainted with so many discoveries "caused him such palpitations of the heart that the had to stop reading in order to recover his breath." Malebranche devoted the next ten years of his life to studying mathematics and philosophy, especially of the Cartesian variety. He was particularly taken with Descartes' critique of the Aristotelian philosophy, which he had earlier found so stultifying and sterile.

Those years of study culminated in the publication in 1674–75 of *The Search After Truth* (*De la recherche de la vérité*), Malebranche's most important work. The *Search* represents a grand synthesis of the systems of Malebranche's two intellectual (and spiritual) mentors, Augustine and Descartes. It is a wide-ranging treatise that deals with questions of knowledge, metaphysics, physics, sense physiology, methodology, and philosophical theology. Malebranche's stated goal in the *Search* is to investigate the sources of human error and to direct us toward the clear and distinct perception of truth: truth about ourselves, about the world around us, and about God. He is ultimately concerned to demonstrate the essential and fundamentally active role of God in every aspect – material, cognitive, and moral – of the world he has created. This becomes particularly clear when one considers the three main doctrines to which Malebranche owes his reputation: occasionalism, the vision in God, and his theodicy.

According to the "doctrine of occasional causes," as Leibniz labeled it, all finite created entities are absolutely devoid of causal efficacy. God is the only true causal agent. Bodies do not cause effects in other bodies or in minds, and minds do not cause effects in bodies or even within themselves. God is directly, immediately and solely responsible for bringing about all phenomena. When a needle pricks the skin, the physical event is merely an occasion for God to cause the relevant mental state (pain); a volition in the soul to raise an arm or to think of something is only an occasion for God to cause the arm to rise or the idea to be present to the mind; and the impact of one billiard ball upon another is an occasion for God to move the second ball. In all three contexts – mind-body, body-body, and mind alone – God's ubiquitous causal activity proceeds in accordance with certain general laws, and (except in the case of miracles) God acts only when the requisite material or psychic conditions obtain.

The doctrine of the vision in God demonstrates how we as knowers are as cognitively dependent upon the divine understanding as bodies in motion are ontologically dependent upon the divine will. Malebranche agreed with Descartes and other philosophers that ideas, or immaterial representations present to the mind, play an essential role in knowledge and perception. However, whereas Descartes' ideas are mental entities, or modifications of the soul, Malebranche argued that the ideas that function in human cognition are in God; they just are the essences and eternal archetypes that exist in the divine understanding. As such, they are eternal and independent of finite minds, and our access to them makes possible the clear and distinct apprehension of objective, necessary truth. Malebranche presented the vision in God as the correct Augustinian view, albeit modified in the light of Descartes' epistemological distinction between understanding (via clear and distinct concepts) and sensation. The theory explains both our knowledge of universals and of mathematical and moral principles, as well as the conceptual element that, he argued, necessarily informs our perceptual acquaintance with the world. Like Descartes' theory of ideas – in which God guarantees our rational faculties – Malebranche's doctrine is at least partly motivated by an anti-skepticism, because divine ideas cannot fail to reveal either eternal truths or the essences of things in the world created by God.

Finally, Malebranche, in his theodicy – or explanation of how God's wisdom, goodness, and power are to be reconciled with the apparent imperfections and evils in the world – claimed that God could have created a more perfect world, free from all the defects that plague this one, but that this would have involved greater complexity in the divine ways. God must act in the manner most in accord with his nature. Thus, God always acts in the simplest way possible and only by means of lawlike general volitions; God never acts by "particular" or ad hoc volitions. This means that, while on any particular occasion God could intervene and forestall an apparent evil that is about to occur by the ordinary course of the laws of nature (for example, a drought), he will not do so, for this would compromise the simplicity of his *modi operandi*. The perfection or goodness of the world per se is thus relativized to the simplicity of the laws of that world (or, which is the same thing, to the generality of the divine volitions that, on the occasionalist view, govern it). Taken together, the laws and the phenomena of the world form a whole that is most worthy of God's nature – in fact, the best combination possible. This account explains God's manner of operation, not just in the natural world of body and mind-body union, but also in the moral world of beings endowed with freedom who depend upon grace for their everlasting happiness.

While the Abbé Simon Foucher (1644–97), canon of Sainte Chappelle of Dijon, was the first in a long line of critics of Malebranche's doctrines, the Jansenist theologian and Cartesian philosopher Antoine Arnauld (1612–94) was undoubtedly the harshest, the most acute, and the most dogged. Arnauld approved of the *Search* upon first reading it. However, when he later learned of Malebranche's views on grace and divine providence – only sketchily presented in the *Search* but more fully expounded in the *Treatise on Nature and Grace* (*Traité de la nature et de la grace*) in 1680 – he embarked on a detailed critique of the major elements of the *Search*. Arnauld's *Des vraies et des fausses idées*, published in 1683, and Malebranche's reply, *Réponse du Père Malebranche au livre des vraies et des fausses idées* (1684), were only the opening salvos of what would come to be a long and often bitter public battle on both philosophical and (more important, at least to the participants) theological matters. Although Arnauld succeeded in having the *Treatise* put on the Index of Prohibited Books in 1690 (the *Search* was added in 1709), their exchanges – public and private – continued until Arnauld's death. The Malebranche-Arnauld debate is one of the great intellectual events of the seventeenth century, and it attracted the attention of many, including Leibniz, Locke, and Newton.

After the publication of the *Search*, Malebranche turned to a "justification" of the Catholic religion and morality, presented in suitably Malebranchian terms, published as the *Conversations Chrétiennes* in 1677. This was followed in 1683 by the *Méditations Chrétiennes et métaphysiques*, which consists of dialogues in which "The Word" explains and defends Malebranche's system. That same year, Malebranche also published his *Traité de morale*, in which he undertakes a rigorous demonstration of a true Christian ethic.

By the mid-1680s, Malebranche's reputation as the most important, if highly unorthodox, representative of the Cartesian philosophy was secure. He was corresponding with thinkers such as Leibniz, who criticized the Cartesian account of the laws of motion (as well as Malebranche's occasionalism), and the physicist Pierre-Sylvain Régis, who defended a more orthodox brand of Cartesianism and engaged Malebranche in a debate over some points in natural philosophy and over the nature of ideas.

Having been forced in his polemics with Arnauld, Régis, Foucher, and others to clarify, develop, and even modify his doctrines, Malebranche decided, at the urging of friends, to compose a treatise that both presented an up-to-date and concise picture of his theories and defended them as the proper Augustinian (and Catholic) system. The *Dialogues on Metaphysics* (*Entretiens sur la métaphysique*) were published in 1688 and were supplemented in 1696 by the *Entretiens sur la mort*, which Malebranche wrote after an illness from which he had not expected to recover. In 1699, he was elected to the Académie Royale des Sciences for his *Traité des lois de la communication du mouvement* (1682).

During the last decade and a half of his life, Malebranche remained actively engaged in philosophical, theological, and scientific matters, publishing the *Entretien d'un philosophe chrétien avec un philosophe chinois, sur l'existence et la nature de Dieu* in 1708 and his *Réflexions sur la prémotion physique* in 1715. He also continued to work on the *Search*, producing the sixth edition, the last to appear in his lifetime, in 1712.

On June 20, 1715, Malebranche became ill while visiting a friend in Villeneuve St. Georges. A few days later, he was taken back to the Oratory in Paris, where he died on October 13.

# 1 Malebranche and Method

The title of Malebranche's first, longest, and most important work might well have been *Discourse on Method*, for method is what *The Search After Truth* is most obviously about. Its subtitle adumbrates the centrality of method: *wherein are treated the nature of man's mind and the use he must make of it to avoid error in the sciences.* The importance of finding a method to avoid error is expressed in the first sentence of the *Search's* first book: "error is the cause of men's misery," for from it comes the evil that upsets human happiness. Each of the five major occasions of error is detailed by the first five books of the work, and the last book, on method, indicates "the paths leading to knowledge of the truth" (*Search* VI.1.i, OC 2:245; LO 408). The method that Malebranche proposes is, like his vision of all things in God, a highly original result of correcting Descartes in light of the Christianized Platonism that he received from Augustine.

The seventeenth century was the *belle époque* of method. The prominence of scientific advance in the period was such that extreme epistemic optimism was pandemic. It seemed that among rationalists everything was knowable and would soon be known, and that even among empiricists who set limits to human knowledge, those limits would soon be achieved. A sharp break from all precedent was universally perceived; these moderns felt that they were uniquely doing something right, and somehow doing it systematically given the results being achieved, thus the preoccupation with the discovery and articulation of method. (Whether the break with the past was as sharp as the moderns thought is, of course, another question. Nor did the pandemic optimism preclude the period from also being the *belle epoche* of skepticism.[1])

8

Method had long been viewed as a part of logic, typically occupying the fourth part of logic books, after parts on concept, judgment, and inference. This quadripartite division of logic survives in such disparate seventeenth-century authors as the scholastic Eustache de St. Paul, the empiricist Pierre Gassendi, and the Cartesian Antoine Arnauld. Descartes, who was Malebranche's main source for method as for so much of his work, treated method somewhat differently and generally had contempt for the traditional logic he was taught. Logic seemed at first to have taught him something, "but on further examination I observed with regard to logic that syllogisms and most of its other techniques are of less use for learning things than for explaining to others the things one already knows or even, as in the art of Lully, for speaking without judgment about matters of which one is ignorant."[2] However, Descartes' condemnation of logic is not wholesale, for there is a retrievable kind of logic that he recommends for study. "I do not mean the logic of the Schools, for this is strictly speaking nothing but a dialectic which teaches ways of expounding to others what one already knows or even of holding forth without judgment about things one does not know. Such logic corrupts good sense without increasing it. I mean instead the kind of logic which teaches us to direct our reason with a view to discovering truths of which we are ignorant."[3]

Malebranche treats concept (simple perception), judgment, and inference in stepwise fashion, but he does so almost incidentally as part of the distinction he draws between understanding and will (*Search* I.2.i, OC 1:49; LO 7). They are certainly not the divisions of anything like a logic for him. Indeed, he uses the term "logic," invariably and irretrievably, as a term of abuse.[4] A good example of Malebranche's disdain for what he calls logic is his diagnosis of the empty terms of Aristotelian scholasticism. The physics displaced by seventeenth-century mechanism explained observable qualities by attributing to things powers or occult qualities that produce them. (In Molière's parodical but accurate example, opium produces sleep because of its dormative power.) The scholastics do not explain these powers in terms of mechanism's specific concepts of colliding particles, according to Malebranche, but instead have in mind only the vague idea of being in general. Their terms apply to everything and thus, in an informative way, to nothing at all. Such terms are what Malebranche calls "logical" (*Search* III.2.viii; LO 241–7).

This departure from traditional logic and, at least nominally, from Descartes is indicative of Malebranche's methodological originality. Here he ignored the main thrust of seventeenth-century views on method (section I, the context for method) and rejected key components in Descartes' method (section II, the metaphysical foundations of method). Only with these contrasts in place can the significance of his own novel views be appreciated (section III, the application of method).

## I.  THE CONTEXT FOR METHOD

Method was generally conceived of as a means to gain knowledge. However, to gain knowledge, one must start someplace, and where else but with what is already known? Even to frame a question, something must be known, if only the terms of the question. In the acquisition of knowledge, the rabbinical apothegm holds true: It takes a pair of tongs to make a pair of tongs. As Descartes puts it: "In every problem, of course, there has to be something unknown – otherwise the inquiry would be pointless. Nevertheless, this unknown something must be delineated by definite conditions [*certis conditionibus ... designatum*], which decidedly point us in one direction rather than another."[5] This requirement that the question be conditioned suggests a two-step dynamic, from what is known to what is unknown and back. The general situation is modeled by a jigsaw puzzle. One realizes that a piece is missing, a piece of a certain shape, and one looks for a piece of that shape; having found it, one then fits it into the empty space. The structure of knowledge is like the puzzle; method's two-step dynamic amounts to locating the missing piece and then fitting it into its proper place.

In several respects, this binary conception of method was a legacy conveyed to the seventeenth century. The century inherited both the Ramist conception of method as a guideline for presenting a discipline and the conception from Zabarella of method that yields Aristotelian scientific syllogisms. The latter, which was to be the more influential, might be seen as subsuming the former with a distinction between the ordering of a subject [*ordo*] and the logical technique of discovery [*methodus*]. Method in the latter sense was itself divided into two parts. One was an *a posteriori*, analytic, resolutive technique that was thought of as dealing with Aristotelian *demonstratio quia*, or reasoning from effects to causes. The other part was an *a priori*, synthetic, compositive technique that was thought of as dealing with Aristotelian *demonstratio propter quid*, or reasoning from causes to effects. The shift from the first to the second technique could be achieved only if not just concomitants but necessary causes had been reached. For this, Zabarella invoked a mysterious process he called *consideratio* or *negotiatio*.[6]

Virtually everyone of philosophical interest in the seventeenth century who had anything at all to say about method adopted some version of the binary dynamic. This two-step movement might naturally be thought of as attractive primarily to those thinkers who claimed to move, by means of it, from appearance or the accidents of things to reality or the essences of things and conversely. No less naturally, they are to be found claiming certainty in the resultant knowledge claims. However, the dynamic was found even among those who claimed only probability from their method and who restricted knowledge to appearances or accidents of things. Bacon, with his elaborate "tables," is something of an exception here to the binary conception of method, but it is to be clearly found in such a fallibilist phenomenalists as Hobbes. An especially good example from this class is Gassendi.

Method for Gassendi tended to diminish in importance just because he thought its product is achieved once we have the other three parts of logic: concepts (imagination) yielding propositions (judgment) in turn yielding syllogisms (reason). Even so, his *Institutio logica* (1658) set out three types of method, each of which mobilizes the two-step dynamic. The method of discovery (*inventio*) is aimed at finding a middle term for syllogism. Depending on whether it begins with the major or minor terms (i.e., with the predicate or subject of the conclusion to be demonstrated) it employs synthesis or analysis, "just as a hunting dog, if he cannot see his prey, seizes upon its track and sniffs along until the prey is uncovered."[7] The method of judgment (*iudicium*) employs the same procedures as a check against each other, as in verifying addition by subtraction and conversely, because, "as Aristotle said, it must be the same journey from Athens to Thebes as from Thebes to Athens."[8] Finally, the method of instruction (*doctrina*) is designed to inculcate knowledge, either practical (e.g., building) or theoretical (e.g., geometry). In the first case, one may begin with the nails, planks, and so forth and proceed to the house or conversely; and in the second case with points, lines, and such and proceed to the object or conversely.

It was Descartes, of course, who famously authored the *Discourse on Method* (1637). However, the four rules constituting the alleged method of that otherwise largely autobiographical work seem risibly vacuous. When he distinguished between analysis and synthesis, he succeeded only in emphasizing the deficiencies of his method. At the very end of his *Objections* to the *Meditations*, Hobbes proposed that Descartes set out the entire argument of that work in geometrical fashion so as to be seen "at a single glance." Descartes in reply played two binary cards. One was to distinguish order, which is an arrangement according to dependence in a demonstration, from method of demonstration, which divides into analysis and synthesis (which are "directly opposite"). Analysis is said to be *a priori*, synthesis *a posteriori*, although its proof is said to be more often *a priori* than in analysis. (How Descartes seemingly reversed the *a priori-a posteriori* designations from their traditional meanings is not clear.[9]) According to Descartes, "it was synthesis alone that the ancients geometers usually employed in their writings. But in my view this was not because they were ignorant of analysis, but because they had such a high regard for it that they kept it to themselves like a sacred mystery. Now it is analysis alone which is the best and truest method of instruction [*via ... ad docendum*], and it was this method alone which I employed in my *Meditations*."[10] Although he proceeded, as requested, to give a recognizably synthetic, deductive account of the *Meditations*, his method of analysis, along with its relation to synthesis, remains no less mysterious than that of the ancients. For one thing, the argumentative procedure from self to God to world is not reversed in the synthetic account, which like the *Meditations* argues the existence of God as the cause of his idea of God. Nor could the procedure be reversed, for, while the steps in analysis are necessarily connected, they are not convertible: "We must note that very many necessary propositions, when converted, are contingent. Thus from the fact that I exist I may conclude with certainty that God exists, but from the fact that God exists I cannot legitimately assert that I too exist."[11]

The analytic-synthetic distinction gained greater prominence and wider dissemination from the "Port-Royal Logic" as Arnauld's *Logic or the art of thinking* (1662, with many subsequent editions) came to be known. This is an essentially Cartesian text, interweaving paraphrase and quotation from Descartes at key points on method in particular, but one that is also un-Cartesianly eclectic and conservative. It is divided into the traditional four parts to be found in Gassendi, for example, with the last being method, which is divided into analysis and synthesis. To the traditional contrastive terms of resolution and composition, it adds Gassendi's discovery and instruction. Analysis consists "more in judgment and mental skill than in particular rules," hence the four rules constituting the method of Descartes' *Discourse* get embedded here merely as useful, if sometimes difficult to follow, aids. There are hints of an unusually non-dynamical conception of method as a stationary, passive contemplation. For example, analysis is described as "paying attention to what is known in the issue we want to resolve" such that "truths are taken from a particular examination of the thing we are examining." However, generally the dynamic characteristic of the period is pronounced: In both methods "we should practice proceeding from what is better known to what is less well known ... these two methods differ only as the route one takes in climbing a mountain differs from the route taken in descending from the mountain into the valley, or as the two ways differ that are used to prove that a person is descended from St. Louis."[12] Unfortunately, there is an ambiguity, perhaps an incoherence, with respect to the direction taken by analysis, at least in the hands of geometers. "They assume what is at issue and examine what follows from that assumption. If in this examination they arrive at some clear truth from which the assumption follows necessarily, they conclude that the assumption is true."[13] Either analysis establishes premises from which the demonstrandum follows or it is disproved via a reductio. However, because the steps are not convertible equivalences, it cannot do both – not for Arnauld and Nicole, or for Descartes any more than for Pappus in antiquity, whose method of analysis was infected with the same problem.[14]

The Port-Royal *Logic* is not to be found among the seven works by Arnauld in Malebranche's library. However, he certainly knew the work, for he quotes from it a paragraph concerning the mind's finitude. Although the finite mind can understand proofs of the infinite divisibility of matter, it cannot comprehend that infinity itself.[15] It is good for the mind to exhaust itself in the futile effort to do so,

according to the *Logic*, "in order to tame its presumption and eliminate its audacity ever to oppose ... the truths offered it by the Church
under the pretext that it cannot understand them."[16] However, this
meeting of (finite) minds was in the first edition of the *Search*, nearly
a decade before the outbreak of hostilities with Arnauld. After a
decade of bitter debate, Malebranche returned to the *Logic* in his
*Third letter* (1699) to the now-deceased Arnauld, but only for an *ad
hominem* argument to be discussed below. Otherwise, Malebranche
took nothing from the *Logic*, and most importantly not the two-step
dynamic.

Malebranche, in fact, did not talk about synthesis at all. Further, he
used the term "analysis" in something like a modern sense; analysis
here is the art, revived by Vieta and Descartes as he said, of evaluating
magnitudes, including infinitely small ones, by equations (*Search*
III.1.iii, VI.1.v, VI.2.vi, OC 1:401, 2:293–4, 374–6; LO 209, 435–6,
483).[17] In this departure from the two-step dynamic Malebranche
was not only unique among major methodologists of the seventeenth
century, but also very forward-looking. To be sure, the dynamic continued to be appealed to, as by Newton in Query 31 of this *Optiks*,
and of course by Kant, who characterized the methodological difference between the *Critique of Pure Reason* and the *Prolegomena* in
these terms. However, today one need not be a Popperian to hold that
what was sought by the method of analysis as well as the means to
what is expressed by the method of synthesis are both, not logical,
but psychological matters. That is, our current inclination is to think
that the only light shed on how we discover the truth of a premise or
the proof of a deductive conclusion is likely to come from empirical
psychology. The methodological thrust of the seventeenth century
proved historically to be a dead-end.

An account of how Malebranche avoided this dead-end may be had
by returning to the epistemological problem addressed by the jigsaw
analogy. It was Plato who first identified this problem of coming-to-
know and who attempted to solve it with his theory of anemnesis:
Coming to know is really a matter of recollecting. The apparently
missing piece is there all along. Malebranche followed Plato in denying any real motion in discovery; both are, as it were, methodological
Parmenideans. For Malebranche too, the apparently missing piece
that we seek is always present to us and needs only to be seen more
clearly in order to be seen as such. We see more clearly by paying

closer attention. This notion of attention is obviously very important in Malebranche's account of method.[18]

## II. THE METAPHYSICAL BASIS FOR METHOD

Like Descartes, Malebranche took the mind to be a simple, indivisible substance and followed tradition, rather more closely, in drawing a distinction in it between two faculties. One is the understanding, which is a passive faculty of perception; the other is the will, which is an active power of decision. Malebranche, again like Descartes, primarily grounded his notion of method in the latter. In general terms, this reliance on the will is an indication of seventeenth-century optimism. The difference between knowledge and ignorance or error is entirely up to each individual.

Despite their agreement in these general terms, a radical difference existed between Descartes and Malebranche over the will's freedom, a difference with systematic implications for their conceptions of method. For Descartes, the human will, like the divine, has a freedom of indifference when it acts in the absence of some reason "pushing me in one direction rather than another." However, unlike God's freedom, this indifference in us is the "lowest grade of freedom." The highest grade would be when I am irresistibly pushed out of this indifference. "In order to be free, there is no need for me to be inclined both ways; on the contrary, the more I incline in one direction – either because I clearly understand that reasons of good and truth point that way, or because of a divinely produced disposition of my inmost thoughts – the freer is my choice."[19] For Malebranche also, the will can be free even if it does not have indifferent alternatives available – as the saints' will is vis-à-vis the beatific vision, or as ours is vis-à-vis such evident propositions as twice two is four. However, freedom of indifference is prized by him as "absolutely necessary" if we are to avoid error and if God is to be exculpated from our errors (*Search* I.2.ii, OC 1:54; LO 9–10).[20] Thus he builds indifference into the very definition of the soul's freedom.[21] The discrepant status of indifference points to Malebranche's rejection of Descartes' psychologism, and it is this that has the systematic implications for method.

The rejection of psychologism is also a part of Malebranche's Platonic inheritance. In the *Phaedo*, Socrates distinguished between the causal explanation of why he is in jail in terms of muscle, bones, and sinew, and the normative explanation in terms of why it is best for him to be there. Psychologism collapses this distinction. Specifically, psychologism here is the view that the normative concepts of logic and epistemology are reducible to the nonnormative concepts of psychology. The former tell us what we ought to believe and, in terms of standards, why we ought to; the latter tells us what we in fact believe and, in terms of causes, why we do. For Descartes, the reduction of the former to the latter is a result of the application of his method of doubt in response to skepticism.

Of the four rules comprising Descartes' method (be careful, divide the problem, order the elements, review your work) only the first is of any philosophical interest. He proposed to take care by "including nothing more in [his] judgments than what presented itself to [his] mind so clearly and so distinctly that [he] had no occasion to doubt it."[22] By famously discovering the indubitability of his own existence as long as he was thinking, Descartes sought to overthrow the skeptic's claim that everything could be doubted. But he thereby espoused psychologism. How so?

The clarity and distinctness that make doubt impossible are supposed to be an infallible criterion of truth. This connection is the central argument of *Meditations* II and III.[23] However, clarity and distinctness are psychological concepts, in two senses. First, they are properties of mental states, isolated as such in *Meditations* III before consideration of anything else. Second, they are causal properties: "The minds of all of us have been so moulded by nature that whenever we perceive something clearly, we spontaneously give our assent to it and are quite unable to doubt its truth."[24] Thus it is nature that breaks skepticism – as it did for the ancients and as it would for Hume, whose "gentle force" in the mind is not far removed from Descartes' clarity and distinctness.

Not incidentally, this psychologistic turn comports well with Descartes' highest grade of freedom, when the will is compelled to assent. However, it also opens up a cleavage between clarity and distinctness as a criterion of truth and truth itself, between the mental state and what is supposed to make it true. This cleavage is exploited by the skeptical Gassendi, who argued that the method of doubt must be insufficient because each go to the stake for opposite beliefs that they take to be clear and distinct.[25] In one sense, Descartes does not even try to bridge this gap, for he recognizes that we might have perfect certitude about something that "absolutely speaking" is false.[26] In another sense, he tries to overcome it with a proof of the reliability of clarity and distinctness based on God's inability to deceive. However, this proof, quite apart from the notorious circle that it involves, is itself a matter of what we are compelled to believe and thus overcomes Gassendi's skepticism only in psychological terms.[27]

Descartes' first rule, again, overcomes doubt by restricting acceptance to what we cannot help but accept because of its clarity and distinctness. (Thus freedom of indifference is in effect a faculty of error, always to be suppressed.) He initially framed this rule by saying that he was "never to accept anything as true if [he] did not have evident knowledge of its truth."[28] Now, very early in the *Search*, and more emphatically even than Descartes, Malebranche proposes a general rule for avoiding error that sounds very much like Descartes' first rule. Like Descartes' rule it concerns the proper function of the will: "*We should never give complete consent except to propositions which seem so evidently true that we cannot refuse it of them without feeling an inward pain and the secret reproaches of reason*" (*Search* I.2.iv, OC 55; LO 10).[29] However, from Malebranche we get a very different sort of rule. Perhaps most revealingly, the famous method of doubt does not appear in Malebranche. Nowhere in his work are propositions systematically held up to the indubitability test of clarity and distinctness in the fashion of Descartes' *Meditations*. Moreover, we get a decidedly nonpsychologistic reading of the rule. The "inward pain and secret reproaches of reason" that we feel in refusing to assent to what is evidently true (vs. Descartes' clear and distinct perceptions, to which we *cannot* refuse consent) is not some inner voice different from our own. Still less is it a negative feeling or a Human psychological force. Rather, Malebranche used metaphorical language to indicate that in some instances we know that unless we accept the truth of what we perceive, we are being just perverse. We should not give complete consent, as he puts it, "unless we knew that ill use would be made of our freedom if consent were not willed."[30]

The modal terms that Malebranche used in his various formulations of his rule, or comments on it, indicate that it is to be understood as a *normative* claim. Thus, when something appears entirely evident, the will is "obliged" to rest content with what is being represented and to assent to it because there is nothing further to be represented to it (*Search* I.2.ii, OC 1:51; LO 8). As he puts it in the *Treatise on Ethics*, we should withhold consent until "*invincibly* led to give it," and never believe until evidence *obliges*" us, for "when the mind clearly sees that it has examined all there is to examine . . . it necessarily rests and stops its investigation" (OC 6, 70–2). The kind of invincibility, obligation, and necessity here is not causal, still less metaphysical, but evidentiary.[31]

A good example of the difference between these kinds of necessity is found in Malebranche's theory of natural judgment. When we look at a star, according to Malebranche, what we actually see is not the star in the heavens but an idea that represents the star. It follows, he thinks, that "everyone who sees the stars in the heavens and who then voluntarily judges that they are there performs two false judgments, one of which is natural, the other free. One is a judgment of the senses or a compound sensation, which is within us, occurs independently of us, and even in spite of us, and according to which no judgment should be made. The other is a free judgment of the will, which can be avoided, and which consequently we must not make if we are to avoid error" (*Search* I.14.i, OC 1:156; LO 68). That we see a star as if in the heavens is causally constrained by God (who acts according to metaphysical necessity in producing our sensations of the star's motion), which is why our judgments of it, though not of its color, for example, contain at least "some measure of truth" (*Search* I.10, OC 1:122; LO 48). However, if from this natural judgment we were to infer that the star is in the heavens, our conclusion would come from an act of our indifferent will. Our will would be acting without necessity in the sense that its inference is unwarranted by any compelling evidence, for compatible with such evidence as it has, the star may have ceased to exist or, like the golden mountain, never have existed at all.

In short, Descartes' God is a brute force for truth as the evil genius of *Meditations* II is a brute force for error. As part of the method of doubt, the evil genius nowhere appears in Malebranche, while his God is rather a standard of truth. "The Master who teaches us inwardly wills that we listen to Him rather than to the authority of the greatest philosophers. It pleases Him to instruct us, provided that we apply ourselves to what He tells us. By meditation and very close attention we consult Him: and by a certain inward conviction and those inward reproaches He makes to those who do not submit, He answers us" (*Search* I.3.i, OC 1:60; LO 13). This master is not the kind who forces us slavishly to believe, but the kind who as a teacher shows us what we *ought* to believe. Once again, it is only metaphorically that we hear a voice at all. Less metaphorically, we are not *told* that something is true; we *see* that it is. Our "necessary union ... with universal Reason" was Malebranche's way of expressing out access to objective truth (*Elucidations* 10, OC 3:129–30; LO 613).[32] Not to accept it for what it is is possible only through the epistemic perversity of which we are necessarily aware. This is why neither the method of doubt nor any other is applied by Malebranche to refute skepticism, which he treats only with contempt.[33] For skepticism in this normative sense is simply perverse.

Thus far, the issue of psychologism with respect to Descartes' clarity and distinctness has been focused on their status as causal properties compelling belief. No less important for method is the other sense in which they are psychological concepts, that is, that they are properties of mental states. This status was at the core of Malebranche's long debate with Arnauld. These bitter opponents agreed that we should reason only on the basis of ideas that are clear and distinct, or evident as Malebranche preferred to put it, but disagreed on whether those ideas are mental states in the sense of being modifications of the mind. A good place to begin is with the *ad hominem* argument that Malebranche extracted from the Port-Royal *Logic*.

According to the *Logic*, following Descartes, axioms such as "the whole is greater than the part," which are so clear and distinct as to need no demonstration, depend on the principle that "everything contained in the clear and distinct idea of a thing can be truthfully affirmed of that thing." To deny this axiom principle, as it might be called, leads immediately to skepticism, as follows. "We judge things only by our ideas of them;" to be conceived they must be in the mind, which they are by means of their ideas. If this axiom principle were false, according to the *Logic*, then our judgments might possibly be only about what we *think* concerning things and not about the things *themselves*. We would be trapped in a circle of our own ideas, with no access to a mind-independent reality. Malebranche agreed with all of this. However, according to him, the skeptical result of denying the axiom principle shows that ideas, contrary to Arnauld, must be different from modifications of the mind. Ideas, and thus the things they represent, are not in the mind as modifications of it.[34]

Malebranche took the axiom principle to be the consequence of a still more basic principle that he variously expresses as follows: Nonbeing is not perceptible (*le néant n'est pas visible*); to perceive nothing is not to perceive; falsity or a relation that does not exist cannot be perceived; all that the mind directly perceives exists and exists as the mind perceives it (OC 8–9:953–4). He concludes from this principle that the mind's ideas are different from its modifications because the latter are, like the mind, finite, whereas our idea is infinite when we think of the infinite. Positively expressed, this first principle of all our knowledge, as he called it, shows that the idea of a thing must be prior (*préalable*) to our perception of it (*Search* IV.9.iii; OC 2:99; LO 320. *Conversations chrétiennes* III, OC 4:72). This priority is, of course, the vision of all things in God, expressed by "an infinity" of passages in Augustine (*Search* III.2.vi, OC 1:244; LO 233).

## III.  THE APPLICATION OF METHOD

Malebranche was less than fully clear in the *Search* about the specific aim of his method. "The aim of this final book [six, on method] is to render the mind as perfect as it can naturally be, by supplying the help necessary to extend its scope and make it more attentive and by laying down the rules that it must observe in the search after truth in order never to err, while in time learning all that it possibly can" (*Search* VI.1.i, OC 2:245; LO 408). As is suggested by the subtitle of the work and by the general rule concerning the proper functioning of the will, the aim may be primarily to avoid error. (Any truth encountered would be a happy, but unessential by-product.) Such would be an important aim, for as the opening paragraphs of the first book argue, error is the one and only cause of human misery. However, such a program is too suggestive of skeptical ataraxia to be espoused by this staunch opponent of skepticism. So perhaps the aim is to avoid error precisely by achieving truth. Error is still the main worry, but we avoid it by preempting it with truth. The idea is that the understanding because of its weakness would otherwise pose a constant temptation to precipitate judgment in violation of the will's general rule. As the title of the work suggests, however, the aim might be the even stronger one of truth and not just avoidance of error. The will's general rule would then be only a safeguard.[35]

It is not sufficient in the search after truth merely to follow the will's general rule never to accept the nonevident, which, while it may preserve us from error, does not guarantee arrival at truth. For that, the positive step must be taken of *applying* the mind. The mind's application is sufficient because the other condition, that is, the availability of ideas, is always satisfied. ("The Sun that illuminates minds is not like the sun that illuminates bodies; it is never eclipsed, and it penetrates everything without losing its strength" *Search* VI.i.i, OC 2:247; LO 410.)

Applying the mind takes two forms: (1) attention, and (2) increase in the mind's scope or capacity. Both invoke fundamental principles of Descartes. With respect to the first, "because, as everyone knows, there is nothing that makes [our perceptions] clearer and more distinct than attentiveness [*attention*], we must try to find the means to become more attentive than we are. In this way we shall preserve evidence in our inferences and see at a glance a necessary connection between all the parts of our longest deductions" (*Search* VI.i.ii, OC 2:250; LO 412). In particular, attention depends on a Cartesian theory of ideas. In order to make use of the axiom principle that everything contained in the idea of a thing can be asserted of that thing, we need only attend to the idea. Also, the intentionality of thought, its capacity to be *about* something, is secured by ideas. We intend a thing by attending to its idea.[36]

The mind must make the effort of attending to ideas because they affect it less than do the senses, the imagination, and the passions, which are thus great occasions of error. Even so, these latter kinds of awareness can with care be used as general aids in the search after truth. Vanity, for example, can motivate the search, and the senses and imagination can be employed in geometrical proofs. In addition, there are aids peculiar to certain people such as beverages, meats, places, dispositions of the body, and others (*Search* VI.i.iii-iv, OC 2:309–45; LO 414–30). We know from his biographer André that Malebranche himself relied on coffee and tobacco.

The imagination, like the senses from which it differs only in degree, is an occasion of error.[37] Nevertheless, the connection between ideas and brain traces, on which the imagination depends, gives it important heuristic value. Because there is no naturally necessary connection between our ideas of abstract and spiritual things and any brain traces, these ideas are difficult to understand and retain. Therefore, when we can explain them in relation to material things, the ideas of which do have a natural connection with our ideas of them, we are well-advised to do so.[38] The difference is between algebraic and geometrical representations of figures: the geometric idea of a cube is naturally tied to a brain trace, the algebraic expression $a^3$ is not. (As will be seen, however, algebra has compensating advantages.) A linguistic corollary is that we should adhere to the customary meaning of terms, whose connection to brain traces is already established (*Search* II.1.5, OC 1:220–1; LO 104–5).

"One can discover nothing without attention" (*Search* IV.11, OC 2:87; LO 313), but what is it to *attend* to an idea? The notion of attention here seems rather to resemble Zabarella's mysterious process of *consideratio* or *negotiatio*. The theological language that Malebranche employs perhaps initially heightens the mystery, but it expresses views recognizably lying at the core of his system. "Man participates in and is joined to Sovereign Reason, and the truth is revealed to him to the extent that he attends to and beseeches it. Now the soul's desire is a natural prayer which is always fulfilled, for it is a natural law that ideas are all the more present to the mind as the will more fervently desires them" (*Elucidations* II; OC 3:39; LO 559). The more we desire to think of something, and the quieter are the senses, the clearer becomes the idea of that thing, which is always present to us, however confusedly.[39]

The other way in which the mind is applied, increase in the mind's scope or capacity, is needed because the mind is limited in several respects. It cannot know, at least not perfectly, an infinite object – not just God, but even the infinite divisibility of matter, both of which are nonetheless demonstrable, and it cannot distinctly know several things simultaneously (*Search* III.1.ii, OC 2:390–1; LO 203). To be precise, Malebranche said that we can never actually *increase* the mind's scope or capacity and that all we can do is *preserve* it (*Search* VI.1.v, OC 2:282, 285–6; LO 431, 433). It is like a fixed quantity. He does not explain this quantity other than by explaining why one might be misled into thinking otherwise (e.g., by the number of our thoughts' objects or the frequency of their occurrence). Frequently, Malebranche was more concerned with his illustration than with what he used it to illustrate. In this case, he was concerned with the unique usefulness of arithmetic and algebra in expressing truth, which he took to be a real relation of either equality or inequality. The notion of thought as a fixed quantity may be that thought as an essence is a binary possibility: Either it is had fully or not at all. This comports, certainly, with Descartes' insistence on the indivisibility of essences, a point of very deep disagreement with Gassendi.[40] However, if this was the direction whence Malebranche was coming, then his methodological point was upset. For if in this sense the mind's thought cannot be *increased*, it cannot be *decreased* either, and the injunction to preserve it has no point. Arithmetic and algebra might be uniquely capable of expressing the truth, but their usefulness does not obviously extend to the mind's capacity or scope.[41]

Whatever the proper metaphor to describe the mind's operation here, arithmetic and algebra are "absolutely necessary" (*Search* VI.i.v, OC 2:282; LO 431), and this involves rules of method. Said Malebranche of these rules of method: "we should not expect anything very extraordinary here" (*Search* VI.i.i, OC 2:295; LO 437). One plausible reading of this disclaimer is that Malebranche had minimal expectations of the *results* of his rules.[42] Such a reduction might well follow, for example, from the case argued above for Malebranche's rejection of the two-step dynamic. Another reading, however, is that Malebranche was disclaiming only the exoticism of his rules, their novelty, and their inaccessibility. For the disclaimer continues: "[we should not expect] anything that surprises and taxes the mind very much. On the contrary, in order for these rules to be good, they must be simple and natural, few in number, very intelligible, and interdependent." On this reading, Malebranche might have been staking a great deal on his rules, which in fact he seemed to do, for he began his discussion by saying that they "absolutely must be observed in the resolution of all questions."

The actual rules that Malebranche set out seem on their face hardly more promising than Descartes' own. They derive, however, from the account of truth that he had just given in the previous chapter. There he says that "truth is nothing but a real relation, whether of equality or inequality." This real relation obtains between ideas (twice two is four), between ideas and things (the sun exists), or between things (the earth is larger than the moon). Because the relation obtains between ideas, which are eternal and immutable, truths of the first sort are themselves immutable and eternal, and serve as the standard for truths of the other two sorts. "This is why only these sorts of truths are considered in arithmetic, algebra, and geometry, because these universal sciences both determine and contain all the particular sciences." In this sense, every relation is a magnitude, and conversely, and thus we can clearly express all relations by numbers and represent them to the imagination with lines." Thus, arithmetic and geometry are theoretically capable of expressing all truth. However, they are practically limited in their operation by their complexity and by their limitation to specific solutions. These limitations are overcome by algebra, "which expresses magnitudes of every possible kind, as well as the relations they might have, [and whose calculations] are the simplest, easiest, and at the same time, most universal calculations conceivable" (*Search* VI.1.v, OC 2:282–92; LO 431–5; also, VI.2.viii, OC 2:418–9; LO 509). Not incidentally, this account applies, not only to truth grounded in intelligible extension (i.e., to mathematics and physics), but also to *all* truth, including moral truth, which is no less a matter of relations (e.g., a man is to be valued more than his dog), and which is in principle no less scientific.[43]

Although the language he uses to state his rules is nonmathematical and very general, it seems that algebra is what Malebranche had in mind in stating them. Just as Descartes' algebraic approach developed in his *Geometry* is not merely an exemplification of his method, but also as a source of that method,[44] so Malebranche's rules are not merely guides for discovery of algebraic solutions, but are also constitutive of what it is to be an algebraic solution. (This apparent two-step dynamic is not the method itself, but the basis for the rules governing method.) It is in this sense, perhaps, that "they all depend on each other" (*Search* VI.2.i, OC 2:295; LO 437).[45]

The first two of the eight rules concern the subject of the study, the latter six the manner of resolving questions, and the whole yielding an algebraic solution. Thus, the first rule is, "the state of the question we propose to resolve must be very distinctly conceived." That Malebranche had in mind with this rule an algebraic formulation of the question is tolerably clear from his comment, "we must have sufficiently distinct ideas of our terms to be able to compare them, and thus to recognize the relations we seek among them." The third rule is, "the subject being considered must be carefully simplified in order to avoid examining things that are irrelevant to the truth sought." In other words, what is necessary is that the equation be preserved. "The things that can be so eliminated are all those that do not affect the question and whose elimination leaves the question intact" (*Search* VI.2.i, OC 2:297; LO 438).

Each of the rules has a basis in some text or other of Descartes.[46] They might even be taken as an expansion of Descartes' four rules, but perhaps more clearly connected to algebra, and most importantly, with the psychologism expunged. Thus, although according to the fourth rule "we must divide the subject of our meditation into parts and consider them one after another according to the natural order beginning with the simplest" (*Search* VI.2.i, OC 2:297; LO 438). This is "not only because this method is natural and helps the mind in these questions, but also because as God always acts with order and in the simplest ways, this method of examining our ideas will make us better understand His works" (*Search* VI.2.iv, OC 2:325; LO 455). Simplicity is not just psychologically useful, but has an ontological basis in God's own ideas, which He follows. Conversely, if Malebranche insisted as a general rule that "we must reason only on things of which we have a clear idea" (*Search* VI. 2.1; OC 2:296; LO 437), the concern is with the things we reason about and not our perceptions of them. The major violator of this rule, discussed at great length, is Aristotle, who "reasons only on the confused ideas received through the senses and on other vague, general, and indeterminate ideas that represent nothing in particular to the mind" (*Search* VI.2.ii, OC 2:300; LO 440). Neither sensations nor the qualitative Aristotelian physics gets at a mind-independent, quantitative order of reality; and it is problematic because of this failure, not because it fails to produce indubitability.

In conclusion, it might be noted that Malebranche was not merely an abstract theorist of method. He was a member of the Royal Academy of Sciences. He was *au courant* with the mathematical advances of his time and was a partisan of the infinitesimal calculus against more orthodox Cartesians such as Régis. The register of the Academy shows him to have attended regularly, and been involved in the administration.[47] Within the Academy, there was an identified group around Malebranche that eventually included such names as L'Hospital, Carré, Rémond de Montfort, and Reyneau.

To what extent his scientific activities influenced his views on method (and conversely) is, however, difficult to say. The method is to be found whole in the first edition of *Search* (1674–5). However, while Malebranche's entire career evidenced an interest in science, his concerns with microscopy, mechanics, biology, anatomy, medicine, and others came to predominate only later, when he seems to have sought refuge from theologically stormy waters; and his election to the Academy was only in 1699 upon its reformation by Fontenelle.

Research in this area might address specific questions, both internal or textual, and external or contextual. A good example of the former would be how Malebranche was able, within his Cartesian framework of mechanism, to reintroduce final causes in both human and bestial physiology (*Search* II.1.iv, OC 1:208–9; LO 98–9). In good Platonic fashion, Malebranche insisted that the role of design, especially in biology, cannot be ignored (*Search* V.iii, OC 2:152–3; LO 353). An example of the latter kind of question concerns still another typically Platonic topic, education. Malebranche's philosophy of education was neither the carrot nor the stick. Rewards and punishments (i.e., pleasures and pains) serve only to entrench for a child the significance of the very sort of sensation that most impedes the search after truth. Instead, he recommends sensory deprivation such that truth itself, unadorned by external enticements or threats, will be discerned (*Search* II.1.viii, OC 1:261–5; LO 127–9). The question would concern Malebranche's influence in the Cartesian-influenced schools attempting to compete with the Jesuit schools that were dominated by Aristotelian scholasticism. Specifically, one would like to know whether the abstract methodological issues discussed above were played out at that concrete level.[48]*

NOTES

1 On the former, see Sorell, *The Rise of Modern Philosophy*; on the latter, see Popkin, *The History of Skepticism from Erasmus to Spinoza*.
2 *Discourse on The Method* II; AT VI, p. 17, CSM I, p. 119.
3 *Principles of Philosophy* Preface; AT IX B, pp. 13–4, CSM I, p. 186.

* I am grateful to J. M. Nicholas for valuable discussion relating to this paper.

4 The *Search* at one point contrasts geometry, which perfects the imagination more than the (pure) mind, with arithmetic and algebra, which constitute the "true logic." However, this usage was eliminated from the last edition (*Search* VI.1.v, OC 2:289 var.b).

5 *Rules for the Direction of the Mind* 13; AT X, pp. 434–5, CSM I, p. 54.

6 See Dear esp. pp. 150–1, but also pp. 147–77 for more on the seventeenth-century background.

7 Jones, p. 156.

8 Jones, p. 159.

9 A tentative account is that a synthetic proof is *a priori* in the sense of moving from causes to effects, while the procedure itself is *a posteriori* in the sense of moving from what is epistemically posterior (i.e., from what is learned after what is being proved). See CSM II, p. 110 n.2, p. 111 n.1.

10 AT VII, p. 15b, CSM II, p. 111.

11 *Rules for the Direction of the Mind* 12; AT X, p. 422, CSM I, p. 46.

12 Arnauld, *Logic*, pp. 236–8.

13 Arnauld, *Logic*, p. 238.

14 See Hintikka, "A Discourse," pp. 76–7.

15 For more on the Cartesian distinction between knowing something and comprehending it see, Ariew, "The Infinite."

16 *Search* III.1.ii, OC 1:393 LO 205. *Logic* 4.1, p. 232.

17 For more, see Robinet, *Malebranche de l'Académie des Sciences*, pp. 20–30.

18 Malebranche and Plato would also reject the two-step dynamic by questioning how the first piece of the puzzle could be put in place. Coherence of the resulting whole is not an option before Berkeley, whose claim that he converts ideas into things is methodologically the introduction of coherence as the nature of truth and not just its criterion. Even so, this Platonic intuitionism is not incompatible with a rather Berkeleian instrumentalism. Malebranche insisted that "nature is not abstract; the levers and balls of mechanics are not the lines and circles of mathematics" (*Search* VI.1.iv, OC 2:277; LO 428); that practical usefulness rather than precision is to be sought (*Search* IV.7, OC 2:58–61; LO 295–7); and that "in physics we try to discover the order and connection of effects with their causes, either in bodies, *if there are any, or in our sensations, if they do not exist*" (*Search* VI.2.vi, OC 2:377; LO 484, emphasis added). The exact role of experiment and hypothesis in Malebranche's physics remains a desideratum of research. For a handle on the topic, see Mouy, *Le Développement*, pp. 314–9.

19 *Meditations* III; AT VII, pp. 57–8, CSM II, 40.

20 "There is no other real and true cause [of our errors] but the misuse of our freedom" (*Search* IV.11, OC 2:86; LO 312). The metaphysics of this

misuse is such that Malebranche can also claim that "the general and universal cause of all our errors ... is that since nothingness has no idea representing it, the mind is led to believe that all things of which it has no idea do not exist" (*Search* III.2.ix, OC 1:468; LO 248). However, this account seems to involve a false inference from what he calls the first principle of all knowledge, to be discussed below.

21 *Treatise on nature and grace*; OC 5:118–9. See Kremer.

22 *Discourse on the method* II; AT VI, p. 18, CSM I, p. 120.

23 See also *Principles of philosophy* I, 30; AT VIII A, pp. 16–7, CSM I, p. 203.

24 *Principles of philosophy* I, 43; AT VIII A. p. 21, CSM I, p. 207. The psychologistic reading is supported by Descartes' explication of the key terms. Distinctness is defined in terms of clarity, and clarity is explained by analogy to something physically acting on the eye "with a sufficient degree of strength and accessibility." *Ibid.* 45; AT VIII A, p. 22, CSM I, p. 207.

25 *Objections* V; AT VIII A, pp. 278–9, CSM II, p. 194.

26 *Replies* II; AT VIII A, pp. 144–5, CSM II, p. 103.

27 The literature on these topics is enormous and, needless to say, the pyschologistic reading of Descartes is controversial. Most relevantly, see D. Radner's review of LO. More important, however, is how Descartes was read in the period. In addition to Gassendi, Leibniz read him this way, and so, as will now be seen, did Malebranche. For Leibniz, see Yvon Belaval, *Leibniz: Critique de Descartes* esp. p. 532. For more on Malebranche, see Robinet, *Système et Existence*, pp. 327–31.

28 *Discourse on the Method* II; AT VI, p. 18, CSM I, p. 120.

29 Emphasis Malebranche's.

30 *Ibid.* Note too that consent is given in degrees, unlike for Descartes, whose action of the constrained will is causally on or off.

31 Drawing this distinction may be Malebranche's intention when he says that in evident perception "it is necessary, as it were [*comme nécessaire*], for the will to cease," and that we should "never consent to anything until we are forced to do so, as it were [*comme forcez*], by the secret reproaches of our reason." *Search* I.2.ii–iii, OC 1:53,55; LO 9,10. See Lennon, *Philosophical Commentary*, LO 765–6, whose reading of these passages is here extended to all the relevant passages about Malebranche's rule.

32 This is the significance of Malebranche's citation of Augustine's *Confessions*, bk.12. ch.25: "If we both see the truth of what you say and we both see the truth of what I say, where do we see it? I ask. I do not see it in you nor do you see it in me, but we both see it in that immutable truth that is above our minds." *Ibid.*

33 See Lennon, *Battle of the Gods and Giants*, p. 219.

34 See esp. OC 8–9:924–6.

35 For Descartes, for whom the goal is certainly not just avoidance of error, the rule of clarity and distinctness is not just a safeguard because it functions positively as a criterion. For Malebranche, evidence is not a criterion on the basis of which we accept a proposition as true; we just see that it is true. This difference is preserved even if on the Frankfurt interpretation of Descartes we say that Descartes' goal is not absolute truth but unassailable certainty.

36 For the Cartesian dialectic of intentionality, see Hausman and Hausman *Descartes's Legacy*, esp. ch. 2–4.

37 *Search*,II.1.i, OC 1:192; LO 88. John P. Wright has revealed the importance of Malebranche's account of the imagination to Hume. *The Skeptical Realism of David Hume*. That Humean ideas should differ only in degree from impressions might be part of Malebranche's influence here.

38 "We cannot learn anything if we do not give it our attention, and ... we can hardly be attentive to something if we do not imagine it and do not represent it vividly in our brain." *Search* II.2.ii, OC 1:270; LO 132.

39 The texts referred to by Carr show the importance of the notion of attention to Descartes and Malebranche. He argued an interesting thesis with respect to this notion, indicated by the title of his book. Concerning Malebranche, it is the view of "the Incarnation itself as a rhetorical act. By entering the world of *res extensa* the Divine Reason becomes an instrument for drawing attention toward the intelligible. The Incarnation is at once the rationale and the model for authentic persuasion among fallen humans." Carr, p. 110. The need for attention to be drawn in this way has methodological implications as follows. According to Malebranche, abstract contemplation of the truth is not sufficient; because we are embodied minds, pleasure in the truth is also required, certainly for meritorious action and perhaps even to arrive at truth. This pleasure is what Malebranche calls "prevenient delight." Without it, there are truths of morality "hidden in the folds and recesses of the mind," which it fails to notice (*Search* III.1.iv, OC 1:408–9; LO 213–4). Since Original Sin, this pleasure is a special grace (*Search* I.5, OC 1:70; LO 19), which is to say in nontheological language that, from our point of view, method must rely on what is fortuitous.

40 See Lennon, "Pandora."

41 At one point, Malebranche in fact rejects the indivisibility of essences (*Search* III.2.x, OC 1:476–7; LO 254–5) However, the essences he discusses here are Aristotelian essences like water and wine, which in fact are not essences at all. Applied to real essences, that is, thought and extension, the doctrine may yet hold for him.

42 Hatfield, p. 967.

43 See Walton, *De la recherche du Bien*.

44 Gaukroger, *Descartes*, p. 91.

45 See also Robinet, *Malebranche de l'Académie des Sciences*, p. 25: "La cinquième règle de la méthode malebranchiste ne regarde que [l'algèbre] qui commande tout le développement des règles suivantes."

46 See the notes 141–51 of G. Rodis-Lewis, OC 2: 548–9.

47 Malebranche gives a fairly sophisticated critique of research as a social institution. In the case of chemists, for example, experiment is not guided by a rational pursuit of truth, but by chance, glamour, and profit; it is conceptually limited by circumstance, invites hasty inference and ignores principles; it collapses because of expenses and fatigue (*Search* II.2.viii, OC 1:318–9; LO 159–60).

48 For a handle on the first question, see Robinet, *Malebranche de l'Académie des Sciences*, on the second, see Brockliss, *French Higher Education*.

# 2 Malebranche on the Soul

Few periods are more important in the philosophy of mind than the seventeenth century. The new mechanical picture of the physical world confronted many philosophers with an exciting challenge; they needed to formulate theories of the mind and its place in nature, which were not only more philosophically defensible but also better adapted to the needs of Christian theology than their traditional Aristotelian-Scholastic rivals. Although many of the theories that were advanced are widely rejected today, there is no doubt that they left a decisive mark on subsequent thinking; indeed, they helped to define the contemporary agenda in the philosophy of mind. For instance, current debates over the merits of dualism and materialism are often clearly of seventeenth-century inspiration. Other thinkers in the period may have had a more direct impact on modern philosophy of mind, but few, if any, are more interesting than Malebranche.

Malebranche's interest and importance as a philosopher of mind are in one way surprising. Malebranche is generally classified as one of the Cartesians, and it is certainly true that he accepted much of the Cartesian philosophical framework. It might, then, be expected that Malebranche would offer no more than a series of minor amendments to Descartes' teaching in this area. Such, however, is not the case. Partly under the influence of his other mentor, Augustine, Malebranche was able to break decisively with Cartesian orthodoxy on a number of issues in the philosophy of mind. In the first half of this chapter we shall see that, armed with the theological slogan that the human mind is not a light to itself, Malebranche pioneers anti-Cartesian theses about the nature of the intellect and sensations. In particular, he challenged the still widely held view that intentionality is a mark of the mental. In the second half of the chapter, we shall examine Malebranche's attack on Descartes' claims concerning self-knowledge. Here we shall see that Malebranche advanced a powerful internal critique of Descartes; he argued convincingly that Descartes' famous thesis that the mind is better known than body is inconsistent with some of his central commitments concerning the nature of knowledge.

## I.  MALEBRANCHE AND THE CARTESIAN ONTOLOGY OF MIND

The radicalism of Malebranche's critique of Descartes is not always readily apparent, for in places, such as the first half of *The Search After Truth*, he seemed straightforwardly to accept the basic features of Descartes' ontology of mind. According to Malebranche, the mind is a substance whose whole essence consists in thought (*Search* III.1.i; OC 1 381; LO 198), and it has two principal faculties: the will and the understanding (*Search* I.1; OC 1:40–1; LO 2). In the spirit of Descartes, Malebranche also made a further distinction regarding the understanding. When used without qualification, the term "understanding" must be taken in a broad sense to mean the "passive faculty of the soul by means of which it receives all the modifications of which it is capable" (*Search* I.1; OC 1:43; LO 3); the understanding in this sense is involved in both sense-perception and imagination. However, later in the work Malebranche introduced us to the notion of the pure understanding; it is by the means of this faculty that the mind is aware of wholly intellectual ideas such as the concepts of geometry. As for Descartes, then, the operations of the pure understanding involved nothing like the manipulation of sensory images and they are also causally independent of the activity of the brain (see *Search* III.1.i; OC 1:381; LO 198).

Malebranche never officially broke with Cartesian orthodoxy on these issues in the ontology of mind, but from the beginning of his career his philosophy is subject to the pull of a non-Cartesian theme. Self-consciously following Augustine and other Church Fathers, Malebranche insisted that the mind is not a light to itself (*Search*, III.2.v, OC 1:434; LO 229). Just what such a claim involves may not be clear in matters of detail, but its general tendency is not in doubt: it suggests a much bleaker picture of the mind's native cognitive resources than we encounter in Descartes. Thus, even in early works, such as *The Search After Truth*, we find that the mind, for Male-branche, does not have a pure intellect in anything like the full Cartesian sense; that is to say, it is not stocked with innate ideas and truths that the finger of God has implanted in it. Indeed, it has no native resources for finding knowledge, or even the seeds of knowledge, in itself. At most, it possesses a capacity for attending to objects of thought whose locus – the mind of God – is external to it.

At least in his later writings, Malebranche's break with Cartesian orthodoxy is arguably more radical than this. Malebranche came to deny not merely that the human mind has any native resources for drawing concepts from itself, but also that it has any native resources for apprehending concepts whose locus is external to it. Malebranche now insisted on a very strict interpretation of the patristic doctrine that the mind is a *lumen illuminatum* (illuminated light), not a *lumen illuminans* (illuminating light); it must be understood to mean that the mind achieves knowledge not by exercising any native capacities of its own, but wholly by virtue of God's action in illuminating it by means of efficacious ideas. As Malebranche never tired of repeating, the mind finds only the darkness of sensations in itself:

Created reason, our soul, the human mind, the purest and most sublime intellects can indeed see the light; but they cannot produce it or draw it from their own resources, nor can they engender it from their substance. They can discover eternal, immutable, necessary truths in the divine Word, in the eternal, immutable, necessary Wisdom, but in themselves they can find only sensations often quite lively, yet always obscure and confused, only modalities full of darkness. (*Dialogues* III.4, OC 12:64–5; JS 32–3)

Thus, if we say that Malebranche continues to recognize a faculty of purely intellect, it is only in the very minimal sense of a passive capacity to be affected by God's efficacious ideas.

Malebranche's insistence that the mind finds only the darkness of sensations in itself has a further consequence for his break with Cartesian orthodoxy in the ontology of mind. As we have seen, Malebranche seemed straightforwardly to echo Descartes' famous claim that the mind is an essentially thinking substance; it is doubtful, however, whether this formulation can have quite the same meaning in his philosophy. Descartes is perhaps most usually read as asserting that it is thought in the sense of consciousness that constitutes the whole essence of mind; in this view, abstract thoughts (e.g., of God and triangles) and sensations of pain and hunger are on the same par as modes of thinking. However, as some commentators have noticed, Descartes often seems to intend his central thesis about the mind in a stronger sense: it is thought in the sense of pure intellect that constitutes the essence of mind.[1] In this view, sensations of pain and hunger are not so much modes of thinking as properties of a third substance, the whole human being, which is a composite of mind and body. In addition, in favor of this view, it can be pointed out that, for Descartes, a disembodied mind would have no states that were not purely intellectual in nature. By contrast, Malebranche held that the mind finds only sensations in itself, and it is thus difficult to see how he could hold that it is essential to the mind to be a pure intellect. If Malebranche wished to retain the Cartesian formula that the mind is an essentially thinking substance, it seems that he must understand "thought" in a broad sense that embraces sensations and sense-perceptions.

Perhaps it will be objected that the issue is not as simple as this. It is true that Malebranche was committed to the thesis that sensations alone are intrinsic to the mind; that is, they alone are its nonrelational properties. However, to say that they are intrinsic to the mind is not to resolve the question of the mind's essence. In *The Search After Truth*, Malebranche observed that it is essential to human minds to be related to God (*Search*, Preface, OC 1:10; LO xxxiv), and even in his later writings he never seemed to withdraw this claim. By virtue of this relationship to God, the mind is capable of perceiving ideas or objects of purely intellectual awareness; in this way, then, we might seek to defend the claim that intellect is essential to the mind. However, such a defense of Malebranche's Cartesianism runs into two problems. In the first place, the most that can be said is that intellect is one of the mind's essential properties; it can hardly be said to constitute its whole essence. Secondly, at least in his later writings, the mind perceives ideas in God solely by virtue of the action of God's efficacious ideas.[2] As we have seen, then, to say that the mind has a faculty of pure intellect is thus only to make the minimal claim that the mind has a passive power to be affected by God's efficacious ideas. Such a thesis is very remote from Cartesian orthodoxy.

Whether or not the Malebranchian mind can be said to have a faculty of pure intellect, there is no doubt that throughout his career he held that pure perceptions number among its states; the mind has pure perceptions, for example, when it apprehends the concept (idea in God) of a triangle or a circle (*Conv. Chrét* III, OC 4:75–6). Malebranche's insistence that the mind has such perceptions, in addition to obscure sensations, gave rise to a problem of consistency. On one hand, Malebranche claimed that the mind has pure perceptions to the extent that it is enlightened by ideas in God. On the other hand, he was no less insistent, as we have seen, that the mind finds in itself only confused and obscure sensations. Martial Gueroult stated the problem by saying that Malebranche's argument for the vision in God seems to commit him to saying that the soul both is and is not enlightened by divine ideas.[3]

One commentator, Tad Schmaltz, tried to solve the problem of consistency by drawing on the fact that perception, for Malebranche, is essentially relational; that is, it involves a relation between the human mind and ideas in God. However, any perception can be considered in terms of its intrinsic or nonrelational properties, and when it is considered in this way, it is merely a sensation, and as such, obscure and confused.[4] Schmaltz's point here can be clarified by means of an analogy: To speak of someone as a father is of course to characterize him in relational terms, but any father can also be considered apart from the relation of paternity; for example, he can be described in terms of intrinsic features such as height, eye-color, and DNA. With the help of this distinction, the problem of consistency can be resolved. Thus, the soul has no intrinsic states that are not obscure and confused sensations, but at least some of these states, considered in terms of their relation to ideas, are pure perceptions.

Although this interpretation effectively resolves the problem of consistency, it receives no direct support from the texts; moreover, it suggests that any modification of the soul – no matter how obscure and confused – is capable of serving as a ground to a relation to ideas, and we may wonder whether Malebranche would wish to assert this. It is, I think, natural to embrace an alternative solution to the problem. When Malebranche said that the mind finds in itself only confused and obscure sensations, he is considering its plight in abstraction from the contribution of God's action in illuminating the soul with divine ideas. Sensations are the only properties which the soul has in abstraction from this contribution. To say this, however, is not to say that pure perceptions are grounded in obscure

and confused sensations. Perceptions are indeed relational properties, but when God illuminates the soul, these perceptions, considered in terms of their intrinsic features, are not simply obscure and
confused sensations. It is a merit of this interpretation that it does
justice to Malebranche's metaphorical insistence that the human intellect is an illuminated light, not an illuminating light. When a place
that was in shadow comes to be illuminated by the sun's rays, then
it undergoes a change in its intrinsic and not just its relational properties; it comes to be bright and sunny. However, to say this is not
to deny either that the sun's illumination is a causal relation or that
the same place, when considered apart from the sun's contribution,
is dark and gloomy.

This interpretation stays closer to the text, but it raises philosophical difficulties of its own. It poses the problem of whether
Malebranche was entitled to distinguish in this way between sensation and pure perception in terms of God's contribution. It is true
that Malebranche appears to have the resources for distinguishing
between sensations and the perceptions of ideas in terms of their
causal source; sensations arise in us by virtue of the laws of the union
of mind and body, whereas the perceptions of ideas arise in us by
virtue of the laws of the union of the soul with God (*Dialogues* XIII.9,
OC 12:319; JS 252–3). However, when Malebranche spoke of these
psychophysical laws, he was discussing matters at the level of occasional causality; states of the brain cannot be genuine causes of
sensations, but only occasional ones. Thus, there is a sense in which
even sensations have God as their genuine cause. Perhaps it will be
said, on Malebranche's behalf, that though God is indeed causally
responsible for producing sensations, the causal action in question
does not consist in illuminating the soul. Thus, we can say that, apart
from divine illumination, the soul finds only obscure and confused
sensations in itself while still recognizing that God is their genuine
cause. This is perfectly correct, but it is fair to note that in his later
writings Malebranche tended to minimize the distinction between
the ways in which sensations and perceptions are produced in the
soul. He wrote as if even sensations, no less than pure perceptions,
are the result of the efficacy of divine ideas. Certainly the only difference between sensations and pure perceptions is in terms of how
ideas touch or affect the soul (*Conv. chrét.*, III, OC 4:75–6).[5] Thus,
on this view, very little is left of the soul when it is considered in

abstraction from the contribution made by God's ideas. It is not for
nothing that the French scholar, Alquié, remarks that the soul, so
considered, is no more than a pure potentiality.[6]

## II.  THE ADVERBIAL THEORY OF SENSATIONS

Malebranche thus broke with the Cartesian doctrine of pure intellect: Not merely is the human mind not stocked with innate ideas
and beliefs, but it has no active, native faculty for attending to such
objects of thought. As an illuminated light, the Malebranchian mind
has a pure intellect at most in the very minimal sense that it possesses a purely passive power of being affected by the light of divine
ideas. Malebranche further broke with Descartes in a philosophically significant way in his theory of sensations; for Malebranche,
sensations constitute a distinct class of mental states that have no
object or content. The moral of this theory is the controversial anti-
Cartesian thesis that intentionality is not one of the marks of the
mental. In this way, Malebranche stands aside from a tradition of
thinking about the nature of the mental that spans Descartes and
Husserl.

   Perhaps the best way of bringing out the originality and interest of
Malebranche's theory of sensations is by means of a notorious passage in the Elucidations to *The Search After Truth*. On the strength of
this passage Malebranche was ridiculed as a believer in the rainbow-
colored soul:

> You even make a fool of yourself before certain Cartesians if you say that
> the soul actually becomes blue, red, or yellow, and that the soul is painted
> with the colors of the rainbow when looking at it. There are many people
> who have doubts and even more who do not believe, that when we smell
> carrion the soul becomes formally rotten; and that the taste of sugar, or of
> pepper or salt, is something belonging to the soul. (*Search*, Elucid. 11, OC 3:
> 166; LO 634)

The idea that the soul becomes red in perceiving something red is
not original with Malebranche; it has precedents in Aristotle's own
very different theory of perception.[7] However, despite, or perhaps because of, its Aristotelian roots it is not difficult to see why the theory
of the rainbow-colored soul should have encountered resistance. The
theory does indeed sound odd to the ears; it sounds odd for the reason

that ordinary language embodies the commonsense assumption that it is firetrucks and English pillarboxes, for example, that are red, not minds or souls. However, orthodox Cartesians would not be satisfied with this objection from ordinary language, for they are committed to the view that ordinary language is a repository of philosophical mistakes. Moreover, even if Cartesians agree that colors are in some sense in physical objects themselves, they cannot concede that they are present in such objects in the way unreflective common sense takes them to be; on the side of bodies they are simply dispositions to cause sensory ideas (sensations) in our minds by virtue of the surface textures.[8] Nonetheless, although this objection is debarred to the Cartesians, it is still possible to see why they should have philosophical scruples about the doctrine of the rainbow-colored soul. An orthodox Cartesian will insist that even though they are confused, sensations are still ideas, and that it is essential to ideas as such to have objective reality, in technical jargon. In other words, ideas by their very nature have intentional content. Just how this intentional content is to be specified is controversial, but on one interpretation it will be in terms of the body's primary qualities. To have a sensory idea of red is to have an obscure and confused representation of the surface texture of a red body. It was just this feature of orthodox Cartesian teaching that Malebranche was concerned to deny. To have a sensation of red is not strictly to have a sensation of anything – in this respect ordinary language is misleading – it is simply for the soul to be in a certain sensory state. When I look at the setting sun, my soul may more accurately be said to sense redly. Thus, Malebranche was advocating what we may call an adverbial theory of sensation.

The claim that Malebranche advanced an adverbial theory of sensation may be viewed with some skepticism. It may be pointed out that Malebranche regularly spoke of sensations in Cartesian language as obscure and confused. In the *Dialogues on Metaphysics*, for example, he says that there is always a clear idea and confused sensation in the view we have of sensible objects (*Dialogues* V.1, OC 12:113; JS 74). It is natural to object that such a characterization of sensations makes sense only on the Cartesian assumption that sensations, like ideas in general, have intentional content. For example, to say that I have an obscure and confused idea of a right-angled triangle, might mean a number of things. It might mean that I am unable to perceive that the Pythagorean theorem is true. Or it might mean that I am unable to discriminate perceptually between a right-angled triangle and one that has an acute angle of eighty-five degrees. However, in each case there is some intentional object or content of which I have an imperfect apprehension.

It is always possible that in pioneering an adverbial theory of sensations Malebranche retained relics of Cartesian habits of thought without seeing that they had no place in his thinking. However, in fact I believe it is not difficult to see how appealing to the obscurity and confusion of sensations might have a real point in Malebranche's new theory. For one thing, Malebranche may have meant that sensations are characteristically accompanied by false judgments; when I have a sensation of red that is occasionally caused by a fire truck, I tend to judge falsely that there is something on the surface of the fire truck that corresponds to my sensation of red. Or Malebranche may mean that such sensations are cognitively empty; thus, there is nothing in my sensation of red itself that enables me to infer to the nature of the surface texture of the particles on the body that we would pretheoretically call red. Indeed, as Schmaltz has shown, according to Malebranche, there are not even strong correlations between particular shades of color and particular surface textures.[9]

Malebranche's tendency to follow the orthodox Cartesians in saying that sensations are confused is thus not evidence against his subscription to the adverbial theory. Nor need we suppose that such expressions are simply unassimilated relics of the Cartesian thesis that sensations have intentional content. However, it may be doubted how clearly Malebranche saw the implications of holding an adverbial theory of sensation. Steven Nadler observed that on occasion Malebranche spoke of sensing or perceiving ideas as colored, as red for example. He even wrote as if ideas were like pictures onto which sensations could be attached or projected like a painter's colors (OC 6:78). However, according to Nadler, such expressions betray an element of confusion in Malebranche's thinking.[10] As is shown in Chapter 6, Malebranchian ideas are properly construed as logical concepts; they are, for example, typically geometrical concepts of circles and triangles. Now we might say (at least pretheoretically) that a given circular figure is red and blue, but logical concepts are not the sort of things that can be perceived or sensed redly or bluely or onto which color can be projected.

There is no need to deny that Malebranche sometimes wrote as if ideas were like pictures onto which the mind can project colors. However, it is a mistake to suppose that such expressions point to a real confusion in his thought. On the contrary, Malebranche may be availing himself of a convenient, if somewhat misleading, shorthand expression. To say that ideas are sensed redly is simply a *façon de parler*. What Malebranche really means is expressed more carefully in an important passage from *The Search After Truth*:

When we perceive something sensible two things are found in our perception: sensation and pure idea. The sensation is a modification of our soul, and it is God who causes it in us. He can cause this modification even though he does not have it himself, because he sees in the idea he has of our soul that it is capable of it. As for the idea found in conjunction with the sensation, it is in God, and we see it because it pleases God to reveal it to us. God joins the sensation to the idea when objects are present so that we may believe them to be present and that we may have all the feelings and passions that we should have in relation to them. (*Search* III.2.vi, OC 1:445; LO 234)

Thus, to say that ideas are sensed redly is to say that a sensation of red occurs in conjunction with the perception of an idea (a geometrical concept) in such a way that I take my experience to be of a red, circular body, for example. Malebranche may have been led to adopt the formulation to which Nadler rightly objects by a desire to do justice to the tight phenomenological connection between two elements in my sensory experience that are really discrete and heterogeneous. It is this tight connection that is expressed in our pretheoretical judgment that when I perceive a setting sun, I am perceiving a body that is both red and circular.

Malebranche, then, advanced an adverbial theory of sensation, but in one way he may seem to be an adverbialist with a difference. Characteristically, the motivation for introducing adverbial theories is a desire to honor Ockham's razor – the principle that entities are not to be multiplied unnecessarily. Such philosophers seek to avoid a commitment to dubious or suspect entities such as sense-data. Instead of saying that in seeing a red patch I immediately perceive a red sense-datum, the adverbialist will insist that I am simply in a certain sensory state. By contrast, Malebranche offered a theory of sense-perception that seems to proliferate with just the dubious entities that the adverbialist seeks to avoid. He insisted that in every act of sense-perception, I am immediately related to extramental entities (ideas) whose locus is God. Thus Malebranche's theory of sensation can hardly be motivated by concerns of ontological economy. However, this verdict may be mistaken, for it fails to take account of the structure of Malebranche's theory of sense-perception. It fails also to recognize that, for Malebranche, every act of sense-perception involves an irreducibly intellectual element of judging or seeing that. According to Malebranche, we cannot give a satisfactory account of this feature of sense-perception unless we recognize the mind's relationship to extramental ideas whose locus is God. Malebranche can plausibly insist that his appeal to ideas involves no violation of the principle of Ockham's razor, for it is not gratuitous. By contrast, matters are different when what is at issue is the strictly sensory side of sense-perception. Here there is no such philosophical pressure to postulate the existence of entities over and above mental states. Malebranche can agree with the adverbialist that sense-data are dubious entities which we can, and should, do without. Malebranche's brand of adverbialism may be unfamiliar, but it is premature to suppose that it is not motivated by a desire to honor Ockham's razor.

Before we leave Malebranche's theory of sensation, let us note one interesting implication of the theory for the status of animals. His theory has the resources, which he never developed, to offer a radical alternative to Descartes's notorious thesis that animals are just machines or automata.[11] Consider one way in which Malebranche's theory of sensations departs from Cartesian orthodoxy. According to Descartes, sensations are confused ideas or modes of thinking that arise from the mind's union or, as it were, intermingling with the body.[12] That is to say, they are intellectual states that have become corrupted or polluted by being admixed with something extraneous to the mind. In terms of this theory, then, Descartes could not consistently ascribe sensations to animals without also endowing them with a capacity at least in principle for purely intellectual awareness. Understandably, Descartes was unwilling to grant animals such a capacity. However, Malebranche, by contrast, broke with Cartesian orthodoxy in his theory of sensation. In his theory, at least according to *The Search After Truth*, sensation is wholly heterogeneous from perception, which is by its nature intellectual. Perception involves the mind's relationship to ideas, and ideas, as

*Animals*

has been seen, are entities in God. Thus, there can be no perception without divine illumination. Sensation, by contrast, is a non-intentional and nonrelational state of the soul. Thus, by virtue of his innovations in this area Malebranche had the resources to avoid the Cartesian doctrine of the beast-machine. Indeed, it seems that Malebranche was in a position to advance a rather intriguing theory of animal consciousness. He said that though animals have no capacity for judgment, or seeing that, they do have the capacity to feel sensations such as pain and hunger. The cat, for example, could not see that there was a circular dish in front of her, but she could sense patches of color. The mental life of animals could be one of buzzing, blooming confusion. It is true that such a theory would ascribe a more minimal form of consciousness to animals than that which most of us are inclined to attribute, but at least it would do justice to the profoundly anti-Cartesian intuition that animals feel pain and hunger.

Malebranche, in fact, did not exploit the resources of his theory in this way; he continued to toe the party line of the beast-machine doctrine. Indeed, he stated it perhaps more dogmatically than Descartes himself did:

> Thus in animals there is neither intelligence nor souls as ordinarily meant. They eat without pleasure, cry without pain, grow without knowing it; they desire nothing, fear nothing, know nothing; and if they act in a manner that demonstrates intelligence, it is because God, having made them in order to preserve them, made their bodies in such a way that they mechanically avoid what is capable of destroying them. (*Search* VI.2.vii, OC 2:394; LO 494–5)

However, his reasons for toeing the Cartesian party line had less to do with the philosophy of mind than with theological considerations. According to Malebranche, the ascription of sensations to animals is inconsistent with the principle that under a just God the innocent will not suffer. It is important to see, then, that Malebranche's loyalty to the party line has little to do with pressures from the philosophy of mind.[13]

### III.  KNOWLEDGE OF THE SOUL

It is tempting to say that the main themes of Malebranche's philosophy of mind are encapsulated in two slogans: (1) the mind is not a light to itself and (2) we have no idea of the mind or soul. Malebranche sometimes ran these two claims in tandem, but strictly speaking this is misleading, for they seem to be logically independent. It is true of course that if the mind is not a light to itself, we cannot have a clear idea of the mind in the Cartesian sense; that is, the idea in question cannot be a psychological possession with which we are, perhaps innately, endowed. However, from the fact that we are not a light to ourselves, it does not follow that we are not capable of having epistemic access to God's idea of the mind. In addition, in the other direction, from the fact that we have no idea of the mind in this sense, it does not follow that we have no native resources of our own for attaining knowledge. It might be the case that though self-knowledge was debarred to us, we could discover within ourselves the resources for a science of the physical world. Thus, in focusing here in this section on the second of Malebranche's two main themes we shall be studying a new and distinct strand in his philosophy of mind.

In his case for his negative thesis, Malebranche mounted a powerful, even annihilating, critique of Descartes. This critique embodies the remarkable insight that there is a serious muddle at the heart of Descartes' whole theory of knowledge. We may bring out the force of Malebranche's point by considering Descartes' famous appeal to clarity and distinctness as a criterion of truth. If we look for the paradigm cases of clear and distinct ideas in Descartes, it is natural to turn to the case of geometry. The idea of a right-angled triangle is clear and distinct in the sense that various properties are deducible from it. The Pythagorean theorem, for example, can be derived from the axioms and definitions of Euclidean geometry. On this account, then, the role of clear and distinct ideas is to ground *a priori* knowledge. However, Descartes also appealed to clear and distinct perception to ground the certainty of his own existence; but here what is at issue is something very different: the source of certainty in this case is simply the incorrigible and self-verifying nature of such a judgment as "I exist." Descartes' whole conception of clear and distinct perception, as a criterion of truth, thus involved a conflation of two radically distinct kinds of knowledge: what Malebranche called knowledge through idea and knowledge through consciousness or internal sensation (*Search*, Elucid. 11, OC 3:167; LO 635). Knowledge of the second kind may indeed achieve the highest kind of certainty *scientia* (as in the case of the *cogito*), but it is only knowledge of the first kind, knowledge through idea, that is capable of issuing in *scientia* – that is, a systematic body of demonstrative truths of the sort that was traditionally held to constitute science.

Malebranche was well-placed to distinguish these two kinds of knowledge by his resolute antipsychologism – that is, by his insistence on distinguishing between the provinces of logic and psychology. When Malebranche appeals to knowledge through idea, he drew our attention to a kind of knowledge that is conversant about logical concepts whose locus is God. Although Malebranche sometimes spoke of ideas as if they were psychological items, we know that this is not his considered position. Knowledge through consciousness or sensation, by contrast, involves nothing that is not psychological. For Descartes, however, all knowledge is concerned with psychological items. He was committed to denying the existence of a Platonic third realm. Thus, it is easier for Descartes than it is for Malebranche to blur the distinction between the provinces of *a priori* and incorrigible knowledge.

Malebranche's key distinction between the two kinds of knowledge is at work in his justified critique of one of Descartes' defenses of his claim that we know the nature of the mind better than the nature of the body. In the Fifth Objections, Gassendi complained that Descartes had not succeeded in establishing this proposition.[14] In reply, Descartes explained how our knowledge of the nature of the mind necessarily outruns our knowledge of the body's nature; in knowing any property of a body, such as the piece of wax, I necessarily know a corresponding property in my mind. By contrast, the converse is not true:

As for me, I have never thought that anything more is required to reveal a substance than its various attributes; thus the more attributes of a given substance we know, the more perfectly we understand its nature. Now we can distinguish many different attributes in the wax: one, that it is white; two, that it is hard; three, that it can be melted; and so on. And there are correspondingly many attributes in my mind; one, that it has the power of knowing the whiteness of the wax; two, that it has the power of knowing its hardness; three, that it has the power of knowing that it can lose its hardness (i.e., melt), and so on.... The clear inference from this is that we know many more attributes in the case of our mind than we do in the case of anything else. For no matter how many attributes we recognize in any given thing, we can always list a corresponding number of attributes in the mind which it has in virtue of knowing the attributes of the thing; and hence the nature of the mind is the one we know best of all.[15]

Intuitively Descartes' defense of his position here is most unappealing. I may be able to list more properties of my computer than of my pencil-sharpener, but it would hardly be convincing to say that I thereby know the nature of the former better than the nature of the latter. In terms of his distinction between two kinds of knowledge, Malebranche was able to suggest why even on his own grounds Descartes is not entitled to this simple-minded kind of defense. Malebranche insists that the ability to enumerate properties in this way involves knowledge by consciousness only: It does not amount to knowledge by idea, that is, *a priori* knowledge (*Search*, Eluc. 11, OC 3:167; LO 635). Malebranche's point was that Descartes was implicitly committed to agreeing that knowing the nature of *x* requires or even consists in *a priori* knowledge. Clearly on Cartesian principles, geometry is a paradigm case of a discipline where we know the nature of the objects of study, and if we ask what such knowledge involves, it seems obvious that it is the ability to derive theorems from axioms and definitions. Further, such knowledge is *a priori* knowledge or knowledge through idea in Malebranche's terms.

When Malebranche denied that we have a (clear) idea of the soul, it is *a priori* knowledge that is at issue; it is such knowledge as issues in *scientia*, as in geometry. Malebranche offered several arguments to show that we have, and can have, no such knowledge of our mind. In the first place, he argued from our inability to know *a priori* the properties or modifications of which the mind is capable:

Surely we have no idea of our mind which is such that, by consulting it, we can discover the modifications of which the mind is capable. If we had never felt pleasure or pain we could not know whether or not the soul could feel them. If a man had never eaten a melon, or seen red or blue, he would consult this alleged idea of his soul in vain and would never discover distinctly whether or not it was capable of these sensations or modifications. (*Search*, Elucid. 11, OC 3:164; LO 634)

It is only through experience that we discover that the mind has a capacity for feeling pain or sensing the taste of melon. To borrow an example from Locke, when a person tastes a pineapple for the first time, he experiences a new kind of sensation, and thus, learns that he was capable of this experience.[16] However, he could not discover *a priori* that his mind was endowed with such a capacity. As Malebranche pointed out, the situation is wholly different in the case of geometry; we do not need to rely on experience to discover that a square is capable of being divided into two right-angled triangles. We can deduce that it has this property from the axioms and definitions of Euclidean geometry.

Malebranche offered a second, related argument for the thesis that we have no idea of the mind from the status of sensible qualities. Unlike the first, this argument does not turn on a denial that we are lacking in *a priori* knowledge about the mind in a certain area. Allowing that we can have some knowledge of this kind, it turns rather on the denial that such knowledge proceeds from the idea of the mind (as opposed to the idea of extension). As we have seen, Malebranche rightly insists that experience is necessary to tell us what sensations our mind is capable of; experience, however, leaves us wholly in the dark about the ontological status of sensible qualities such as color, taste, and odor. This is an issue that can be resolved *a priori*, but it can be resolved only by consulting the idea of extension:

> In order to determine whether sensible qualities are modes of the mind, we do not consult the alleged idea of the soul – the Cartesians themselves consult, rather, the idea of extension, and they reason as follows. Heat, pain, and color cannot be modifications of extension, for extension can only have various figures and motion. Now there are only two kinds of beings, minds and bodies. Therefore, pain, heat, color and all other sensible qualities belong to the mind. (*Search*, Elucid. 11, OC 3:165; LO 634)

Malebranche's aim here was to show how the reasoning of the Cartesians themselves provides support for the premise that we cannot determine the status of sensible qualities *a priori* by consulting the idea of the mind. Malebranche's reasoning seemed to take the form of inference to the best explanation. The Cartesians take a roundabout way of arguing that sensible qualities are modes of mind, and the best explanation for their taking this detour is that the direct route to this conclusion is blocked. In other words, they do not have epistemic access to an idea of the mind that would allow them to argue in a straightforward way for the conclusion that sensible qualities are merely modes of mind.

In the Elucidations, Malebranche offered a final argument that turns on the claim that knowing the nature of a thing necessarily involves the ability to discover its relations with other things of the same kind. However, in the case of the mind's modifications, no such comparison is possible. We cannot express relations between our sensations in the way that we can express the relations between numbers and between geometrical figures:

> But we cannot compare our mind with other minds in order to discover clearly some relation between them. We cannot even compare the modes of our mind, its own perceptions. We cannot discover clearly the relation between pleasure and pain, heat and color, or to speak only of modes of the same kind, we cannot exactly determine the relation between green and red, yellow and violet, or even between violet and violet. We sense that the one is darker or more brilliant than the other, but we do not know clearly either by how much or in what being darker or more brilliant consists. (*Search*, Eluc. 11, OC 3:168; LO 636)

There may be an objection that in the case of some sensible qualities, such as sounds, an ordering of this kind is in fact possible. A musician, for example, can determine that a particular interval is an octave or a fifth. Malebranche effectively responds to this objection by arguing through a dilemma. Any such ordering is either by means of physical properties with which the sounds are correlated or it is purely empirical, and hence, lacking in the mathematical precision of the relation between vibrations.[17] However, in neither case is there any parity with the kind of precise *a priori* knowledge that is possible with regard to numbers and geometrical figures.[18]

Malebranche's case against the Cartesian thesis that mind is better known than body was a powerful one, but it was subjected to a savage attack by Arnauld. Arnauld displayed his characteristic wit and dialectical skill. There is no doubt that he was an able proxy for Descartes himself, but it is fair to say that his attack left Malebranche's thesis largely unscathed. Indeed, Arnauld never really succeeded in coming to grips with the heart of Malebranche's case, which is that we have no *scientia* with regard to the mind.

Perhaps Arnauld's most telling point against his opponent was that in comparing our knowledge of mind and body Malebranche tends to operate with a double standard.[19] When Malebranche insisted that we do not have a clear idea of the soul, he sets the epistemological bar high. The criterion he employed is that of knowledge *par simple vue*. In other words, to have a clear idea of the soul would be to have something like an intuitive knowledge of those properties that derive from its essence. By contrast, when he argued that we do have a clear idea of body, he lowered the bar considerably, so that even pre-Pythagoreans can jump over it despite their ignorance of the famous theorem. Obviously, such people do not satisfy the condition of intuitive knowledge of the properties that derive from the essence of geometrical figures. The point is rather that in some sense they have a potential knowledge of such properties as the one that is proved with respect to right-angled triangles in the case of the Pythagorean theorem. Arnauld seemed justified in claiming that Malebranche equivocated in this way, but this equivocation was not seriously damaging to Malebranche's case. For even if the epistemic bar is lowered in the case of the idea of the mind, it is still fair to say that we have no knowledge of the soul that meets the standard. That is, we have an *a priori* science of geometry, but we have no *a priori* science of psychology. Arnauld never succeeded in grasping this point or its importance.

Arnauld was equally strident in his critique of Malebranche's argument from the ontological status of sensible qualities. Recall that, according to Malebranche, even the Cartesians are implicitly committed to holding that the status of such qualities can be determined only by appealing to the idea of extension. Thus, they are implicitly committed to holding that they do not have a clear idea of the soul. Arnauld responded by charging Malebranche with a gross *ignoratio elenchi* here. It is silly to suppose that the Cartesians ever argued in this way; indeed no one has ever needed to appeal to the idea of extension in order to resolve the status of sensations of pain and color, for no one has ever doubted that these are mind-dependent entities.[20] But in fact, for all the heat that he generates, it is Arnauld rather than Malebranche who is guilty of misrepresenting the issue. In his argument against the Cartesians, Malebranche spoke, not of sensations, but of sensible qualities, and he was surely right to claim that the status of these qualities was a subject of controversy between the Cartesians and their Scholastic opponents. The Cartesians may have disagreed as to whether sensible qualities are dispositional properties of bodies or purely mind-dependent items, but they are at one in supposing that they are not straightforwardly manifest properties of bodies in the way common sense takes them to be, and that this fact about them needs to be established against the Scholastics by philosophical argument. Moreover, a case can be made for saying that Malebranche was accurate in his account of the strategy of argument adopted by the Cartesians. They did appeal to the idea of extension in order to determine that such sensible qualities cannot be manifest physical properties.

How did Arnauld come to misread Malebranche in this way? The answer may well be that Malebranche's list of the sensible qualities includes pain, and that pain seems obviously and uncontroversially a mental item. In the spirit of Descartes, we might say that pain is nothing over and above a private sensation. Philosophers who have absorbed Cartesian doctrine may well think in these terms, but we should beware of supposing that this intuition is universally shared. Some people seem to think of painfulness as a sensible quality in pretty much the Scholastic sense; with the rest of us they say that their arm is painful when it is jabbed by a needle, but (unlike the Cartesians) they mean that there is a straightforwardly physical property that is present in the affected part of the body. Thus, the inclusion of pain on Malebranche's list of sensible qualities may not be an oversight; even here there is an issue that needs to be resolved by philosophical argument.

Somewhat harder to assess is Arnauld's objection to Malebranche's claim that our mental modifications cannot be ordered or compared. Arnauld complained that Malebranche was demanding the impossible here; he was unfairly requiring that sensations, which are essentially nonquantitative, stand in precise quantitative relations.[21] Sensations can of course differ among themselves in terms of intensive magnitude: one shade of green is deeper or brighter than another. However, it is merely silly (and confused) to complain that such intensive magnitudes lack the precision of extensive magnitudes. Indeed, as Robert Adams observes,[22] it was precisely the fact that sensations were not amenable to mathematical treatment that was one important motive for kicking the phenomenal qualia out of the physical world and into the mind.

Once again Arnauld's objection sounds initially impressive, but further reflection suggests some doubts about its adequacy. Indeed, it may be argued that this is a case where Arnauld leads with his chin. Arnauld may be implicitly conceding that sensations are not candidates for *scientia*, that is, a systematic body of knowledge. Rather, the only knowledge of which we are capable in this area is of the incorrigible kind, which Malebranche is prepared to concede. Perhaps it will be said that *scientia* is not necessarily quantitative, and that sensations and the mind's modifications are candidates for a *scientia* of this sort. However, then the onus of proof will be on Arnauld to show us what such a kind of *scientia* would look like; here the presumption is very much in Malebranche's favor that no such *scientia* is available.

Malebranche's critique of Descartes' account of self-knowledge is powerful, perhaps even unassailable. Certainly, there are good grounds for thinking that Malebranche's polemic compares favorably with Gassendi's otherwise similar critique of Descartes on the score of self-knowledge. Gassendi complained that Descartes had not succeeded in discovering the nature of the mind because he had not revealed its internal substance or constitution. Gassendi famously insisted that a kind of chemical labor was needed to reveal this internal substance.[23] However, arguably Descartes dismissed this criticism as misguided on the ground that it is of the essence of the mental to have no internal constitution; there is no analogy with body in this respect. Malebranche, by contrast, was not vulnerable to this kind of response; in saying that we have no idea of the mind, the contrast that he invoked was not with our ability to know the internal structure of bodies but rather with our ability to have an *a priori* science of geometry. Descartes could not without embarrassment reasonably dismiss Malebranche's point by saying that it is of the essence of mind to be resistant to *a priori* knowledge, for to concede this point would be tantamount to admitting the impossibility of a *scientia* of the mind.

At the heart of the debate between Malebranche and orthodox Cartesians is thus the possibility of systematic *a priori* knowledge of the mind of the kind we have in geometry. This interpretation of the debate is seemingly challenged by Schmaltz who holds that the key contrast is not between the *a priori* and the *a posteriori* but rather between the objective and the subjective view. On this account, Malebranche's central point is that whereas we have an objective view of bodies, we have only a subjective view of mental states.[24] Now in one way the two approaches to Malebranche are on a par. Any commentator must take account of the fact that, for

Malebranche, there is an idea of the human mind to which God alone has epistemic access. By virtue of this idea God has *a priori* knowledge of mental states, and he also an objective knowledge of them without of course experiencing them. Thus, no discrimination between the two approaches is possible in these terms. However, if we consider Malebranche's polemical target, there are grounds for preferring the approach that stresses the centrality of the issue of *a priori* knowledge. To insist on the subjectivity of mental states is to insist on something that Descartes concedes; to insist on our lack of *a priori* knowledge in this area is rather to insist on something that is controversial and damaging to the Cartesian project.

## IV. SPIRITUALITY AND IMMORTALITY: THE DEMONSTRATION OF PROPERTIES

On one set of issues Arnauld was able to throw down a pointed challenge to Malebranche. Malebranche claimed to be able to demonstrate the freedom, spirituality, and immortality of the soul, yet it is difficult to see how this is possible if we have no clear idea of its nature. Indeed, Arnauld argued that it is in fact a contradiction to hold that we have no clear idea of the soul and that we can nonetheless demonstrate these properties. Obviously, as a self-styled Christian philosopher, Malebranche needed to tread carefully through this theological minefield. It might seem that the safest, or at least most consistent course, would be to adopt a fideistic position; he could take the line that the immortality of the soul, for instance, is a truth of faith for which no rational justification is possible. Yet Malebranche did not avail himself of this option. In what follows we shall take up the question of whether Malebranche can justify his confidence in the possibility of demonstrating the spirituality and immortality of the soul (the issue of freedom of the will is discussed in Chapter 8 of this volume). Malebranche's attempts at demonstration may not be convincing, but at least his strategy is instructive.

   The issue of strategy is obviously crucial for Malebranche, because as Arnauld sharply observes, he debarred himself the obvious recourse of basing a proof on the idea of the mind. Yet to say this is not to mean he has no philosophical resources available for demonstrating properties of the soul. The direct route via the idea of the mind may be blocked, but it remains open to him to appeal to inner consciousness or to the idea of extension. As we have seen, Malebranche held that an appeal to the idea of extension is necessary to determine the ontological status of sensible qualities.

It is to the deliverances of inner consciousness that Malebranche appealed in *The Search After Truth*:

Although our knowledge of our soul is not complete, what we do know of it through consciousness or inner sensation is enough to demonstrate its immortality, spirituality, freedom, and several other attributes we need to know. And this seems to be why God does not cause us to know the soul, as he causes us to know bodies, through its idea. The knowledge that we have of our soul through consciousness is imperfect, granted; but it is not false. (*Search* III.2.vii, OC 1:453; LO 239)

Malebranche here appeals to the Cartesian principle that we have incorrigible knowledge of our mental states; thus, if I believe that I am in pain, for example, then it is true that I am in pain. However, obviously it is a far cry from asserting such incorrigibility to demonstrating the spirituality and immortality of the mind. As we shall see, Malebranche became dissatisfied with this strategy of appealing to inner consciousness, and this is hardly surprising, for it raises a number of difficulties.

In the first place, the difficulty of proving that the mind is a spiritual substance on his principles is complicated by the issue of his commitment to Platonism. For Malebranche, the spirituality that he seeks to prove with regard to the soul cannot be simply equated with the property of being immaterial. Ideas in God are immaterial – they are not at all like tables and chairs – but they are not spiritual in the sense in which the soul is supposed to be a spiritual substance; that is, they are not purely thinking or conscious beings. Perhaps it is possible to mount a defense of Malebranche's position here, which would take something like the following form. Anything that is immaterial is either an idea or it is spiritual. Now when I turn my consciousness on myself, I discover not merely that the object of such consciousness is immaterial but also that it is not an idea, for I find that it does not have the properties of infinity, necessity, and the like, which can be predicated of all ideas. Nonetheless, although it is possible to see how Malebranche might defend his position, it is fair to say that he did not adequately attend to the issue of the relationship between the properties of being immaterial and spiritual. In the

context of the mind-body problem, Malebranche tended to write like
an orthodox Cartesian who recognized only two kinds of substance
and ignored the complicating factors introduced by his commitment
to a kind of Christian Platonism.

The fact that Malebranche often approached the mind-body problem in the spirit of Cartesian orthodoxy points to a more specific
difficulty with his proof that the soul is spiritual. As Schmaltz has
argued, Malebranche may have inherited some of Descartes' difficulties in this area.[25] Having established the certainty of his own existence in the Second Meditation, Descartes proceeds to argue that
he is a thinking thing. Unfortunately, as critics since Gassendi have
observed, Descartes seems guilty of a damaging slide here; he seems
to move illicitly from "I am only certain that I am a thinking thing"
to "I am certain that I am only a thinking thing" (that is, a thing
whose whole essence consists in thinking).[26] It seems that in some
of his formulations Malebranche may have been guilty of an analogous mistake, expressed in terms of the deliverances of consciousness or inner sensation. That is, he may have moved from the weak
thesis that inner consciousness acquaints him with the fact that he
is a thinking thing to the stronger thesis that inner consciousness
acquaints him with the fact that he is only a thinking thing.

A further difficulty is suggested by Malebranche's claim that our
knowledge of the soul is imperfect or incomplete; he invited us to
think of self-knowledge in terms of a model to which he is not
entitled. Consider the case of a schoolboy geometer who knows
just enough Euclidean geometry to be able to demonstrate the
Pythagorean theorem; however, he does not know enough to be able
to demonstrate more difficult theorems. By saying that our knowledge of it is incomplete, Malebranche led us to suppose that our
epistemic position with regard to our soul is rather similar to that of
the schoolboy geometer. We know just enough of its nature through
inner consciousness to demonstrate its spirituality and the like, even
though there are *a priori* truths about the soul that are hidden from
us. However, this overlooks the fact that the distinction between
knowledge by idea and knowledge by consciousness or inner sensation is officially supposed to be a difference of kind, not a difference of
degree only. Our knowledge by consciousness may allow us to make
incorrigible judgments about our occurrent mental states, but there
is no reason to suppose that this kind of knowledge can allow us to

demonstrate truths about its nature or essence. The demonstration of such truths belongs to the sphere of knowledge through idea, or *a priori* knowledge, and it is Malebranche's official position that such knowledge of the soul is debarred to us.

Whether and how far Malebranche was conscious of these difficulties is not entirely clear. Schmaltz recently suggested that Malebranche may have been more impressed by another difficulty with his appeal to consciousness or inner sensation; Malebranche may have been struck by the implausibility of maintaining that inner consciousness can establish the spirituality and immortality of the mind while denying that it can resolve the question of the ontological status of sensible qualities.[27] As we have seen, Malebranche is insistent that it is the idea of extension that is needed in order to resolve this issue. In any case, whatever his reasons for dissatisfaction, Malebranche came to abandon the strategy of appealing to inner sensation or consciousness. In 1693, Malebranche wrote to Régis that the soul:

senses only that it is, and it is evident that it can sense only what it is in itself. It sees itself and knows itself if you will, but exclusively through inner sensation, a confused sensation that discovers to it neither what it is nor what is the nature of any of its modalities. This sensation does not reveal to it that it is not extended, still less that color, that the whiteness, for example, that it sees in this paper, is really only a modification of its own substance. This sensation is thus only shadowy (*tenebres*) in this regard. (OC 17–1:298)

Instead, Malebranche adopted the only remaining strategy available to him. He has recourse to the idea of extension in order to prove the spirituality and immortality of the mind.

Malebranche offered somewhat different versions of the argument in different places, but one version takes the following form:

(1) Thoughts are not relations of distance.
(2) Anything which is not a relation of distance is not a modification of extension.
(3) Therefore, thoughts are not modifications of extension (*Dialogues* 1, OC 12:32–3: JS 7).[28]

This argument seems vulnerable to several objections. In a brilliant short work called "Conversation of Philarète and Ariste,"

which is a continuation of Malebranche's *Dialogues on Metaphysics,*
Leibniz observed that a reductive materialist would challenge the
first premise:

[Malebranche's spokesman] holds that no thoughts are relations of distance,
because we cannot measure thoughts. But a follower of Epicurus will say
that this is due to our lack of proper knowledge of them, and that if we
knew the corpuscles that form thought and the motions that are necessary
for this, we would see that thoughts are measurable and are the workings of
some subtle machines.[29]

It is only fair to observe, however, that Leibniz was using one of his
speakers to play devil's advocate here. Leibniz may have sought to
criticize the argument from the standpoint of the reductive materialist but he had no intention of defending such a position himself.

   In a more Lockean spirit, it is also natural to observe that, even
if sound, the argument establishes less than the Cartesians suppose.
With the Cartesians, Malebranche was of course committed to identifying extension with the essence of matter; thus the conclusion of
his argument is really a subconclusion from which it is supposed to
follow straightforwardly that thought is not a modification of matter. However, it is just this last step in the argument challenged
by Locke and others who rejected the Cartesian doctrine that the
essence of matter is extension. Thus, even if thought is clearly not
a way of being extended, it does not follow that it is not a modification of matter. In the *Essay Concerning Human Understanding,*
Locke further broke with the Cartesian framework by challenging
the principle that any property of a substance must be a determinate
modification of its essence. He argued that, for all we know, thought
may be a property which is superadded by God to certain material
substances.[30]

   Malebranche also appealed ultimately to the idea of extension to
prove the immortality of the soul. Employing a strategy of proof that
goes back to Plato's *Phaedo,* Malebranche argued that "if the mind is
not extended, it will not be divisible, and if it is not divisible, it must
be agreed that in this sense it will not be corruptible" (*Search* IV.2.iv,
OC 2:24; LO 274); thus, the immortality of the soul is supposed to
follow from its spirituality. The argument is parasitic on the prior
proof of the mind's spirituality, and as we have seen, Malebranche
came to believe that such a proof is dependent on an appeal to the

idea of extension. The idea of extension plays a similarly indirect role in a second proof, which turns on general considerations concerning the indestructibility of substances (OC 6:163). Lacking a clear idea of a thinking substance, we must turn to the idea of extended substance to furnish us with a model of what is involved in being a substance. When we consult such an idea, we are supposed to see that it is of the very nature of substance to be indestructible. It is natural to object of course that even if extended substance is necessarily indestructible, it does not follow that it is indestructible by virtue of being a substance. Hence, the idea of extended substance offers no basis for proving the immortality of the soul. However, Malebranche had a response to this: Extended substance is not indestructible by virtue of being extended because there are extended items – particular bodies, for example – which can be destroyed; Malebranche need not deny that the human body, for example, is corrupted and destroyed at death. It is thus supposed to follow that extended substance is indestructible precisely as substance.

Malebranche, then, had a strategy for proving the spirituality and immortality of the mind that provides an answer to Arnauld's challenge. This strategy remains at least formally consistent with his thesis that we have no idea of the mind. No one of course today is likely to find these proofs impressive, but their weaknesses should not blind us to the real strengths of Malebranche's anti-Cartesian position on the idea of the mind. His critique of Descartes in this area, is powerful, perhaps even unassailable. As Malebranche saw, surely correctly, it is the pursuit of *scientia* that really animates the Cartesian project of first philosophy. It is this project that Descartes announced on the first page of the *Meditations* when he said that his aim is to establish the sciences on new and secure foundations. Descartes could not admit that no *scientia* of the mind is possible without thereby conceding that with respect to the highest kind of knowledge, it is simply false that mind is better known than body. Further, to make such an admission would surely be an embarrassment.

Malebranche's critique of Descartes on the issue of self-knowledge also suggests a different moral. Although he may never make the point explicitly, Malebranche seemed to see that Descartes' philosophy was really driven by a new conception of matter. Matter not only offers the paradigm of the intelligible; it also gives rise to a new conception of the mental. Descartes subscribed to what might be called a dustbin or grabbag conception of the mind. The items that fall under the umbrella of the mental, for Descartes, are whatever is left over from the picture of the world once matter is defined in purely geometrical terms. Modern philosophers who are highly critical of Descartes' dualism have nonetheless often inherited its account of the sphere of the mental, while failing to see how this account is shaped by a new conception of the material world. Malebranche was one of the few philosophers to recognize that any serious challenge to Descartes' philosophy of mind must also understand its roots in his philosophy of matter.

### NOTES

1 See, e.g., M. Wilson, *Descartes*, pp. 181, 200–1.

2 On the theory of efficacious ideas, see Robinet, *Système et existence dans l' oeuvre de Malebranche*, pp. 259–62. See also N. Jolley, "Intellect and Illumination in Malebranche."

3 Gueroult, *Malebranche* I, pp. 189–90.

4 Schmaltz, *Malebranche's Theory of the Soul*, pp. 102–3.

5 This passage was added in a later edition. See also *Dialogues* V.5, OC 12:116; JS 77.

6 Alquié, *Le cartésianisme de Malebranche*, p. 105.

7 Tad Schmaltz has shown that Malebranche's discussion of the rainbow-colored soul has its roots in a series of philosophical conferences at Commercy. See *Malebranche's Theory of the Soul*, p. 82.

8 Descartes, *Principles of Philosophy* IV.198, AT IXB 322; CSM 1, p. 285.

9 See Schmaltz, "Malebranche's Cartesianism and Lockean Colors," 387–403.

10 Nadler, *Malebranche and Ideas*, pp. 64–5.

11 For Descartes's view that animals are just machines or automata, see *Discourse on Method* V.

12 Descartes, *Meditations* VI, AT VII 81; CSM II 56.

13 For a very different view of Malebranche's reasons for holding that animals are just machines or automata, see D. and M. Radner, *Animal Consciousness*, pp. 70–91.

14 Gassendi, Fifth Objections, AT VII 275–6; CSM II 192–3.

15 Descartes, Fifth Replies, AT VII 359–60; CSM II 249.

16 Locke, *Essay Concerning Human Understanding*, III.iv.11.

17 For further discussion of Malebranche's argument, see Schmaltz, *Malebranche's Theory of the Soul*, p. 75.

18 Tad Schmaltz has recently observed (*Malebranche's Theory of the Soul*, p. 75) that Malebranche here anticipates Robert Adams who draws attention to the implausibility of supposing that there is a unique objectively valid spectrum in which all phenomenal qualia are ordered (see R. M. Adams, "Flavors, Colors, and God," pp. 257–8). A relevant difference, however, is that Adams is concerned to argue that such an ordering is in principle impossible, whereas Malebranche's point is rather that it is contingently unavailable to us. God, by contrast, has access to an idea of the soul which presumably allows him to order these sensations in a way in which we cannot.

19 Arnauld, *Des Vraies et des Fausses Idées*, ch. XXIII, pp. 321–2.

20 Arnauld, *Des Vraies et des Fausses Idées*, ch. XXIII, pp. 310–11.

21 Arnauld, *Des Vraies et des Fausses Idées*, ch. XXIII, pp. 314–15. See Schmaltz, *Malebranche's Theory of the Soul*, p. 76.

22 Adams, "Flavors, Colors, and God," p. 258.

23 Gassendi, Fifth Objections, Descartes, AT VII 276–7; CSM II 193.

24 Schmaltz, *Malebranche's Theory of the Soul*, ch. 1, pp. 41–3. Perhaps Schmaltz is in danger of conflating the thesis that mental phenomena are subjective with the very different thesis that in the case of such subjective phenomena no objective knowledge is possible.

25 See Schmaltz, *Malebranche's Theory of the Soul*, ch. 4.

26 See Gassendi, Fifth Objections, AT VII 276; CSM II 192. The offending passage is *Meditations* II, AT VII 27; CSM II 18. See also Descartes' explanation at AT IX A 215–6; CSM II 276–7.

27 Schmaltz, *Malebranche's Theory of the Soul*, p. 134.

28 Cf. OC 6:163.

29 Leibniz, "Conversation of Philarèthe and Ariste," *Die Philosophischen Schriften von G. W. Leibniz*, VI, p. 587.

30 Locke, *Essay Concerning Human Understanding*, IV.iii.6.

# 3    Malebranche on Ideas and the Vision in God

One of the most controversial of the claims in Malebranche's first published work, *The Search After Truth*, is that "we see all things in God" (*nous voyons toutes choses en Dieu*) (III.2.vi, OC 1:437; LO 230). It is true that this text restricts that particular claim by noting that "we see in God only the things of which we have ideas," and in particular, only bodies and their properties.[1] Yet even given this restriction the doctrine that we see all things (that is, bodies) in (that is, through ideas in) God scandalized Malebranche's most prominent critic, the Augustinian theologian and Cartesian partisan Antoine Arnauld (1612–94). Arnauld protested in particular that such a doctrine has the "bizarre" consequence that "we see God when we see bodies, the sun, a horse or a tree."[2]

Arnauld was objecting here not only to the placement of ideas of material objects in God, but also, and more basically, to the reification of ideas. As an alternative to Malebranche's claim that the ideas we perceive are "representative beings" distinct from our perceptions, he offered the position, which he plausibly ascribed to Descartes, that such ideas are identical to those perceptions. It is difficult not to prefer Arnauld's parsimonious account of ideas to Malebranche's more exotic doctrine of the "Vision in God" (as I call his thesis that we see bodies by means of ideas in God). Yet Malebranche did not simply overlook Arnauld's alternative to his doctrine. Indeed, he came to insist that such an alternative cannot explain how our perception of the nature of bodies can reach beyond our finite experience.

This chapter attempts to give Malebranche's admittedly foreign doctrine of the Vision in God a fair hearing. It begins with a discussion of the connection of this doctrine to what Malebranche found most valuable in the work of his two philosophical heroes, namely, Saint Augustine and Descartes. While Cartesian opponents such as Arnauld tended to invoke the views of Descartes to counter Malebranche's position that ideas are distinct from our perceptions, Malebranche himself indicated consistently that the primary inspiration for this position was the theory of divine illumination in Augustine. He noted in particular that the Augustinian identification of ideas with "archetypes" of objects in the divine mind supports his own claim that nothing in us can serve to represent material objects. By contrast, the influence of Descartes is most evident in Malebranche's view that we perceive the nature of body by means of an intellectual idea of extension. He further inherited from Descartes the problem of relating a "pure" or nonsensory idea of extension to our ordinary sensory experience of the material world.

Nonetheless, Malebranche did not inherit from Descartes the conclusion that this pure idea exists in God. This chapter considers three main arguments that Malebranche offered for the Vision in God over the course of his philosophical career. His initial argument in the 1674 *Search* attempts to establish the doctrine by eliminating all competing explanations of our perception of material objects. While Arnauld unfairly claimed that this argument begs the question by assuming from the start that ideas are objects distinct from our perceptions, he did have a point when he protested that it distracts attention from the central issue of the nature of ideas.

In the 1678 "Elucidation 10," his commentary on the discussion of ideas in the *Search*, Malebranche offered a second argument for the Vision in God that appeals directly to the necessity, immutability, and infinity of the ideas we perceive. The specific emphasis on infinity is connected to the introduction in this text of the controversial claim that we know bodies through a single "intelligible extension" that exists in God. Malebranche later qualified this claim by holding that this extension differs from God's substance "taken absolutely," thereby indicating that he is committed to a vision *in* God rather than a vision *of* God. However, "Elucidation 10" leaves him with the unsettled position that what we see in God is rendered sensible by our sensations.

The final stage of the development of the Vision in God was triggered by the objection of a Cartesian critic, Pierre-Sylvain Régis (1632–1707), that Malebranche had done nothing to explain how we perceive the material world through a "union" with God. In his 1693 *Response to Régis*, Malebranche countered by suggesting a third argument for the Vision in God on which divine ideas are the objects of our thought in the sense that they cause our perceptions of bodies. This final argument involves a shift in Malebranche from a vision *in* God to a vision *by* God,[3] one which takes him further from the consequence, so scandalous to Arnauld, that we "see God" when we perceive bodies. Such an argument also provides the material for an account that reconciles Malebranche's commitment to the intellectual nature of the idea of extension with his claim that such an idea informs our sensory perception of the world.

## I.  AUGUSTINIAN IDEAS AND CARTESIAN VISION

The exchange between Malebranche and Arnauld on the issue of the nature of ideas, which was one of the major intellectual events of the early modern period, appears at times to be a battle for the soul of Descartes. In the work that opened the debate, the 1683 *On True and False Ideas*, Arnauld cited Descartes explicitly in support of the position that our idea of an object is simply a perceptual modification of our soul that represents – or is "of" – that object.[4] No doubt irritated by the invocation of this authority, Malebranche claimed in response that Descartes himself did not in fact affirm the principle in Arnauld that "the modalities of the soul are essentially representative" (OC 6:172). In a later response to Arnauld, Malebranche conceded that Descartes did in fact say that "ideas are modalities of minds," though he added that Descartes said this only "because, unlike me, he does not take the word "idea" to signify exclusively the "representative reality," but for those sorts of thoughts by which one perceives a man, an angel, etc." (OC 6:217). The reference here is to the distinction in the "Third Meditation" between the *formal reality* of an idea as a mode of our mind and the *objective reality* in virtue of which that idea represents a particular object.[5] Malebranche's claim is that Descartes simply confused the idea as formal reality, which exists only as a modification in us, with the idea as objective or representative reality, which is distinct from our perceptual modifications.

Arnauld had little difficulty drawing from Descartes' texts the position that the objective reality of a perception of an external object is simply the internal "form" of the perception that serves to relate it to that object.[6] Given Arnauld's considerable intellect and intimate knowledge of Descartes' system, there was little chance that Malebranche would show him up in Descartes exegesis. Yet it must be said that Malebranche was not overly concerned to connect his account of ideas to Descartes' writings. It is telling, for instance, that when Arnauld charged that this account is dangerously novel, Malebranche responded that "it is principally [Augustine's] authority which has given me the desire to put forth *the new philosophy of ideas*" (OC 6:80). Indeed, he had emphasized in the *Search* itself that Augustine had proven in "an infinity of passages [that] we already see God in this life through the knowledge we have of the eternal truths" (III.2.vi, OC 1:144; LO 233). Moreover, he had offered in the preface to this work the Augustinian position that God's "eternal wisdom" is the source (*principe*) of our understanding and that God alone "can teach us the truth through the manifestation of His substance ... and without the mediation of any creature" (OC 1:17ff; LO xxiiiff).[7]

Malebranche took Augustine to hold that the divine substance is revealed to us through "the exemplars or the archetypes of creatures" contained in God that provide the models for his creation of the world (OC 12:11ff). He further explicated the Augustinian position that the archetypes are contained in God by appealing to the view in Thomas Aquinas that "God's ideas of creatures are ... only His essence, insofar as it is participable or imperfectly imitable, for God contains every creaturely perfection, though in a divine and infinite way" (OC 3:149; LO 625).[8] The last point that God contains creaturely perfections "in a divine and infinite way" indicates that He contains perfections that are limited and diverse in creatures in an unlimited and absolutely simple manner. How God can so contain these perfections is something that Malebranche admitted "seems incomprehensible," though he added that he is not bothered by his lack of comprehension because "I long stopped worrying about problems that are beyond me" (OC 6:204). This attitude is understandable given his reliance on the traditional view that God, as a supremely perfect being, can depend on nothing external to Himself for his perfect knowledge of creatures. Because he took reason to reveal that God knows creatures by means of His own perfection, Malebranche felt no need to worry that he cannot comprehend how precisely He contains the perfections of creatures.

Arnauld objected that the claim that creaturely perfections are "in" God is equivocal. He conceded that the perfections must be *objectively* in God, because for them to be present in this way is simply for them to be known by God. However, he took Malebranche to offer the problematic view that these perfections are also *formally* in God, that is to say, that God actually contains the perfections.[9] Malebranche responded that such a view is a mere "phantom" concocted by Arnauld, and that his own position is that the perfections of creatures are present in God not formally but *eminently* (OC 6:118ff).[10] Here Malebranche was drawing on Descartes' stipulation that an object eminently contains a property just in case it both lacks that property and contains something that "is such that it can stand in the place of such [a property]."[11] Descartes himself tended to ignore the condition that an eminently contained property "stand in the place of" that property, requiring only that the former exist in an object that is higher on the ontological "scale of reality" than any object that formally contains the property.[12] However, this condition was important for Malebranche, who held that God eminently contains created perfections, and thereby has something that can stand in place of them, in virtue of the fact that he has ideas that serve as the archetypes for such perfections. Thus Malebranche inferred, as Descartes did not, that it follows from the fact that God eminently contains perfections that He has ideas or archetypes that represent these perfections to Him.[13]

The link in Malebranche between eminent containment and representation explains his otherwise puzzling inability to comprehend Arnauld's seemingly intuitive proposal that our mind represents bodies to itself by means of its own ideas. Certainly for Malebranche our "ideas" or perceptions cannot represent external objects by serving as the archetypes for these objects, as is the case with God's ideas.[14] Nor can bodily perfections be said to be contained in our mind in the manner in which they are contained in God's mind.[15] The basic argument in Malebranche, then, is that our perceptions cannot represent external objects given that they cannot stand in place of those objects in the way in which God's ideas do. This argument is similar in structure to Malebranche's argument in the *Search* that creatures cannot be real causes because they cannot be necessarily related to effects in the manner in which God's volitions are related to their upshots (VI.2.iii, OC 2:309–20; LO 446–52). While the refutation of the "dangerous" claim of "the philosophy of the ancients" that there are real causes other than God occurs only in the final book of this text, long after the defense in the third book of the Vision in God, in later years Malebranche came to appeal to his views concerning divine causality in order to explicate the manner in which God's ideas represent external objects to us (see §4).

One reason that the Arnauld-Malebranche debate proved to be so intractable is that the two thinkers had such fundamentally different starting points. Arnauld began his discussion of Malebranchean ideas by invoking the certainty of the cogito in Descartes.[16] The reflective Cartesian self provided the basis for his account of representation. By contrast, Malebranche began his response to Arnauld by citing the conclusion, which he claimed to find in Augustine, that "the universal Reason in which all minds participate is the *Word* or the *Reason* of God Himself" (OC 6:50). He thus took Augustine to anticipate his own "God centered" approach to our perception of external objects.

Malebranche conceded to Arnauld that Augustine himself did not say that we see bodies in God. However, he went on to downplay this difference by noting:

What prevented this holy doctor from speaking as I have done [in saying that we see all things in God] is that being in the prejudice that colors are in objects ... as one sees objects only by colors, he believed that it was the object itself that one saw. He could not say that one saw in God these colors that are not of a nature immutable, intelligent, and common to all minds, but sensible and particular modifications of the soul, and according to Saint Augustine, a quality that is spread out on the surface of bodies. (OC 6:68)

The suggestion here is that Augustine did not say that we see bodies in God simply because he was in the grip of the prejudice that sensation reveals that colors are "spread out on the surface of bodies." Malebranche assumed that Augustine would have held that we see bodies in God had he recognized that colors and other sensible qualities are only "sensible and particular modifications of the soul."

This assumption is admittedly questionable; Augustine himself seems to have had little interest in using the theory of divine illumination to explain our knowledge of the material world. Moreover, Malebranche allowed that post-Augustinian advances in the understanding of bodies were made possible by a novel conception of matter. Thus he noted in the preface to the *Search* that

although one must agree that [Augustine] explained the properties of the soul and the body better than all those who preceded him and who have followed him until our own time, nonetheless he would have done better not to attribute to the bodies surrounding us all the sensible qualities that we perceive by means of them, for in the final analysis these qualities are not clearly contained in the idea that we have of matter. As a result, it can be said with some assurance that the difference between the mind and the body has been known with sufficient clarity for only a few years. (OC 1:20; LO xxvi)

The recently discovered idea to which this passage alludes clearly is that of Descartes. Descartes had argued that matter is simply extension by contrasting the idea of extension with the idea of shape. He noted that while the idea of shape is "incomplete" because he cannot conceive shape apart from extension, "the idea I have of a substance with extension and shape is a complete idea, because I can conceive it entirely on its own and deny of it everything else of which I have an idea" (AT 3:475; CSMK 202). This line of argument informs Malebranche's claim in the *Search* that although we cannot conceive of roundness without extension, because roundness is only extension itself existing in a certain way, we can conceive of this extension apart from anything else; thus this extension "is not a mode of any being, and consequently is itself a being." The conclusion here is that because matter is a single being and "not composed of several beings – as a man, who is composed of body and mind – matter clearly is nothing other than extension" (III.2.viii, OC 1:462; LO 244).

Malebranche explained the remark in the preface that sensible qualities "are not clearly contained in the idea we have of matter" when he wrote in the first book of the *Search* that because the idea of extension "can represent only successive and permanent relations of distance, that is to say, instances of movements and shapes," it cannot represent "relations of joy, pleasure, pain, heat, taste, color, or any other sensible qualities, although these qualities are sensed when a certain change occurs in the body" (I.10, OC 1:123; LO 49). Later in this same book, Malebranche emphasized that any account of sensation must rely on a conception of body derived from "pure intellection" rather than from sensation.

In order thus to judge soundly about light and colors, as well as the other sensible qualities, one must distinguish with care the sensation of color from the movement of the optic nerve, and recognize by reason that movements and impulsions are properties of bodies and that hence they can be encountered in the objects and in the organs of our senses; but that light, and the colors we see, are modifications of the soul quite different from the others, and of which also one has quite different ideas. (I.12, OC 1:141; LO 59)

The particular argument in this passage is linked to the principle – central to the first book of the *Search*, "On the Senses" – that one must reject "the prejudice common to all men, *That their sensations are in the objects that they sense*" (I.16, OC 1:169; LO 75). Malebranche held that this very prejudice was the source of Augustine's projection of color sensations onto bodies. He also emphasized that Descartes provided the means to eradicate such a prejudice when he discovered an intellectual idea of matter that entails that there is nothing in bodies that resembles such sensations.

Malebranche's conclusion that *sensible qualities* are nothing more than "particular and sensible modifications of the soul" does seem to go a bit beyond Descartes, who suggested at times the more Lockean position that such qualities are dispositional properties in bodies that produce the relevant sensations in us.[17] Yet what is most important for Malebranche's departure from Augustine is the claim that we know "by reason" that our sensations differ from bodily properties. Such a claim is deeply connected to Descartes' own views, and in particular to his conclusion in the "Second Meditation" that bodies are "strictly perceived neither by the senses nor by the faculty of the imagination, but by the intellect alone."[18] Descartes' argument for this conclusion draws on the memorable example of the piece of wax. He noted initially in the "Second Meditation" that the determinate features of the wax that he apprehends through the senses – its taste, smell and color, and also its size and shape – cannot be essential to it because such features change even while the wax remains. The nature of this wax thus consists only in being a determinable entity, "nothing other than something extended, flexible, mutable." Yet Descartes further claimed that while he can imagine some of the changes in shape that the wax can undergo, still "I would not judge correctly what the wax is, unless I take this [wax] to admit of more varieties of being extended than I ever would encompass [*complexus*] by means of imagination." The result is that the nature of the wax as infinitely (or, as Descartes preferred to say, indefinitely) determinable is something that is perceived not by means of the sensory faculties but rather "by the mind alone" (*sola mente percipere*), that is to say, by pure intellect.[19]

The insistence in the "Second Meditation" on the possibility of the perception of body through pure intellect is reflected in Malebranche's own discussion of ideas in the *Search*. This discussion is found in a section devoted to the "pure understanding," that is, to "the mind's faculty of knowing external objects without forming corporeal images of them in the brain" (III.1.i, OC 1:381; LO 198). It is this independence from bodily images that distinguishes such a faculty from the faculties of sense and imagination, the latter of which involve "the understanding perceiving objects through the organs of the body" (I.1, OC 1:43; LO 3). Malebranche further claimed, in line with the view in the "Second Meditation," that it is the pure understanding that grasps the nature of "material things, extension with its properties" (I.4, OC 1:66; LO 16ff). He added that this faculty alone is involved in the perception of "a shape of a thousand sides," an example that brings to mind Descartes' appeal in the "Sixth Meditation" to the case of the chiliagon. In this text, Descartes applied his results cocerning the piece of wax to that particular case by noting that we can intellectually apprehend distinguishing properties of the chiliagon even though we cannot form a picture of this figure that clearly differs from the picture of a myriagon or any other polygon with many sides.[20] For both Malebranche and Descartes, then, it is the intellect that apprehends the nature of extension and its modes.

The intellectualist thrust of the Vision in God is reinforced by Malebranche's caveat in the *Search* that when he says that "we see material and sensible things in God, it must be carefully noted that I am not saying that we have sensations of them in God." Indeed, later in this passage he distinguished our sensations from the "pure idea" of body found "in conjunction with" or "joined to" those sensations (III.2.vi, OC 1:445; LO 234). I have already touched on, and will return to, the ontological point here that the pure idea differs from sensations in virtue of the fact that the former exists in God rather than as a modification of our soul. What I want to emphasize now is the different suggestion that a "pure" or nonsensory idea of body somehow informs our sensory experience of the material world. There is a similar suggestion in the "Second Meditation," where Descartes indicated that purely intellectual perception of the wax is present not only when we clearly and distinctly understand the nature of the wax but also when we have an "imperfect and confused" sensory perception of the wax itself.[21] What is required of both Malebranche and Descartes, however, is an explanation of how the clear intellectual conception of the material world is involved in our confused sensory experience.

One tidy explanation in the literature is that Malebranche took the pure idea of body to be restricted to our experience of the so-called "primary" qualities (e.g., sizes, shapes, and motions), with the senses covering the remaining "secondary" qualities (e.g., colors, tastes, and smells).[22] Yet Malebranche himself distinguished our sensation of determinate shapes from the intellectual idea that represents a shape that is determinable in an infinite number of ways.[23] He therefore indicated that our perception of determinate primary qualities is sensory, recalling Descartes' own claim in the "Second Meditation" that we initially perceive the particular shape and size of the wax through the senses.[24] There remains for Descartes and Malebranche alike the problem of the relation of the intellectual idea of extension to our sensory perception of the material world.

Malebranche was initially at a disadvantage in providing a solution to this problem because he said relatively little in the *Search* about the manner in which the soul "sees" pure ideas in God. It is only in light of the emphasis in his mature thought on the causal efficacy of ideas that we can begin to discern a clear account of the manner in which pure ideas serve as the objects of our own sensory modifications. Thus, any discussion of Malebranche's solution to the Cartesian problem concerning the relation of intellectual ideas to our sense experience must await a consideration of his development of (what he took to be) his Augustinian theory of the Vision in God.

## II.    VISION IN GOD IN THE *SEARCH*

The discussion of the nature of ideas in the second part of the third book of the *Search* begins with the assertion that "everyone agrees that we do not perceive objects external to us by themselves" because it can hardly be the case that "the soul should leave the body to stroll about the heavens to see the objects present there" (III.2.i, OC 1:413; LO 217). Arnauld, for one, took exception to the claim of universal agreement, countering that "ideas, taken in the sense of representative beings, distinct from perceptions, are not needed by our soul in order to see bodies."[25] The objection here is that Malebranche is stacking the deck in favor of the conclusion that we see ideas in God by assuming from the start that these ideas are objects distinct from our perceptions rather than, as Arnauld would have it, something identical to these perceptions.

The definition in the first edition of the *Search* of an idea as "the immediate object or what is closest to the mind when it perceives some thing" (III.2.1, OC 1:414a) does indeed appear to assume that ideas are objects as opposed to perceptions. However, the claim that an idea is an immediate object has a more innocuous sense indicated by Arnauld's own remark that "*the perception* of a square indicates more directly the soul as perceiving the square and *the idea* of a square indicates more directly the square insofar as it is objectively in the mind."[26] As Malebranche subsequently indicated to Arnauld, an idea of a body is simply the *objective reality* of that body, the body as represented to the mind.[27] This object-as-represented must differ from the object itself given Arnauld's own admission that the objective reality of a body differs from the formal reality it has in the material world.[28] Of course, Arnauld further insisted that this objective reality is nothing distinct from our perception of the body, which is itself merely a modification of our soul. Yet Malebranche allowed that the conclusion that we must perceive external objects through ideas does not itself preclude this option when he noted that such a conclusion leaves open the question of whether an idea is "a *modality of the soul*, according to the sentiment of Mr. Arnauld; or an *express species*, according to certain philosophers, or an *entity created* with the soul, according to others; or finally *intelligible extension rendered sensible by color or light*, according to my sentiment" (OC 6:95).[29]

It is not at all clear from the remarks in the *Search* what it means to say that "intelligible extension is rendered sensible by color or light," and indeed this characterization broaches certain difficulties for Malebranche (see §3). However, the list of alternatives to the Vision in God that Malebranche presented to Arnauld is drawn explicitly from this text, which provides a proof of this doctrine that has the form of an "argument from elimination." According to this particular proof, there are the following four possible alternatives to the conclusion that we see bodies through ideas in God: (1) Bodies transmit resembling species to the soul (III.2.ii); (2) Our soul has a power to produce ideas when triggered by nonresembling bodily impressions (III.2.iii); (3) Ideas are created with our soul or produced in it successively by God (III.2.iv); and (4) Our soul sees both the essence and the existence of bodies by considering its own perfections (III.2.v).[30] Malebranche claimed to Arnauld that because this list constitutes "an exact division ... of all the ways in which we can see objects" beyond seeing them in God, and because each of the alternative accounts yields "manifest contradictions," his argument from elimination yields an indisputable proof of the Augustinian doctrine of the Vision in God (OC 6:198ff).

In his posthumously published reading notes on the *Search*, Locke objected that there is no proof in Malebranche's text that the enumeration of the possible ways of perceiving external objects is exhaustive. In the absence of such a proof, according to Locke, we cannot exclude the possibility that there is some way of perceiving bodies other than the Vision in God that we cannot comprehend but that an omnipotent God can bring about.[31] Indeed, it is difficult to determine from the remarks in the *Search* itself precisely how Malebranche arrived at his enumeration. Yet Desmond Connell has produced evidence for the somewhat surprising result that the enumeration was guided by the account of angelic knowledge in the work of the early modern scholastic, Francisco Suárez.[32] Particularly crucial for Malebranche's enumeration is Suárez's claim that angels must know material objects through species that God adds to their mind given that God alone can know them through His own substance. In light of this claim, we can take Malebranche's first three hypotheses to cover the various ways in which we could perceive bodies through immaterial species "superadded" to our soul, and his fourth hypothesis to cover the possibility that we perceive bodies in the perfections of our own soul.

So read, Malebranche's argument from elimination proceeds in the following manner: We must see material objects either (a) by immaterial species distinct from our soul's perfections (hyp.1–3), or (b) in the perfections of our soul (hyp.4), or (c) in a being that contains the perfections of all creatures in a perfect manner (the Vision in God). If (a), then the species must be either (i) drawn from material species sent from bodies (hyp.1), or (ii) produced ex nihilo by our own soul (hyp.2),[33] or (iii) created in our soul by God either simultaneously with the creation of the soul or successively thereafter (hyp.3). Because (i)–(iii) are all unacceptable for various reasons, either (b) or (c) must be the case. However, given that a finite being can see in itself neither the infinite nor an infinite number of beings (as Suárez had argued in the case of angels),[34] and also that we can in fact perceive both the infinite and an infinity of beings external to us, it must be that we see external objects by means of perfections contained in the only being that can possess ideas of an infinity of beings, namely, God Himself.[35]

From a Cartesian standpoint, the first three hypotheses are particularly odd because they involve an appeal to immaterial species that are not themselves spiritual substances but also, as superadded, not straightforwardly modes of such a substance.[36] Moreover, Arnauld noted that Malebranche's argument for a particular account of the nature of ideas begins strangely with hypotheses concerning the production of ideas. He objected that the argument thus violates the rule that questions concerning the nature of an object, which are to be answered in terms of the formal cause of that object, not be confused with questions concerning the origin of an object, which are to be answered in terms of the efficient cause of that object.[37] This objection is related to the peculiarity that the argument in the *Search* makes little use of the Augustinian point in this text that the ideas we perceive are "uncreated, immutable, immense, eternal, above all things" (III.2.vi, OC 1:444; LO 233).[38] Surely, it would have been preferable to argue more directly for the Vision in God, especially given Locke's point that there is no proof that Malebranche's enumeration of the alternatives is complete. Malebranche himself never explicitly disowned his indirect argument for this doctrine in the *Search*. However, in his later writings he said little more about this argument, devoting his energies instead to finding less circuitous routes to the Vision in God.

### III. INFINITE INTELLIGIBLE EXTENSION IN "ELUCIDATION 10"

In "Elucidation 10," first published with the third edition (1678) of the *Search*, Malebranche claimed that he would not have offered reasons for the Vision in God beyond those he provided in his first text

were it not for the fact that its importance for religion "indispensably
obliges me to explain and defend it as far as it is possible for me" and
thus to propose "several more arguments for the sentiment that I
have established in the chapters on which I am now writing" (OC
3:128ff; LO 613). Whereas the *Search* infers to the Vision in God
from the inadequacy of alternative accounts of the origin of ideas,
"Elucidation 10" offers the new Augustinian argument that the ideas
we know must exist in an "immutable and necessary Reason" because they are themselves necessary and immutable (OC 3:129ff;
LO613ff).

   This text also includes the argument that the Reason by which
we know the truth must be infinite given that our mind "will never
lack for ideas of shapes, and that it will discover new ones, even if it
were to attend only to these kinds of ideas for all eternity" (OC 3:130;
LO 614). Though some have denied that Malebranche endorsed from
the start the position that ideas in general are infinite,[39] the emphasis on infinity in "Elucidation 10" is anticipated by the Augustinian
point in the initial edition of the *Search* that we can know "abstract
and general truths only through the presence of Him who can enlighten the mind in an infinity of different ways" (III.2.vi, OC 1:441;
LO 232). Moreover, the remarks in "Elucidation 10" reinforce the
claim in this first edition that "a simple piece of wax is capable of an
infinite, or rather of an infinitely infinite number of different modifications" (*Search* III.1.i, OC 1:384; LO 199). This claim is connected
in turn to Descartes' conclusion in the "Second Meditation" that
the nature of the piece of wax is unlimited in virtue of the fact that
this object is capable of countless shapes (see §1). Descartes did not
himself make the further Malebranchean inference that ideas of inexhaustible natures must be distinct from our mind. Yet he did suggest
in the "Second Meditation" that the unlimited idea of the wax cannot be identified with any of the limited perceptions of it that derive
from the senses or the imagination. Malebranche could be seen as
arguing, along similar lines, that an unlimited idea of the wax cannot be identified even with our limited intellectual perceptions of
this object. Indeed, he stressed in the *Search* that the piece of wax is
capable of an infinite number of modifications "that no [finite] mind
can comprehend" (III.1.i, OC 1:384; LO 199). On his view, then, our
intellectual perceptions can no more exhaust the nature of the wax
than can perceptions deriving from our sensory faculties.

Malebranche later appealed to the infinity of ideas in order to respond to the claim in the work of his Cartesian critic Régis that our perceptions can represent infinity without being themselves infinite. Arnauld used this response as the occasion to return to the account of ideas that he had proposed to Malebranche over a decade before. In an open letter published in 1694 – the last year of his life – Arnauld claimed that a simple distinction undermines the argument against Régis.

[I]t is not true that a modality of our soul, which is finite, cannot represent an infinite thing; and it is true, on the contrary, that however finite our perceptions may be, there are some which must pass for infinite in this sense, that they represent the infinite. This is what M. Régis correctly maintained to you, and what he meant by these terms, that they are finite *in essendo*, and infinite *in repræsentando*. You are not happy with this distinction. Too bad for you.[40]

In his *Third Letter* to Arnauld, published five years after the death of his critic, Malebranche rejoined that this distinction does not undermine his original argument against Régis because only that which is infinite *in essendo* can be infinite *in repræsentando*.

[S]ince [the modalities of the soul] are finite modalities, we cannot find the infinite there, since nothingness is not visible, and one cannot perceive in the soul what is not there. Similarly, from the fact that I perceive in a circle an infinity of equal diameters, or rather, from the fact that there are equal diameters therein *in repræsentando*, I must concede that they are really there *in essendo*. For, in effect, a circle contains the reality of an infinity of diameters. In order, then, for the reality to be present to the mind, for it to affect the mind, for the mind to perceive or receive it, it necessarily must really be there. (OC 9:954)

Because the soul is finite, it cannot perceive at one and the same time infinitely many circles. Given the principle that properties can be in the soul *in repræsentando* only if the soul actually perceives them, it follows that the unperceived properties of the circle cannot exist there in this manner: "One cannot perceive in the soul what is not there." Because ideas of shapes include the reality of an infinity of properties that we do not in fact perceive, according to Malebranche, the ideas themselves cannot be found in our soul.

In "Elucidation 10" Malebranche had applied this argument not only to ideas of shapes but also to the idea of extension itself, noting that our mind "even perceives infinity in extension, for the mind cannot doubt that its idea of space is inexhaustible" (OC 3:130; LO 614). This text also includes the first mention of the controversial notion of "intelligible extension." Malebranche introduced the notion somewhat incidentally there in order to respond to the objection that the soul can contain the bodies that represent them. His specific response is that "the soul does not contain intelligible extension as one of its modes" given that one cannot conceive of extension as a mode (OC 3:148ff; LO 624ff). However, he continued by claiming that God contains in Himself "an ideal or intelligible infinite extension" (OC 3:152; LO 626). It is this claim that prompted critics to charge that Malebranche's system entails the Spinozistic identification of God with the extended world, a charge Malebranche himself vigorously denied by emphasizing that ideal extension differs from extension as it is present in the material world.[41]

In "Elucidation 10" Malebranche further denied that "there are in God certain particular ideas that represent each body individually" on the grounds that He contains a single idea of extension that serves to represent all bodies to Him (OC 3:154; LO 627). Arnauld insisted that the denial that God has particular ideas of bodies involves a retraction of the view in the *Search* that "we see each thing by a particular idea of it in God."[42] Malebranche responded that what Arnauld sees as a retraction is merely an explication of his earlier views,[43] and one could perhaps defend this response by stressing the claim in the first edition of the *Search* that God sees particular beings by means of His own perfectly simple "absolute being" (III.2.vi, OC 1:439). Yet Arnauld seems to have been correct in drawing attention to the oddity of the argument in "Elucidation 10" – absent from the *Search* – that our soul cannot contain intelligible extension because this extension is divisible into "intelligible parts" whereas "one sees nothing in the soul that is divisible" (OC 3:148; LO 625). To this argument he offered the clever retort:

Is it not even clearer that there is nothing in God which is divisible? Therefore, if he believes that he has the right to conclude ... that intelligible extension cannot be a way of being of our mind, how much more reason has he to conclude also that it cannot be God or an attribute of God.[44]

However, we need to understand Malebranche's argument in light of his assertion that our soul cannot eminently contain bodies in the way in which God does (see §1). Malebranche took the only other sort of containment to be formal containment. Our soul cannot formally contain bodies, because in order to do so, it must be divisible in the same way as the bodies. Such an argument does not rule out the containment of bodies in God given that those bodies are contained there only eminently; in particular, they are contained in the archetype of extension in the divine substance that stands in place of them.

Admittedly, one complication was introduced by Malebranche's claim to Arnauld that intelligible extension "is not at all the divine substance in itself" because it is "the divine substance only insofar as it is participable by corporeal creatures," and thus that "intelligible extension is neither a substance nor a modification of substance, notwithstanding the axiom of the Philosophers" (OC 6:245). The last point is particularly strange given that Malebranche himself repeatedly endorsed throughout his career the metaphysical principle that everything is either a substance or a mode of substance.[45] Yet he did indicate to Arnauld that intelligible extension is not a substance only in the sense that it is not the divine substance considered *in itself*, and he noted elsewhere that God's idea of extension differs from His substance only "as we see it."

We can explain this restriction to our conception in terms of Malebranche's position that God does not contain extension formally, as it exists in the external world, but only eminently "in the simplicity of His infinitely infinite substance" (OC 6:118). While he claimed that what we see in God reveals to us the formal reality of extension, Malebranche also emphasized to Arnauld that it does not allow us to comprehend the manner in which God eminently contains these perfections in His own supreme perfection.[46] It is thus for the epistemological purpose of safeguarding divine incomprehensibility that Malebranche distinguished between intelligible extension and God's absolutely simple substance.

This sort of distinction applies to the case of intelligible extension a point that Malebranche makes in the *Search*, namely, that it does not follow from the fact that our mind see all things in God that it sees God's "essence," which is "His own absolute Being" (III.2.vi, OC 1:439; LO 231). Such a point reveals that

Malebranche could not have accepted Arnauld's claim that the Vision in God has the consequence that we "see God," at least where this is taken to mean that we perceive God's essence. Even so, it cannot be said that "Elucidation 10" provides a clear account of how we actually do perceive intelligible extension. What seems particularly problematic is Malebranche's claim in the initial edition of this text that intelligible extension "becomes sensible and particular by color, or by some other sensible quality that the soul attaches to it" (OC 3:152c). While it is not anticipated in the *Search*, the suggestion that sensation involves the sensible apprehension of intelligible extension is replicated in other works that post-date "Elucidation 10."[47] Yet it is not immediately evident what it could mean to say that a pure or nonsensory idea "becomes sensible" by means of sensation. Likewise, the claim that the soul "attaches" colors to such an idea requires further explanation, a point which Malebranche himself may have admitted when he referred elsewhere to the sensations that we attach "so to speak" (*pour ainsi dire*) to the idea of extension (OC 6:78). It was in fact only after he had settled on his final theory of efficacious ideas that he had the means to fully unpack these metaphorical claims concerning the relation of our sensations to intelligible extension.

## IV.  EFFICACIOUS IDEAS AND THE *RESPONSE TO RÉGIS*

At one point in his popular Cartesian textbook, the 1690 *System of Philosophy*, Régis objected that the "modern philosopher who teaches that we see bodies in God" provides no intelligible account of the union between God and the soul. He further noted that this union would have to bear some resemblance to the union between finite mental and bodily substances. Yet God obviously is not related to the soul by contact, as different bodies are, and because He is not passive He cannot be related to it by a mutual dependence of states, as a human mind and its body or as different minds are related.[48] God can be united to the soul only as a totally independent cause is to its effect, as one who "has created it, has conserved it, and has produced in it all its ideas and all its sensations in virtue of being the first cause."[49] However, Régis urged that this understanding of the union with God does not preclude the claim that we see bodies "by means of ideas that are in us, and that depend on the bodies that they represent."[50]

Malebranche's rejoinder in his 1693 *Response to Régis* begins with the point that we cannot see (*voir*) material extension because "it cannot act efficaciously and directly on our mind" and thereby "is absolutely invisible by itself." It is only "intelligible ideas that can affect intelligences" (OC 17–1:282ff). Malebranche repeated the Augustinian argument in "Elucidation 10" that the intelligible idea of extension must exist in God rather than in our soul given that it is "eternal, immutable, necessary, common to all minds and to God himself, and thus ... different from the changing and particular modalities of our mind" (OC 17–1:284). What is new, and what serves to address Régis' challenge, is the point that God's idea of extension is intelligible in the sense that it "acts on" our mind, "affecting" it with our limited perceptions of the nature of extension. To Régis' point that the soul can be united to God only as an effect to its first cause, therefore, Malebranche replied that there is a distinctive sort of union with God that derives from the fact that there is "an intelligible reality of the sovereign Reason that can act on minds and communicates to them some understanding of the Truth" (OC 17–1:294).

The notion of a "union with God" can be found in the 1674 preface to the *Search*, where Malebranche started by citing the Augustinian position that the mind is united not only to bodies below it but also to God above it. He insisted that while the union with the body "debases man and is today the cause of all his errors and miseries," the union with God "raises the mind above all things" and is the source of "its life, its light, and its entire felicity" (OC 1:9; LO xix). This distinction between the two unions is reflected to some extent in the view in the *Search* that our sensations differ from pure ideas in God (III.2.vi, OC 1:445; LO 234), yet the chapter on the Vision in God in this text says almost nothing about the intellectual features of the soul that serve to relate it to God's ideas. In the 1688 *Dialogues on Metaphysics*, however, Malebranche attempted to further explicate the nature of the soul's intellectual union with God by appealing to the general laws of nature by means of which God acts. He claimed in this text that while the sensory changes in a human mind are coupled with changes in its body through the laws of the soul-body union that govern God's action, the intellectual thoughts that the mind has when it attends to ideas are governed by the laws of the union with God, through which God gives the mind "the power to think of what it wills, and to discover the truth" (OC12:319; JS 252ff). This nomological account of the union with God serves to connect, in a manner more explicit than Malebranche had ever previously suggested, his occasionalist conclusion that God is the cause of all real changes in us and the conclusion of the Vision in God that we depend on God's ideas for our thoughts.

With the introduction of this nomological account there is a new emphasis on the special nature of the effects in the soul that derive from its union with God. In particular, Malebranche began to stress that this union gives rise to "pure perceptions" in the soul that differ from the sensory modifications it has in virtue of its union with the body.[51] Thus, in the 1699 *Third Letter*, the response to Arnauld containing the most definitive statement of his mature account of ideas, Malebranche claimed that the divine idea of extension "affects" the mind with a "pure perception ... in consequence of the general laws of the union of mind with sovereign Reason" (OC 9:959). On the view here, this idea communicates to us "some intellectual comprehension of the truth" by producing in our soul a limited but nonsensory perception of extension and its modes. While the *Search* emphasized that the soul has a "pure understanding" distinct from its sensory faculties (see §1), it did not stress the position in the *Third Letter* that the soul has pure perceptions deriving from a distinctive sort of intellectual union with God.

What further distinguishes the *Third Letter* from the 1674 *Search* is the fact that the former relies on a theory of "efficacious ideas," according to which the intelligibility of divine ideas is to be explained in terms of the way in which these ideas "affect" or "touch" the soul. The French scholar André Robinet was one of the first to recognize the importance of this theory for Malebranche's mature thought.[52] While Robinet has set the introduction of the theory at 1695,[53] it is clear that there are anticipations of the emphasis on the efficacy of ideas both in the nomological account in the *Dialogues* of the union with God and in the view in the *Response to Régis* that divine ideas become intelligible to us by "affecting" our soul. These earlier remarks prepare for the claim added to the final edition (1712) of the *Search* that an idea is "the immediate object of mind" in the sense that it "touches or modifies the mind with the perception that it has of an object" (III.2.i, OC 1:414; LO 217). Here indeed we have a contrast with the position in the 1674 edition of this text that "we see [an idea] because it pleases [God] to reveal it to us" (III.2.vi, OC 1:445; LO 234). Whereas the earlier passage suggests that ideas are inert objects of perception, the later addition reflects the view that they are the vehicles for divine causation. On such a view, to say that a divine idea is present to mind or that it constitutes the objective reality of a perception is to say that the idea produces a certain sort of perceptual effect. Drawing on Robinet's work, Ferdinand Alquié has noted that the emphasis on the efficacy of ideas reveals the significant shift in Malebranche's thought from a *vision dans Dieu* to a *vision par Dieu* in which "the character of the causality and the efficacy of an idea replaces that of its visible character."[54]

I have noted the denial in the *Search* that pure ideas in God are "visible" in the sense of being "sensible." However, this denial seems to be compromised by the claim in "Elucidation 10" that intelligible extension "becomes sensible and particular" by means of color sensations (see §3). Moreover, Malebranche indicated in his later writings that the theory of efficacious ideas applies even to the realm of sensation. Thus, he noted in the *Third Letter* that these ideas affect the mind not only with pure perceptions governed by the laws of the union with Reason, but also with "sensible perceptions, which one calls color, taste, odor, and the rest ... in consequence of the general laws of the union of the soul and the body" (OC 9:959). In this passage and others, it is the same idea that is said to cause different intellectual and sensory states in us by affecting our soul in different ways.[55]

The implication in Malebranche's later writings that the doctrine Vision in God extends to the realm of the soul-body union does seem to conflict with the suggestion, sometimes in the very same writings, that the doctrine is restricted to the soul's union with God.[56] I will return to this apparent conflict presently, but for the moment I want to indicate that Malebranche had good reasons for extending the Vision in God to sensation. By so extending the doctrine, for instance, he was able to provide an explanation of the manner in which sensations "sensualize" intelligible extension that does not compromise his principle that God's pure ideas are intellectual rather than sensory. Thus, Malebranche explained, in a 1700 addition to the passage from "Elucidation 10" cited toward the end of §3, that a particular

figure becomes sensible "through color or some other sensible perception by which its idea affects the soul" (OC 3:152; LO 626). The
suggestion here is that a pure idea is sensible merely in the sense
that it produces sensory perceptions in us. Malebranche claimed repeatedly that the sensible features of our perceptions belong to our
soul rather than to the pure idea.[57] Yet such a claim is consistent
with the point that sensations bear a causal connection to the pure
idea through which we understand the nature of extension.

That particular point is reflected in the claim in the *Dialogues*
that sensations "awaken our attention, and thereby lead us indirectly [*indirectement*] to an understanding of the truth" (OC 12:118;
JS 79). We can explicate this position in terms of the comment in
this text that "intelligible extension becomes visible and represents
some body in particular only through color, since it is only from
the diversity of colors that we judge the difference in the objects we
see" (OC 12:46; JS 17). Rough sensory discrimination draws our attention to the boundaries of particular colored objects, and in this
way aids in an understanding of the nature of the shapes. However,
given the principle in Malebranche that God alone "can enlighten
us, by representing everything to us" (*Search* III.2.vi, OC 1:447; LO
235), the admission that sensations can lead us to the truth commits
him to the conclusion that they derive in some manner from divine
ideas. Thus, he was bound to hold that even sensory experiences
deriving from the soul-body union involve a Vision in God. The theory of efficacious ideas allowed him to understand such a vision in
straightforwardly causal terms.

However, it is significant that the *Dialogues* passage above states
that sensations lead us to the truth only *indirectly*. Sensory discrimination may bring about an understanding of the various shapes we
see, but it does not itself constitute such an understanding. At best
such discrimination prompts the apprehension of the nature of those
shapes through pure perception. Malebranche can therefore claim, in
a manner compatible with his extension of the Vision in God to the
soul-body union, that ideas become intelligible to us only through
the union of our soul with God. Yet just as the theory of efficacious
ideas allows him to say that these ideas are sensible in the sense
that they cause sensations in us, so it allows him to hold that they
are intelligible in the sense that they produce our pure perceptions.
In the end, then, the claim that we see ideas in God becomes for

Malebranche the claim that our soul has intellectual and sensory modifications that directly or indirectly yield an understanding of the truth in virtue of their causal relation to divine ideas.[58]

In this way, the account of efficacious ideas provides the material for a further response to Arnauld's initial charge that Malebranche was committed to the "bizarre" view that we see God when we see that material world. On this account, moreover, the Vision in God can be extended broadly given that all of our perceptions are produced by divine ideas, but also can be restricted to intellect given that our pure perceptions involve a direct apprehension of the truth that is lacking in the case of our sensations. If we are to give the doctrine of the Vision in God its full due, we must see it through all the way to the theory of efficacious ideas that Malebranche adopted toward the end of his life.

Even when modified by this theory, the doctrine no doubt remains less immediately compelling than Arnauld's alternative account of ideas. However, the use of this theory to extend the doctrine of the Vision in God to sensation does alleviate a difficulty arising from Descartes' view of sensory experience that Arnauld seems not to have considered. In particular, such a use provides the means for Malebranche to draw on Augustine in order to reconcile the conclusion in the "Second Meditation" that the inexhaustible idea of body is purely intellectual and the claim in this same text that such an idea is present to us even in our most basic sensory contact with the material world.[59]

### NOTES

1 On the view there we see neither our soul nor other souls nor God himself through ideas in God, but rather see God "through Himself" (*par lui-même*), our own soul through "consciousness or inner feeling" (*conscience ou sentiment interieur*), and other souls similar to ours "through conjecture" (*par conjecture*) (*Search* III.2.vii, OC 1:448–55; LO 236–40).

2 OA 38:286; Arnauld 1990, 108. Arnauld emphasized in a letter to Malebranche that the belief that we see bodies in God involves a *bizarre pensée* (OA 9:1013), while Malebranche repeated several times in his brief response that his purportedly *bizarre sentiment* is just what results when the Augustinian theory of divine illumination is qualified by the account of body and sensation in Descartes (OA 9:992, 998, 999).

3 I borrow this characterization of the shift in Malebranche's views from Alquié; see the passage cited in note 54.

4 Cf. OA 38:198ff and 205ff; Arnauld 1990, 20 and 26ff.

5 See AT 7:40ff; CSM 2:27–9.

6 OA 38:200; Arnauld 1990, 21, modelled on Descartes' remarks on objective reality at AT 7:102ff; CSM 2:74ff.

7 For the most part, Malebranche cited passages from Augustine in the 1667 *Philosophia christiana*, edited by the Cartesian Oratorian André Martin (pseud. Ambrosius Victor). Gouhier has provided the authoritative discussion of the influence of Martin's collection on Malebranche's thought (*La Philosophie de Malebranche et son expérience religieuse*, 279–311), as well as a complete collation of passages from Augustine cited or quoted by Malebranche (ibid., 411–20).

8 Elsewhere Malebranche cited explicitly St. Thomas' account of divine ideas in *Summa Theologiæ* Ia. 14, 6, and Ia. 15, 2; see OC 6:224, OC 9:950.

9 OA 38:246ff; Arnauld 1990, 67ff.

10 Cf. *Search* III.2.v, OC 1:434; LO 228; OC 9:952.

11 AT 7:161; CSM 2:114.

12 See, for instance, his suggestion in the "Sixth Meditation" that "some creature more noble than a body" can eminently contain what is formally contained in bodies simply because it is more noble than body (AT 7:79; CSM 2:55). While Descartes sometimes offered a relatively simple ontological hierarchy of infinite substance, finite substance, and mode (e.g., at AT 7:185; CSM 2:130), moreover, this particular passage reveals that he sometimes assumed a more complex hierarchy that places certain finite (presumably incorporeal) substances above bodily substances.

13 For a discussion of this difference between Malebranche and Descartes, see Cook, "The Ontological Status of Malebranchean Ideas."

14 OC 17–1:287.

15 Cf. *Search* III.2.v, OC 1:435; LO 229. See also OC 6:223, 250–5; OC 9:954ff.

16 OA 38:183; Arnauld 1990, 5. Arnauld also emphasized the anticipations of the cogito in Augustine, and he insisted that Augustine himself would have rejected Malebranche's account of ideas in terms of the Vision in God. I do not propose to adjudicate here the dispute between Arnauld and Malebranche over the proper interpretation of Augustine.

17 See, for instance, AT 8–1:33; CSM 2:217. But cf. Descartes' claim that "colors, odors, tastes, and so on, are merely sensations existing in my thought" (AT 7:440; CSM 2:297). For further discussion of the complexities of the relation between Descartes and Malebranche on this issue, see my "Malebranche's Cartesianism and Lockean Colors."

18 AT 7:34; CSM 2:22.

19 AT 7:30ff; CSM 2:20ff.

20 AT 7:73; CSM 2:51.

21 AT 7:31; CSM 2:21.

22 See, for instance, Jolley, *Light of the Soul*, 91ff.

23 For example, in OC 12:58; JS 26ff.

24 Descartes' position is complicated somewhat by his claim elsewhere that the determination of the shape and size of an object occurs at a stage of sensation that is intellectual rather than sensory because it is distinct from the stage that includes all the immediate sensory effects produced in the mind by the body (AT 7:436–38; CSM 2:294ff). However, in this same passage he admitted that the sensory stage includes the perception not only of qualities such as light and color, but also of "the extension of the color and its boundaries together with its position in relation to the parts of the brain" (AT 7:437; CSM 2:295). He therefore consistently indicated that there is some perception of extension that is properly attributed to the senses.

25 OA 38:197; Arnauld 1990, 18.

26 OA 38:198; Arnauld 1990, 20.

27 See, for instance, OC 6:172, 216ff.

28 See OA 38:200; Arnauld 1990, 21.

29 This position is undermined by the claim, added to the final edition (1712) of the *Search*, that an idea is by definition that which "touches and modifies the mind with the perception that is has of an object" (OC 1:414; LO 217). This rider, which reflects Malebranche's later theory of efficacious ideas (see §4), entails that an idea of an object is distinct from the perception of it on the assumption that a cause differs from its effect. Such a rider illustrates that the *Search* is to some extent a palimpsest in which later additions do not always fit easily with views retained from earlier editions.

30 In the third edition (1678) of the *Search* Malebranche identified the first hypothesis with the view of the "peripatetics," while in a note added to the fifth edition (1700) he identified the fourth hypothesis with the view in Arnauld's *On True and False Ideas*.

31 "Examination of P. Malebranche's Opinion of seeing all Things in God," in *Works of John Locke*, 8:212.

32 *Vision in God*, 110–29.

33 My claim that hypothesis 2 is a species account conflicts with Nadler's conclusion that Malebranche understood this hypothesis to represent the Cartesian innatist account of ideas in the Port-Royal *Logic* (Nadler, *Malebranche and Ideas*, 115–25; cf. his "Malebranche and the Vision in God"). Nadler admits that Malebranche explicitly identified hypothesis

4 with Arnauld's Cartesian view (for the identification, see note 30), but claims that because this hypothesis concerns only the *nature* of ideas it is perfectly compatible with hypothesis 2, which by contrast concerns only their *origin*. However, the *Search* certainly appears to present the hypotheses as competing alternative accounts of our perception of external objects. I take it to be an advantage of my reading of Malebranche's enumeration that it yields the result that the hypotheses are in fact competitors.

34 See *Vision in God*, 116–29.

35 Here I depart from the view, prominent in the French literature, that Malebranche's enumeration depends on two logical principles, the first that ideas either come from experience or are innate and the second that the soul must be either active or passive in the generation of ideas (cf. Gueroult, *Malebranche*, 1:102, Robinet, *Système et Existence*, 218–20, and Rodis-Lewis' editorial comments in OC 1:527ff n.359). I think that these principles are not clearly reflected in Malebranche's own discussion of the hypotheses. For instance, his remarks indicate that the first hypothesis allows for the contribution of the active intellect in the creation of ideas. Moreover, the experiential nature of ideas is not prominent in his criticism of the second hypothesis, which focuses almost exclusively on the point that the soul has the power to create ideas. Finally, Malebranche's critique of the fourth hypothesis does not stress the activity of the soul. For a discussion of the argument from elimination in the *Search* that makes some of these same points against the standard reading, see Nadler, *Malebranche and Ideas*, 108–40 (but cf. note 33).

36 See, for instance, Malebranche's awkward claim that though ideas as species are "lesser and insignificant beings, still they are beings, and spiritual beings at that," and that while such an idea is not a substance, "it is still a spiritual being" (*Search* III.2.iii, OC 1:423; LO 223).

37 OA 38:182, 184; Arnauld 1990, 4, 5ff.

38 However, Malebranche's refutation of some of the alternative hypotheses does make use of the point that ideas involve some kind of infinity; see *Search* III.2.iv, OC 1:432; LO 227; III.2.v, OC 1:435; LO 229. As I indicate in §3, this property plays an important role in the argument in "Elucidation 10" for the distinction of pure ideas from our perceptual modifications.

39 Gueroult has urged that Malebranche accepted a theory of finite and created ideas in the first edition of the *Search* and only later adopted the view that ideas are eternal, uncreated, and infinite; see *Malebranche*, 1:62–81. Cf. Robinet, *Système et Existence*, 213ff, and Alquié, *Cartésianisme de Malebranche*, 218–20. I am sympathetic, however, to Rodis-Lewis' claim

that Malebranche never denied that the ideas we perceive are infinite and uncreated; see her "La connaissance par idée chez Malebranche" and her responses to Gueroult in the accompanying "Échange de vues."

40 OA 40:88ff. In his *Système*, Régis had argued that while the idea of God is finite "according to its formal being," it is infinite in the sense that it represents the infinite perfections of its object (see the passage from the 1691 edition, retitled *Cours entiers de philosophie*, at 1:194). It was Malebranche who, in his response to Régis, introduced the *in essendo/in repræsentando* distinction (see OC 17–1:302).

41 The charge was made by Malebranche's former student, J.J. Dortous de Mairan, who exchanged four letters on Spinoza with his teacher between September 1713 and September 1714. The eight letters are reprinted in OC 19:852–65, 870–9, 882–9, 890–912. For a discussion of this exchange, see Moreau, "Malebranche et le spinozisme." The charge of Spinozism is found also in Arnauld (OA 38:517), and in response Malebranche anticipated his claim to de Mairan that ideal and real extension are distinct (OC 6:232).

42 OA 38:247; Arnauld 1990, 69. Arnauld also claimed that the new account of knowledge in terms of intelligible extension is even more problematic than the old account in terms of particular ideas in God.

43 See, for instance, OC 6:111ff.

44 OA 38:254; Arnauld 1990, 76.

45 For texts endorsing this axiom that span Malebranche's career, see "Eluc. 12", *Search*, OC 3:174; LO 639ff; OC 12:33; JS 7; OC 16:58. I owe my awareness of this oddity, and my own response to it, to the discussion in Cook, "The Ontological Status of Malebranchean Ideas."

46 See OC 6:52, 235, 252; OC 9:950, 955.

47 See, for instance, OC 6:97ff; OC 9:961ff; OC 17–1:284.

48 See *Cours entiers de philosophie*, 1:184ff.

49 Ibid., 1:185.

50 Ibid., 1:188.

51 For more on this notion in Malebranche, see Robinet, *Système et existence*, 275–84.

52 Ibid., 259–72.

53 Robinet takes this date to mark the emergence of the theory "in its precise sense," that is, in the sense that makes explicit that ideas are intelligible in virtue of their causal efficacy (ibid., 259 n.2). Alquié notes one other text that may indicate that Malebranche adopted this theory in this precise sense even prior to 1695; see *Cartésianisme de Malebranche*, 210 n.8.

54 *Cartésianisme de Malebranche*, 209ff.

55 Cf. the additions to the fifth edition (1969) of the *Christian Conversa-tions* (OC 4:75ff) and to the fourth edition (1711) of the *Dialogues on Metaphysics* (OC 12:116; JS 77).

56 Thus, the texts cited in the previous note also contain passages suggest-ing that the Vision in God is restricted to intellectual states. For the claim that there are in fact conflicting accounts of the Vision in God in Malebranche, see Jolley, *Light of the Soul*, 110–3.

57 See, for instance, *Search* I.12, OC 1:139; LO 59; "Eluc. 6," *Search*, OC 3:56; LO 569; OC 6:55ff; OC 9:1058.

58 For more on how the theory of efficacious ideas is related to Malebranche's mature account of sensation and pure perception, see my *Malebranche's Theory of the Soul*, §3.2.2.

59 I would like to thank Steve Nadler for helpful comments on earlier ver-sions of this chapter, and to acknowledge that work on the chapter was made possible by a fellowship from the Research Triangle Foundation of North Carolina and the support of the National Humanities Center.

# 4    The Malebranche-Arnauld Debate

## I.    PRESENTATION

From 1683 to 1694, a long and furious polemic took place between Malebranche and Antoine Arnauld.[1] When the debate began, Malebranche was still a "young" philosopher (*The Search After Truth* was published in 1674), identified by the public as one of the leading lights of the new generation of Cartesians. Antoine Arnauld (1612–1694), on the other hand, was an "old" thinker, known mainly for his theological (rather than philosophical) writings. These can be divided into two general periods: from 1640 to 1668, Arnauld was one of the principal protagonists of the battles over efficacious grace that took place after the publication of Jansenius's *Augustinus*, appearing as the leader of the "Jansenist" camp. After the "Peace of the Church" in 1668, Arnauld devoted himself essentially to the campaign against the Protestants, in collaboration with Pierre Nicole. Philosophically, Arnauld had written very little: the *Fourth Objections* to Descartes' *Meditations* in 1641, and the *Grammar* of 1660 and the *Logic* of 1662 – both called *de Port-Royal*, the first in collaboration with Claude Lancelot, the second with Pierre Nicole. All three of these texts had earned him a well-established reputation as a Cartesian. Thus, the ideological proximity of Arnauld and Malebranche defined and delimited the domain of their confrontation. They were both Catholic priests and both referred constantly to Descartes and St. Augustine.

The initial occasion of the debate was a text, the *Treatise on Nature and Grace*, that Malebranche published in 1680 without waiting for Arnauld's opinion, which he had initially sought in 1679. It is absolutely certain that it was this treatise that provoked Arnauld

into attacking Malebranche; a dozen letters from Arnauld's correspondence testify to this.[2] However, this poses a problem for our
understanding of the development of this polemic. In 1683, the first
work that Arnauld published against Malebranche is the famous *On
True and False Ideas*. It is basically a text on the theory of knowledge,
in which Arnauld attacks, in the name of Descartes, Malebranche's
theory that has traditionally come to be called, quite spectacularly,
the "vision in God." Now, the theory of knowledge plays no role
in the *Treatise on Nature and Grace*. And thus our difficulty: Why
would Arnauld, who notoriously detested what he found in the *Treatise*, choose to begin the debate with a work that apparently has
nothing to do with that text? At first glance, the question seems to
be purely factual or historical. However, I will show that, in fact,
answering it is essential to understanding the celebrated polemic.
Moreover, it will become clear that it is a rather problematic question when considered in relation to the interpretive tradition that,
at least since Thomas Reid in his *Essay on the Intellectual Power of
Man*, has focused in its account of the debate only on the question
of ideas.

The following chronology provides a general overview of the debate and of the different texts produced by the protagonists.

## I. PRELIMINARIES

### 167?–1679
Malebranche and Arnauld are "friends."[3]

### 1679
Malebranche and Arnauld meet at the home of a mutual friend,
the Marquis de Roucy (in May); they disagree over the theses that
will, later that year, appear in the *Treatise on Nature and Grace*.
Arnauld leaves France because of his opposition to Louis XIV in
the "Regale" affair. At the end of the year, Malebranche sends a
copy of the manuscript of the *Treatise* to Arnauld to ask for his
opinion.

### 1680
Without waiting for Arnauld's opinion, Malebranche decides to publish the *Treatise*.

**1681**

There are many critics of the *Treatise*, (including Arnauld, Bossuet, Fénelon, Fontenelle, Nicole, and Madame de Sévigné). Arnauld announces his intention to refute the work.

**1682**

Nicole tries (unsuccessfully) to mediate between Arnauld and Malebranche.

## 2. IDEAS AND THE INTELLIGIBLE EXTENSION

**1683**

Arnauld publishes *On True and False Ideas*; Malebranche publishes the third edition of the *Treatise*.

**1684**

Malebranche publishes his *Réponse de l'auteur de la Recherche de la Vérité au livre de Monsieur Arnauld Des vraies et des fausses idées* (hereafter, RVFI).

Arnauld publishes his *Défense de Monsieur Arnauld Docteur de Sorbonne contre la Réponse au livre des vraies et des fausses idées* (DRVFI).

Malebranche: *Treatise*, fourth edition; and *Treatise on Morality*, first edition.

In his *Nouvelles de la République des lettres*, Pierre Bayle begins his reviews of the debate (he is generally favorable to Malebranche).

Malebranche: *Trois lettres de l'auteur de la Recherche de la vérité touchant la défense de Monsieur Arnauld.*

Leibniz: *Méditations sur la connaissance, la vérité et les idées.*

## 3. THE ORDER OF NATURE-PROVIDENCE

**1684**

Arnauld: *Dissertation de Monsieur Arnauld sur la manière dont Dieu a fait des miracles par le ministère des anges.*

Malebranche: *Réponse à une Dissertation de monsieur Arnauld* ...

Arnauld: *Neuf lettres de Monsieur Arnauld Docteur de Sorbonne au révérend Père Malebranche* and *Réflexions philosophiques et théologiques sur le nouveau système de la nature et de la Grâce, Livre I touchant l'ordre de la nature* (henceforth, Refl. I).

Beginning of the debate between Arnauld and Bayle on the pleasure of the senses.

**1686**
Malebranche: *Trois lettres du Père Malebranche à un de ses amis dans lesquelles il répond aux Réflexions philosophiques et théologiques de M. Arnauld . . .* (henceforth, Rep.Refl.).
Beginning of the Leibniz-Arnauld correspondence.
Fontenelle: *Doutes sur le système physique des causes occasionelles.*

### 4. GRACE

**1686**
Arnauld: *Réflexions philosophiques et théologiques sur le nouveau système de la nature et de la Grâce, Livre II touchant l'ordre de la Grâce* (henceforth, Refl. II); and *Réflexions philosophiques et théologiques sur le nouveau système de la nature et de la Grace, Livre III touchant Jésus-Christ comme cause occasionnelle* (henceforth, Refl. III).

**1687**
Malebranche: *Quatre lettres du Père Malebranche touchant celles de M. Arnauld* (a response to Arnauld's *Neuf lettres* of 1685); and *Deux lettres du père Malebranche touchant le deuxième et le troisième volume des Réflexions philosophiques et théologiques.*
Arnauld: *Dissertation sur le prétendu bonheur du plaisir des sens;* end of the polemic with Bayle.
Fénelon: *Réfutation du système du Père Malebranche* (unpublished; date uncertain).
Bossuet: *Lettre au marquis d'Allemans* of May 21, 1687 (sometimes called the Lettre à un disciple de Malebranche).

**1688**
Malebranche: *Entretiens sur la métaphysique et sur la religion* (*Dialogues on Metaphysics and on Religion.*)

**1689**
The *Treatise on Nature and Grace* is placed on the Index, along with the *Trois lettres en réponse aux Réflexions* and the *Trois lettres de l'auteur de la Recherche de la vérité.*

## 5. PLEASURE AND IDEAS

### 1693

Beginning of the polemic between Malebranche and Pierre Sylvain Régis, with Régis' articles on the polemic between Arnauld and Bayle.

Locke: *An Examination of P. Malebranche's opinion of seeing all things in God* (unpublished).

### 1694

Arnauld: *Première lettre de Monsieur Arnauld, Docteur de Sorbonne, contre le R. P. Malebranche, prêtre de l'Oratoire; Seconde lettre de Monsieur Arnauld ...*

Malebranche: *Première lettre du Père Malebranche, prêtre de l'Oratoire à M. Arnauld, Docteur de Sorbonne; Seconde lettre du Père Malebranche ...*

Arnauld: *Troisième lettre de Monsieur Arnauld ...; Quatrième lettre de Monsieur Arnauld ...* (published in 1698).

Arnauld dies on August 8.

### 1699

Malebranche: *Réponse du P. Malebranche à la troisième lettre de Monsieur Arnauld ... touchant les idées et les plaisirs* (published in 1704).

### 1704

Malebranche: *Recueil de toutes les réponses à Monsieur Arnauld*, first edition, containing some unedited pieces, including the *Contre la prévention* and the *Abrégé du Traité de la nature et de la grace*.

### 1709

Malebranche: *Recueil de toutes les réponses du P. Malebranche à Monsieur Arnauld* (new edition of all of the texts written by Malebranche in the course of the debate).

This chronology suggests, first of all, that the polemic between Arnauld and Malebranche was an intellectual event of considerable importance. Many great minds of the period – and I have only mentioned the most well-known; the list is far from exhaustive – took sides and thus found themselves implicated, to one degree or another, in the duel. By studying and classifying their reactions, something that goes beyond the scope of this essay, one would doubtless find the various philosophical camps and tensions of the 1680s. Second, and contrary to the interpretive tradition that focuses only on the question of "ideas," it should be noted that one of the main characteristics of this controversy is the profusion of themes involved. As the dispute developed (and became more venomous), it was not uncommon to find, in the span of twenty pages, reflections on the theory of knowledge, divine freedom, causation, miracles, the role of pleasure in moral life, and the efficacy of grace, along with both a little mockery for one's adversary and erudite commentary on the Church fathers. However, again, it is impossible to provide, in the limited confines of this essay, an exhaustive presentation of this ensemble of issues.

Those exchanges that concern grace (section 4 in the chronology) and the pleasure of the senses (number 5) will not be discussed here. Anything that pertains to grace would be of concern more to theologians than to philosophers; moreover, after over forty years of debates over the theory of efficacious grace developed by Jansenius in his *Augustinus*, it very quickly reached a high degree of complexity and technicality. As for the discussions about the pleasure of the senses, they have a rather epiphenomenal status in the evolution of the quarrel between Arnauld and Malebranche, because it was mainly Pierre Bayle, a "third man" in the debate, who was responsible for introducing the issue when, in the *Nouvelles de la République des lettres* of August 1685, he took Malebranche's side after Arnauld had devoted several pages to criticizing the Oratorian's views on this subject.[4] Besides, each of these themes has been well studied.[5] Rather, I will concentrate, in my presentation, on the first two sections of my division of the controversy, ideas and nature. Then I will show the connection that unites them and provides the logic to the unfolding of these debates.

## II.  TRUE AND FALSE IDEAS

From 1683 to 1685, the polemic between Malebranche and Arnauld opened with a famous episode, an episode that acquired its name from the work of Arnauld that fired the opening salvo: the quarrel over "true and false ideas." What is initially striking here is the

contrast between the apparent simplicity and clarity of the disagreement between Malebranche and Arnauld over ideas and the complexity of the extremely voluminous critical literature that this part
of their quarrel generated (and continues to generate). One could
practically write a history of the debates about this debate, which,
oddly enough, has interested Anglo-American philosophers more
than their colleagues on the continent.[6]

To simplify, it can be said that the discussion between Arnauld
and Malebranche consisted of their divergent interpretations of a
single Cartesian text: an early passage in the Third Meditation, where
Descartes distinguishes between two ways of describing our ideas:

In so far as ideas are considered simply modes of thought, there is no recog-
nizable inequality between them: they all appear to come from within me
in the same fashion. But in so far as different ideas are considered as images
which represent different things, it is clear than they differ widely. Undoubtedly, the ideas that represent substances to me amount to something more
and, so to speak, contain within themselves more objective reality than the
ideas that merely represent modes or accidents.[7]

Thus, if one is considering what Descartes called the "formal reality" of our ideas (that is, our ideas in so far as they are mental events,
modifications of the mind), then all of these ideas are alike. They
can be described, in an ontologically correct manner, as modifications inherent in me, a thinking thing. However, another mode of
description is available, one that introduces a distinction among our
ideas. The basis for this distinction is what Descartes calls the "objective reality" of ideas, their representational content. From this
second point of view, ideas are quite distinct. One can, for example, order them hierarchically, because some ideas represent more
("contain in themselves, so to speak, more objective reality") than
others. This Cartesian text is rather ambiguous, because one can say
either that ideas are all the same (in terms of formal reality) or all
different (in terms of objective reality), depending on the descriptive point of view one adopts. The passage was, thus, discussed for
many dozens of pages by both Malebranche and Arnauld, and their
disagreement was grounded, initially, on this ambiguity.

Arnauld insisted right away on the ontological equality among
ideas.[8] To be sure, they represent, but they are all nothing but modifications of our mind: "Those diverse thoughts must be no more than
different modifications of the thought which is my nature" (VFI, OA

38:184; K 6). Arnauld was thus led to identify idea and perception, explaining that these two terms denote the same mental event ("to think about something") but differ in their connotation: We speak of "perception" when referring to its aspect as "modification of the mind"; and we speak of "idea" when referring to its representative relation to the object of which it is the idea.

> I have said that I take the perception and the idea to be the same thing. Nevertheless, it must be noted that this thing, although only one, has two relations: one to the soul which it modifies, the other to the thing perceived insofar as it is objectively in the soul; and that the word 'perception' indicates more directly the first relation and the word 'idea' the second. So the *perception* of a square indicates more directly my soul as perceiving a square and the *idea* of a square indicates more directly the square insofar as it is *objectively* in my mind. (VFI, OA 38:198, K 20)

Thus, in order to explain the way in which an act of knowing works, there is no need to interpose a third term between the idea understood as the perception of the object and the object of which the idea is the idea: "We can know material things, as well as God and our soul, not only *mediately* but also *immediately*, i.e., we can know them without there being any intermediary between our perceptions and the object" (VFI, OA 38:210, K 31).

In contrast with this strict identification, for Arnauld, between idea and perception – that is, between the modification of the mind and the representative structure of the idea – Malebranche offered a different commentary on the Third Meditation by radicalizing the distinction introduced by Descartes. He dissociated quite cleanly between perception, on the one hand, and, on the other hand, representative idea.[9] "Perceptions are not at all representative of objects, and the ideas that do represent them are quite different from the modifications of our soul" (*Réponse à la troisième lettre de Monsieur Arnauld*, OC 9:905). Why is this the case? Certainly, it can be conceded to Arnauld that when I think of something, there is in me, a thinking substance, a mental event that can be called a "modification" or a "perception."

> When I see this centaur, I notice two things in me. The first is that I see it, the second that I am aware that I see it ... I am aware that I see the centaur, that it is I who sees it, that the perception that I have of it belongs to me, and that it is a modification of my substance. (RVFI, OC 6:60)

However, if I analyze the content of this perception, that is, the idea, I notice that this idea is ontologically irreducible to its being-thought. The idea is perceived, but it is not in itself a perception. The perception is, in effect, a modification of my mind, but the idea perceived cannot – because of its properties (for example, in the particularly clear case of a geometric figure, its immutability, necessity, eternity and universality) – be derived from or connected with what I am, namely, a thinking substance that does not possess these characteristics. The idea is thus a being whose intrinsic characteristics are such that it cannot be dependent upon my thought. It must be situated, rather, in a place that will allow us to understand these properties that it does possess: God, or more precisely, the divine understanding. It is thus in God that we see ideas.[10]

Without going into great interpretive detail, the major traits of the opposition between Malebranche and Arnauld on the question of ideas can be summarized as follows: Malebranche defended a kind of representationalist position, whereby the "direct and immediate objects of perception are never independently-existing physical entities, but nonphysical [mind-independent] representative entities; physical objects are perceived indirectly, by means of these immediately-perceived entities."[11] Malebranche's philosophical originality lies in his placing these immediately perceived entities *in God*. Arnauld seemed much closer to a direct realist theory of knowledge, that is, "the view that the direct and immediate objects of normal veridical perception are external physical entities existing independently of any perceiving mind.... For the direct realist ... the perceiver is (in veridical perception) in direct, non-mediated (non-inferential) perceptual contact with the objects of the physical world."[12] This is due, perhaps, to Arnauld's more empiricist tendencies.[13]

### III.  THE *TREATISE ON NATURE AND GRACE*: DISORDER AND DIVINE WAYS, WISDOM AND POWER

In order to introduce the second major stage of the Arnauld-Malebranche polemic – less celebrated than the first but quantitatively more substantial, as it occupies almost two-thirds of the texts – let us return to the question posed above: Why did Arnauld, who was notoriously vexed over the *Treatise on Nature and Grace*, in

which the question of "ideas" is never broached, begin his attack on
Malebranche by devoting two years and 1,500 pages to the
Oratorian's theory of knowledge? In order to answer this question, we
need to turn back to what Malebranche said in the *Treatise* (I shall focus only on the first discourse, that is, the part concerning "nature").

What do we find in the *Treatise?* First, there is an extremely original theodicy, to my knowledge, unique among seventeenth-century
Catholic thinkers.[14] Malebranche explained that our world is not
the best of all possible worlds, and that there actually are real and
positive disorders and evils in it. This is clear from a number of texts:

"The present world is a neglected work." (*Méditations Chrétiennes* VII.12,
OC 10:73)

"God could make a world that is more perfect than the one we inhabit. He
could, for example, make it such that the rain, which makes the earth fertile,
falls more regularly on prepared soil rather than in the sea, where it is not
as needed." (TNG, I.14, OC 5:29)

"Shadows are necessary in a painting, just as dissonances are in music.
Therefore, women must give birth to still-borns and create an infinite number of monsters. I would reply boldly to philosophers who reason thus, What
a consequence! ... All these disastrous effects that God allows in the universe are not at all necessary. And if there is black with the white, dissonance
with the consonance, it is not because these give more force to the painting,
and more sweetness to the harmony. What I mean is that, at bottom, all
this does not render God's work more perfect. On the contrary, it disfigures
it, and makes it disagreeable to those who prefer order ... I do not hesitate
to repeat it: the universe is not the most perfect that could be, absolutely
speaking.... It is an evident flaw that a child should come into the world
with superfluous members that prevent it from living." (*Trois lettres du
Père Malebranche à un de ses amis dans lesquelles il répond aux Réflexions
philosophiques et théologiques de M. Arnauld*, III, OC 8:765–8)

These pronouncements constitute a considerable innovation in
terms of theodicy, because they represent a clean break with the theses of Augustine and St. Thomas on the order of the world and the
perfection of creation, as well as with those that Leibniz would take
up. Arnauld, in fact (and quite rightly), draws our attention to this
point: "It is a little surprising that no one has noticed how this language must offend Christian ears" (*Réfl* I.6, OA 39:225).

However, Malebranche's break with classical theodicy is neither
autonomous nor brought about lightly. He has, in fact, a theory of

divine action that allows him to explain why there are such evils and disorders in the universe.[15] God, Malebranche explained, wants to create the best, the most perfect. However, the intrinsic perfection of the world, of the creation itself, is not the only variable that God – who must keep in mind what would best glorify him – considers when he creates. He must also take into account the perfection of what Malebranche calls his "ways [*voies*]," that is, the manner of acting that he employs to create and sustain the world. In other words, God, in his quest for overall maximum perfection, must consider not only the created world itself, but, in order to optimise it, the compound world/ways.

God wills that his work honor him . . . Note, however, that God does not will that his ways dishonor him . . . God wills that his action as well as his work bear the character of his attributes. Not content that the universe honors him with its excellence and beauty, he wills that his ways glorify him. . . . (*Dialogues* IX.10, OC 12:213–14; JS 162–3)

The creative (and sustaining) ways are promoted to the role of being the expression of divine perfection. Far from being simply means that are indifferently utilized for the sake of a result (the creation) that alone has value, God's ways must be integrated by God into his search for maximal perfection. What, then, for God would be the most perfect ways or means of creation possible? In sum, it would be those that are the most simple, those which "glorify him through their simplicity, their fecundity, their universality, their uniformity, through the characteristics that express the qualities that he is glorified in possessing" (*Dialogues* IX.10, OC 12:214; JS 163), because, on the one hand, "God must act in a manner that bears the character of the divine attributes" (TNG I.19, OC 5:32) – especially simplicity. On the other hand, the simplicity of ways of acting testifies equally to the wisdom of the agent.

An excellent craftsman must proportion his action to his work: he does not do by very complex means that which he can executed by more simple ones . . . It follows from this that God, who discovers among the infinite treasures of his wisdom an infinitude of possible worlds . . . determines himself to create that which could be produced and conserved by the most simple laws, or which must be the most perfect, relative to the simplicity of ways necessary for its production or conservation. (TNG I.13, OC 5:28)

However, it is not the most absolutely simple laws that God chooses. It must not be forgotten that it is the total perfection of the compound world/ways that must be maximized. According to Malebranche, herein lies the explanation of the evils and disorders found in the creation: The respective perfections of the world and the means employed to actualize it vary in an inverse manner. In effect, in order to actualize an absolutely perfect work, one without any evils or disorders, God would have to will or create each of its most minute details in particular, and thus he would have to multiply his particular creative volitions and ways. This is just what he does not do, lest he sacrifice the simplicity of his ways. "If a world more perfect than ours could be created and conserved only in ways that are correspondingly less perfect ... I am not afraid to say this to you: God is too wise, he loves his glory too much ... to prefer this new world to the universe he has created" (*Dialogues* IX.10, OC 12:214–5; JS 163). Inversely, absolutely simple and thus perfect ways would be so general and would so stand in the way of a detailed organization of the world, that the product that they would generate would inevitably be catastrophic. Thus, this is not what God did, in order not to produce a work that would dishonor him. The explanation for the nature of our world must be found between these two extremes: It is neither the most perfect possible, nor created and conserved by the most perfect ways possible. It is the best compound (or compromise?) possible; that is, it is the world that corresponds to the pair "work/ways" that, taking into account correlative and inverse variations among its two constituents, offers the maximum overall perfection. The created world is therefore not "the most perfect that could possibly be." If God had not taken his ways into consideration, and had thus created by more complex ways, then the world would have been, in itself, much better. This explains, the presence – limited, to be sure, but nonetheless real – disorders within the world.

All of this leads toward one conclusion: If God acts as he does, it is because he must conform his activity to what his wisdom dictates as being worthy of him – he must act through simple and general ways – rather than will what would be the perfection of the created world. Thus, we find here a specific conception of the freedom of a God who "cannot will to do what his wisdom forbids" (*Réponse à une Dissertation*, IX.13, OC 7:533). To put it negatively, we can say that God constrains himself; this allowed Malebranche to present him as "prevented" (*Rép. Réfl* I.1.ix, OC 8:676: "The wisdom of God prevents him from complicating his ways"), as submitting to duty (RVFI iv.12, OC6:40: "God must not upset the order and simplicity of his ways ... He must not act ... by particular volitions"), and to obligation ("When the order that is his inviolable law does not oblige him to use them otherwise").[16] In a more positive vein, divine freedom must not be conceived as an absolute capacity for choice, but rather as the *autonomy* of a God who "gives laws to himself" and who "truly obeys only his own laws" (*Réponse à une Dissertation*, XII.8, OC 7:562). Thus, the famous phrase that would scandalize Arnauld but that is really only a terse way of reminding his readers that the divine wisdom limits the exercise of omnipotence: "[God's] wisdom renders him, so to speak, impotent" (TNG I.38, OC 5:47).[17]

### IV.  ARNAULD'S REPONSES

All of the innovations in Malebranche's theodicy were attacked, one by one, by Arnauld in his *Neuf lettres ... au révérend Père Malebranche* and, above all, in his *Réflexions philosophiques et théologiques sur le nouveau système de la nature et de la grâce*, perhaps Arnauld's greatest anti-Malebranchist work.

### 4.1.  Theodicy

Arnauld – in a cursory fashion, as if his points were self-evident – took issue with the results of Malebranche's theodicy, recalling the classical arguments of St. Augustine and St. Thomas in order to reaffirm the goodness and order of creation.

Every substance is necessarily good, as St. Augustine often says, and only Manicheans believe that there are any evils in it. Those that we call "defective" are such only in comparison to those that are more perfect. "Nothing is to be condemned," says St. Augustine, "except by comparison with something better" ... A monstrous animal is, if you will, a dissonance in the harmony of the universe. But it does not fail to contribute to this harmony. (*Réfl* I.2, OA 39:203–5)

It is certain, at least, that St. Augustine found it hard to tolerate speaking so crudely of the "irregularities" and "disorders" that some claimed to discover in the works of God. He believed that the Manicheans put these sorts of claims to good use, and he always denied, contrary to these heretics, that there could be any evil in nature other than that which originates in the free will of intelligent creatures, that is, in sin and concupiscence. (*ibid.*, I.6, OA 39:225)

One needs a perverse sense of judgment in order to find something to say against [God's] works. (*Réfl.* I.6, OA 39:225)[18]

### 4.2.  *Miracles, Providence, Volitions*

Arnauld's attacks, however, focused above all on the thesis of "general volitions," and in two ways. First, Arnauld tries to show how this thesis causes difficulties – indeed, even renders incoherent – certain classic notions of Christian theology. Second, he shows how Malebranche redefines the notion of God in an inadmissable way.

Malebranche's claims about God's general volitions, Arnauld argued, make it hard to make sense of certain classic doctrines. This is the case, first of all, with miracles. When one affirms, as Malebranche did, that the laws of physics that govern the universe have been chosen and put into place by God as the best because they are the most general possible, it becomes difficult to understand how there can be exceptions to these laws, that is, how miracles are possible.[19] Providence is the second notion threatened by Malebranche's views: If God is content to organize the course of events in a general way and cannot (or must not) decide as to details, then any providential planning and, even more so, any divine intervention at the level of particulars seems to be at least improbable, if not downright impossible.

[If God acts only by general volitions], how then can I conclude that if I keep faith in God, then he will not fail to clothe me, feed me and protect me throughout the time that he has ordained that I should live on this earth? ... Need one have a great deal of confidence in God in order to allow oneself to be carried along according to the laws of nature? (*Réfl.* I.17, OA 39:335)

From this perspective, Arnauld's attack seems, above all, motivated by preoccupations of a religious nature. He feared that Malebranche's philosophy would keep us from thinking of the personal God who is spoken of in the Bible, the God of whom we can say *Pater noster* without misusing the common notion of paternity, which involves a personal and particular concern for the child. In consequence of this – and this moves into more speculative terrain – Arnauld is trying to reestablish the possibility of particular volitions in God. Malebranche's mistake was to make an identification between the voluntary and the legal in his explanation of the way in which God acts. "He takes 'acting by general volitions' to be the same thing as 'acting according to general laws.'" Now, Arnauld explained, "laws are the order according to which things come about; and volitions (above all, those in God) are that by which things come about" (*Réfl.* I.1, OA 39:175). The distinction he established here is difficult to define, but two examples from the *Dissertation sur les fréquents miracles de l'ancienne loi* where these questions had been already addressed provide some clarification.

Although I am subject to a general law to pray to God every morning, this does not mean that each time I do not do it by a particular volition.

God has set himself a law to create a soul and attach it to a human body as soon as this human body is formed in the womb of a woman ... Does it therefore follow that the birth of each and every one of us, and the creation of each person's soul is not the effect of a particular volition in God? (OA 38:734, 737)

It is a matter, then, of driving a wedge into one of the fundamental assumptions of Malebranchian theology – namely, the presumed identity between the generality of the ways of divine agency (the laws that govern creation) and the generality of the volitions that organize that creation. God's volitions, Arnauld insisted, are general in the sense that they are in accordance with general laws, and not *ad hoc*. However, they are not general in the sense of not being directed at particular states of affairs.

If, as Arnauld here attempts, one can succeed in differentiating between legal generality and generality of volition, it becomes possible once again to think that, within the legal-general framework that obviously governs all creation, particular volitions of God intervene, reaching to the details of created beings. *A parte Dei*, the characterization of the form of the volition is not exhausted by the legal generality that it expresses. Without in any way denying that the world is governed by laws, it can be affirmed that the beings and events that constitute it have been willed "by a particular purpose in God," "by a positive, direct and particular volition" (*Réfl.* I.2, OA 39:204).

Malebranche was sensitive to these objections, and tried to respond to them, as much in the texts written directly against Arnauld as in the modifications that he introduced into his books when he reedited them (e.g., the Fourth Elucidation of the *Treatise on Nature and Grace*, concerning miracles) or in his new works. Thus, in 1688, he devoted four of his *Dialogues on Metaphysics and Religion* (dialogues ten, eleven, twelve, and thirteen) to a recapitulation and clarification of his views on providence, notably insisting on the fact that God foresaw everything that would take place in the world that he choose to create. "His foreknowledge has no limits and is the rule of his providence" (*Dialogues* XII.10, OC 20:291; JS 228). Concerning miracles, Malebranche was, to all appearances, ill at ease. God, he explained from 1685 onwards, brings about a miracle, that is to say, acts by a particular volition, when the global perfection of the compound world/ways is so threatened by an imperfection in the work itself as a result of the generality of his ways that it would be better for God to abandon at that moment this generality of ways, in order to augment, by means of a particular volition, the perfection of the world and maintain the optimal perfection of the whole.[20] Arnauld, implacable as ever, then asked why, if God can presume to act by particular volitions, he does not do so all the time.[21] Sensing the danger of a massive invasion of particular volitions, Malebranche, in a second line of defense, counter-attacked and forced himself to appeal once again to the practically inviolable generality of divine ways. "I claim that it is *very rare* for God to act by particular volitions" (*Rép. Réfl.* I.6, OC 8:661; emphasis added). The example of miracles makes it clear that Malebranche, in these texts of his polemic with Arnauld, seemed sometimes to oscillate between the structural demands that follow from the reformulations and clarifications[22] that he never stopped supplying in order to respond to his adversary, and the desire not to abandon the central themes of his thought.

### 4.3.  Freedom, Power and the Attributes of God

The second major axis of attack by Arnauld bore more directly on some fundamental questions of theology. A number of texts show, first of all, that Arnauld vehemently refuses the Malebranchian affirmation of divine impotence.

Nothing is more unreasonable than what you say in your *Treatise* ... that [God's] wisdom renders him impotent by obliging him not to act by particular volitions.[23]

There are three reasons for this resistance. First, Arnauld refuses to submit God, as Malebranche does, to the necessity or obligation of acting by general volitions.

How can he [Malebranche] thus take this mass of circumstances, which gives birth to monsters, as a reason that proves that God cannot act by a positive, direct and particular volition, but only by a kind of necessity? ... There is nothing more contrary to the idea of the sovereign being than making him act with a kind of necessity. (*Réfl.* I.2, OA 39:204)

Second, in contrast with the Malebranchian conception of divine liberty as autonomy, Arnauld wants to maintain a conception of divine liberty that could be called absolutist and voluntarist.

He fears not to set limits to the freedom of God, and to subject it to the imaginations of a new metaphysics ... He fears not to proclaim that *God freely forms his plan, but that the plan having been formed, he necessarily chooses the general ways that are the most worthy of his wisdom* [citation of TNG II.50]. And thus God will have no freedom in his choice of ways necessary for the execution of his designs ... But on what basis could a doctrine so injurious to divine freedom be grounded? (*Réfl.* II.26, OA 39:594–5)

It is indeed that strange that someone should so easily take the liberty to provide arbitrary boundaries to the freedom of God. (*Réfl.* II.27, OA 39:603)

Thus, the source of the Malebranchian error in these questions is probably the overly strong distinction between the divine attributes. This leads Malebranche to believe in "a kind of struggle between the reason and the power of God" (*Réfl.* II. 19, OA 39:544). In opposition to this Malebranchian distinction, Arnauld endeavors on numerous occasions to reunite the divine attributes ("Can there be a thought more unworthy of God than to imagine such a disagreement between his wisdom and his will, as if his will and his wisdom were not the same thing?" (*Réfl.* II.2, OA 39:748)) and to forge expressions that seem destined to express their intimate identity and their functional interpenetration. He thus speaks of God's "rational will," and affirms that "God willing nothing except with wisdom, he wills nothing that his wisdom does not will." There is evident in these texts of Arnauld a kind of echo of the concern expressed by Descartes when he refuses to distinguish the understanding from the will in God, or rather understanding and willing, "not even by means of a distinction of reason."[24] Malebranche, for his part, seems closer to a position like that of Duns Scotus in recognizing something like a "formal distinction" between wisdom and will in God. This allows him to distinguish among the attributes in God prior to any differentiations made by our thought.[25]


## V.  THE CONNECTION: UNIVOCITY

Before concluding, we must return to the question that has guided us from the start: what connection is there between the two principal stages of the quarrel, between the dispute over ideas and these long and drawn out discussions over the *Treatise on Nature and Grace*?

We can answer this question by looking closely at what is, for us as well as for a classical thinker, a most surprising aspect of the first discourse of the *Treatise* – namely, the Malebranchian insistence on describing the divine actions and making assured judgments, sometimes pejorative, on their products. An Augustinian or a Cartesian (such as Arnauld) would say that we have an imprudent (even impudent) transgression of the limits of possible human knowledge. God is "incomprehensible," his designs remain "hidden" to us; it is, consequently, "rash" to presume to judge and evaluate God's actions.

However, to take Malebranche's point of view, this accusation is unjustified. We do see, in God and as God, our ideas; we are thus well-grounded in our evaluations of what God wants and does. Put another way, because we know as God knows, at least partially, and because God's knowledge governs his will and his actions, it is not at all "rash" to judge, and in certain cases to criticize, the creative behavior of God and its results.

Were I not persuaded that all men are rational only because they are enlightened by the Eternal Wisdom, I would, without a doubt, be rash to speak about God's plans and to want to discover some of his ways in the production of his Work. But because it is certain that the Eternal Word is the universal Reason of minds, and that by the light that it shines on us incessantly we can all have some communication with God, I should not be blamed for consulting this Reason, which, although consubstantial with God himself, does not fail to answer those who know how to interrogate it with serious attention. (TNG I.7, OC 5:24–5)

It is in God and in an immutable nature that we see beauty, truth, justice, since we are not afraid to criticize His work, to note the defects in it, and even to conclude thereby that it is corrupt. Indeed, the immutable order, which we see partly, must be the law of God Himself, written in His substance in eternal and divine characters, since we are unafraid of judging His conduct by the knowledge we have of that law. (*Dialogues* IX.13, OC 12:221; JS 169)

The knowing process called "vision in God" makes legitimate our judgments on the value of creation and on the quality of the ways of divine agency. What would otherwise appear to be an impudent theological promethianism, finds its methodological justification and its theoretical legitimacy in Malebranche's analysis of the foundational operations of human knowledge. This makes the expositional structure of the *Méditations chrétiennes* – a dialogue between a philosopher and the Word – very significant. Because there is a dialogue – that is, a coextensivity – between the philosopher's reason and the divine reason, the evaluative considerations brought to bear on the action and the works of God in the *Treatise on Nature and Grace* and the *Méditations* are conceivable, and – when they have been performed correctly – valuable.

To summarize, without paying too much attention to nuance: One of the conditions for the possibility of Malebranche's theodicy and, more generally, for the ensemble of theses formulated in the *Treatise on Nature and Grace* is what a more contemporary thinker would call the "univocity of knowledge" between the human being and God, as is implied by the operation called "vision in God." We cannot hope to understand Malebranche's theodicy, both in its contents and in the conditions for its possibility, without connecting it to the theory of knowledge that authorizes its development. Consequently, an efficacious and complete refutation of this theodicy cannot do without a critique of that theory of knowledge and of the notion of the union of human reason with divine reason. Understandably, Arnauld, who was deeply opposed to the conclusions of the *Treatise on Nature and Grace*, thought it necessary first to write a text devoted to the question of "ideas" in order to carry out his grand project of refutation.

We can thus see the unity of the quarrel and the logic of its development. We can reread the debates over ideas while thinking of this question of the univocity of knowledge between human and God.

When Arnauld reduced the idea to the perception itself, he was try-ing to break and forestall every possibility of intellectual complicity or homogeneity between human reason and divine reason. If ideas are nothing but modifications of our mind, then there is, in an act of knowledge, no obligatory coideation between God and myself. The univocity presupposed by Malebranche was thus, at the very least, contestable. Further, the assertions of the *Treatise on Nature and Grace* become "presumptuous" and "rash." From ideas that are mine and only mine, with what right can I judge what God knows and what his wisdom demands? Thus with what right can I affirm that "the wisdom of God renders him impotent"? All of Arnauld's work in the *Réflexions philosophiques et théologiques* consisted in drawing out the theological consequences of the epistemic conclu-sions established in *On True and False Ideas*.


VI.   CONCLUSION

There are three points on which I would like to conclude, all indicat-ing ways in which this study – which, I hope, has at least suggested the great interest these long and complex debates hold – could be expanded.

First, it is hard to provide a global interpretive matrix for this controversy between Arnauld and Malebranche. However, we can envisage different ways of reading it, without implying that these frameworks are mutually exclusive. One involves pitting the Jansenist and classic "hidden God" against a more "molinistic" God – that is to say, a "bourgeois"[26] God – which paves the way for the "deism" of the moderns in the eighteenth century. Or perhaps it is just a new version of Plato's "gigantomachy" (*Sophist*, 245) between the friends of the Forms (seeing Malebranche as an "idealist") and the partisans of "matter" (Arnauld as the "realist"). Still yet another way of looking at the debate regards it simply as a clash between compet-ing interpretations of some themes that are ambiguously introduced in Descartes. I want to suggest here only that, as is often the case in the seventeenth century, we must seek the final word on the discord between our two protagonists in the way they conceive the distinc-tion and relations between divine attributes.[27] For Malebranche, the establishment of a strong distinction between understanding and will in God allows him to envisage the preexistence in the divine understanding of an infinite number of possibles, all offered to the creative will as "choosable." Consequently, it implies a determination of the divine will by the divine understanding, which translates into a limitation by the understanding of the effective capacities of God's power, as well as a restriction of the ways in which divine freedom can be deployed. It constitutes, moreover, the condition for the possibility of the vision in God: because God's understanding is separated from the rest of his being as a kind of autonomous realm, the human being can access ("see in God") that understanding without this implying that he can apprehend the totality of the divine being ("see God").

For Arnauld, the absence of a distinction (other than a "distinction of reason") between understanding and will in God prevents him from conceiving a logical and determining priority between the former and the latter. Because God is determined by nothing other than his own unitary and necessary essence, he can be conceived as absolutely omnipotent and free. Thus, this absence of a distinction between divine attributes demands, or at least permits, a refusal of the Malebranchian vision in God. Taking for granted the classical assumption that there can be no knowledge of what God's volitions are, the inaccessibility of this will flows over, so to speak, on to the understanding which is not distinct from it, and cuts off any possibility of cognitive sharing between human being and God.[28]

What we have here is incontestably a wonderful debate of great philosophical interest. It is important that this interest not be reduced to the question of "ideas," as so many commentaries on it have done. Not that this aspect of the debate is superfluous or unimportant. However, the technical dispute over the nature of ideas as representative modalities makes sense only in the context of a larger framework. In fact, the quarrel over true and false ideas is justified only by the ensemble of questions implied by the Malebranchian thesis of the vision in God, including the issue of the univocity of knowledge between the human being and God and its numerous metaphysical and theological ramifications.

Second, the questions broached in the polemic between Malebranche and Arnauld are not all original. By 1684, there had already been debates between Cartesians and their adversaries over the themes that we have examined (the status of ideas, miracles, providence) and others, themes that Arnauld and Malebranche discuss but which were not examined here because of the limited scope of this paper (e.g., the validity of evidence as a criterion of truth, causality, the relationship between reason and revelation). And yet this polemic performed a revelatory function. It contributed to clarifying the questions that would become the major problems for eighteenth-century philosophers.[29] If one must specify only two concepts that this debate brought to the forefront on the philosophical scene, it would be the notion of representation in the theory of knowledge[30] – which Kant would go on to investigate further, citing Malebranche in his famous "Letter to Marcus Herz" of February 21, 1772 – and the issue of general will, which was of interest to Montesquieu as well as Hume, and which, at the end of a process of secularization, became the central element in Rousseau's *The Social Contract*.[31]

Third, at the very least, reading this debate is also of great interest for the study of the philosophy of Malebranche himself. Arnauld was a worthy adversary, and his attacks revealed, with an impressive precision, the originalities and/or difficulties of the Malebranchian system. A number of passages from Malebranche's mature works (from the *Dialogues on Metaphysics and Religion* to the *Réflexions sur la prémotion physique*) can be read as attempts to respond to the problems raised by Arnauld. A familiarity with Arnauld's objections is, thus, indispensable for understanding and appreciating Malebranche's philosophy after 1685.

Malebranche himself willingly concedes this point; "Monsieur Arnauld," he claims, was a formidable adversary. The pitiless fire of Arnauld's attacks brought Malebranche's system, over the years, to the point of incandescence. The real question, however, was whether this test would prove to reinforce that system, or extinguish it.[32]

NOTES

1 Arnauld died in 1694, but his friends continued to publish his anti-Malebranchiste texts posthumously. Malebranche responded to them up until 1704. Thus, the debate has the distinctive characteristic of continuing long after the death of one of its protagonists.

2 See, for example, the letter to Neercassel of January 13, 1681 (OA 2:95); the letter to the Marquis de Roucy of May 26, 1681 (OA 2:101); and the letter to the Marquis de Roucy of January 4, 181 (OA 2:116).

3 See OA 43:250, and André 1886, p. 78.

4 See *Réflexions*, OA 39:360–97.

5 On grace, see Laporte 1922 and 1923. On the pleasure of the senses, see Adam 1995, pp. 92–7; Bouillier 1954, vol. 2, pp. 203–5; MacKenna 1982; Montcheuil 1946, 162–206; and Solère 1995.

6 This history can be schematised into four parts:

   a) Locke is probably the precurser of all commentators on the debate, being greatly interested in Arnauld, Malebranche and their quarrel. He owned copies of *On True and False Ideas*, the *Logic*, the *Treatise on Nature and Grace*, and several editions of the *Search After Truth*; see Harrison and Laslett 1971, pp. 75 and 182–3. Gibson (1917) suggests that Locke's "Examination of Père Malebranche's Opinion" has an Arnauldian inspiration. On the relations between Locke and Arnauld, see Bonno 1955.

   b) The real point of departure for the Anglo-American tradition, however, is Thomas Reid, who refers to Arnauld as a precurser of his own philosophy of common sense. See the *Essay on the Intellectual Powers of Man*, II. 13, in Reid 1863.

   c) In the 1920s, there was in fact a "quarrel about the quarrel." See Laird 1920 and 1924, Ginsberg in Malebranche 1923, and Lovejoy 1923 and 1924.

   d) This debate between Lovejoy, Ginsberg, and Laird has been taken up by more recent scholars; see, for example, Nadler 1989.

7 AT 7:40; CSM 2:27–8.

8 For some of the principal commentaries by Arnauld on the passage from the Third Meditation, see VFI VI, OA 38:205–7; DRVFI, OA 38:386–9; *Neuf lettres*, OA 39:138–9.

9 For Malebranche's commentary on the passage from the Third Meditation, see *Trois lettres*, OC 6:214–8. For a fine analysis, see Delbos 1958, pp. 184–5. For a comparison of the different commentaries on this Cartesian text by Arnauld and Malebranche, see Ganault 1992 and Wahl 1988.

10 I am, of course, here summarizing in a very superficial manner the famous demonstration given by Malebranche in the *Search*, Elucidation 10 – much more than the merely residual argument of *Search* III.2.i–vi – for the vision in God. See also the *Dialogues*, OC 12:45.

11 Nadler 1989, 12. However, Nadler later moves away from this representationalist reading of Malebranche and offers a radically different reading of his theory; see Nadler, 1992.

12 Nadler 1989, 12.
13 See Bouillier 1954, vol. 2, p. 161; Ollé-Laprune 1890, vol. 2, pp. 25–6 and
   p. 33; Bridet 1929, ch. 7; Jacques 1976, p. 452; and Ndiaye 1991, p. 160.
   I have here summarized in basic outline the dominant interpretation
   of Arnauld's view, that which follows the readings of Reid and Laird; see
   Cook 1991, Nadler 1986 and 1989, Radner 1978, Schulthess 1986, and
   Yolton 1984. Recently, however, this interpretation has been contested
   by scholars who argue that Arnauld's position was not really that of a
   direct realist, and who favor Lovejoy's reading that both Malebranche and
   Arnauld were representationalists; see Kremer 1994 and Moreau 1999.
   It is also worth mentioning the provocative reading of Bracken (1991),
   who argues that there is no Arnauldian theory of ideas in the polemical
   writings against Malebranche.
14 For a fuller study of Malebranche's theodicy, see Rutherford's essay in
   this volume, and Moreau 1999, chapters 3 and 4.
15 This point having been well-studied, I remind the reader only of the principles of Malebranche's theodicy that constitute the essential axes of his
   polemic with Arnauld. For more detail, see Alquié 1974, pp. 243–95,
   307–24, 419–27; Dreyfus 1958, pp. 11–118; Gouhier 1978, pp. 37–93;
   Gueroult 1955–9, vol. 2, pp. 137–207; Riley 1986, pp. 26–46, 99–137;
   Robinet 1965, pp. 17–44, 68–114; and Rodis-Lewis 1963, pp. 287–318.
16 See also TNG, Elucidations 3, 26, OC 5:189.
17 The "so to speak" was added only in the 1712 edition. The text that
   Arnauld originally read said "His wisdom renders him impotent."
18 At the beginning of Book I of the *Réflexions philosophiques et
   théologiques*, Arnauld's references to the texts of Augustine (*Confessions*
   VII, *De Ordine* I and II, and *De Vera Religione*, ch. 40) are matched by an
   equal number of references to the texts of St. Thomas. See, for example,
   chapter 2, which cites the *Summa Theologiae* Ia, q. 22, art. 2 and q. 49,
   art. 12.
19 See, for example, the *Dissertation sur les miracles de l'ancienne loi*, the
   first four letters in the *Neuf lettres*, and chapters 7–12 and 16–7 of Book
   I of the *Réflexions*. Malebranche's principal responses to this objection
   are the *Réponse à la Dissertation; Rép. Réfl.* II. 1, II. 3 and III; and *Contre
   la Prévention* (OC 9:1114–6).
20 The argument is developed initially (and in great haste) in the *Réponse
   à une Dissertation*, chapter 3, and made more precise in the *Dialogues*
   XII. 12, OC 12:293.
21 In 1685–6, in Book I of the *Réflexions*.
22 On the reformulations that Malebranche makes in his thought in general
   and in his theory on the relation between divine attributes in particular,
   see Robinet 1965.

23 *Neuf lettres*, II, OA 39:32. See also *Réfl*. II. 25, OA 39:585. There are, in fact, over twenty texts of this nature in the *Réflexions* alone.

24 See the letter to Mersenne of May 27, 1630, AT 1:153: "In God, it is one and the same thing to will, to understand and to create, without one preceding the other, *ne quidem ratione*."

25 I am following here a suggestion made by Laporte (1951).

26 See Groethuysen 1927.

27 See Malebranche, *Dialogues* VII. 16, OC 12:170: "In my opinion, it is of the utmost importance to try to acquire some knowledge of the attributes of this divine being, since we depend on him so strongly."

28 See Gouhier 1964, pp. 239–40.

29 On the influence of Malebranche on the eighteenth century, see Alquié 1974 and McCracken 1983.

30 Arnauld and Malebranche agree that our ideas "represent" the objects of which they are ideas. However, Arnauld believes that the Malebranchian conception of "idea" renders this representative function impossible; see DRVFI, OA 38:584–5. See Glauser 1988.

31 For a history of the notion of general will (a notion that Arnauld probably invented!), see Riley 1986.

32 I would like to thank Philippe Desoche for his remarks on this paper, and Steven Nadler, who was kind enough to translate it.

# 5 Malebranche on Causation

Questions about the nature of causality occupy a rather central place in early modern philosophy. There had been, of course, a concern with causality in ancient philosophy (especially Aristotle) and in medieval thought (particularly in the sacramental context). However, the topic took on even greater urgency in the seventeenth century. In large measure, this was due to a problem specific to the period: how to reconcile an emerging scientific view of the natural world – mechanistic physics – with traditional and still-compelling beliefs about the relationship between God and his creation. On the one hand, natural philosophers of the period saw their task as one of identifying the underlying causal structures of observed phenomena and of framing explanations in terms of matter and motion alone. On the other hand, it was generally recognized that an omnipotent God is responsible not just for creating the world and its contents, but also for sustaining them in existence. Against this background, in which philosophy, physics, and theology merge, the problem of causation arises in several contexts: (1) in the realm of purely physical inquiry (How does one body produce changes in another body?); (2) in regard to relations between the mind and the body (Are mental events true causes of physical states of affairs, and do bodily states cause effects in the mind?); and (3) in philosophical inquiry into the mind alone (Are there real causal relations among thoughts and other mental activities? Does the mind cause its own states of being?) In all three contexts, the answers to these specific questions hang upon the answer to the more general question as to how God's omnipotence and role in sustaining things in being can be reconciled with granting creatures true causal efficacy.

Before Hume, no one gave deeper and more systematic attention to these issues than Malebranche. If his contemporaries often seem more concerned with the "enthusiasm" of his theory of ideas and the doctrine of the vision in God, his subsequent importance in the history of philosophy rests mainly on his analysis of causality and the doctrine with which he tried to resolve the general question raised above, the so-called theory of occasional causes, or "occasionalism." Occasionalism was not, in fact, an entirely new doctrine, emerging *ex nihilo* onto the philosophical scene only in Malebranche's works. It has its immediate sources in Descartes' own metaphysics of matter, motion, and God, and more ancestral roots in medieval Arabic and Latin philosophy, particularly the radical voluntarist tradition. In the seventeenth century, before Malebranche, Cartesians such as Géraud de Cordemoy, Louis de la Forge, Arnold Geulincx, and Johannes Clauberg, all occasionalists to one degree or another, used the doctrine to account for the motion of bodies and/or to explain the relationship between the mind and the body in a human being.[1] However, it was not until Malebranche that occasionalism became a full-blown system incorporating a sophisticated analysis of causation, a detailed philosophical theology, and a positive solution to the various metaphysical, physical, and theological problems surrounding natural causality. As Gouhier elegantly puts it, "lorsque nous pensons d'occasionalisme, c'est à Malebranche que nous pensons.... Les 'causes qui donnent occasion' reviennent à Descartes; l'"occasionalisme' est l'*oeuvre* de Malebranche."[2]

## I.   THE ANALYSIS OF CAUSATION

One of the central ingredients of the philosophical analysis of causation traditionally has been necessity. A causal relation is a necessary relation. When two objects or events are causally related, if one occurs, the other does not just invariably follow – it *must* occur. If *a* is the cause of *b*, then *a*, in some sense, necessitates *b*. In this regard, there is nothing unusual about Malebranche's analysis of causation. "A true cause as I understand it is one such that the mind perceives a necessary connection [*liaison nécessaire*] between it and its effects" (*Search* VI.2.iii, OC 2:316; LO 450). It is clear, moreover, that for Malebranche the necessity at the heart of causality is a *logical* one. Two things or events are causally related only if there is a logically necessary relation between them such that if the one occurs it is logically (absolutely) impossible that the other does not follow. When he argued that finite substances, such as the mind or a body, are not real causes, he did so on the basis of the fact that for any two such substances, it is always possible to conceive, without contradiction, that the one occur without the other. Likewise, when he tried to demonstrate that only God is a true cause, he argued that it is absolutely inconceivable that God should will something to occur and that event not occur.

This way of construing causal necessity is not without precedent. Some medieval Aristotelians (Avicenna, for example) believed that all causal relations were, by nature, absolutely necessary. Similarly, Avicenna's greatest critic, the anti-Aristotelian al-Ghazali, argued against real natural causality by showing that the required logical necessity could never be found in nature.[3] However, Malebranche's identification of causal with logical necessity does seem strange today, and, I suggest, *should* have seemed strange to a seventeenth-century Cartesian. Between al-Ghazali in the eleventh century and Malebranche, there was a clear and dominant philosophical tendency to distinguish causal or natural necessity – grounded in the operations of real efficient causes – from logical necessity. What is necessary on account of the natural order (that is, what is necessary *ex hypothesi* or *secundum quid*) is not absolutely or logically necessary, because God, in his absolute power, could have established a different natural order.[4] In other words, there is a distinction between nomological necessity (that is, necessity relative to some non-necessary set of laws – for example, the laws of nature) and logical necessity. Thus, even assuming that Malebranche, like al-Ghazali, was arguing against a neo-Aristotelian causal picture on its own terms, as he surely was, it would be one that was informed by intervening developments.

Why, then, does Malebranche conflate causal necessity with logical necessity? Perhaps it is the result of an extreme causal rationalism, a commitment to the principle that the entire order of nature as embedded in its causal relations is thoroughly perspicuous to logical reasoning. Or, in a more elevated vein, it may be due to a belief that the laws of nature are eternal truths and discoverable through universal, *a priori* science. This could lead one to claim that the causal laws found in nature are absolutely necessary, and could not have been otherwise. Neither of these explanations, however, are useful in explaining Malebranche's move. First, as we shall see, he clearly does not believe that the order of nature *is* perspicuous to logical reasoning.⁵ Second, Malebranche, despite his general fealty to Descartes, did not follow his philosophical mentor in believing that the laws of nature can be discovered *a priori* from a consideration of God's nature alone.

While the logic of causality involves a necessary connection between events, the metaphysics of causality involves power. These two aspects of causality are intimately related. The necessity of the connection has to be grounded in a real power or nature in the agent. *Natures necessitate*: This is an assumption that Malebranche shared with the Aristotelian system he opposes. If one event, *a*, is the genuine cause of another event, *b*, then *b* follows necessarily from *a* just because *a* by its nature has the power or force to bring about *b*. Malebranche had in mind here a real ontological foundation for causal necessity, which was far from a reductionist account of causal power or force in terms of epistemic necessity alone. "If we consider attentively our idea of cause or of power [*puissance*] to act, we cannot doubt that this idea represents something divine. For the idea of a sovereign power is the idea of a sovereign divinity ... the idea of a genuine power or cause" (*Search* VI.2.iii, OC 2:309; LO 446). Bodies lack causal efficacy because, ontically, active force cannot conceivably be a property of passive extension, the essence of bodies. God *is* the cause of every event because infinite power is an essential attribute of the divine nature.

## II. OCCASIONALISM

Occasionalism is the doctrine that all creatures, finite entities that they are, are absolutely devoid of any causal efficacy, and that God is the only true causal agent. Or, as Malebranche so piously puts it in the title of the fifth of his *Méditations Chrétiennes*, "God alone is the true cause of all that occurs in the world. He acts regularly according to certain laws, in consequence of which it can be said that secondary causes have the power to do that which God does by means of them." Bodies do not cause effects in other bodies or in minds, and minds do not cause effects in bodies or even within themselves. God is directly, immediately, and solely responsible for bringing about all phenomena. When a needle pricks the skin, the physical event is merely an occasion for God to cause the appropriate mental event, a pain; a volition in the soul to raise an arm or to think of something is only an occasion for God to cause the arm to rise or the appropriate idea to become present to the mind; and the impact of one billiard ball upon another is an occasion for God to put the first ball at rest and move the second ball. In all three contexts – mind-body, body-body, and mind alone – God's ubiquitous causal activity proceeds in accordance with certain general laws, and (except in the case of miracles) he acts only when the requisite material or psychic conditions obtain.

Occasionalism has often been portrayed as an *ad hoc* solution to a Cartesian mind-body problem. Because seventeenth-century Cartesians, with their commitment to mind-body dualism, could not explain how two such radically different substances as mind and matter could causally engage each other and interact, the traditional story runs, they had recourse to God as a *deus ex machina* to explain why there is a lawlike correspondence between states of the body and mental states. However, any close examination of Malebranche's arguments will easily show that the doctrine is supposed to follow not from some specific problem about interaction in a dualist system, but rather from general philosophical considerations of the nature of causal relations, from an analysis of the Cartesian concept of matter, and, perhaps most importantly, from theological premises concerning the essential ontological relationship between an omnipotent God and the created world that he sustains in existence.[6] Above all, Malebranche's occasionalism was motivated by a desire to combat the Aristotelian-Scholastic picture of natural causality, according to which ordinary objects in nature are endowed with real natures, powers, forces, and inner principles of activity that often seem to work as occult qualities. Such an opinion is not only scientifically spurious, but also theologically offensive. It fosters an impious worship of finite entities rather than the true and proper worship due their creator.

If we assume, in accordance with [the philosophers's] opinion, that bodies have certain entities distinct from matter in them, then ... we can easily imagine that they are the true or major causes of the effects we see. That is even the general opinion of ordinary philosophers; for it is mainly to explain these effects that they think there are substantial forms, real qualities, and other similar entities. If we next consider attentively our idea of cause or power to act, we cannot doubt that this idea represents something divine. For the idea of a sovereign power is the idea of sovereign divinity but a genuine one, at least according to the pagans, assuming that it is the idea of a genuine power or cause. We therefore admit something divine in all the bodies around us when we posit forms, faculties, qualities, virtues or real beings capable of producing certain effects through the force of their nature. (*Search* VI.2.iii, OC 2:309; LO 446)  *Leib says, " Yes,"*

Because we believe that "we should love and fear what can be the true cause of good and evil," that we should direct our reverence or disdain to that which can make us happy or unhappy, this "most dangerous error of the philosophy of the ancients" can lead only to idolatry, to the adoration of ordinary objects, and to "rendering sovereign honor to onions and leeks."

Occasionalism's initial claim, then, is a universal negative thesis: No finite creature is a genuine cause of any effect. Malebranche's first argument for this claim was based on the logical component of his analysis of causality: "A true cause as I understand it is such that the mind perceives a necessary connection between it and its effects." Malebranche insisted, in a line of reasoning that clearly foreshadows Hume, that we can find no such connection between any two objects or events in nature. This conclusion was supported both by *a priori* inquiry and by empirical considerations. There is, for example, no necessary connection between any mental event and a corresponding physical event, say, between a volition to move my arm and my arm actually rising.

Since the idea we have of all bodies makes us aware that they cannot move themselves, it must be concluded that it is minds that move them. But when we examine our idea of all finite minds, we do not see any necessary connection between their will and the motion of any body whatsoever. On the contrary, we see that there is none and that there can be none. We must therefore also conclude ... that there is absolutely no mind created that can move a body as a true and principal cause. (*Search* VI.2.iii, OC 2:313; LO 448)

In this stage of the argument, Malebranche seems to be relying on an assumption about the essential nonomnipotence of a finite will: to be nonomnipotent means that if one wills x, it does not (logically) necessarily follow that x obtains. Therefore, there is no necessary connection, hence no real causal connection, between my will and the movement of my body because it is always possible to conceive, without contradiction, that I will to raise my arm and my arm does not rise. Similarly, no necessary connection can be found between any state of the body and any subsequent mental event alleged to be its effect. "I cannot understand how certain people imagine that there is an absolutely necessary relation between the movements of the spirits and blood and the emotions of the soul. A few tiny particles of bile are rather violently stirred up in the brain – therefore, the soul must be excited by some passion, and the passion must be anger rather than love" (*Search* V.1, OC 2:129, LO 338–9). Given the "remoteness" and radical dissimilarity between the two events, Malebranche failed to see any necessity in their correlation, and believed that none can possibly be found. Not even in the realm of matter alone can the requisite necessary connections be discovered. If a body moving with a certain speed in a given direction should strike another body at rest, there is no absolute necessity that the second body should move one way rather than another, or even move at all (*Dialogues* VII.12, OC 12:163–4; JS 118).

Our senses are no more informative on this score than our powers of conception. Experience, whether of a single or multiple instances, reveals only a sequence of events, what Hume more famously called "succession" and "constant conjunction." It does *not* exhibit necessary relations between those events. In the *Méditations Chrétiennes*, the World warns us that

what your eyes, in truth, tell you, is that when a body at rest is struck by another body, it begins to move. You can believe here what you see, for it is a fact and the senses are good enough whenever it comes to such facts. ... But you go wrong, my son, when you judge that your desires produce your ideas because your ideas never fail to follow your desire. Today you are making a similar mistake, for you imagine that, just because a body is never struck without being moved, bodies move each other ... Renounce, my son, your prejudices and never judge with regard to natural effects that one thing is the effect of another because experience teaches you that it never fails to follow it. (Meditation V, OC 10:48, 58–9)

At one point, Malebranche considered an objection that was first raised by one of his contemporaries, Bernard le Bovier de Fontenelle, in his *Doutes sur le système physique des causes occasionelles*. The objection was intended to demonstrate that there are indeed, independently of any action or decision by God, necessary connections between the motive states of physical bodies. On the assumption that bodies are impenetrable, when a moving body strikes a body at rest, something must happen, even if God has not yet established any law for the communication of motion or committed himself to moving bodies directly in specific ways. Perhaps, in our ignorance of the laws, we may not know exactly what the subsequent states of the two bodies will be. However, because the bodies are impenetrable, there *must* be *some* determinate change in their states after impact. Hence, if there is such a necessary connection between their states before and after impact, then there is a real causal relationship. If body *a* runs into body *b*, which is concave and molded to fit *a*, then

> what will become of body *a* on encountering *b*? Either it will rebound, or it will not rebound. If it rebounds, we shall have a new effect of which *b* is the cause. If it does not rebound, this will be even worse; for then we shall have a force which is destroyed or at any rate ineffectual. Hence, the impact of bodies is not an occasional cause but a very real and true cause, since there is a necessary connection between the impact and whatever effect you choose. (*Dialogues* VII.12, OC 12:163; JS 118)[7]

Malebranche's reply, unfortunately, did not really address the objection, and seems almost question-begging: "Given that bodies are impenetrable, it is a necessity that, at the instant of impact, God make up his mind to choose between the alternatives you have proposed. That is all." Outside of the framework of the positive thesis of occasionalism, concerning God's unique causal efficacy with regard to the motion of bodies, Malebranche seems incapable of grasping the force of Fontenelle's argument.

Malebranche's second argument for the negative thesis of occasionalism focused on the metaphysical dimension of his conception of causality, and was based on the "inconceivability" that any natural cause, any finite body or mind, should have "a force, a power, an efficacy to produce anything." Relying on Descartes' reductive metaphysics of matter, he began by considering the intrinsic inertness of bodies. A Cartesian body is pure extension, or spatiality. As Descartes insisted, "the nature of matter, or body considered in general, consists not in its being something which is hard or heavy or colored, or which affects the senses in any way, but simply in its being something which is extended in length, breadth and depth."[8]

A body is thus capable of possessing only those properties that can be properties or modifications of extension – shape, size, divisibility, and motion or rest. "Consult the idea of extension and judge by that idea, which represents bodies if anything does, whether they can have some property other than the passive faculty of receiving various shapes and various motions. Is it not evident to the last degree that properties of extension can consist only in relations of distance?" (*Dialogues* VII.2, OC 12:150; JS 106). Because the notion of active causal power or force cannot be reduced to or explained in terms of shape, size, or divisibility (that is, in terms purely of "relations of distance") – and these are all essentially passive features – it follows that such an active power cannot be a property of extended bodies. Bodies, therefore, are essentially inert and inactive. They cannot causally act on other bodies nor on minds.[9]

Malebranche went on to note that even if a bodily substance did have motive force, that force would have to be a modification belonging to it. Also, Cartesian metaphysics precludes modifications being transferred from one substance to another. Thus, if for one body to cause motion in another were to mean that the former would communicate its moving force to the latter (and Descartes, as Malebranche reads him, occasionally suggests as much), then clearly no body can be the cause of another body's motion. "If moving force belonged to bodies, it would be a mode of their substance, and it is a contradiction that modes go from substance to substance."[10] On the other hand, if a body were to cause motion in a second body not by communicating its own moving force but by creating *ex nihilo* moving force in the second body, this would be to admit in bodies a power to create, which is likewise inconsistent with our clear and distinct idea of extension, as well as with our idea of finite, created substances.

A similar causal inefficacy on the part of the human soul is revealed by inner consciousness. Whatever knowledge I have of my soul – and for Malebranche, unlike Descartes, such knowledge is minimal and not based on any clear and distinct idea – does not involve the perception of any power, whether to move the body or even to produce its own ideas. In voluntary action, all I perceive through introspection, or *sentiment intérieur*, is an actual volition to move my arm upwards, and all I notice in my body is that my arm subsequently rises. However, I perceive, either by inner consciousness or by reason, no power on the part of the soul by means of which it might effect this motion (*Search*, Elucidation 15, OC 3:227–8; LO 670–1). It is in this sense that "those who maintain that creatures have force and power in themselves advance what they do not clearly perceive" (*Search*, Elucidation 15, OC 3:204; LO 658). Indeed, according to Malebranche, I perceive a general incompatibility between the idea of a created finite being and such a power or productive faculty. Finite creatures are essentially impotent. Only in my idea of the will of an infinite being do I clearly and distinctly recognize any element of causal power whatsoever.

Malebranche had a third argument against natural causality, one that seems to be based on a presumably intuitive premise that sets an epistemic condition on the notion of "cause." In order to qualify as the cause of an effect, the premise runs, a thing must know how to bring about the effect. Without ever stating such a principle explicitly, Malebranche appeared to use it to argue against the causal efficacy of minds and bodies.

Let us grant, Malebranche suggested, that the soul *does* have the power to move the body. Still, he replied, it is an obvious matter of fact that we clearly lack the knowledge of how to do so.

For how could we move our arms? To move them, it is necessary to have animal spirits, to send them through certain nerves toward certain muscles in order to inflate and contract them, for it is thus that the arm attached to them is moved.... And we see that men who do not know that they have spirits, nerves, and muscles move their arms, and even move them with more skill and ease than those who know anatomy best. Therefore, men will to move their arms, and only God is able and knows how to move them. If a man cannot turn a tower upside down, at least he knows what must be done to do so; but there is no man who knows what must be done to move one of his fingers by means of animal spirits. How, then could men move their arms? (*Search* VI.2.iii, OC 2:315; LO 449–50)[11]

The mind does not have adequate knowledge of the physiological and neurological processes that mediate between the volition and the motion of the arm. In the *Méditations Chrétiennes*, the Word notes that uneducated jugglers and peasants, as much as the most learned anatomist, know how to raise an arm in the sense that if asked to do so, they could perform the act successfully – they know what to do in this very broad and unspecific sense. However, despite his knowledge of the body's mechanisms for movement and the laws of motion, not even the anatomist can have all the specific knowledge required to *cause* the arm to rise: knowledge of which muscle to move by bringing about what expansions and contractions of which nerves through directing the flow of which particles of animal spirits. In the face of such irremediable ignorance, Malebranche concluded that the mind is not the real cause of the body's movements. As the Word rhetorically asks,

> Can one do, can one even will what one does not know how to do? Can one will that the animal spirits expand in certain muscles, without knowing whether one has such spirits and muscles? One can will to move the fingers, because one sees and one knows that one has them. But can one will to impel spirits that one does not see, and of which one has no knowledge? Can one move them into muscles equally unknown, by means of nerve channels equally invisible; and can one choose promptly and without fail that which corresponds to the finger that one wants to move? (VI.11, OC 10:62)

Part of the problem is the sheer quantity of information that is required. Because matter cannot move itself, the soul, through its volitions, is responsible for moving every single material particle involved in the process. Thus, in order for the soul to move the body, the number of the soul's volitions would have to be as great as the number of collisions or impacts that would occur among the particles composing the activated animal spirits. Malebranche insisted that such an action "is inconceivable, unless we allow in the soul an infinite number of volitions for the least movement of the body, because in order to move it, an infinite number of communications must take place." Further, these volitions must be backed up by an equivalent amount of relevant knowledge. However, he concludes, because the soul is finite, particular and limited – especially in its cognitive capacity – it is necessarily incapable of an infinite number of volitions, as well as of knowing exactly "the size and agitation of an infinite number of particles that collide with each other when the spirits expand into the muscles" (*Search*, Elucidation 15, OC 3:228; LO 671).

Malebranche's point here could be a rather narrow one, confined only to the question of the efficacy of the soul. In his argument, he may have been claiming only that in order for the human mind to cause an effect, it must intend or will that the effect obtain; and that because the will cannot act blindly, the mind therefore must first have an idea of that which it is to will. The mind needs for the intellect to present objects to the will for its approbation or rejection. This is the natural way in which the will and the intellect work together. As Malebranche insisted, "The will is a blind power, which can proceed only toward things the understanding represents to it" (*Search* I.1.ii, OC 1:47; LO 5). Consequently, what the mind does not, or cannot have knowledge of, it cannot will, hence cannot cause.

If that was Malebranche's argument, then its implications for a general analysis of causation are limited. His demonstration would touch only on the causality of intelligent, volitional agents, on the question of why such agents cannot be the causes either of the motion of their bodies or of their own mental states or modalities. Intelligent, volitional agents require knowledge for *their* causality, and the knowledge needed to move their bodies or cause their ideas simply exceeds their capacity. This certainly seems to be the message of the following passage from Elucidation 15 of the *Search*:

I deny that my will is the true cause of my arm's movement, of my mind's ideas, and of other things accompanying my volitions, for I see no relation whatever between such different things. I even see clearly that there can be no relation between the volition I have to move my arm and the agitation of the animal spirits, i.e., of certain tiny bodies whose motion and figure I do not know and which choose certain nerve canals from a million others I do not know in order to cause in me the motion I desire through an infinity of movements I do not desire. I deny that my will produces my ideas in me, for I do not see even how they could produce them, because my will, which is unable to act or will without knowledge, presupposes my ideas and does not produce them. (OC 3:225–6; LO 669)

There is, however, another context for Malebranche's argument here, a context in which knowledge is required not just for causality on the part of intelligent, volitional agents, but for causality *per se.* Some philosophers, as far back as certain early medieval Islamic theologians, have insisted that there is an epistemic condition on causality *tout court*, according to which the cause of an effect must have productive knowledge of the effect. In order to qualify as the real cause of some effect, a thing must know how to bring that effect about. In the case Malebranche was interested in above, he could be appealing to the evident fact that the epistemic condition is *not* satisfied by our minds in order to show that the mind, therefore, does not in fact cause those bodily motions that we consider voluntary. The same reasoning would rule out, *a fortiori*, any causal efficacy one might want to attribute to bodies, because, as nonthinking beings, they necessarily cannot satisfy the relevant epistemic conditions. (Only God, the final stage of the argument would run, has the requisite knowledge; hence, only God is the cause of bodily motions or mental events.)

Although Malebranche's texts do not strongly support this broader reading of his argument, it is indeed a tempting one. Consider, for example, the following exchange from the *Conversations Chrétiennes*:

THEODORE: ... Tell me, Aristarque, what does the fire cause in you?
ARISTARQUE: It warms me and causes me pleasure.
THEODORE: The fire, then, causes pleasure in you?
ARISTARQUE: I swear it.
THEODORE: Whatever causes some pleasure in us in some way makes us happy, for actual pleasure makes us actually happy.
ARISTARQUE: It's true.
THEODORE: Whatever makes us in some way happy is, in some way, our good; it is, in some way, above us; and it deserves, in some way, our love and a kind of respect or attention. What do you think, Eraste? Is the fire, in some way, above you? Can the fire act upon you? Can it cause in you pleasure that it does not possess, that it does not feel, *pleasure of which it has no knowledge*? (OC 4:15–6, emphasis added)

Moreover, in the light of some contemporary Cartesian thinking on causation, it may even be a plausible way of understanding Malebranche's argument. Arnold Geulincx, another seventeenth-century occasionalist (some years before Malebranche), explicitly set an epistemic condition upon causality. The fundamental causal principle, according to Geulincx, is that *impossible est, ut is faciat, qui nescit quomodo fiat ... quod nescis quomodo fiat, id non facis*: "It is impossible for someone to bring about something if they do not know how it is to be brought about ... You are not the cause of that which you do not know how to do."[12] On the face of it, with its personal references to "someone" and "you," this simply looks like the more restricted version of the claim at work in Malebranche's argument, a premise tailored to fit only the causality of intelligent, volitional agents. Geulincx uses the principle initially to argue that the human

*Kx of producing effects*

mind is not the real cause of the sensation of warmth that one feels
when the body is near the fire, because the mind is clearly ignorant of
how to bring about such sentiments. However, he then immediately
went on to argue that, for exactly the *same* reason, neither is the fire
itself the cause of the sensations in the soul; because it is an unthink-
ing thing, it necessarily – and trivially – lacks the knowledge of how
to bring about the effect. "Fire, the sun and rocks are all only brute
things, which I know to be without sensation, devoid of consciousness ... they are totally ignorant of how to produce such effects, and
in general they have no knowledge of any sort."[13] The real cause of
the sensory effects in the mind must be a thinking and willing agent
endowed with the relevant knowledge of how to bring them about –
in a word, it must be God. Possibly, some unstated intuition about
a relationship between knowledge and causation in general, similar
to Geulincx's principle, lies behind Malebranche's argument.[14]

One would naturally like to know, however, why anyone would
adopt the general principle – as Geunlicx and, perhaps, Malebranche
did – that sets an epistemic condition upon causality? It seems to be
a not-unreasonable assumption to make when what is in question is
the causal activity of intelligent, volitional agents, particularly when
these are understood on the Cartesian model. However, it seems to be
a category mistake to extend the epistemic condition to causation
by corporeal agents, such as fire and stones, that is, to causation
*generaliter* – unless, of course, one takes volitional agency to be *the*
paradigm case of causality, as some medieval thinkers did.[15]

Because finite things, material and spiritual, had been denuded
of all causal power, it remained for Malebranche to establish the
positive thesis of occasionalism: *Dieu fait tout.* He relied primarily on two arguments to this end. The first was a continuation of
the argument that purported to show that there are not real causal
connections between finite things because there are no necessary
connections between them. Because God is an infinitely perfect and
omnipotent being, it is necessarily the case that what God wills obtains. Thus, the (logically) necessary connection essential to causality that was lacking between natural objects and events clearly and
indubitably exists between acts of the divine will and their objects. It
is logically impossible that an omnipotent God should will to move
a body, for example, and it does not move. Such is the nature of
omnipotence.

A true cause as I understand it is one such that the mind perceives a necessary connection between it and its effects. Now the mind perceives a necessary connection only between the will of an infinitely perfect being and its effects. Therefore, it is only God who is the true cause and who truly has the power to move bodies.... God needs no instruments to act; it suffices that He wills in order that a thing should be, because it is a contradiction that He should will and that what He wills should not happen.... There is a necessary connection between the will of God and the thing He wills. (*Search* VI.2.iii, OC 2:316; LO 450)

Malebranche's most powerful and sweeping argument for God as the sole causal agent in the universe, however, appears to rest on an analysis of causality different from that which underlies the "necessary connection" argument. It appeals to God's role as the creator and sustainer (that is, recreator) of the universe, and represents an attempt to demonstrate that it is an "absolute contradiction" that anything besides God should move a body (and, by extension, cause a mental state).

Situating himself in a long and generally orthodox tradition that runs from early medieval philosophy through the end of the seventeenth century, Malebranche insisted that God's activity is required not only to create the world, but also to sustain its existence. To insist otherwise is to mistake the kind of dependence that creatures have upon God. This is the doctrine of divine sustenance, and it is as essential to the foundations of St. Thomas's theology as it is to Descartes' metaphysics.[16] As Malebranche elegantly puts it, "As the universe is derived from nothing, it depends to such an extent on the universal cause that, if God ceased to conserve it, it would necessarily revert to nothing. For God does not will, and indeed the cannot make, a creature independent of his volitions" (*Dialogues* VII.8, OC 12:157; JS 113). God, in other words, is not a mere *causa secundum fieri* of his creation, a "cause of coming into being" that produces an effect that will continue to exist even after the activity of the cause has ceased (as a house will persist even after the builder has stopped working). Rather, he is a *causa secundum esse*, a "cause of being" that must continually operate causally in order for its effects to continue in being (as the light and the warmth of the sun persist only as long as the sun is actively causally generating them).[17]

By Malebranche's time, moreover, the distinction between God's initial act of creation and God's subsequent causal activity as conserver largely has disappeared, and divine conservation of the world and its contents has become identified as a kind of continuous creation.[18] The activity by which God conserves finite creatures in their being requires no less of a divine operation than the original act of bringing them into being out of nothing. God sustains them by a continuous exertion of his creative powers. Descartes, in fact, insists that "the distinction between preservation and creation is only a conceptual one," and that "the same power and action are needed to preserve anything at each individual moment of its duration as would be required to create that thing anew if it were not yet in existence."[19] In the *Dialogues*, Malebranche had Theodore, his spokesman, make precisely this point, with his usual rhetorical flourish.

'The instant of creation past'! ... Be careful of what you say. God wills that there be a world. His will is all-powerful, and so the world is made. Let God no longer will that there be a world, and it is thereby annihilated. For the world certainly depends on the volitions of the Creator. If the world subsists, it is because God continues to will that the world exist. On the part of God, the conservation of creatures is simply their continued creation. I say, on the part of God who acts. For, from our perspective, there appears to be a difference, since, in creation, they pass from nothing to being whereas, in conservation, they continue to be. But, in reality, creation does not pass away because, in God, conservation and creation are one and the same volition which consequently is necessarily followed by the same effect. (*Dialogues* VII.7, OC 12:157–8; JS 112)

The proposition, "the conservation of creatures is simply their continued creation" is the key to Malebranche's argument for occasionalism. For when God conserves/recreates a body, he does not sustain that body in abstraction ("God cannot create a body that is nowhere"); rather, it must be recreated at each moment in some particular place and in some specific relations of distance to other bodies. If God conserves a body in the same place relative to other bodies from one moment to the next, it is a body at rest. If God recreates it successively in different relative places, it is a body in motion.[20] However, because only God (as the sole creator of the world and its contents) is and can be the conserving or recreating cause of bodies, it follows that only God is and can be the cause of the motion of bodies. As Malebranche puts it, the motion of a body is only its being transported by a divine act (or, perhaps, by a series of divine acts). "The

moving force of a body is, then, simply the efficacy of the volition of God who conserves it successively in different places.... Hence, bodies cannot move one another, and their encounter or impact is only an occasional cause of the distribution of their motions" (*Dialogues* VII.11, OC 12:161–2; JS 117). Further, what applies to bodies as apparent causes of motion applies also to minds. As Theodore says to Aristes,

Here you are in the world without any power, as incapable of motion as a rock, dumb as a log, as it were. Your soul can be united to your body as closely as you please ... yet what advantage will you derive from this imaginary union? What will you do to move merely the end of your finger, to utter merely a one-syllable word? If, alas, God does not come to your aid, you will only make efforts in vain.... It is only the Creator of bodies who can be their mover. (*Dialogues* VII.13, OC 12:165; JS 119–20)

Presumably, because God is required to sustain not only bodies in existence but also minds, similar considerations would establish God as the sole cause of the states – sensations, perceptions, and volitions – of finite minds.[21]

In various contexts, Malebranche suggested that a proper analysis of causation would reveal that it is tantamount to creation. To his mind, causal action was a kind of production, the generation by one substance of a new mode or state of being in another substance. This is especially clear when we keep in mind that the alternative, the transference of modes from one substance to another, is ruled out. The argument for occasionalism on the basis of God's conservation of creatures by their continuous creation takes this suggestion to an even deeper metaphysical level. The argument implies that the power to cause, to give new modalities to finite things, belongs only to the being that creates and sustains them. Malebranche unequivocally identifies God's creative and sustaining activity with God's causal activity with respect to modes or properties. God brings about the particular motive properties of a body just by conserving it in the same or different relative places. It just *is* the continuous creative activity of sustaining a body that gives its specific place(s) and motive (and, presumably, other) properties. More generally, the action by which God recreates anything is numerically the same as the action by which God gives modalities or properties to that thing. Therefore, all causality in nature is ultimately and essentially creation, in

the strongest sense of the word.[22] Malebranche's refusal to concede
causal powers to finite things thus stems from his belief that, by its
nature, such a power is exclusively divine.

In his presentation of occasionalism, Malebranche makes it abun-
dantly clear that the real target of his attack is the concurrence theory
of natural causation held by many important Scholastic philosophers. The concurrentist argues that the created beings that God sustains have their own proper causal powers, but that the possession
and exercise of those powers is wholly dependent upon God's own
coorperating causal action. God, in other words, actively "concurs"
in the actions of things. This is not, on most accounts, a matter of
division of labor. Divine concurrence is supposed to maintain God's
full contribution to the causation of natural effects without dimin-
ishing the real causal powers of creatures. To Malebranche, the whole
notion of "divine concourse" was unintelligible; it "rouses not a single distinct idea in an attentive mind" (*Search* III.2.vi, OC 1:440; LO
231). The partisans of the theory lack an understanding both of the
true nature of divine conservation and of the essence of causality.
God's sustenance of creatures rules out their having real causal powers (even with God's concurrent support), and God certainly cannot
communicate or lend his own causal powers to finite beings. Even if
creatures did have real causal powers, what causal contribution could
they possibly make to the production of any effect if, for every effect, God's willing that effect is the necessary and sufficient cause of
its obtaining? The doctrine of divine concurrence, Malebranche concluded, is nothing but the result of a well-intentioned but confused
effort by theologians to reconcile the teaching of Scripture – which
tells us that God alone acts – with the testimony of the senses, which
(reinforced by an Aristotelian philosophy) *seem to tell us that bodies
are real causes* (*Search*, Elucidation 15, OC 3:237–8; LO 676–7).

### III.  OCCASIONALISM AND SCIENCE

According to Malebranche, then, "there is only one true cause because there is only one true God; the nature or power of each thing
is nothing but the will of God; all natural causes are not *true* causes
but only *occasional* causes ... that determine the Author of nature to
act in such and such a manner in such and such a situation" (*Search*
VI.2.iii, OC 2:312–3; LO 448).

This does not mean, however, that for Malebranche, natural philosophy – what today we would call natural science – has been reduced to a single theocratic claim. Malebranche was as committed to the program of the new mechanistic science as any other seventeenth-century Cartesian. Deeply antagonistic to the immaterial (and apparently occult) powers and active virtues placed in physical bodies by Scholastic-Aristotelian philosophers, the proponents of the mechanical philosophy insisted that all natural phenomena, no matter how complex, and all the sensible and insensible properties and behaviors of bodies are the result of the arrangement and motion or rest of minute, invisible particles of matter. Each particle is characterized exclusively by certain fundamental and irreducible properties, namely, size, shape, and mobility. All other properties, powers, and phenomena, such as color, odor, viscosity, texture, gravity, magnetism, and combustability, can be understood reductively as the result of the shape, movement, position, and collision of individual material corpuscles or relatively stable collections of corpuscles. The resulting explanations of natural phenomena, by appealing to only a few simple and clearly conceived principles (matter, motion, and impact), will be informative and perspicuous.

Malebranche was very careful to stress that, despite God's ubiquitous and exclusive causal activity, it is not the case that mechanical considerations have no place whatsoever in explanation. On the contrary, the role of "secondary" or "occasional" causes is an essential one. "It is certain that all things are produced through the motion of either visible or invisible bodies" (*Search* VI.2.iii, OC 2:313; LO 448). When God acts on bodies, his activity is not arbitrary and *ad hoc*. Rather, in the ordinary (i.e., nonmiraculous) course of nature, God always acts in accordance with general physical (and psychophysical) laws that he chose at creation. These laws specify how bodies in motion behave upon impact with stationary or other moving bodies. Thus, when God moves a body that has collided with another body (and the collision itself is, of course, brought about by God), he is simply carrying out the dictates of some law; and he will not move the stationary body unless it *is* struck by another body – otherwise it would be a violation of the laws of nature. The collision of the two bodies is the occasional cause that determines the real cause (God) to move the struck body in a determinate way, as commanded by the law. Thus, a complete explanation of any natural phenomenon will refer not just to the true efficient cause of the phenomenon (in all cases this will be God), but also to the motions, structures, and mechanical processes that occasion the operation of that omnipotent cause, as well as to the law that links those material conditions with the effect wrought by God on that occasion.

In fact, Malebranche insisted that in ordinary physical inquiry, all that is really sought are the mechanical secondary "causes" that occasion the effect being investigated; and that scientific explanation need not go so far as to include the will of God.

> I grant that recourse to God as the universal cause should not be had when the explanation of particular effects is sought. For we would be ridiculous were we to say, for example, that it is God who dries the roads or who freezes the water of rivers. We should say that the air dries the earth because it stirs and raises with it the water that soaks the earth, and that the air or subtle matter freezes the river because in this season it ceases to communicate enough motion to the parts of which the water is composed to make it fluid. (*Search*, Elucidation 15, OC 3:213; LO 662)

When offering an explanation of a specific phenomenon of nature, it is true but vacuous to claim that its cause is the will of God – God is the cause of *every* phenomenon. Rather, one should specify just those occasional or secondary causes whose structures and motions are to be nomologically conjoined with the *explanandum* as a mechanical operation. At the level of physics proper, explanation employs "the natural and particular cause of the effect in question," and must proceed mechanistically. "It could be said that this body is the physical or natural cause of the motion which it communicates, since it acts in accordance with natural laws" (*Méditations Chrétiennes*, OC 10:54).

For Malebranche, then, occasionalism leaves the task of the natural philosopher fundamentally unchanged: to uncover regularities in nature and formulate the laws that govern the correlations between events. The scientific program of the mechanical philosophy, to which Malebranche enthusiastically subscribed, still motivates the search into hidden mechanisms that underlie observed phenomena and requires the investigator to frame explanations by referring to secondary causes described solely in terms of matter and motion.

Malebranche's occasionalism does, however, contribute an important supplementary framework for the mechanical philosophy.

Motion, the primary explanatory element in the new science, must have a causal ground outside the passive, inert extension of Cartesian bodies. If matter is just extension, as Cartesian mechanists insist, then, as Malebranche points out, bodies – whether they be macroscopic substances or microscopic particles – are not genuine causal agents; they are necessarily inactive beings, and thus cannot be the source of either their own motions or the motions of other bodies. Bodies, that is, do not have force as an inherent property. However, how do they move, and why do they move in the particular ways that they do? What *is* the proper account of force? Put another way, if there is a problem bequeathed by Cartesian dualism to which "the system of occasional causes" is supposed to be a solution, it is not a mind-body problem but a body-body problem. What occasionalism provides is a metaphysical framework within which the motion of bodies is given a true causal basis outside the limits of physics proper. Malebranche placed the locus of force in the will of God. Bodies move and behave the way they do because that is how God, following the laws of nature that he has established, moves them around. The kinematic phenomena and the laws of nature are thereby dynamically grounded in God's efficacious will. Occasionalism, in other words, provides the metaphysical foundations of Cartesian physics.[23]

Malebranche actually employed occasionalism to modify some important details of Descartes' physics. Descartes claimed that every body has a force to remain in the state that it is in, whether it be in motion or at rest. "What is at rest has some power [*puissance*] of remaining at rest and consequently of resisting anything that may alter the state of rest, and what is in motion has some power of persisting in its motion."[24] If force for Descartes is nothing but God's willing each body to remain in its current state (and this is how Malebranche reads him), then God must will a body to be at rest with as positive a volition as that with which he wills a body to be in motion. This, Malebranche insisted, is simply false, and is based on a misconception of the way in which God's will is engaged in sustaining and moving bodies. There is a crucial difference between the way in which God causes a body to move and the way in which God causes a body to be at rest.[25] For a body to be at rest is just for God to sustain it in existence, nothing more. For a body to be in motion, however, is for God to sustain it in existence *and* actually to put it in motion.

I have no certain proof that God wills, through a positive volition, that bodies remain at rest; and it seems to suffice that God wills matter to exist, in order not only that it exist, but also that it exist at rest. Such is not the case with motion, because the idea of matter in motion certainly includes two powers or efficacies to which it is related, to wit, what created it, and further, what activated it. But the idea of matter at rest includes only the idea of the power that created it, without the necessity of another power to put it at rest. . . . Therefore, there has to be in God a positive will to put a ball in motion or to cause a ball to have such a force to be moved, and it is sufficient for it to be at rest that He stops willing it to be moved. (*Search* VI.2.ix, OC 2:428–30; LO 515–6)

"There must be in God a positive will to put a ball in motion," he insisted. However, if a ball in motion comes to rest, it does so not because God positively wills it to be at rest; all God needs to do is cease willing it to be moving. Therefore, Malebranche concludes, "rest has no force that causes it. It is nothing but a pure privation that assumes no positive will in God."[26]

It follows from this, he claims, that in a void, the tiniest body in motion "will contain more force and power than the rest of the largest body." The latter has no force whatsoever to resist the motor force of the former, and *this* means that three of Descartes' seven rules of collision and of the resulting distribution of motion are false.[27] Here we have, Malebranche insists, a fine demonstration of "the utility" of his principles.

## IV.   MALEBRANCHE AND HUME

In 1737, David Hume wrote to a friend and suggested that he prepare himself for reading the manuscript of the *Treatise on Human Nature* by studying Malebranche's *Search*. Hume frequently (if not always explicitly) revealed his familiarity with Malebranche's ideas, and he clearly benefitted from reading the unorthodox Cartesian's work.[28] Nowhere is this more apparent than in the matter of causation. Hume's discussion of causation is perhaps the most important and influential in the history of philosophy. In addition, some of his well-known arguments showing that causal reasoning lacks philosophical justification seem to come straight out of Malebranche. It is, in fact, no exaggeration to say that Malebranche prepared the ground for Hume's work on necessary connections. However,

Hume was also one of Malebranche's more rigorous early modern critics.[29]

Like Malebranche, Hume stressed the centrality of the idea of necessary connection to our understanding of causation. The mere proximity and succession of two things is not sufficient to lead us to call the one the cause of the other. "Shall we then rest contented with these two relations of contiguity and succession? By no means. An object may be contiguous and prior to another, without being consider'd as its cause. There is a NECESSARY CONNECTION to be taken into consideration; and that relation is of much greater importance, than any of the other two above mentioned."[30]

Hume, also – and in a manner distinctly reminiscent of Malebranche's arguments – insisted that the requisite necessity will never be discovered, either by reason or by the senses, between any two objects or events. Reason cannot find necessary connections in nature because for any two discrete objects, one can always conceive or imagine, without contradiction, the one without the other.

> There is no object, which implies the existence of any other if we consider these objects in themselves, and never look beyond the idea which we form of them. Such an inference wou'd amount to knowledge, and wou'd imply the absolute contradiction and impossibility of conceiving anything different. But as all distinct ideas are separable, 'tis evident there can be no impossibility of that kind. When we pass from a present impression to the idea of any object, we might possibly have separated the idea from the impression, and have substituted any other idea in its room.[31]

Neither will sense experience ever uncover necessary connections. No matter how many times one may encounter two objects together, one following the other – whether it be a single instance or multiple instances (what Hume calls "constant conjunction") – all one will ever find is that the two are "contiguous in time and place, and that the object we call cause precedes the other we call effect."[32]

Hume insisted that, in fact, there can be no solid reasons for attributing causal powers to either minds or bodies. Although his ultimate conclusion is purely epistemological and not ontological – the skeptic Hume did not adopt the negative thesis of occasionalism and *deny* that things have causal powers – his arguments again seem thoroughly Malebranchian. The mind has no discoverable power either for moving the body or for producing its own ideas.

Do we pretend to be acquainted with the nature of the human soul and the nature of an idea, or the aptitude of the one to produce the other? This is a real creation; a production of something out of nothing: Which implies a power so great, that it may seem, at first sight, beyond the reach of any being, less than infinite. At least it must be owned, that such a power is not felt, nor known, nor even conceivable by the mind.[33]

The case of body is no better. We cannot derive any idea of causal power from the concept of matter. "In reality, there is no part of matter, that does ever, by its sensible qualities, discover any power or energy, or give us ground to imagine, that it could produce anything, or be followed by any other object, which we could denominate its effect. Solidity, extension, motion; these qualities are all complete in themselves, and never point out any other event which may result from them."[34]

The crucial difference between Malebranche and Hume, of course, is that Malebranche goes on to claim that we *do* discover a necessary connection between the will of God and any event willed by God, and causal power in our idea of an infinite being, whereas Hume's stunning maneuver is to turn Malebranche's arguments right back on occasionalism itself. Hume argued that there can be discovered no more necessary a connection between the divine will and an event than between any other two things. All objects and events, including divine volitions and their objects, are, if truly discrete, really and logically separate from one another, and none implies the existence of any other. To claim otherwise, he insisted, is simply to beg the question.

In saying that the idea of an infinitely powerful being is connected with that of every effect, which he wills, we really do no more than assert, that a being, whose volition is connected with every effect, is connected with every effect; which is an identical proposition, and gives us no insight into the nature of this power or connexion.[35]

Moreover, because all of our ideas derive either immediately or mediately from impressions, and because we have never had, in any circumstance, an impression of anything even remotely like power, we have no idea of power. Thus, *a fortiori*, "we have no idea of a being endow'd with any power, much less of one endow'd with infinite power."[36] In Hume's eyes, consistency requires that an occasionalist like Malebranche drop the positive thesis of his doctrine.

For Malebranche, there was more to the problem of causality than making sense of the correspondence between the natural states of things in the world around us. Occasionalism is not just a doctrine of causal relations in nature, and Malebranche's concern with causality goes beyond the problems of physics and metaphysics discussed above. Occasionalism is a grand system that informed Malebranche's thinking on a host of philosophical and theological issues. In an important sense, it is motivated not by any worries over a particular mind-body or body-body problem, but by the urge to make sense of God's operations in the realms of nature and grace, in other words, by the theodicy question in all its dimensions. These grander aspects of Malebranche's system are addressed in the following essay.

### NOTES

1 For various accounts of the development of occasionalism in the seventeenth century, see Gouhier 1926, chapter 3; Prost 1907; Clair 1976; Battail 1973; Weier 1981; Balz 1951; and Nadler 1998. For an account of the medieval precedents, see Nadler 1996.

2 Gouhier 1926, p. 123.

3 See al-Ghazali, *Tahafut al-Falasifah* [*The Incoherence of the Philosophers*], Problem 17.

4 See St. Thomas, *De potentia Dei*, Q. 1, art. 3–5.

5 Leibniz, in fact, in his objections to occasionalism, accuses Malebranche of entirely undermining the rational order of nature; see, for example, *Theodicy*, §§ 207, 305. For a discussion of this aspect of Leibniz's critique, see Rutherford 1993.

6 For a correction of the traditional account of the philosophical motives behind occasionalism, see Lennon 1980, 810ff; and Nadler 1997.

7 See *Doutes sur le système physique des causes occasionelles*, in Fontenelle 1818, pp. 618–9. Fontenelle's work was first published in 1686; Malebranche replied directly to Fontenelle with his *Reflexions sur un livre imprimé à Rotterdam 1686, intitulé Doutes sur le systeme des causes occasionelle* (OC 7–1).

8 *Principles of Philosophy* II.4.

9 See also *Search*, Elucidation 15, OC 3:208–9; LO 660.

10 *Réponse à une Dissertation de Mr. Arnauld contre un Eclaircissement du Traité de la Nature et de la Grace*, VII.6, OC 7:515–6.

11 See also *Dialogues* VII.13.

12 *Metaphysica vera*, Part I, Quinta Scientia, in Geulincx 1892, vol. 2, 150–1.

13 Ibid.

14 Scholarly opinion, however, seems to run against such a reading; see Mc-Cracken 1983, p. 105; and Radner 1978, pp. 17–8, both of whom believe that Malebranche is concerned here only with the causality of volitional agents.

15 For more on this, see Nadler 1999.

16 St. Thomas, *Summa theologiae*, 1a, q. 104, art. 1, resp.; Descartes, *Meditations*, III and *Replies to Fifth Objections*, AT 7:369.

17 See St. Thomas, *Summa theologiae*, 1a, q. 104, art. 1, resp.

18 This, too, may have its source in St. Thomas, who insists that "God does not maintain things in existence by any new action, but by the continuation of the act whereby he bestows being [*esse*]; an act subject to neither change nor time" (Ibid.)

19 *Meditations* III, AT 7:49.

20 *Dialogues* VII.6–11; *Méditations Chrétiennes* V.9.

21 Oddly, Malebranche does not extend the "divine sustenance" argument to the case of minds in this way. It is, however, a natural and, indeed, compulsory extension of the argument; see Nadler 1998.

22 As Gouhier notes, "en confrontant sa doctrine des causes occasionelles avec celle du concours divine, Malebranche a vu se préciser les caractères de l'idée de cause. *Causer*, c'est vraiment *créer*; une cause est une puissance créatrice ou mieux une toute-puissance créatrice" (Gouhier 1926, p. 118).

23 In this regard, Malebranche's account is perhaps just a logical extension of the role Descartes gives to God as "the universal and primary cause of motion"; see *Principles of Philosophy* II.36–43. For a discussion of this aspect of Descartes' system, see Hatfield 1979.

24 *Principles of Philosophy* II.43.

25 Given Malebranche's account of divine sustenance and the conclusions he draws from it about the motion and rest of bodies, however, it is not clear that he is entitled to such a distinction.

26 This conclusion, he insists, is confirmed by purely physical considerations. If force = mass × speed (as Descartes claimed and Malebranche agreed), then when speed = 0 – that is, when the body is at rest – so does force = 0; see *Search* VI.2.ix, OC 2:429–30; LO 516.

27 Rules four, six, and seven (*Principles of Philosophy* II.49, 51, 52), which all rely on attributing to bodies a force to remain at rest. Leibniz, in his general critique of Cartesian physics, praises Malebranche for recognizing Descartes' errors. He insists, however, that because Malebranche was still wedded to Descartes' conservation law – where what is conserved is quantity of motion (mass × speed) rather than quantity of motive force (mass × the square of the velocity) – Malebranche has failed

to see that all except the first of Descartes' rules, along with the new rules he substituted for the ones he rejected, were wrong. In 1692, Malebranche published his *On the laws of the communication of motions*, in which he concedes that Leibniz is right about the rules themselves but continues to maintain the old conservation law. It is not until a letter to Leibniz in 1699 and the 1700 edition of the *Search* that Malebranche admits that Descartes' conservation law was false.

28 McCracken believes that certain passages in Hume "suggest that Hume not only kept the *Search* in mind as he wrote on causality, but that he even had it open for consultation while writing" (McCracken 1983, p. 258).

29 For studies of the philosophical relationship between Malebranche and Hume on causality, see McCracken 1983, pp. 257–69; Wright 1991; and Church 1938.

30 *Treatise*, Book I, Part 3, section 2, p. 77.

31 *Treatise* I.3.6, p. 86–7.

32 *Treatise* I.3.14, p. 155.

33 *An Enquiry Concerning Human Understanding*, 68.

34 *An Enquiry Concerning Human Understanding*, 63.

35 *Treatise* I.4.5, p. 249.

36 *Treatise* I.4.5, p. 248.

# 6   Metaphysics and Philosophy

The main theses of Malebranche's philosophy are well-known today. The theory of vision in God of ideas, the doctrine of occasionalism, the philosophy of will, the function of intelligible extension, as well as the relationship of Malebranche's thought to Descartes' or Leibniz's have all been carefully studied. Very little work, however, in either France or the United States, has explicitly investigated the status and the function of metaphysics in the work of the Oratorian. The question of the definition and the role of a Malebranchian metaphysics gives rise to two distinct but inseparable lines of investigation.

First, is it legitimate to search for a definition and systematic use of the word *métaphysique* in Malebranche? This investigation requires us to determine the relation of any possible Malebranchian metaphysics to the history of metaphysics in the classical period. The other issue is whether Malebranche's metaphysics constitutes a new and original figure in the evolution of metaphysics in the seventeenth century. This essay will seek to address these two questions simultaneously.

As a preliminary step, it seems wise to establish a fact: That the majority of commentators have kept silent on the subject of a Malebranchian metaphysics is all the more surprising as the Oratorian explicitly affirms the preeminent and decisive role of metaphysics in the architecture of his philosophy. While he first published the *Méditations Chrétiennes* in 1683, these become *Chrétiennes* and *Métaphysiques* in their third edition in 1690. This addition to the title suggests that the work, which reexamines a good part of Malebranche's philosophical theses, possesses an admittedly metaphysical character. In 1688, the Oratorian collected his *Dialogues on*

*Metaphysics and Religion*, thus dedicating one of his major works to the definition and explanation of a metaphysics. In a letter to his friend Pierre Berrand dated 23 December 1686, the philosopher announced his goal of writing dialogues on metaphysics and justified his project in these terms: "They want me to undertake a metaphysics. I believe that in fact this is necessary and that I am more capable than most people. A good metaphysics is one which must regulate everything, and I will try to establish the principal truths which are the ground of religion and morality."[1] Even though this letter affirms both the regulative role of metaphysics that must regulate everything and its founding character in matters of religious and moral truths, a complete and meaningful definition is nevertheless not to be found. These lines lead us to place Malebranche's interest for metaphysical questioning at the forefront of our investigation.

It is without a doubt in the *Dialogues on Metaphysics and Religion* themselves that we can find clear evidence.[2] "For by metaphysics, I do not mean those abstract considerations of certain imaginary properties. . . . By this science, I mean the general truths which can serve as principles for the particular sciences" (*Dialogues* VI.2, OC 12:133; JS 92). This text provides several decisive pieces of evidence. First of all, metaphysics is a *general science* that transcends the whole of the *particular sciences*, in other words, the forms of knowing attached to the examination of types of being or more determined objects. Secondly, this science does not aim to examine a precise object, but to confer on the whole of the sciences the principles that will guarantee their own truth. This is why on the same page of the *Dialogues*, Malebranche can still write "this general science rules over all the others" because its proper task, as we will see, is to define the epistemological conditions for the certainty of the other forms of knowing. As a consequence, the whole of Malebranche's philosophy will be indebted to metaphysics.

In order to comprehend what Malebranche's metaphysics might be, it is therefore appropriate to explicate this founding epistemological function.[3]

## I.   METAPHYSICAL ABSTRACTION

A quick lexical investigation reveals that in a number of occurrences, the word *métaphysique* is joined with the theme of abstraction:

"It is well known that I have devoted more attention to abstract and metaphysical questions than to learning what is said in the Fathers," Malebranche ironically responded to Arnauld.[4] Evoking the first principle of morality, the Oratorian cautioned us: "This principle is abstract, metaphysical, purely intelligible; it is not sensed or imagined" (*Search* VI.2.iii; OC 2:20; LO 271). This text therefore yields three related determinations of the first principle of morality: its intelligibility, its abstract character, and therefore its belonging to metaphysics.[5] What immediately follows this sequence clarifies more precisely the nature of the metaphysical abstraction: A principle is not *sensed* and is not *imagined*.

The first principle is metaphysical because it excludes sensible and imaginative knowledge. This double exclusion constitutes the difficulty proper to metaphysics: "Those who are unaccustomed to abstract or metaphysical truths are easily persuaded that we are trying only to lead them astray when we would enlighten them" (*Search*, Elucidation 10, OC 3:128; LO 612). By excluding the senses and the imagination, metaphysical abstraction ensures that the knowledge thus obtained will possess the maximum of evidence: "Metaphysical truths and arguments contain nothing sensible, men are not affected by them, and as a result they do not remain convinced by them. Nonetheless, it is certain that abstract ideas are the most distinct and metaphysical truths the clearest and most evident" (*Search*, Elucidation 6, OC 3:53–4; LO 568).

Let me note at once that the process of abstraction concerns simultaneously the mode of knowledge required by metaphysics – namely, the pure intellectual idea – and the object known by this idea. If, as we will see, the thing is known only in and through the epistemological mediation of the abstract idea, and if on the other hand, metaphysics proceeds only by means of these same ideas, then we anticipate that metaphysics will concern simultaneously the object known by the idea and the idea itself. Before defining this or that object, the word *métaphysique* qualifies a certain type of knowledge applicable to different objects.

In taking abstraction to be the first operation of knowledge, the Oratorian confirms the metaphysical rootedness of his thought in relation to a twofold tradition. First of all, he assumes the scholastic characterization of metaphysics as the most abstract science. We know that Suarez, for example, distinguished three degrees of abstraction, each corresponding to a determinate science. The metaphysical abstraction operates at once in reason and in being. Metaphysics thus contemplates an object totally separate from sensible and intelligible matter. "For this knowledge abstracts from sensible or material things, which are called physical, because they are the subject matter of natural philosophy; it is concerned with divine things, both those separated from matter and the common notions of things which can exist without."[6] Whereas physics considers a sensible object and mathematics is still attached to intelligible matter, metaphysics alone is totally abstracted from all relation to any matter. "For physics should consider things made of sensible matter. Mathematics abstracts from that matter according to reason, but not however according to being . . . Metaphysics abstracts from both sensible and intelligible matter, not only according to reason, but also according to being."[7]

Malebranche is just as much the heir of Descartes. For the latter, the rule of metaphysics begins at the point where that of matter and sensible knowledge stops. That is to say, metaphysics is deployed in and through the *abductio mentis a sensibus*, in and through recourse to a strictly intellectual knowledge.[8] Metaphysical knowledge implies renouncing both sensation and imagination: "Metaphysical thoughts, which exercise the pure intellect, help to familiarize us with the notion of the soul; and the study of mathematics, which exercises mainly the imagination in the consideration of shapes and motions accustoms us to form very distinct notions of the body."[9] Thus, we are free to consider Malebranche as a direct descendant of Descartes when he characterizes the object of metaphysics as immaterial and consequently intelligible.[10] The evidence relating to abstraction provides a decisive marker: What is abstract first of all in Malebranche is the purely intelligible idea. The pure idea is abstract not only because it does not require any mediation from the senses, but also because it is purely immaterial. Therefore, it before all else is what permits abstraction; the knowing procured by it is thus immediately identified with the abstract knowing required by metaphysics. In a quite precise text, the Oratorian joins together the epistemological abstraction of metaphysical knowledge and the correlative abstraction of the known object. He thus indicates that metaphysical knowledge is obtained first by the vision in God of archetypal ideas: "Finally, I call it [the mind] pure mind, or pure understanding, when it receives from God entirely pure ideas of the truth, with no admixture of sensations and images, through its union not with the body but with the Word, or the Wisdom, of God" (*Search*, OC 1:489; LO 261).

A more thorough inquiry concerning the occurrences of the word *métaphysique* reveals that the idea is not simply the means by which the abstraction operates. In a more original way, the idea becomes in itself an object of investigation for metaphysics.

## II.  IDEA AS OBJECT OF METAPHYSICS

In several particularly clear texts, metaphysics is not only defined as the knowing that is acquired through the intermediary of the idea, but more profoundly as the science of the idea itself: "A serious reflection on the difference between knowing by *feeling* and knowing by *idea*, ... between numbers and their properties ... and feeling pleasure ... forces those who are accustomed to the mediation on Metaphysical truths to judge ... that to feel ... pain, a representational *idea* is not at all necessary" (RVFI, OC 6:55). In this text, the distinction between the clear idea and the confused feeling, and correlatively, the distinction between the objects corresponding to these types of knowledge, arises explicitly from metaphysics. The latter thus concentrates on examining modes of knowledge, on analyzing the power and the domain of the diverse cognitive faculties. Evoking the debate about ideas, the point of entry for the polemic between Malebranche and Arnauld, Malebranche writes: "Monsieur Arnauld did not have to hoodwink people on false pretexts by criticizing only the most abstract parts of *The Search After Truth*, ... in order to prejudice against me the vast number of those who would prefer to take it on his word, rather than exert themselves too much on a Metaphysical proceeding" (RVFI, OC 6:18). This "metaphysical proceeding" concerns precisely the discussion about the essence of human knowledge, more especially about the nature and the origin of our ideas.[11] Thus, Malebranche can declare that "perhaps the most abstract subject of Metaphysics is that of the nature of our ideas. The majority of Philosophers do not take the trouble to illuminate this matter, and though they define man as *animal rationis particeps*, there are few who know that this universal Reason in which all men participate is the Word or the reason of God himself" (RVFI,

OC 6:50).[12] Before investigating a possible object, metaphysics questions the conditions of its own possibility, that is to say knowledge by pure idea. Metaphysics thus finds its primary object in the investigation of knowledge – which first investigates the essence of the object in general before elucidating this or that being.

This prioritized epistemological orientation of metaphysics that becomes a general theory of the conditions of knowing is confirmed by two reasons. Recall that Malebranche retains as true knowledge only the vision in God of ideas, the unique objects of divine and human intellections.[13] Before affirming vision in God, the Oratorian has carefully eliminated all the empiricist options.[14] Vision in God therefore exhibits a type of knowledge that is originally abstract. As a determination of the divine essence itself, the idea is metaphysical in origin, because it remains indifferent to the creation of any possible nature.[15] Vision in God therefore answers quite precisely to what metaphysics requires as a mode of knowledge. It is thus the sole mode of knowledge that really counts, and as such, vision in God becomes the true ground of all philosophy: "If I consult Him in all metaphysical, natural and purely philosophical questions ... I will always have a loyal master who will never deceive me" (*Search*, OC 1:491; LO 262). In this text, the questions that belong to metaphysics are found to be previously submitted to vision in God and the attentive investigation of the Word.[16]

The elaboration of philosophy thus depends on elucidating the nature and powers of the idea. Reflecting on its own conditions of possibility, metaphysics will first be a theory of the idea and the correct use of the understanding.[17] We should note that this inclination of metaphysical inquiry toward the examination of the idea before all else is not something Malebranche alone accomplished in the second half of the seventeenth century. The Oratorian could have read it in a text that he knew well, the *Logique ou l'art de penser*: "There is nothing of greater importance in metaphysics than the origin of our ideas, the separation of spiritual ideas and corporeal images, the distinction of the soul and the body."[18]

In this text, the question of the origin of the idea comes before the proof of the distinction between the soul and the body because this distinction is grounded in the immateriality of the idea, which implies the spirituality of the soul that knows it. In the Cartesian school, metaphysics comprised by and large the questions relative to the origin of knowledge. If for Pierre-Sylvain Régis, the first book of *Metaphysics* treats chiefly the mind, the existence of bodies and God, the second examines the theory of ideas: "The second book of metaphysics treats in general the faculties of the soul. The first part treats in particular the understanding. We examine what this faculty is; we divide it into its kinds.... We explain the nature, the origin and the properties of ideas and sensation.... We show that natural ideas always conform with their objects."[19] In Arnauld himself, questions connected to the doctrine of knowledge seem to hold one of the first roles in metaphysics. This is testified to by the complete title of the *Régles du bon sens: Régles du bon sens pour bien juger des écrits polémiques dans des matières de sciences appliquées à une dispute entre deux théologiens touchant cette question métaphysique si nous pouvons voir les vérités nécessaires et immuables dans la vérité souveraine et incréée.*[20] In one text at least, Descartes himself asserts that metaphysics has as its principal task the elucidation of the principles of knowledge. He speaks of "philosophy whose first part is metaphysics, which contains the principles of knowledge, including the explanation of the principal attributes of God, the non-material nature of the soul and all the clear and distinct notions which are in us."[21]

Metaphysics therefore explores the idea, understood as its first object, and the beings knowable through these same ideas. Metaphysics can thus become "general science" because it includes the determination of the conditions through which objects can appear and give themselves to be known. Metaphysics is therefore not simply the first of sciences, but a meta-scientific knowing; it is, as it were, the science of sciences.

We have therefore arrived at an initial explanation of metaphysics as general science. As confirmation, we could evoke a text that illustrates the affirmations of the fifth of the *Dialogues*: in Book IV (6.ii) of the *Search*, the Oratorian illustrates metaphysics' relationships with the other sciences. It is important therefore to grasp what exactly he means when he qualifies metaphysics as general science.

### III.   METAPHYSICS AS GENERAL SCIENCE

The generality of metaphysics seems to reside in its particular and supereminent function of being the sole discipline equipped to ground the certainty of the whole of the sciences. A text from the *Search* helps clarify this. In the text, Malebranche decides that the principle of evidence, inherited from Descartes, is the first metaphysical axiom, by thus explaining the assimilation of metaphysics to the theory of knowledge. The discredit into which metaphysics fell is also what determines its worth: "Metaphysics is a similarly abstract science that does not flatter the senses ...; for the same reason this science is very much neglected, and one often finds people foolish enough to boldly deny common notions. There are even some who deny that we can and should assert of a thing what is included in the clear and distinct idea we have of it" (*Search* IV.11.ii, OC 2:90; LO 315).

The rejection of metaphysics is witnessed paradoxically in that of the common notions that are its skeleton. From this collection of notions, one always stands out: "we can assert of a thing what is included in the clear and distinct idea we have of it." This notion will quickly become an axiom," then will be brought to the rank of "general principle of all the sciences." The principle of evidence, which confers on the idea an immediate access to evidence, is also "the first foundation of all our clear and evident knowledge" and the "first axiom of all the sciences." If metaphysics can be defined as the search for and the science of the foundation, this first principle is doubly a foundation. It is the first and most evident, but also the most general and therefore counts universally.

We will observe in this collection of texts, a close connection between the discovery of a first principle of metaphysics and the determination of this same principle as principle of the sciences. The metaphysical principle thus exhibited can count universally for the sciences because it does not exactly state the property of an object. It consists inversely in the affirmation of the universal conveyed in knowledge by ideas as the sole real mode of authentic knowing: "And yet this metaphysical axiom, i.e., that one can be certain of something one clearly conceives to be included in the idea that represents it ..., is more evident than the axiom that states that the whole is greater than its parts, because this latter axiom is not so much an axiom as a conclusion from the first axiom ... the first cannot be proven by any other" (OC 2:92; LO 316).

The first axiom or principle therefore states a thesis about the essence of knowledge: from knowledge by idea to the being of the thing, the conclusion is correct, so long as we stick with the evident idea that manifests the nature or essence of the thing.[22] The first axiom therefore confirms what Descartes had established.[23] By demonstrating and putting into operation the principle of evidence, metaphysics ensures its superiority over the other sciences depending on this universal principle. With precise examples, Malebranche will show the principal and universal scope of the evident idea: "Ask all the men in the world [if] the whole is greater than its parts, and I am sure that not one will be found who will not give the appropriate answer right away. Then ask them if one can in the same way, without fear of error, be certain of a thing one clearly conceives to be included in the idea that represents it, and you will see that few will agree to this without hesitation. . . . And yet this metaphysical axiom . . . is more evident than the axiom that states the whole is greater than its parts, because this latter axiom is not so much an axiom as a conclusion from the first axiom. . . . The first cannot be proven by any other. It is absolutely the first and the foundation of all our clear and evident knowledge" (OC 2:92; LO 316).

In this text, the Oratorian affirms the founding value of evidence in relation to the forms of knowing that the evident idea renders possible. The sciences as systems of evident truths acquire value and certainty only because the idea, with its rights and privileges, is recognized previously.[24] By demonstrating the proof of the first axiom, metaphysics therefore appears as the general science that surpasses, so as to better ground, the whole of particular sciences. It thus bears in itself the requirement for its own comprehension. It is raised to the essence of scientificity.

We now understand why elucidating the nature and the origin of the idea turns out to be so crucial to the constitution of metaphysics. In effect, the idea with the maximum level of evidence becomes the unsurpassable criterion of truth. Metaphysics thus brings together under its jurisdiction the totality of the sciences that depend on the objectivity whose definition is the mission of metaphysics. This is testified to by the examples that Malebranche offers in the text we are commenting on. The truths of logic are themselves subordinate to the evidence of the ideas that manifest their truths to us: "they [men] think it is evident that the whole is greater than its parts, that a mountain of marble is possible and that a mountain without a valley is impossible, and that it is not equally evident that there is a God." The level of evidence for each of these propositions is equal because they are all "equally removed from the first principle." The first three conclusions here concern logic and the modes of existence of certain beings; the fourth is more concerned with natural theology and the proof for the existence of God.

These four questions stand at an equal distance from an epistemological dependence on the principle of evidence that guarantees them. This first principle, by its greater generality, acquires in a certain sense a surplus of evidence. All the truths become evident and therefore true in dependence on a more primordial truth, stated precisely by the founding axiom of metaphysics. The principle of contradiction itself becomes operative only because it is in turn validated by a clear and distinct, metaphysically certain, idea. The proof for the existence of God enjoys no particular evidence, but like the other conclusions is led back to its previous validation by the general science. The proof for the existence of God presupposes the unconditioned validity of the evident idea.[25]

The first axiom is indeed metaphysical and not simply epistemological because it has in itself an ontological value. That is, this first axiom ensures the concept's equivalence to the essence by positing that all that we conceive in evidence is such as we conceive it. The metaphysical value of evidence is grounded immediately on the vision in God of the idea. By seeing in God, we reach absolute essences, such as God knows them. When Malebranche enumerates the objects that belong within metaphysics, the nature of knowledge, especially the proof for our union with God, always figures in a prominent place: "What does the ordinary man think, for example, when most metaphysical truths are proved to him, when we demonstrate for him the existence of God ... that there is only one sovereign Reason in which all intelligences participate, ... metaphysical truths and arguments having nothing to do with sensation? These men are not affected by them" (*Search*, Elucidation 6, OC 3:53; LO 568).

The thesis of vision in God therefore becomes the principal affirmation of general metaphysics. This vision becomes an "unshakable foundation." "But it seems to me that the principle that only God enlightens us, and that He enlightens us only through the manifestation of an immutable and necessary wisdom or reason so conforms to religion, ... is so absolutely necessary if a certain and unshakeable foundation is to be given to any truth whatsoever, that I feel myself under an indispensable obligation to explain it" (*Search*, Elucidation 10, OC 3:128; LO 613 [modified]).[26] The primacy of the foundation therefore no longer coincides with that of a privileged being, but is found in the unconditioned epistemological workings of a first principle to which the exploration of the different regions of being will be submitted. Any error in metaphysics will therefore endanger the whole of the structure: "It is dangerous in metaphysics to only half-comprehend things ... and the smallest errors in this part of philosophy are of infinite consequence" (*Méditations chrétiennes* XIII, OC 10:101).[27]

However, metaphysics cannot confine itself to being only a science of the idea. Let us not forget the first function of the idea is *to represent,* to manifest an essence in truth. On this condition,  knowledge will fulfill its fundamental function by enabling us to determine what kind of relation we should maintain with other beings. Now it seems appropriate for us to explore the whole of the objects accessible to the different ideas, with the aim of locating the limits to the field of competence and the validity of the general science.

## IV. THE DOMAIN OF METAPHYSICS

At the beginning of *Dialogues* VI, after having evoked the general science and having fixed its definition, Malebranche announces a research plan for the subsequent *Dialogues*: "there are only three kinds of beings about which we have any knowledge and to which we can have any connection: God, or the infinitely perfect being, ... minds, ... and bodies, of the existence of which we are assured by the revelation we have of them" (*Dialogues* VI.3, OC 12:135; JS 93).[28]  I propose that these three objects belong explicitly to metaphysical knowledge. To show this, and because metaphysics proceeds by means of representative ideas, it is appropriate to show simultaneously that the field of knowledge by ideas is not, as is often assumed, limited just to knowledge of bodies by intelligible extension. I suggest that the workings of knowledge by *ideas* is not irreconcilable with the famous distinction between the four modes of knowledge stated in the *Search*.

### 6.1.   Knowledge of Bodies

The case of knowledge of bodies is explicit. For Malebranche, the essence of bodies is knowable in and through the idea of extension, or *intelligible extension*. The existence of bodies, on the other hand, is revealed to us by a feeling which, beginning in 1693, is engendered by a stronger affection, a more powerful efficacy of intelligible extension over the mind.[29] "Through illumination and through a clear idea, the mind sees numbers, extension, and the essences of things. Through a confused idea or through sensation, it judges about the existence of creatures and knows its own existence" (*Search*, Elucidation 10, OC 3:142; LO 621).

Intelligible extension, the archetype or essence of bodies, has as its mission *to represent* local and created extension, invisible in itself. "It must be realized that God contains in Himself an ideal or intelligible infinite extension; for since He has created it, God knows extension, and He can know it only in Himself. Thus since the mind can perceive a part of this intelligible extension that God contains, it surely can perceive in God all figures.... Furthermore, we see or sense a given body when its idea, i.e., when some figure composed of intelligible and general extension, becomes sensible and particular through color or some other sensible perception by which its idea affects the soul" (OC 3:152; LO 626).

In this text, intelligible extension is first of all the foundation of geometry because it allows us to think shapes; it is the representation of a space that is in itself invisible.[30] The existence of bodies is revealed by the increase in the efficacy of the extended idea itself. The feeling that manifests existence is itself thought as "confused idea." Intelligible extension thus gives us access to the mathematical essences: "having the idea of extension, it depends only on us to assiduously consider the connections to it" (RVFI, OC 6:126). The essence of the circle is nothing other than its idea through which we conceive all possible circles.[31] Intelligible extension does not *actually* contain shapes, but permits their construction. This ideal extension is therefore not the image of created extension; rather it is the concept in and through which all representation of an extended being can occur. Intelligible extension is simultaneously what is known and what makes geometrical space knowable. It is at one and the same time an idea and an essence, an object of knowing. With this example, we understand how the science of the idea (i.e., metaphysics) is also understood as a science of objects.

Intelligible extension does not merely found geometry; it also makes physics possible. By assuming the Cartesian identification of matter and geometrical extension, by determining intelligible extension as the archetype of this same matter, Malebranche confers a common metaphysical ground to mathematics and physics. Extension is indeed the object of the physicist and the mathematician. "We could extract from the idea of extension properties which belong to the body because this idea represents their nature as being the archetype according to which God created them, and because we must judge things according to their ideas" (*Réponse à Régis* II.11, OC 17–1:287).

More explicitly, Malebranche specifies that "the idea of extension is so clear and so intelligible, so rich in truth that the geometers and physicists extract from it all knowledge that they have of geometry and physics" (*ibid.*, 297). Intelligible extension is thus the essence of bodies, an essence which determines the law of their possible existence:[32] "... with respect to corporeal beings, I claim that we can see or know them only in intelligible extension – the idea which represents all their essences or what they are, and which is found only in God" (RVFI, OC 6:108).[33] Though unchangeable, intelligible extension is called *mobile*, which is to say that it furnishes the means to represent the movement of created bodies. It follows that certain physical properties of bodies will be *a priori* deducible from the idea of extension. It is from a purely static conception of movement that the Oratorian can ground its metaphysical representation in an unchangeable extension: "But although we might suppose that the intelligible parts of the idea of extension always maintain the same relation of intelligible distance between them ..., nonetheless, if we conceive of a given created extension to which there corresponds a given part of intelligible extension as its idea, we will be able through this same idea of space (though intelligibly immobile) to see that the parts of the created extension are mobile, because the idea of space ... necessarily represents all sorts of relations of distance and shows that the parts of a body can fail to maintain the same situation relative to each other" (*Search*, Elucidation 10, OC 3:153; LO 627). This representation of movement is made possible by the mathematization of the physical definition of the body: a body is defined as the identity of a relation of distance between parts in relative rest. For the purpose of conceiving movement, it is a matter of conceiving some change in this relation of distance.[34]

Intelligible extension is therefore not the local extension objectively present to the mind, but the eternal and unchangeable idea, the essence of a potentially created extension.[35] The knowledge of physical extension therefore does not in any way presuppose the creation of this same extension. Intelligible extension is sufficient to ground a metaphysical theory of corporeal being.[36]

In this way, the submission of one type of created being to the type of knowledge defined by metaphysics is confirmed for the first time. To be sure, the latter does not give physics its principles or its laws; these laws are still not deducible from the Word and will be known only through *experience*. However, more decisively perhaps, metaphysics fixes the conditions under which representation of the physical object is possible. The Oratorian denounces, moreover, the false physics that pretends to exhibit essences on the basis of sensible givens alone.[37] Prolonging the paradox inscribed in his doctrine of representation (we reach the essence of things by ignoring the things themselves), Malebranche proposes the possibility of a physics independent of the existence of the bodies it studies.[38] Malebranche can thus reproach physicists for not inquiring about the foundations of their own certainties: "Finally, most physicists and chemists consider only the particular effects of nature. They never ascend to the primary notions of things that compose bodies. But, it is indubitable that we cannot know ... the particular things of physics without the more general, and without ascending even to the level of Metaphysics" (*Search* II.2.viii, OC 1:319; LO 159–60). The foundations of occasionalism are thus often evoked in the list of metaphysical truths, which are indispensable to founding physics.[39] The demonstration for physical occasionalism can be carried out *a priori* in the name of the inconceivability of force immanent in the finite, on the one hand, and from the demonstration of divine immutability on the other. Now the latter must be demonstrated metaphysically by the examination of the attributes of God.[40] Physics therefore postulates its own rootedness in metaphysics. For that matter, the latter guarantees the work of the physicist by providing him the object of his own speculation.

## 6.2.  The Knowledge of Souls

In contrast to the knowledge of bodies, it seems that access to our soul refuses representation in an idea. We know our soul "by interior feeling or consciousness" without an idea and immediately, by a permanent revelation without distance dividing the soul from itself.[41] The idea of our soul is, it seems, refused by God in this life.[42]

Nevertheless, it is not absolutely certain that we can, while respecting these texts, reject every function to the idea of our soul. Let us observe that the soul is not the cause of its own appearing in the immanence of an unmediated lived experience. The feeling that reveals our soul to us does not result from self-affection. By virtue of the occasionalist conception of causality, the soul, a finite substance, cannot by itself produce the feeling that reveals it. It therefore belongs to God, an omnipotent cause, to support the soul's presence to itself: "it is thus that the soul knows itself only confusedly and by an interior feeling. It feels itself, but though it might be inseparable from itself, it never knows itself ... until it sees itself in God, until God reveals the ideal or intelligible mind to it, that is to say, the eternal model on which it was formed" (*Lettre à Arnauld*, OC 9:956).

Donation by feeling is always effected by the efficacious idea, always operative, but never fully manifest. "If I feel myself, it is because it touches me" (OC 10:19), the *Méditations chrétiennes* clearly state. In its indetermination, this *it* witnesses the necessary mediation of the power of the affecting idea to produce feeling in our soul. "The soul is a substance which thinks; it is an intelligence which perceives; but it perceives only that which touches it, only that which affects it; and it is not what affects it, it is not formally its own light ... Nothing can affect or touch it besides the divine ideas ... Nothing can act in it except what is above it, and nothing is superior to the soul but God" (*Lettre à Arnauld*, OC 9:921). The soul, in order to appear, requires the inescapable mediation of its archetype; it can be thought only through the invisible but active mediation of its idea in God.

Another important thesis again manifests the rootedness of knowledge of the soul in the noetic schema of metaphysics. Not being able to reach the clear idea of our soul immediately, Malebranchian philosophy turns to two procedures in order to grasp it in terms of the idea of extension.[43]

(a) The Oratorian has recourse to an analogical process: since the beginning of the *Search*, he compares the faculties of the soul (understanding and will) with the two properties of extension manifest by its idea (shapes and motions).[44] He then tries to set up an analogy between matter's relations to its modes on the one hand and spiritual substance's relation to its own modes on the other. The properties of the soul will be thought on the basis of the body's relation to its own properties. Just as the body is susceptible to two types of modifications, the soul is endowed with two inseparable faculties: the understanding which corresponds to figuration in matter, and the will defined as a spiritual movement, a tension leading straight toward the good that corresponds to the movement of the parts of matter in a straight line. Material figures correspond to the pure perceptions of the soul, the configurations to the sensible perceptions. It is therefore an issue of *representing* the soul in terms of the properties known clearly in extension.

(b) In other texts (*Dialogues* I.1–2), Malebranche claims to describe the essence of our soul in terms of the negation of the properties known clearly in intelligible extension. While this extension is divisible, composite, and material, the soul will be indivisible, simple, and immaterial. By means of this process, the possibility of a rational psychology opens up, one based on the metaphysical doctrine of extension. As it passes through the detour of these two processes, the soul becomes the possible subject of a metaphysical discourse.

### 6.3. Knowledge of God

Ordinarily, one takes pains to be sure that God is not submitted to knowledge by ideas. It therefore behooves us to comment on the famous denial of an idea of God in *Search After Truth*: "Only God do we know through Himself ... Only He can act on our mind and reveal Himself to it. Only God do we see in immediate and direct sight" (III.2.ii, OC 1:449; LO 236–7). In this way, the mind would be in *immediate* contact with God known *directly*. Just like the soul,

Kx God by idea

God would reject the gap constitutive of representation.[45] What I want to propose, however, is that God does *not* make an exception to knowledge by idea – if one takes care to note the modifications that the definition of idea undergoes so as to be applicable to knowledge of God. To be sure, we have to acknowledge that Malebranche's position is ambiguous. When the Oratorian denies that God can be known by an idea, it is always in a precise context where the definition of "idea" does not include the characteristics that Malebranche elsewhere sees in the idea. In a word, knowledge of God by ideas is rejected when the idea is defined as "different" from God, when it is thought as created, finite, and particular.

A quite clear text from the *Réponse aux livre des vraies et des fausses idées* permits us to grasp the motives and the real meaning of Malebranche's refusal: "...I sometimes take the word 'idea' generally for that which is the immediate object of the mind when it thinks; I want, nevertheless, for us to see the infinite, for us to know God by means of an idea, but certainly this idea will be God himself, for there is no other idea of God besides his Word ... I want us to see God or the infinite by means of an idea, but an idea which is consubstantial with him, an idea which contains all his substance.... Finally, I deny that we can see the uncreated, infinite universal being in a created, finite, and particular being" (OC 6:166–7).

The Word is therefore at one and the same time a divine person and the representation that God engenders of his own substance. In reaching the Word through vision in God, one therefore reaches the representation that God has of himself. The refusal of an idea of God is therefore grounded in the refusal to have God let himself be represented by a finite idea, particular and different from himself. Now, it is well-known that starting with Elucidation 10, Malebranche breaks definitively with the definition of the idea as modality or finite being, which still partially prevails in the *Search*.[46] Starting with the tenth Elucidation, the idea is immutable, eternal, and infinite. Malebranche's rejection of an idea of God will henceforth seem incompatible with the proper determinations that the Oratorian grants to ideas. In a word, Malebranche denies the idea of God when "idea" means what he himself refuses to see in this word. From the *Search* on, he granted the possibility of a distinct idea of God; let us not forget that the "ontological" argument and the proof by "mere sight" are equally grounded in "the idea of the infinitely perfect being." The third Elucidation produces a definition of idea that will be compatible with what the knowledge of God demands: "Thus the word *idea* is equivocal. Sometimes, I take it as anything that represents some object to the mind whether clearly or confusedly. More generally, I take it for anything that is the immediate object of the mind" (OC 3:44; LO 561). In the second sense of idea indicated by this text, it becomes the absolutely undetermined and obligatory form of all thoughts.

We should note finally that by acceding to the divine ideas, we know the very perfections of the divine essence. Knowledge by idea therefore always presupposes the knowledge of God. Intelligible extension is thus at once an idea of corporeal things and a perfection of the divine essence. The Word that contains the totality of representative perfections thus becomes the "natural and necessary object of our thoughts" (*Traité de morale* I.3.xiv, OC 11:45). In fact, it is appropriate to distinguish two ideas of God: the idea of the God-Word, included in all our representations, and the idea of God as undetermined and universal being, more vague and confused because it encompasses confusedly the totality of the divine being.[47]

In summary, an idea of God is admissible as soon as God is his own idea. Malebranche refuses the idea of God when idea is defined as an archetype that is different from the object it represents. So as not to have to reject a knowledge of God by ideas, God becomes his own archetype: "For being has no idea that represents it. It has no archetype containing all its intelligible reality. *It is its own archetype*" (*Dialogues* II.5, OC 12:54; JS 23, my emphasis). Knowledge of God quite obviously implies the transgression of all the sensible and imaginative mediations; in order to make right judgments about God, one has to have recourse to a pure and abstract idea, such as metaphysics has defined it in advance.[48] Thus understood, the idea of God has the sense of a self-manifestation of God, as a rational revelation of the divine to the mind. It is therefore important not to let oneself abuse the vocabulary of *immediacy* and of *direct* knowledge. Immediate knowledge is not the result of mystical union. The word *immediate* in Malebranche's vocabulary is quite frequently associated with the lexicon of the idea. Even in the beyond, in the face-to-face vision, God unveils himself to the mind only through the always operative mediation of his idea, producing pleasant feelings in the mind of the elect.

Several texts testify to the effectivity of an idea of God: "[Reason] tries to envision Him in Himself, or through that great and vast idea of infinitely perfect being that He contains" (*Search* V.5, OC 2:174–5; LO 367). The metaphysical exploration of the divine attributes can happen only under the control of the idea of God. Philosophical theology proceeds conceptually, and the idea of God determines the attribution to the divine essence of its principal properties.[49] The idea of God grounds the possibility of an *a priori* theodicy and more particularly the deduction of the principle of the simplicity of means.[50]

The three types of being that we can know (God, the soul, and bodies) are therefore susceptible to knowledge by idea.[51] This result immediately calls for a remark concerning the structure of Malebranchian metaphysics.

The preceding analyses enable us to point out two chief orientations of the metaphysics. First, we brought to light a metaphysics understood as general science understood as theory of knowledge and the power of the idea. This metaphysics then rises to the rank of the ground of the particular sciences. In addition to this role of the foundation, metaphysics can be defined as speculation on the essence of the three principal objects that coincide at least partially with the objects of the particular sciences. We are therefore free to point out  two clearly articulated moments in the Malebranchian constitution of metaphysics. Metaphysics, defined as science of the idea, validates more specific investigations as to the types of knowable beings. One such articulation, noticeable in the internal structure of the principal work Malebranche consecrated to metaphysics (the *Dialogues* of 1688), will enable us to confirm our previous analyses.

### V.  METAPHYSICS IN THE *DIALOGUES*

It might be surprising to see a work dedicated to metaphysics not open with a definition of it, with at least a statement of its subject matter and its field of competence. The most complete definition comes only at the beginning of the sixth of the *Dialogues*. It should not be concluded from that, however, that the first five dialogues do not belong to the elaboration of metaphysics.[52] "By the metaphysical truths we have discovered in our foregoing discussions, you can judge whether the truth of philosophy contradicts religion." What then are these metaphysical truths evoked by Theodore and brought to light in the first five dialogues?

The first presents the distinction of the soul and the body, the inquiry into the nature of ideas and the distinction between sensible and intelligible objects. It is incumbent that one not make a mistake about the status of the distinction between the soul and the body. It is not, in this first step, a matter of grasping the nature of humankind, but of affirming the possibility for a purely spiritual or intellectual knowledge, independent of the body. It is important at the outset of metaphysical inquiry to lay bare the optimal conditions for illumination by divine ideas. Paragraph four of the first dialogue explores the nature of the idea. The fundamental character of the latter remains abstraction. We do not see objects, but solely their archetypes. The same paragraph asserts the supereminent dignity of the idea, as well as its necessarily representative status.[53] It is here that the first formulation of vision in God comes up. Paragraphs six and seven will establish the status of the idea as essence and unique object of the mind. The first of the *Dialogues* is therefore dominated by the question of the origin and the nature of intellectual knowledge. The "metaphysical ideas" evoked at the end (OC 12:47) concern the doctrine of knowledge far more than the illumination of a determinate object.

The second of the *Dialogues*[54] broaches the existence of God only to the degree that God grounds the possibility of the vision of ideas. Paradoxically, it is the demonstration of vision in God that permits establishing the existence of God. The latter is therefore considered first as the absolute ground of clear knowledge, as is attested by the movement through which the proof of his existence is established on the basis of the analysis of the conditions of representation in and through intelligible extension: "Infinite intelligible extension is not a modification of my mind. It is immutable, eternal, necessary. I can doubt neither its reality nor its immensity. Everything immutable . . . is not a creature. . . . Thus it belongs to the creator and can be found only in God. Therefore there is a God, and a Reason" (OC 12:50–1; JS 20). The God exhibited here is first attained as reason and ground of knowing. It is on the basis of the idea and its real conditions for existence (eternity and immutability) that the existence of God is demonstrated. God is therefore shown against the background of an analysis of the human condition. His metaphysical status is first of all that of a ground for clear knowledge. The metaphysical analysis of the conditions for this knowledge thus brings it to the point where it considers God as privileged object.[55]

Paragraphs two and three examine the idea of extension – without however seeking to constitute, at least for the moment, a genuine science of bodies. This science will come up later when metaphysics determines its objects in dialogues seven and ten. In the Malebranchian version of the ontological argument, God does not come up through the analysis of properties inscribed in a concept, but through the necessities of representation by vision in him. The God of the second dialogue is therefore not the supreme being so much as he is the being through which all beings become knowable.[56]

The third of the *Dialogues* develops at length the distinction between confused feeling and clear idea. The value of representation by idea is strongly affirmed as ground of all judgments about things: *things are to be judged only by the ideas that represent them.* More broadly, dialogues three through five investigate the diverse modes of knowledge. The language of section eleven of *Dialogues* III shows well that the explanation of knowledge remains the inevitable preliminary exercise to the explanation of the objects of metaphysics. Only the idea is equipped to deliver the real.[57]

With *Dialogues* VI, we enter into the second major stage of the work. Once the theory of knowledge has been established, it is asked what we can and should know. The prologue and the first three paragraphs reinterrogate the status of metaphysics, which is now turned toward its objects. The third paragraph enumerates the plan that served as the guiding line for our investigation into the objects of metaphysics.[58] The bodies and the laws of their connection will be studied in *Dialogues* VII, the essence of God will be the object of VIII, and his action in Creation is the specific object of *Dialogues* IX through XI. The scholastic systematization of metaphysics in Germany will arrive, with Wolff, at the distinction between a general metaphysics, or ontology understood as science of the concept of being, and a special metaphysics. The latter is characterized by a threefold division between a rational psychology, a natural theology, and a cosmology. Malebranche, in his own way, is part of the evolution of metaphysics that ends in such an organization.

The final dialogues (twelve through fourteen) constitute more especially the rational exploration of the revealed deposit with a view to "founding religion." The founding principles of Christianity are themselves claimed as falling under the jurisdiction of metaphysics.

It is in this way that it is appropriate to "make metaphysics serve religion" (XIV.13, OC 12:354; JS 284).

Thus, *Dialogues* I through V state the principles of metaphysics, while the ones that follow are dedicated to shedding some light on its objects.


## VI.    METAPHYSICS AND PHILOSOPHY

For Malebranche, metaphysics was therefore the most noble part of philosophy. We saw how this general science determined the certainty of the derived forms of knowing. If it grounds (from an epistemological point of view) mathematics and physics, it appears just as decisive for the elaboration of a philosophical ethics and for confirmation – indeed the demonstration – of religious dogma.

The Oratorian clearly affirms the subordination of ethics as theory of action to metaphysics. The morality that is divided into a doctrine of virtue and a theory of obligations toward other beings is grounded on the correct evaluation of the different loves that we should show the beings with whom we find ourselves in relation. The axiological evaluation is immediately organized by the ontic determination of what is loved. The principle of evaluation is written into the Order that determines the hierarchy of divine perfections. However, to the degree that these perfections are representative (through vision in God) of different beings, representation permits us to accede to the nature, and also the value, of beings, then to determine our attitude toward them. Therefore, the *Traité de Morale* (Book I, chapter 1) establishes at the outset that the Order is known in God like the other truths. The knowledge of this Order falls within metaphysics because the order is seen in God.[59] The relations between the perfections that constitute the Order are seen in God, as are the "relations of greatness" that constitute the mathematical truths.[60] Moral knowledge henceforth illuminates the will in its choice and its orientations. Before being a quality of will, virtue is a strength of mind, a capacity to be attentive to clear and distinct ideas.

Finally, metaphysics grounds the belief in a future life and then confirms the truths of faith: "... it is necessary that there be another life where God satisfies that which his justice demands of him. ... Metaphysics demonstrates this to us."[61] The eternal life is at issue in metaphysics because metaphysics claims to ground religion.

Malebranche was not content to affirm a bland peaceful concord between revealed truths and natural reason. To the degree that reason is rooted in the contemplation of divine ideas, this reason and the philosophy that proceed from it can reinforce, indeed duplicate, the  givens of faith.[62] Thus, "... it is necessary to be a good philosopher to gain understanding of the truths of faith; ... the stronger we are in the true principles of metaphysics, the stronger we are in the truths of religion" (*Dialogues* VI.2, OC 12:133; JS 92).[63] To do metaphysics is to unite oneself to God in the highest way possible. Metaphysics becomes a sort of rational revelation.

At the end of this investigation, it has been shown that metaphysics constitutes a decisive moment in the construction of Malebranchian philosophy. With the Oratorian, metaphysics clearly experiences an evolution, largely anticipated by Descartes. If metaphysics can still be, in a certain sense, a doctrine of beings, it proceeds on the basis of a "general idea of being" of which the particular ideas will be only secondary determinations. However, being, such as Malebranche's metaphysics understands it, is knowable only by its idea. More than a science of being, metaphysics thinks being in and through its concept. If Malebranchian metaphysics can be defined as an ontology, the latter understands being as what the idea gives to be conceived, in conformity to the meaning the word *ontology* has in the second half of the seventeenth century. In laying hold of Being as an *object*, metaphysics continues to assume its ontological task, all the while becoming chiefly a theory of the general principles of knowledge. From now on, metaphysics is understood as a "critique" of our power to know, as an evaluation of its pertinence and its scope. Though he might, on this point, be particularly sensitive to his Cartesian inheritance, Malebranche does not therefore reassume the previous definitions of metaphysics. Let it at once be noted that the latter tends in a certain sense to identify itself with the whole of philosophical practice. This relative identification would accentuate the indetermination from which all definitions of metaphysics perhaps suffer.

By affirming the unknowability of force, Malebranche foreshadows Hume's analysis of causality. More broadly, by defining metaphysics as an analysis of the powers of the understanding, he anticipates the transformation of philosophy that it will fall to Kant to complete, though by other means.

NOTES

1 See the letter to P. Berrand, 23 December 1686, OC 18:42.
2 We should note that, contrary to the final syntheses of scholastic philosophy, the *Dialogues* do not open with an examination of the definition and subject matter of metaphysics. It is only at the beginning of the sixth dialogue that the most precise definition is found.
3 I have attempted such a detailed examination of Malebranche's philosophy in my recent book; see Bardout 1999. The present essay summarizes the main findings of chapters 1 and 2.
4 See *Lettre touchant la Défense de M. Arnauld* (LD), OC 6:282.
5 The fact of being *intelligible* suggests the greatest knowability and simultaneously the greatest intellectuality, to the exclusion of the senses and the imagination.
6 *Disputationes Metaphysicae*, Disputatio I, in Suarez 1856, vol. 25, p. 2.
7 *Ibid.* I.1.xiv, p. 7.
8 *Abductio mentis a sensibus* is frequently evoked by Descartes, notably in the Preface and Synopsis of the *Meditations*; see AT 7:9.
9 *To Princess Elizabeth*, 28 June 1643, AT 3:692, CSM 3:227; *To Mersenne*, 13 November 1639, AT 2:622.
10 See the letter that serves as a preface to the French translation of the *Principia philosophiae*, AT 9-2:10. See also, the *Second Set of Replies*, AT 9-1:104. Descartes already joins immateriality together with intelligibility; see *Meditations* IV, AT 7:53.
11 For a similar characterization of the debate about ideas, see *Quatre Lettres* III, OC 7:421, 448. Malebranche also speaks of "metaphysical proceeding," LD, OC 6:329. See also *Réponse à Régis*, OC 17-1:303; the posthumous letter to Arnauld of 19 March 1699, OC 9:901; and *Search*, Elucidation 17, OC 3:307.
12 The distinction between knowing and feeling arises from metaphysics: *Dialogues* III.9, OC 12:69.
13 See *Search* III.2.vi; *Dialogues* I and II.
14 *Search* III.2.ii-v.
15 Malebranchian abstraction is therefore fundamentally different from an abstraction that starts from sensible knowledge: *Dialogues* II.9, OC 12:58.
16 The truths of morality, metaphysics, and geometry are all seen in God: *Réponse au livre des Vraies et des Fausses Idées* (RVFI), OC 6:146.
17 The principle of clear ideas will itself become the object of a metaphysical proof: *Dialogues* III.15, OC 12:81.
18 See *Discours Préliminaire* II, Arnauld and Nicole 1996.
19 See Régis 1691, vol. 1, pp. 10-1.
20 See OA 40, p. 153.

21 *Preface to the French edition of Principia philosophiae*, AT 9–2:14; CSM 1:186.

22 Concerning the idea's power to represent the essence, see *Méditations chrétiennes* IX.12, OC 10:100.

23 The *regula generalis* of *Meditations* III, AT 7:33.

24 This knowledge is explicitly metaphysical: "we do not see with our eyes the truth of the first axiom of all the sciences"; OC 2:93; LO 316.

25 The proof for the existence of God always rests on the "first axiom of metaphysics," *Lettre à Arnauld*, OC 9:947. See *Search* IV.6.iv, OC 2:55.

26 See RVFI, OC 6:181. "He alone illuminates us, he alone animates us . . . these are evident truths that metaphysics teaches us," *Quatre Lettres*, OC 7:361.

27 Vision in God is therefore a metaphysical thesis par excellence: *Dialogues* III.12, OC 12:76.

28 The program imparted to metaphysics is designed in terms of what can be known.

29 This arrangement recurs in the *Réponse à Régis*, in the preface to the *Dialogues* added to the addition of 1696, or again in *Entretien sur la Mort* II.

30 Intelligible extension is "the object of geometry"; see RVFI, OC 6:68; *and Dialogues* I.10, OC 12:47.

31 *Dialogues* II.4, OC 12:53.

32 See *Réponse à Régis*, OC 17–1:307–8.

33 See also *Méditations chrétiennes* X.12, OC 10:100.

34 For such a definition of body, see *Dialogues* I.10, OC 12:47; X.12, OC 12:236.

35 *Méditations chrétiennes* VI.6, OC 10:60.

36 On this point, see Alquié 1974, p. 221.

37 *Search* I.16.ii–iii.

38 *Search* VI.2.vi, OC 2:373, 377.

39 See notably Elucidation 6, OC 3:53–4.

40 *Dialogues* X.7, OC 12:234.

41 Concerning the absence of a clear idea of our soul, see *Search* III.2.vii, OC 1:451; Elucidations 11, OC 3:166; *Entretien sur la mort* II, OC 13:401; and *Méditations chrétiennes* XI.20.

42 Elucidation 11, OC 3:170; *Méditations chrétiennes* XVI.14, OC 10:181.

43 See Gueroult 1987, and more recently Schmaltz 1996.

44 *Search* I.1.i, OC 1:40.

45 Concerning the absence of an idea of God, see Robinet 1965, II.4; Alquié 1974, 111–1181; Rodis-Lewis 1967; and Nadler 1992.

46 See on this point, Robinet 1965, 211–17; Rodis-Lewis 1963, 88ff.; Elungu 1973, 82–3.

47  See *Search* III.2.v, OC 1:432; III.2.iv, OC 1:473; *Entretien d'un philosophe chrétien et d'un philosophe chinois*, OC 15:3–4. "Being is the idea of God," *Dialogues* II.4, OC 12:53; JS 22.

48  *Réponse à la Dissertation*, OC 7:541. The knowledge of God by himself will be interpreted in terms of representation; the divine essence is the *immediate object* of the divine understanding; see *Dialogues* VIII.7, OC 12:183.

49  "They must attribute to God only that which they conceive clearly to be contained in the idea of an infinitely perfect being": *Search*, Elucidation 8, OC 3:86.

50  See *Réponse aux Réflexions*, OC 8:752.

51  It would be fair, however, to make an exception of others, who are known only through conjecture on the basis of oneself: *Search* III.2.vii.5.

52  *Dialogues* VI.2, OC 12:134; JS 93.

53  See §5, OC 12:36.

54  *De l'existence de Dieu, que nous pouvons voir en lui toutes choses et que rien de fini ne peut le représenter.*

55  The metaphysical investigation of the properties and the essence of God will be conducted until *Dialogues* VIII.

56  *Dialogues* II.6, OC 12:55.

57  *Dialogues* III.11, OC 12:73.

58  *Dialogues* VI.3, OC 12:135.

59  See *Search*, OC 1:491; Elucidation 10, OC 3:137.

60  See *Méditations chrétiennes* IV.8, OC 10:39.

61  *Entretiens sur la mort*, OC 13:377–8.

62  Faith and reason proceed ultimately from the same source: the assertion of vision in God overwhelms the traditional economy of their relations.

63  See *Dialogues* XIV. 13, OC 12:353; JS 283: "It is not necessary ... that we know exactly the reasons for our faith, I mean the reasons with which metaphysics can furnish us." The rules of reasoning are valid indifferently for philosophical and revealed truths: *Réponse aux Réflexions*, OC 8:632.

# 7 Malebranche's Theodicy

The topic of theodicy looms large in Malebranche's thought. His distinctive views on the subject form the basis of one of his most famous books, the *Treatise on Nature and Grace* (1680), and occupy a prominent place in important later works such as the *Dialogues on Metaphysics and Religion* (1688). Embracing issues of the relation of the divine will to creation and our knowledge of that will, Malebranche's theodicy is inextricably linked to his signature doctrines of occasionalism and vision in God. Together, they form a single comprehensive theory that attempts to explicate the existence and nature of the world, and the special place of human beings within it, in relation to God as creator.[1]

What has come to be called the problem of theodicy signifies a cluster of issues, some of which any theological explanation of the world's existence must confront, others of which are specifically associated with the tenets of Christian theology. Of the first sort are basic questions about the world's imperfection and what this implies about God's apparent lack of concern for the welfare of human beings. If God is all powerful, all wise, and all good, why does he permit natural circumstances (floods, earthquakes, and drought) that are unworthy of his perfection and that bring harm to human beings, particularly the innocent who have done nothing to earn God's punishment? Why does God allow wicked people to exercise their wickedness in harming the innocent, and then, apparently, fail to punish the wicked, who profit from their evil deeds? Questions such as these strike at the fundamental justice of God's action: How could God allow such things to happen, unless he is in some way limited by less than supreme goodness, knowledge, or power?

Malebranche's answers to these questions lead directly to the central thesis of his theodicy: the doctrine of the simplicity and generality of God's will. His preoccupation with the theodicy problem, however, cannot be disentagled from a second set of issues deriving specifically from Christian theology, particularly God's distribution of the grace necessary for salvation. It is an established part of Christian doctrine that no human being merits salvation; thus those who are saved owe their salvation to God's mercy alone, which is communicated through his grace. How God distributes this grace was one of the most bitterly contested topics of seventeenth-century theology. Scripture teaches both that God wills to save all human beings and that not all human beings are saved (*TNG* I.39; OC 5:47; R 127).[2]

The Jansenist cause, defended by Blaise Pascal and Antoine Arnauld, had maintained strenuously that any grace received from God must be efficacious and that God limits this grace to his "elect." Given this position, Jansenists were forced to deny the most straightforward reading of the claim that God wills to save all human beings. Citing Augustine as their authority, they allowed that God might will to save all *types* of human beings but not every human being; for granting that not every human being is saved, this would undermine the efficaciousness of God's will. Malebranche, by contrast, was committed to the view that, in accordance with Scripture, God wills to save all; consequently, he was faced with the task of explaining why all human beings are not saved and why this result does not jeopardize God's perfection.[3]

The boldness and originality of Malebranche's theodicy was contained in his conception of a single doctrine capable of addressing both dimensions of the theodicy problem. In both cases, the justice of God's action can be understood in terms of the simplicity and generality of his will, a will that is guided by God's infinite wisdom. It is this wisdom, above all, that Malebranche is concerned to defend as the basis of our knowledge and love of God. As he writes in the anonymous letter that prefaces the *Treatise on Nature and Grace*, "The author . . . avows that his main plan is to make God lovable to men, and to justify the wisdom of his conduct in the minds of certain philosophers who push metaphysics too far, and who, in order to have a powerful and sovereign God, make him unjust, cruel, and bizarre" (OC 5:3–4; R 107). In his writings on theodicy, Malebranche is principally concerned to reject the claims of those who subordinate

God's wisdom to his power and make his will alone the final justification for his actions. The theory Malebranche offers is a remarkable
attempt to account for the revelation of Christianity within a theological framework that stresses the generality of God's will, from
which follows "a constant and lawful order, according to which he
has foreseen, through the infinite extent of his wisdom, that a work
as admirable as his is, ought to come into existence" (TNG I.37; OC
5:46; R 127).

In what follows, Malebranche's theodicy will be examined in three
stages: first, God's original motivation for creation (section I); second,
the doctrine of God's general will as the governing principle of the
order of nature (section II); and third, the order of grace (section III).

## I. CREATION

Considered theologically, the world's existence suggests two basic questions. Why should God choose to create this world rather
than any other world he might have created? Also, more fundamentally, why should God, an infinitely perfect being, create at all?
Malebranche, to his credit, takes this second question very seriously.
Beginning from an understanding of God as an infinitely perfect being, sufficient unto himself, there is no necessity that God should
create anything.[4] For Malebranche, this is sufficient reason to reject
the ancient view, revived in his time by Spinoza, that the world is a
necessary emanation of God. "God suffices fully to himself – for the
infinitely perfect Being can be conceived alone, and without any necessary relation to a single one of his creatures" (TNG II.51; OC 5:110;
R 162). Given his self-sufficiency, God's choice to create is entirely
free; creation is in no way required for God to be God. Malebranche
argues in a similar way against the eternity of the world: "Eternity
is the mark of independence; thus it was necessary that the world
begin" (TNG I.4; OC 5:18–9; R 113). Because God has produced the
world in time, we see that "creatures are not at all necessary em-
anations from the divinity, and that they are essentially dependent
on a free will of the Creator" (TNG II.52; OC 5:110; R 162). At the
same time, once produced, such created substances never perish absolutely, for the destruction of what has been created would be "a
mark of inconstancy in him who has produced them" (TNG I.4; OC
5:18–9; R 113).

Acknowledging that God is no way obliged to create, how are we to understand the fact that he nonetheless chooses to do so? What would motivate God to act in this way? Malebranche stresses that this action cannot be understood in terms of God's need for created beings, or even the love his infinite goodness might inspire for such creatures. As Theodore argues in the *Discourse*, as an infinitely perfect being, God can be motivated by nothing but himself:

It seems evident to me that … his will is but the love he has for himself and for his divine perfections; that the movement of his love cannot, as with us, come to him from without, nor consequently lead him outside himself; that being uniquely the principle of his action, he must be its end; in short, that in God all love other than self-love would be disordered or contrary to the immutable order which he contains and which is the inviolable law of the divine volitions. (*Dialogues* IX.3; OC 12:200–1; JS 151)

Whatever God creates, therefore, is only for himself: "God cannot will except through his will, and his will is simply the love he bears for himself. The reason, the motive, the end of his decrees can be found only in him" (ibid.).

Malebranche interpreted this motive as God's glory: "As God esteems and loves himself invincibly he find his glory and takes gratification in a work which in some way expresses his excellent qualities" (*Dialogues* IX.4; OC 12:203; JS 153). Creation is thus an expression of divine self-love in which God is pleased by the perfection of his own will. For God to enjoy this glory, he does not need to be admired by his creatures: "it is based simply on the esteem and love he has for his own qualities" (ibid.). Furthermore, while his glory supplies a sufficient reason for God to create, it does not "invincibly determine him to will to act" (*Dialogues* IX.4; OC 12:203; JS 154). Whether God chooses to create remains an entirely free decision. At most, therefore, we can say that *if* God wills to act, he acts only for his own glory, "since he can only act according to what he is and through the love he has for himself and his divine perfections" (ibid).

This explanation of the motivation for creation, following directly from the idea of God as an infinitely perfect being, leads to a final, critical question: If God acts solely for himself, how can the creation of the world possibly serve as an adequate basis for his glory? As Theodore observed again, "however perfect the universe might be, insofar as it is finite it will be unworthy of the action of God, whose worth is infinite" (*Dialogues* IX.4; OC 12:203–4; JS 154). This was, in many ways, the defining moment of Malebranche's theodicy, for in response to this question he offered the unequivocal answer that the *only* thing that could justify God's creation of the world, an act that must necesarily entail his glory, is the production of a divine person:

There must be some relation between the world and the action by which it is produced. Now the action by which the world is drawn from nothingness, is the action of a God; his worth is infinite; and the world, however perfect it may be, is not infinitely lovable, and cannot render to God an honour worthy of him. Thus, separate Jesus Christ from the rest of created beings and see if he who can act only for his own glory, and whose wisdom has no limits, can form the plan to produce anything outside himself. (*TNG* I.3; OC 5:15; R 112–3)[5]

Malebranche closely associated Christ's appearance with the founding of the Catholic Church, and in the opening article of the *Treatise* goes so far as to claim that it is the establishment of the Church that justifies the creation of the world (*TNG* I.1; OC 5:12; R 112). This claim, however, must be understood elliptically in terms of Christ's role in the world. By the "Church," Malebranche meant no temporal institution but the Church everlasting, composed of the souls of those who have been saved through the intercession of Jesus Christ and whose worship of God is unconstrained by the limits of a bodily existence. Nevertheless, it remains the case that no assembly of finite souls could provide a glory sufficient to motivate God's will. Only the presence of Christ, the "man-God" can do this, and Christ himself fulfills the role of savior by serving as a mediator between God and created beings.[6] Thus, Malebranche concluded, "it was necessary that God create the universe for the Church, the Church for Jesus Christ, and Jesus Christ in order to find in him a victim and a sovereign priest worthy of the divine majesty. No one will doubt this order in the plans of God, if one takes care to notice that there can be no other end of his actions than himself" (*TNG* I.6; OC 5:20; R 114).

The appearance of Jesus Christ in the world is fundamental to Malebranche's theodicy at several levels. As noted, Christ alone provides a sufficient reason for God to create: Only the realization of a divine person can offer a glory proportionate to God's infinite perfection. Equally important, however, Christ himself is a direct manifestation of God's wisdom in the world. As the second person of the Trinity, the Word incarnate, Christ *is* God's wisdom made flesh.[7] Thus, the point is underscored that creation is not simply an exercise of God's arbitrary will, a demonstration of his infinite power, but rather the realization of divine wisdom in the person of Jesus Christ:

God, loving himself by the necessity of his being, and wanting to procure for himself an infinite glory, an honour perfectly worthy of himself, consults his wisdom concerning the accomplishment of his desires. That divine wisdom, filled with love for him from whom it receives its being through an eternal and ineffable generation, seeing nothing in all possible creatures (whose intelligible ideas it contains) that is worthy of the majesty of its Father, offers itself to establish an eternal cult in his honour and as sovereign priest, to offer him a victim who, by the dignity of his person, is capable of contenting him. (*TNG* I.24; OC 5:38; R 120)

Finally, in addition to embodying Wisdom itself, Christ serves as the essential mediator by which there is raised the "eternal cult" that is God's crowning glory.[8] Only through Jesus Christ are human beings saved for the eternal worship of God, a circumstance that at once allows Christ to be Christ and that enables the world as a whole to acquire a perfection it would not otherwise possess. The corruption of humankind through Adam's sin was foreseen and permitted by God, for the simple reason that "the universe, restored through Jesus Christ, is worth more than the same universe in its initial construction" (*Dialogues* IX.5; OC 12:204; JS 155).[9]

The means by which Christ's historical mission is carried out bring us to the next stage of Malebranche's theodicy, which is concerned with God's governance of the created world through the parallel orders of nature and grace. Malebranche's appeal to the incarnation of the Word as God's "first and principal design" in creation (*Dialogues* IX.6; OC 12:207; JS 156) is an account that, by itself, might justify any plan for the rest of the world, provided that it can be understood as furthering this highest end. At one level, this reflects an important point about Malebranche's position, for, as we shall see, he conceived of the order of grace as contributing in an essential way to the fulfillment of Christ's mission, and the order of nature as subordinate to the order of grace. Yet Malebranche insisted that both of these orders also directly express God's perfection and are chosen by him for that reason. Although they serve as means to the realization of the highest end, the orders of nature and grace are only worthy of God insofar as they bear marks of his infinite wisdom. This provided the starting point for Malebranche's answer to the two main species of theodicy problem. We turn now, then, to how God's wisdom is manifested in his governance of the created world, first in the order of nature and then in the order of grace.

## II. THE ORDER OF NATURE

Nature is marked by a complex set of regularities: planetary motions, seasonal changes, cycles of birth and death. Such regularity has long suggested to human beings the design of a wise and good God, who exhibits his intelligence in the order of nature and his goodness in the benefits this order brings to human life. Yet nature also contains many apparent irregularities, flaws in the divine order, which thwart the purposes of human beings: rain falls on the ocean instead of on newly sown fields; earthquakes and volcanos destroy entire cities; infants are born with terrible deformities. How can these events be reconciled with nature's governance by a wise and good God?

Various answers have been proposed to this classical theodicy problem. Some have simply deferred to God's inscrutable ends; others have found greater perfection in the balancing of order with disorder. Malebranche's answer is defined by the emphasis he placed on the essential relationship between God's will and his wisdom, a wisdom expressed in God's preference for a world governed by simple and universal laws. Guided by his infinite wisdom, God determines the order of nature solely through "general volitions" (volontés générales), which give rise to exceptionless laws of nature.[10] Creation itself is the product of a "particular volition" (volonté particulière) that establishes the initial conditions of the world. Thereafter, nature unfolds according to a small number of "constant and immutable" laws that God wills knowing fully the consequences that will follow from them, including natural events harmful to human beings.[11] Malebranche insisted that God cannot be blamed for these unfortunate circumstances.

As God does not act in nature through particular volitions, he has not directly willed that these events should occur (*TNG* I.18–9, 22; OC 5:31–2, 35; R 118–20). Instead, we must understand that had God not acted through general laws that have these events as their consequence, he would have acted in a manner unworthy of his perfection. In order to make a world in which everything turned out best from a human point of view, God would have had to have "changed the simplicity of his ways" and "multiplied the laws of the communication of motion, through which our world exists." However, then, Malebranche argued,

> there would no longer be that proportion between the action of God and his work, which is necessary in order to determine an infinitely wise being to act; or at least there would not have been the same proportion between the activity of God and this so-perfect world, as between the laws of nature and the world in which we live; for our world, however imperfect one wishes to imagine it, is based on laws of motion which are so simple and so natural that it is perfectly worthy of the infinite wisdom of its author (*TNG* I.14; OC 5:29; R 117).

Thus, although the world contains many circumstances that threaten the welfare of human beings, these could not have been changed without altering the condition under which alone the world is worthy of God.

Malebranche's account of the relationship between God's will and the order of nature reflects the basic commitments of his occasionalism. According to that doctrine, God is the only real causal power in the world; finite things, minds and bodies, are merely "secondary" causes that occasion the effects of God's general laws. The order of nature, therefore, is identical with the "ways" (*voies*) in which God efficaciously wills the continued existence of created beings. "Properly speaking," Malebranche wrote, "what is called *nature* is nothing other than the general laws which God has established to construct or to preserve his work by very simple means [*voyes*], by an action which is uniform, constant, perfectly worthy of an infinite wisdom and of a universal cause" (*TNG*, "Premier Éclaircissement," 3; OC 5:148; R 196). Given this identity, it is obvious that the order of nature can contain nothing unworthy of God. Malebranche's emphasis on the generality of the laws of nature stems from his conception of God's wisdom as an essential attribute that guides the actions of his will. It is characteristic of a limited intelligence, he argued, to act by particular volitions, in ways that respond to the circumstances of a given situation. An unlimited intelligence, on the other hand, acts by general volitions that take into account all possible circumstances. Such an intelligence governs by laws that are "general for all times and for all places ... laws so simple and at the same time so fruitful that they serve to produce everything beautiful that we see in the world" (*TNG* I.18; OC 5:31–2; R 118).[12]

Reasoning in this way, Malebranche was forced to admit that "God could ... make a world more perfect than the one in which we live" (*TNG* I.14; OC 5:29; R 116). By this he means not only that nature is replete with events and deeds that fall short of the standard of God's perfection, but also that created beings collectively could have enjoyed greater perfection had this not conflicted with the simplicity of God's ways (*Dialogues* IX.10; OC 12:213–5; JS 162–4). On this point, his position was at odds with that of Leibniz, who maintained that the created world is the best of all possible worlds – the world of the greatest intrinsic perfection – and that it is God's choice of the "most fitting" laws of nature that allows this maximization of perfection to occur. Malebranche, by contrast, saw an inherent conflict in the relationship between the perfection of created beings and the simplicity and generality of the laws of nature: to have increased the former, it would have been necessary to sacrifice the latter; but this is something God cannot do as God.[13]

In spite of this, within the limits of his theory, Malebranche also recognized at least two senses in which the created world is the best world that God could have created. In the *Treatise*, in a passage that almost certainly had an important influence on Leibniz, Malebranche affirmed that the world is the "most perfect" (*le plus parfait*) with respect to the laws that govern it:

God, discovering in the infinite treasures of his wisdom an infinity of possible worlds (as the necessary consequences of the laws of motion which he can establish), determines himself to create that world which could have been produced and preserved by the simplest laws, and which ought to be the most perfect, with respect to the simplicity of the ways necessary to its production or to its conservation. (*TNG* I.13; OC 5:28; R 116)

Beyond this, we have seen that in a deeper sense this must be the best possible world, because it alone is the world in which God has chosen to realize the perfection of his wisdom in the person of Jesus Christ, the founder of the Church dedicated to God's eternal glory. Where the world falls short in perfection is only in the particular circumstances of finite creatures, who, from the perspective of divine wisdom, have no grounds for criticizing God's action.

If this conclusion seems to offer insufficient consolation to those who suffer from natural evils, Malebranche was prepared to admit at least that, "in a very true sense ... God wishes [*souhaite*] that all his creatures be perfect" (*TNG* I.22; OC 5:35; R 119–20). As noted, God does not bring about the imperfections of created things through particular volitions, nor does he will the laws of nature with the intention of bringing about such imperfections indirectly. We can be sure that if God "had been able (by equally simple ways) to make and to preserve a more perfect world, he would never have established any laws, of which so great a number of monsters are necessary consequences" (ibid.). None of this, however, implies that God ought to abandon the generality of his will in order to correct the imperfections of created things. To hold God responsible on a case-by-case basis for events in the world, would be to eliminate the essential relationship between God's will and his wisdom, which is reflected in the generality of his volitions.

Malebranche pursued this point by stressing the connection between God's general will and the existence of an objective standard of perfection. He framed the issue in terms of a version of the question posed by Socrates in the *Euthyphro*: Does the perfection of creation derive solely from the fact that God wills it, or does God will this world because his wisdom determines it to be the most perfect way of acting? To insist that God preserves the world through discrete, particular volitions, Malebranche contended, rather than general volitions prescribed by his wisdom, is to place the ground of the world's perfection in God's will alone. According to this principle, Theodore argued in the *Dialogues*,

the universe is perfect because God willed it. Monsters are works as perfect as others according to the plans of God.... However we invert the world, whatever chaos we make out of it, it will always be equally admirable, since its entire beauty consists in its conformity with the divine will, which is not obliged to conform to order. (*Dialogues* IX.13; OC 12:221; JS 169)

In interpreting creation as the effect of an infinite series of particular volitions, Malebranche claims, one commits oneself to the view that the perfection of the world depends solely on God's will exercised independently of his wisdom. However, if this is so, we have no basis for believing that the present world is more perfect than any other world God could have created. Rather, we must accept that whatever world God should create, no matter how disorderly and chaotic it might be, it would be the most perfect for the simple reason that God willed it. For Malebranche, this amounted to a *reductio ad absurdum* of the view that God acts in the best possible manner, for it is to abandon any coherent notion of the perfection of God's ways and of the world he creates.

In the *Treatise*, Malebranche invariably interpreted the wisdom of God's action in terms of certain formal characteristics of his will: God is "obliged to act always in a way worthy of him, through simple, general, constant, and uniform means – in a word, means conformed to the idea we have a general cause whose wisdom has no limits" (*TNG* I.43; OC 5:49; R 128–9). In other writings, however, he made clear that there is also a determinate *content* to the principle that regulates God's action. This principle, which he designated "order," reflects God's understanding of the eternal relation among his perfections and those of his creatures, who "as [they] participate unequally in his being, imitate unequally his perfections, have more or less relation to him" (*Traité de l'Amor du Dieu*; OC 14:7).[14] Order is the ultimate principle governing both the divine and human will:

This immutable order is undoubtedly the inviolable rule of divine volitions, that is, the eternal law, but it is also the natural and necessary law of all intelligent beings.... Nothing therefore is just, reasonable, agreeable to God, except what conforms to the immutable order of his perfections. (OC 14:7–8)

The principle of order allows us to penetrate Malebranche's fullest answer to the problem of theodicy. In the strictest sense, justice *is* order, for Malebranche. Thus, the justice of God's action can consist of nothing other than his acting as order, the immutable relation of his perfections, demands. Here, however, we encounter an important subtlety in his position. Nature is marked by an order whose simplicity and generality reflect the influence of God's wisdom on his will. In its effects, however, nature falls far short of what order itself demands. Although the form of the laws of nature mirrors God's wisdom, the sequences of events that those laws determine do not. To take a crucial example, the inclination of the human will toward some particular good (bodily pleasure) rather than the universal good (God) constitutes a disorderly movement of the will that is nonetheless governed by the general law of the union of the soul and the body. Thus, natural events – those determined by the laws of nature – are not necessarily in conformity with order.[15]

Malebranche explained this discrepancy by appealing to an "arbitrary" element in the laws of nature that are the product of God's general volitions (*TNG* I.20; OC 5:33; R 119).[16] God wills these laws for the sake of their simplicity and generality, *not* for the sake of the justice (or order) that is inherent in the sequences of events they entail. In point of fact, many *prima facie* injustices occur within the order of nature: natural disasters destroy the lives of thousands; the lusts of the wicked bring grief to the victims on whom they prey. Cases such as these suggest a final, pointed challenge to the justice of God's action. Even if we accept Malebranche's claim that for the sake of his wisdom God must act through simple and general laws, how can the consequences of these laws be reconciled with God's commitment to order? If order demands anything, it is a balancing of merit and treatment. If God even *allows* the order of nature to bring suffering to persons who are truly innocent, can he be regarded as acting justly?

Malebranche's answer to this question was, somewhat surprisingly, no. If God had, through the effects of the order of nature, allowed the innocent to suffer, God would have acted unjustly. The crucial proviso, however, is that no human being is truly innocent: All are marked by Adam's sin. Consequently, nothing that God allows to happen through the order of nature counts against the justice of his action. If man had not sinned, Malebranche conceded, "then, order not permitting that he be punished, the laws of the communication of motion would never have been able to make him unhappy" (*TNG* I.20; OC 5:33; R 119). In the absence of Adam's fall, God's plans would have had to have been different, for a truly innocent person could not be subjected to unjustified suffering through the order of nature. Because all human beings are sinners, however, our treatment at the hands of nature is not undeserved. Thus, God's justice is not compromised.

In sum, while the laws of nature do not further the ends of order, they also do not violate those ends. In and of themselves, the laws of nature determine an immutable order within which natural events frequently thwart human purposes and human beings act for immoral ends. While expressive of God's wisdom in their form, the laws of nature do no more than set the stage for the drama of creation. Since Adam's fall, the world has been corrupt and the laws of nature have perpetuated this corruption. Creation is repaired only through the actions of Jesus Christ, whose appearance in the world signals the beginning of our redemption. To understand how this occurs, we must turn to the general laws by which God governs the order of grace, for it is by means of this order that God fulfills the promise of creation and thereby realizes the full expression of his wisdom.

### III. THE ORDER OF GRACE

The present world is an imperfect world, a world of physical and spiritual corruption. However, this world is not the totality of God's plan for creation. It is no more than a prelude to the "future world," in which the souls of the blessed will be reunited, under the rule of the Jesus Christ, in the eternal Church dedicated to God's glory.[17] For Malebranche, creation is only worthy of God in virtue of this goal. Thus, to fully understand his theodicy, it is necessary to understand the means by which God selects for eternal life those of his creatures who will become the members of his Church.

No human being deserves the reward of eternal life. As a consequence of Adam's sin, salvation is only possible for human beings in virtue of God's grace.[18] Malebranche and his Jansenist opponents agreed that no human being is able to earn this grace through her own efforts alone. Thus, the "future world" is, in Malebranche's words, "a work of pure mercy" (*TNG* I.35; OC 5:44; R 126). The crucial point of disagreement between the two parties concerns the manner in which God communicates his grace to human beings. Jansenists such as Arnauld maintained that God's mercy is selective ("many are called but few are chosen"), and that his grace is necessarily efficacious: It cannot be without its intended effect. It follows that God cannot be understood as willing to save all human beings without exception. If God wills to save all and not all are saved, then God's will would be inefficacious, which implies a lack of power in God. For Arnauld, the essence of God's mercy is that he distributes his grace as he sees fit through *particular* volitions, which express his desire for the salvation of the "elect."

Malebranche's account of God's distribution of grace was very different. He too insisted on the necessity of divine grace for salvation and accepts that not all human beings are saved; however, he strongly rejected Arnauld's claim that it is the particularity of God's volitions that explains his discrimination between those who receive grace sufficient for salvation and those who do not. In light of his infinite wisdom, God is no more inclined to act by particular volitions in the order of grace than in the order of nature. Because it is the same God who is the author of both orders, Malebranche argued, it is necessary that they contain marks of "the same wisdom and the same will" (*TNG* I.23; OC 5:37; R 120).[19] Thus, God establishes the order of grace solely through general volitions, the first of which is that all human beings be saved (*TNG* I.42; OC 5:49; R 128). Given this, Malebranche had to face the question of why, if God wills that all human beings be saved, it happens that not all are saved. How is it that despite God's general will, the "rain of grace" often falls on hearts that fail to benefit from it? (*TNG* I.41; OC 5:48; R 128).

Framed in this way, the problem of God's justice in the order of grace is exactly parallel to the analogous problem in the order of nature. What recommends God's action in both cases, and defines it as worthy of his wisdom, are the simplicity and generality of his ways: "God being obliged to act always in a way worthy of him, through simple, general, constant, and uniform means – in a word means conformed to the idea that we have of a general cause whose wisdom has no limits – he had to establish certain laws in the order of grace, as I have proved him to have done in the order of nature" (*TNG* I.43; OC 5:49; R128–9). Because God is determined to distribute his mercy according to the simplest, most general, and most fruitful laws, his grace inevitably falls on those who are unprepared to receive it: souls whose degree of corruption outweighs the grace they receive.[20] This, Malebranche argued, is a circumstance God could correct through an infinite number of particular volitions, alloting his grace to match the particular needs of the sinner, but this would undermine the simplicity and generality of his laws. In this respect, the parallel between the orders of nature and grace is complete:

[Just] as one has no right to be annoyed that the rain falls in the sea where it is useless, and that it does not fall on seeded grounds where it is necessary ... so too one ought not to complain of the apparent irregularity according to which grace is given to men. It is the regularity with which God acts, it is the simplicity of the laws which he observes, it is the wisdom and uniformity of his conduct, which is the cause of the apparent irregularity. It is necessary, according to the laws of grace that God has ordained, on behalf of his elect and for the building of his Church, that this heavenly grace sometimes fall on hardened hearts, as well as on prepared grounds. If, then, grace falls uselessly, it is not the case that God acts without design.... Rather the simplicity of general laws does not permit that this grace, which is inefficacious in this corrupted heart, fall in another heart where it would be efficacious. This grace not being given at all by a particular will, but in consequence of the immutability of the general order of grace, it suffices that order produce a work proportional to the simplicity of his laws, in order that it be worthy of the wisdom of its author. (*TNG* I.44; OC 5:50–1; R 129–30)[21]

Malebranche readily acknowledged that one consequence of this view is that the "grace of feeling" bestowed by God is not always sufficient to secure the salvation of its recipient. Such grace inevitably has some effect on the soul, inclining it toward God, but "it does not always produce the whole effect which it could cause, because concupiscence opposes it" (*TNG* III.19; OC 5:132; R 182). Again, he believed this supports no serious objection, for in willing the distribution of grace, God is acting not for the sake of individual sinners but for his own glory, which is found only in the perfection of his ways. God's mercy is expressed in his choosing to will grace at all and in his willing it universally; that not all sinners benefit equally from this grace is a sign neither of God's injustice nor his inequity. No sinner can claim to deserve divine grace; and though God's acting by simple and general laws has the *effect* of electing some and not others for salvation, this election cannot be construed as preferential treatment of the former, for God does not act by particular volitions with the intention of bringing about the salvation of those souls alone. He simply acts in the wisest possible manner, for the sake of his own glory, foreseeing and permitting whatever effects follow from his general volitions. Given this, Malebranche argued, we owe God our love regardless of the outcome of his action:

> Let men ... love and adore not only the good will of God, by which the elect
> are sanctified, but also the secret judgments of his justice, through which
> there is so great a number of rejected ones. It is the same order of wisdom, it
> is the same laws of grace, which produce the effects which are so different.
> God is equally adorable and lovable in all he does: his conduct is always full
> of wisdom and of goodness. (TNG I.47; OC 5:52; R 131)[22]

The grace necessary for salvation and for the establishment of
the Church originates in God, who is the sole cause of everything
in the created world (TNG II.1; OC 5:66; R 138). Yet Malebranche
held that the realization of these ends would be impossible without Jesus Christ. As we have seen, at the most fundamental level,
Christ alone justifies creation as the incarnation of the Word: the
"man-God" who serves as the head of the Church devoted to God's
eternal glory. Christ, however, is also deeply implicated in the process by which this end is brought about. Both as a terrestrial being,
Jesus of Nazareth, and as a celestial being, the resurrected Son of
God, Christ serves as the essential mediator between God and human beings, and through him alone an order of grace is possible.
Summarizing the multiple roles played by Christ within the order
of grace, Malebranche declares, "What he said, what he did, what he
suffered has thus been to prepare us to receive the celestial rain of
grace through his doctrine, through his example, through his merits,
and to make it efficacious" (TNG I.49; OC 5:53–4; R 132).

Malebranche assigned three distinct functions to Christ within
the order of grace. Through his teachings and example, Jesus brings
the Word of God to human beings. He shows them what it is to be a
Christian, one worthy of entering the Kingdom of God. By accepting
his teachings, by following his example, human beings cannot guarantee their salvation, but they thereby prepare themselves to receive
God's grace should it be forthcoming:

> That which is most opposed to the efficacy of grace, is pleasures of sense
> and feelings of pride: for there is nothing which corrupts the mind so much,
> and which hardens the heart more. But did not Jesus Christ sacrifice and
> destroy, in his person, all grandeurs and sensible pleasures? ... To what is his
> doctrine reducible; which way do his counsels tend? Is it not to humility and
> to penitence, to a general privation of everything which flatters the senses,
> of everything which corrupts the purity of the imagination, of everything

which sustains and which fortifies the concupisence of pride?... Thus [sinners] can remove some impediments to the efficacy of grace, and prepare the ground of their heart, such that it becomes fruitful when God pours his rain according to the general laws which he has prescribed to himself. (*TNG* I.49–50; OC 5:53–4; R 131–2)

Jesus Christ is also the "meritious cause" of grace. It is Christ's sacrifice alone, his atonement for the sin of Adam through his crucifixion and death that establishes a proportionality between humanity and divine grace. God's grace is pure mercy in relation to the merit of human beings; it is *earned* through Christ's sacrifice of himself: "Since all men are enveloped in original sin, and they are by their nature infinitely beneath God, it is only Jesus Christ who, by the dignity of his person and by the holiness of his sacrifice, can have access to his Father, reconcile us with him, and merit his favours for us" (*TNG* II.2; OC 5:66; R 138–9).

From the point of view of Malebranche's philosophy, it is the third of Christ's functions that is of greatest interest. It is a fundamental claim of Malebranche's occasionalism that God, the only true cause, acts through general volitions, which bring about their effects only insofar as they are determined through particular occasional causes.[23] As the order of grace is an order defined by certain general laws governing God's distribution of grace to human beings, it is necessary in this case as well that there be occasional causes that serve to determine the efficacy of God's general laws. According to Malebranche, order further demands that these causes have some relation to the plan [*dessein*] for which God has established the order of grace: the formation of his Church through Jesus Christ (*TNG* II.4; OC 5:68; R 139–40). Thus, "the rain of grace" is not diffused in our hearts according to the different positions of the planets or the natural movements of bodies, but must be occasioned by the actions either of Jesus Christ or of "the creatures united by reason to him." We know, however, that "grace is not given to all those who wish for it, nor as soon as they wish for it," and that it is sometimes even given to those who do not ask for it; thus the efficacy of the laws of grace is not determined by the volitions of human beings (*TNG* II.5–7; OC 5:68–70; R 140–1).[24] It follows that only Christ can fill this role: "Since God had a plan to make his Son the head of his Church, it was appropriate that he make him the occasional or natural cause of the grace that sanctified it; for it is from the head that life and movement must be diffused in the members" (*TNG* II.9; OC 5:70; R 141).

The Christ who is the occasional cause of grace is neither the terrestrial Jesus nor Christ in his divinity, but rather Christ in his "resurrected humanity" as the "Son of God." As resurrected humanity, Christ lacks the power to bring about the Church through his own efforts; he can do no more than "desire" and "pray" that the necessary grace be bestowed on men by God (*TNG* II.13; OC 5:72; R 143). Because his soul "has not at all an infinite capacity, and he wants to place in the body of the Church an infinity of beauties and ornaments," Christ prays ceaselessly that grace be given to human beings (*TNG* II.11; OC 5:71; R 142); and his prayers are always answered. His Father refuses him nothing, "for faith teaches us that God has given to his Son an absolute power over men, by making him head of his Church; and this cannot be conceived, if the different wills of Jesus Christ are not followed by their effects" (*TNG* II.12; OC 5:71; R 142).

Thus, the Church, the final tribute to God's glory, is formed through the combination of God's general will and power and Christ's particular desires for the salvation of individual souls.[25] Because his soul is united to eternal wisdom, Christ's desires are "always conformed to order in general, which is necessarily the rule of divine wills and of all those who love God." Order determines for Christ the goal of raising to the glory of God, "the greatest, the most magnificent, the most finished Temple that can be" (*TNG*, Premier Éclaircissement, 14; OC 5:162–3; R 208). To this end, Christ wills the salvation of an infinite variety of souls, from saints to inveterate sinners, "by the means most in conformity to order." Yet Christ, focusing on the beauty of particular "ornaments," and willing that particular degrees of grace be conferred on particular souls, does not have in view the plan of the Temple as a whole. Consequently, "it is necessary that he incessantly change his desires – it being only an infinite wisdom which can prescribe general laws to itself in order to execute its plans" (*TNG*, Premier Éclaircissement, 14; OC 5:164; R 209). The result is that only in the fullness of time will the "mystical body of Jesus Christ" – the members of his Church – form "the perfect man" (*TNG* II.16; OC 5:74; R 144). Thus, the Church is a work in progress; but once completed, it will endure forever.

Although Christ is cast by Malebranche as an enlightened servant of God, he is a servant with whom God as creator cannot dispense. As abstract, infinite wisdom, God is limited to acting through general volitions, which by themselves cannot bring about determinate effects such as the formation of the Church. Only Christ can exercise the particular volitions necessary to realize this end. Malebranche's masterstroke was to stress here Christ's identity as the concrete embodiment of wisdom: the one soul whose volitions conform perfectly to order. Thus wisdom, which had constrained God to act according to general laws, redeems itself in Malebranche's scheme as a concrete subject capable of acting by particular volitions:

It is in this way that eternal wisdom returns, so to speak, to its Father that which it had taken away from him – for not permitting him to act by particular wills, it seemed to make him impotent. But being incarnate it so brings it to pass that God, acting in a way worthy of him by quite simple and quite general means, produces a work in which the most enlightened intelligences will never be able to observe the slightest defect. (*TNG*, Premier Éclaircissement, 14; OC 5:165; R 210)

Malebranche interpreted creation as an act by which God glories in his own perfection, expressing his infinite wisdom both in his "ways" and in the person of Jesus Christ, who in a "future world" rules the Church dedicated to God's eternal glory. To achieve this goal, he believed, the Fall was an essential event within human history. Without the corruption of man by sin, there would be no role for Christ to play in creation, no place for the man-God who alone renders the created world worthy of God and serves as the head of his Church. Without the Fall, human nature would have remained in its original state of perfection and eternal life would have been our just reward. "If man had remained in a state of innocence, since his wills would have been meritorious of grace and even of glory, God would have had to establish in man the occasional cause of his perfection and of his happiness – the inviolable law of order will have it so." The result, Malebranche sardonically remarked, is that "Jesus Christ would not have been the head of the Church, or at least he would have been a head with whose influence all the members would have been able to dispense" (*TNG* II.9; OC 5:70; R 141). Thus, for God to create at all, man had to sin, to be redeemed by the man-God. Only in this way, does eternal wisdom find its proper place within the future world, in the form of Jesus Christ united to the members of his "mystical body." Through Christ and the order of grace, wisdom completes the work of creation, rendering it a fitting tribute to God.

## IV. CONCLUSION

What is most impressive about Malebranche's theodicy was his distinctive attempt to give equal weight to the demands of philosophy and faith, reason, and Scripture. In justifying the ways of God to man, Malebranche's starting point is the philosopher's God: an infinitely perfect being, who acts according to the dictates of supreme wisdom. It is God's wisdom alone that renders him lovable to human beings, and without this wisdom in which we partake, we would have no basis for understanding and appreciating the work of creation (*Treatise* I.7; OC 5:25; R 114). As Theodore declared in the *Dialogues*, "everything is inverted if we claim that God is above Reason and has no rule in his plans other than his mere will. This false principle spreads such blanket darkness that it confounds the good with the evil, the true with the false, and creates out of everything a chaos in which the mind no longer knows anything" (*Dialogues* IX.13; OC 12:220; JS 168).

At the same time, Malebranche strongly resisted the inclination, to which Leibniz arguably succumbs, of allowing reason to overwhelm the revelation of Christianity. There can be no satisfactory explanation of the existence and nature of the created world without appeal to the appearance of Jesus Christ: "God has let his work be corrupted. Reconcile this with his wisdom and with his power. Extricate yourself from this problem without the aid of the man-God, without admitting a mediator, without conceiving that God had principally the incarnation of his Son in view. I defy you to do it with all the principles of the best philosophy. For my part I find myself at a loss every time I try to philosophize without the aid of faith" (*Dialogues* IX.6; OC 12:207). Malebranche's theodicy was thus, fundamentally, a Christian theodicy. The existence of the world, particularly in its historical dimension, cannot be understood apart from God's intention to realize a divine person that renders the world worthy of him.

Throughout his writings, Malebranche was quick to criticize an excessive reliance on what he calls the "anthropologies" of Scripture:

its attribution to God of human characteristics, emotions, and foibles. To foster a proper attitude of love and reverence for God, he believed, one must begin – as his philosophy does – with "the abstract idea of an infinite wisdom, of a universal cause, of an infinitely perfect being" (*TNG* I.57; OC 5:62–3; R 136–7). The central tenet of Christianity, the divinity of Jesus Christ, adds to the philosopher's God the paradox of God become man. Within this paradox Malebranche located the basis of his theodicy. As the concrete embodiment of wisdom, Jesus Christ in union with his Church forms the sole end for the sake of which God could create, the only end that accounts for the existence of a world. For Malebranche, the *justice* of God's creation is defined by wisdom itself, which, as order, provides the standard by which justice is conceived: "nothing is just, reasonable, agreeable to God, except what conforms to the immutable order of God's perfections" (OC 14:8). Thus, the crux of Malebranche's theodicy is that creation is justified precisely in virtue of culminating in wisdom's perfect expression of itself, Jesus Christ and his Church, through which God's greater glory is affirmed.

NOTES

1 To speak of Malebranche's theodicy is to impose on him a term most closely associated with his younger contemporary Gottfried Wilhelm Leibniz, the author of the work that introduced the term "theodicy" (*theos* = god; *dike* = justice) to the philosophical lexicon: *Essais de Théodicée, sur la bonté de Dieu, la liberté de l'homme et l'origine du mal* (1710). Since the eighteenth century, the term has acquired a broader meaning that eliminates any specific reference to Leibniz's thought. It is in this sense that I use it here. The issue is complicated, however, by the close intellectual relationship between Malebranche and Leibniz. Although many of the central doctrines of Leibniz's theodicy were in place by the early 1670s, he clearly drew considerable inspiration from his reading of Malebranche's *Treatise on Nature and Grace*, an influence that is reflected in both the *Discourse on Metaphysics* (1686) and the *Theodicy* itself. Despite this debt, there remain significant differences between the views of the two philosophers. For further discussion, see Robinet, *Leibniz et Malebranche*; C. Wilson, "Leibnizian Optimism"; Sleigh, *Leibniz and Arnauld*; Rutherford, "Natures, Laws, and Miracles"; Nadler, "Choosing a Theodicy"; Riley, *Leibniz' Universal Jurisprudence*.

2 For the former, see I Timothy 2:4; for the latter, Matthew 22:14.

3 For a helpful account of the theological background to Malebranche's theodicy and further references to the literature, see Patrick Riley's "Introduction" to his translation of the *Treatise on Nature and Grace*.

4 In the *Dialogues on Metaphysics and Religion*, Malebranche's spokesman Theodore poses the question bluntly: "But how can God will that we exist, he who has no need of us? How can a Being who lacks nothing, who is entirely self-sufficient, will anything? That is what creates the difficulty" (*Dialogues* IX.3; OC 12:200; JS 151).

5 "Scripture and reason teach us that it is because of Jesus Christ that the world exists, and that it is by the dignity of this divine person that it receives a beauty which makes it pleasing in the sight of God" (*TNG* I.27; OC 5:41; R 122).

6 "[S]ince a finite world, a profane world, still contains nothing divine, it cannot have any real relation to the divinity; it cannot express the attribute essential to God, His infinity. Thus God can neither derive His gratification from it, nor consequently create it, without denying Himself. What, then, does He do? Religion teaches us this. He renders His work divine through the union of a divine person to the two substances, mind and body, from which He composes it. And he thereby elevates it infinitely and, principally because of the divinity He communicates to it, He receives from it that first glory which is related to that of the architects who constructed a house which does them honor because it expresses the qualities they are proud to possess.... Extricate yourself from this problem without the aid of the Man-God, without admitting a mediator, without conceiving that God had principally the incarnation of His Son in view. I defy you to do it with all the principles of the best philosophy" (*Dialogues* IX.6; OC 12:205–7; JS 155–7).

7 This point is emphasized in the "Additions" to the first article of *TNG*: "But what divine person will sanctify the work of God. It will be the Eternal Word. For it is the Word or wisdom of God which must be, as it were, the first thing consulted in order to regulate divine action and to make it that God could act" (OC 5:12).

8 "Yes, Aristes, vile and contemptible creatures that we are, through our divine leader we render and shall eternally render divine honors to God, honors worthy of the divine majesty, honors which God receives and will always receive with pleasure.... God regards us in Jesus Christ as Gods, as His children, as His heirs, and as co-heirs of His dearly beloved Son. In this dear Son He has adopted us. It is through Him that He gives us access to His supreme majesty" (*Dialogues* IX.6; OC 12:206; JS 156).

9 See *TNG* I.36, 40; OC 5:45, 47; R 126–7.

10 See *TNG*, "Premier Éclaircissement," 1: "I say that God acts by general wills, when he acts in consequence of general laws which he has established" (OC 5:147; R 195).

11 These include laws of the communication of motion and laws of the union of the soul and the body. Of the former, Malebranche writes: "Indeed I am persuaded that the laws of motion which are necessary to the production and the preservation of the earth, and of all the stars that are in the heavens, are reducible to these two: the first, that moved bodies tend to continue their motion in a straight line; the second, that when two bodies collide, their motion is distributed in both in proportion to their size, such that they must afterwards move at an equal speed" (*TNG* I.15: OC 5:30; R 117).

12 "The more enlightened an agent is, the more extensive are his volitions. A very limited mind undertakes new plans at every moment; and when he wants to execute one of them, he uses several means, of which some are always useless. In a word, a limited mind does not sufficiently compare the means with the end, the power and the action with the effect that they must produce. On the contrary a broad and penetrating mind compares and weighs all things: it never forms plans except with the knowledge that it has the means to execute them.... [God] ought not to multiply his wills, which are the executive laws of his plans, any further than necessity obliges. He must act through general wills, and thus establish a constant and lawful order, according to which he has foreseen, through the infinite extent of his wisdom, that a work as admirable as his is ought to come into existence" (*TNG* I.38; OC 5:46; R 126-7).

13 On the contrast between Malebranche's and Leibniz's positions on this point, see Rutherford, "Natures, Laws, and Miracles," and Nadler, "Choosing a Theodicy." For a fuller account of Leibniz's conception of this as "the best of all possible worlds," see Rutherford, *Leibniz and the Rational Order of Nature*, chs. 1–3.

14 "Order is nothing but the relation that the divine perfections, both absolute and relative, have among themselves" (OC 14:8).

15 This point is critical for Malebranche, because it opens a space in which moral action becomes possible for human beings. If order, as the rule of justice, were identical with the order of nature, then one could not "correct" nature (e.g., by saving victims of a natural disaster) without acting against divine law. In the *Traité de morale*, Malebranche uses this as another argument against the view that God acts by particular volitions, for if that were the case God would have to be understood as positively willing every event in nature, and "it would be a crime to avoid by flight the ruins of a collapsing building" (*TM* I.21; OC 11:25). See Riley, "Introduction," pp. 40–1.

16  See also *Méd. Chrét.* VII.18; OC 10:76.

17  Malebranche makes it clear that this "future world" is part of the plan of creation: "God wishes us to learn that it is the future world which will properly be his work [*ouvrage*] or the object of delight and the subject of his glory. The present world is a neglected work. It is the home of sinners, it is necessary that disorder be found in it" (*Méd. Chrét.* VII.11–2; OC 10:73). See also *TNG* I.24 and I.54: "God discovers in the infinite treasures of his wisdom an infinity of possible works, and at the same time the most perfect way of producing each of them. He considers, among other [things], his Church, Jesus Christ who is its head, and all the persons who must compose it in consequence of the establishment of certain general laws" (OC 5:57; R 134).

18  The denial of this claim forms the basis of the Pelagian heresy condemned by St. Augustine. Malebranche defines grace, which is "the principle or the motive of all the lawful movements of our love," as "either a light which teaches us, or a confused feeling which convinces us, that God is our good: since we never begin to love an object if we do not see clearly by the light of reason, or if we do not feel confusedly by the taste of pleasure, that this object is good – I mean capable of making us happier than we are" (*TNG* II.1; OC 5:66; R 138). His position, therefore, is that God is not loved as God, unless our soul has received divine grace. In its absence, our will is guided by the desire for particular goods conducive to human happiness, rather than the one true good: God.

19  See also *TNG* I.37; OC 5:45; R 126.

20  While Malebranche gives greatest emphasis to the simplicity and generality of God's laws, he also commends their "fruitfulness," insofar as they produce the greatest variety of degress of grace: "That which constitutes the beauty of the spiritual edifice of the Church is the infinite diversity of the graces which he who is the head of it distributes to all the parts that compose it: it is the order and the admirable relations which he places between them: these are the different degrees of glory which shine from all sides" (*TNG* I:30; OC 5:42; R 124). Here again we find an idea, the combination of order and variety, that figures prominently in Leibniz's theodicy, although Leibniz had embraced this idea of the "harmony" of divine wisdom prior to reading Malebranche.

21  See also *TNG* I.53; OC 5:56; R 133–4.

22  For elaborations of this theme, see *TNG* I.46; OC 5:52; R 130–1 and *TNG* I.55; OC 5:55; R 134–5: "Someone will say, perhaps, that these laws are so simple and so fruitful that God had to prefer them to all others, and that, loving only his own glory, his Son had to be incarnated – that he has done nothing purely for his elect. I grant it: God has done nothing purely for his elect. For St. Paul teaches me that he made his elect for Jesus Christ,

and Jesus Christ for himself. If, to render God lovable to men, one has to make him act purely for them, or in a way which would not be the wisest, I would prefer to remain silent. Reason teaches me to make God lovable by making him infinitely perfect, and by representing him as so full of charity for his creatures, that he produces none of them with the plan [*dessein*] of making them unhappy." Assuming that God wills the salvation of all human beings, Malebranche argues, the notion that he does so through particular volitions leads to the absurd conclusion that God sometimes intentionally confers on souls a degree of grace that is almost but not quite sufficient for salvation: "to what purpose is it to give three degrees of spiritual delectation to one for whom four degrees are necessary, and to refuse them to him to whom they would be sufficient to convert him? Does this agree with the idea that we have of the wisdom and of the goodness of God?" (*TNG* I.45; OC 5:51; R 130; cf. *TNG* I.52; OC 5:55; R 133). Obviously, this argument only has force against those who accept, as the Jansenists do not, that God wills the salvation of all human beings.

23 "[I]n order that the general cause act by general laws or wills, and that his action be lawful, constant, and uniform, it is absolutely necessary that there be some occasional cause which determines the efficacy of these laws, and which serves to establish them.... The laws of the union of the soul and the body are only rendered efficacious by the changes which take place in one or the other of these two substances. For if God made the pain of a pricking felt by the soul without the body's being pricked, or without the same thing happening in the brain as if the body were pricked, he would not act by general laws of the soul and the body, but by a particular will" (*TNG* II.3; OC 5:67; R 139).

24 Indeed, Malebranche argues, since the advent of sin, we could not perform this function: "Being all in a state of disorder, we could no longer be an occasion for God to give us grace. We needed a mediator not only to give us access to God, but to be the occasional cause of the favours which we hope for from him" (*TNG* II.8; OC 5:70; R 141).

25 Or types of souls; see *TNG* II.17; OC 5:74–5; R 144.

# 8 Malebranche on Human Freedom

Malebranche was deeply committed to the position that human beings have "freedom of indifference." However, he was equally committed to occasionalism, according to which God, and God alone, is the true cause of everything real outside of Himself. As Malebranche put it, "It is God who does all in all things (*fait tout en toutes choses*)" (*TNG*, OC 5:148; R 196). It is hard to see how these two positions are compatible. Malebranche touched upon freedom of indifference and its relation to causality in all of his major works, and in the process worked out an unusual position on human freedom. Although there is reason to disagree with Jean Laporte's judgment that this position is "coherent in all its parts,"[1] it continues to deserve the attention of philosophers and theologians for at least two reasons.

First, it shows one way in which seventeenth-century dualism influenced discussion of freedom of will. Malebranche's dualism was more extreme than Descartes' because Malebranche not only held that mind and body are distinct substances, but that they do not really act on one another. This extreme dualism helps to account for his identification of human freedom with freedom of will, and his narrow focus on freedom of will as opposed to freedom of overt human actions.[2]

Second, central to Malebranche's position is a proposition relevant to current work on free will: that human beings have the freedom to choose their ultimate ends, or as Harry Frankfurt might put it, that we are free to choose what we care about.[3] Like many of his predecessors, for example, Aquinas and Descartes, Malebranche held that we have freedom of choice to assent or not to assent to propositions that are not "fully evident" to us, and that we are in general free to choose what we will do in order to seek what we desire. However,

Malebranche was mainly concerned to defend the position that we are free to choose what we love "absolutely and intrinsically."

## I.   MALEBRANCHE'S IDENTIFICATION OF HUMAN FREEDOM WITH FREEDOM OF WILL

Malebranche's discussion of human freedom was highly focused, and more limited than his language might lead a twentieth-century reader to expect. He wrote as if he intended to provide a general account of free human action. However, his discussion was much more limited. To begin with, he took up the freedom only of acts of will. Indeed, for Malebranche, human freedom *is* freedom of will. Thus, he said that he uses word "freedom" to designate a certain property of will (*Search*, I.1, OC 1:46; LO 4–5), and the only human acts he ever calls "free" are acts of will. He did not often use expressions that would be translated by "freedom of will" or "free will." Rather, he spoke simply of freedom. However, by "freedom" he meant freedom of will, and he almost totally disregarded the freedom of overt, bodily, human actions.

Sometimes Malebranche described overt, public actions in terms that suggested that they are free. But he stopped short of saying explicitly that they are free. Consider the passage, "Only inner sensation (*sentiment interieur*) teaches us that we are and what we are. We must consult this sensation, therefore, in order convince ourselves that we are free. Its response on this matter is clear enough when we are considering some particular good; for nobody can doubt that he is not led invincibly to eat some fruit, or avoid some mild pain" (*Search*, Eluc. 1, OC 3:30; LO 554). Eating a fruit or refraining from doing so, avoiding a slight pain or refraining from doing so, are overt actions, and in this passage Malebranche came close to saying that such actions are free. However, he did not say it explicitly, and his statement that the freedom of such actions is known by inner sensation certainly suggests that it is only the inner, private part of the actions that is, strictly speaking, free.

No doubt this first limitation in Malebranche's discussion reflects his Augustinian conviction that the moral quality of a human being's life is determined by the private, interior life of intellect and will. However, it also shows the influence of his dualism and his occasionalism. Full-blown occasionalism is not present in the first volume of *The Search*, published in 1674. That doctrine first appeared a year later, in the second volume, where Malebranche summarized it in these terms: "that there is only one true cause because there is only one true God; that the nature or power of each thing is nothing but the will of God; that all natural causes are not *true* causes, but only *occasional* causes" (*Search* VI.2.iii, OC 2:312; LO 448).[4] However, from the beginning of his discussion of human freedom, in the opening chapters of *The Search*, Malebranche assumed that in general creatures are not genuinely active, that they operate passively under the domination of divine causality – with one exception, the free volition of human beings, angels, and devils. Thus, he says that "matter is altogether without action; it has no force to arrest its motion or to direct it and turn it in one direction rather than another ... because God impresses its motion on it and controls its direction" (*Search*, I.1; OC 1:46; LO 4). As regards created minds, he divided their operations into those of intellect and those of will, and says that the intellect is "purely passive," while the will is "both active and passive" (*Search*, "Conclusion of the First Three Books," OC 1:488; LO 261). The will is active insofar as it is free. As Malebranche puts it in *Réflexions sur la Prémotion physique* (hereafter *Prémotion*), his last work, published in 1715, "[God] wanted to communicate to us some power or some mastery over our action," and hence gave us mastery over certain acts of will (OC 16:17). So from first to last in his written work, Malebranche emphasized that the only events in which creatures are active are acts of free will.

## II. MALEBRANCHE'S CONCENTRATION ON FREEDOM WITH REGARD TO WHAT ONE LOVES ABSOLUTELY AND INTRINSICALLY

Malebranche's treatment of human freedom was limited in a further way: His repeated attempts to give a philosophical analysis of freedom of will, and to defend the claim that human beings have "freedom of indifference" deal almost exclusively with one exercise of will, that which determines what one loves "absolutely and intrinsically" (*Search*, I.2, OC 1:55; LO 10). The logical opposite of loving something absolutely and intrinsically is loving something in relation to something else. Thus, Malebranche stated that it is a sin to freely love anything other than God absolutely and intrinsically, and he sometimes puts this point by saying that one ought to love creatures only "in relation to" God: If you love the virtue and justice of your friend, then "your love is Christian, for then you love God in your friend, or your friend in relation to [par rapport à] God" (*Conversations Chrétiennes*, OC 4:203).

In general, one loves an object x in relation to an object y if and only if one loves y and loves x because of its relation to y. Thus, to love a creature in relation to God is to love God and to love the creature because of its relation to God. Various relations may be involved. Thus, the passage just quoted continues, "You love [your friend] because he holds fast to God, because he lives according to God, because his will is conformed to God's will." Again, one ought to do one's duty "to one's Prince, to one's father, to all those who have authority," and this involves honoring and loving them. "But the honor one gives them, the love one bears them, ought to terminate in God alone: *Sicut Domino et non hominibus*, says St. Paul: The honor rendered to power is related *to God and not to men*, for power to act is present only in God" (*Traité de Morale*, OC 11:44). Thus, one ought to love one's Prince because one loves God and because the power the Prince exercises is really God's power. Malebranche says that one ought to love not only other human beings, but all creatures, in proportion to their perfection. Such love ought always "terminate in God" (See *Traité de Morale*, Chapter III, OC 11:38, ff.).[5]

Malebranche used the verb "to love" and the noun "love" (French, "aimer" and "amour") to stand for any mental inclination toward something apprehended as good. Desire is a particular form of love, namely, love of an absent good. This is made clear by the many texts in which Malebranche identified the love of the good in general and the desire for happiness. I comment below on his identification of the good in general with happiness. Here, I want to make clear the relation, in Malebranche's discussion, between love and desire. Malebranche typically spoke of "the *love* of the good in general" and "the *desire* for happiness." For example, "The soul is not the cause of its love of the good, or its natural and invincible desire to be happy" (*Réponse à la Dissertation*, OC 7:565). Again, "God creates [the soul] ceaselessly with the invincible desire to be happy, that is, He ceaselessly moves it toward the good in general" (*Prémotion*, OC 16:46). However, in the very next paragraph of *Prémotion*, he spoke instead of "the *love* of happiness" (my italics). The shift is not surprising, given that desire is a specific form of love.

Malebranche said repeatedly that when one is attracted to a determinate good, one is free to "stop at (*s'arrêter à*)" the object or to "go further on (*aller plus loin*)," and that it is a sin to freely "stop at" an object other than God. The theme is first announced clearly in the *First Elucidation to The Search*:

> God is not the author of sin because He constantly impresses the impulse to continue (*aller plus loin*) on whoever sins or stops at (*s'arrêter à*) some particular good, because He gives the sinner the power of thinking of other things and of proceeding to goods other than the one that is actually the object of his thought and love. (*Search*, Eluc. 1, OC 3:21; LO 549)

Malebranche also said that the root of all sin is to freely love a determinate good other than God absolutely and intrinsically (*Search*, I.2, OC 1:55; LO 10). Therefore, to stop at an object apprehended as good is to love it absolutely and intrinsically, in other words, to love it and not love it in relation to anything else.

Malebranche, like Augustine, held that every act of will involves the love of some object absolutely and intrinsically. So whenever one wills in any way, one loves either God or a creature absolutely and intrinsically. But suppose one loves a creature *x* in relation to another creature *y*, and vice versa, loves *y* in relation to *x*, but loves neither *x* nor *y* in relation to anything else. For example, it seems possible that one should love one's son because the son loves one's wife and one's wife because she loves the son, and that one should not love either because of one's love for anything else. Malebranche's answer would have to be that then one loves the created pair consisting of one's wife and one's son absolutely and intrinsically, and that would be a special case of stopping at a particular created good.

### III.   KNOWLEDGE OF FREEDOM BY "INNER SENSATION," BY REASON, AND BY FAITH

I have quoted a text in which Malebranche says that because we can know that we are and what we are only through "inner sensation," we "must consult this sensation in order to convince ourselves that we are free." "Inner sensation" is his phrase for a sort of cognition through which everyone is supposed to have privileged access to the existence of his own mind and its operations. However, he also said, "Even if we were not convinced of our freedom through the inner sensation we have of ourselves, we could discover through reason that man is necessarily created free ..." (*Search*, Eluc. 1, OC 3:28; LO 553). In addition, he says that a theologian "must keep in view the dogmas decided [by the Church]" and avoid anything that would "clash with (*choquer*) one of these dogmas, above all a dogma as essential as that of freedom. For if freedom is rejected, God is made the author of sin, someone unjust and cruel; in a word, this heresy overturns all religion and all morality ..." (*Prémotion*, OC 16:27–8).[6]

However, if we can discover by reasoning that human beings are free, and if that proposition is a dogma of the Church that we ought to believe, why did Malebranche say that we "must" consult inner sensation in order to be convinced that we are free? His position was as follows: We can discover by reason, and by the teaching of the Church, that human beings have freedom of indifference with respect to all determinate goods. However, the conviction that I am free depends on inner sensation in several ways. First, although I can be convinced by faith and by reason that all human beings are created free, neither faith nor reason gives me acquaintance with what it is like to be free. According to Malebranche, only through inner sensation can one know what freedom is like. Second, I cannot be convinced that I am free unless I am convinced that I exist, and I can be convinced that I exist only by inner sensation.

In addition, Malebranche realized that abstract reasoning about freedom and determinism can make one doubt that one has freedom of will:

If instead of listening to our inner sensation we attend to abstract reasoning that distracts us from thinking about ourselves, then perhaps in losing sight of ourselves we shall forget what we are, and in wishing to reconcile God's knowledge with His absolute power over our wills, we shall doubt that we are free and shall fall into an error that upsets all the principles of religion and morality. (*Search*, Eluc. 1, OC 3:30; LO 554)

So he thought that knowledge of freedom by inner sensation is a healthy antidote to any skepticism that might arise from abstract debate.[7]

Malebranche's phrase, "if we were not convinced of our freedom through the inner sensation we have of ourselves, we could discover through reason that man is necessarily created free," suggests that knowledge by reason that man is created free is an unessential supplement to knowledge by inner sensation of the same truth. However, that is misleading. Malebranche recognized that inner sensation can give a person knowledge only about his own case. It is not the source of knowledge of general propositions, such as that all human beings have free will (*Search*, V.7, OC 2:185; LO 374). Such general propositions can be known only through reason and faith.

Malebranche emphasized that although one must rely upon inner sensation in order to know what the exercise of free will *is like*, inner sensation does not give knowledge of *the nature* of free will:

With regard to freedom, the inner sensation of it suffices to demonstrate it. Nothing is more sure than inner sensation, for proving that a thing is; it is useless for knowing what the thing is. (*Réponse au Livre des vrayes et des fausses idées*, OC 6:163)

On the contrary, he holds, inner sensation gives only confused knowledge, and it is impossible for any human being, at least during this life, to understand the nature of freedom.[8]

However, according to Malebranche, philosophical reasoning and writing about freedom requires a notion of freedom more precise and distinct than that provided by inner sensation alone. To this end, he tried to make our notions of will and of freedom more "precise," "distinct," and "familiar," by comparing them with the properties of material things. He said that although comparisons of the mental and the material limp, they can be used "to make the mind more attentive and to make others experience (*sentir*), as it were, what one wants to say" (*Search*, OC 1:41; LO, 2). Later on he suggests that such comparisons are not only useful, but indispensable: "We cannot explain ourselves on this matter [human freedom] clearly, but we can do so only by metaphor..." (*Prémotion*, OC 16:29). In a reply to Arnauld, Malebranche lists a number of expressions he uses in his explanation of will and freedom, and says that they are metaphorical:

Since I know my soul only by inner sensation ... I say that it is not possible [to explain the will and freedom more clearly than I have just done]. If you find that the terms "rest," "movement," "impression," "consent," "efficacy," "power," etc., are obscure and metaphorical, as indeed they are, that is because we do not have a clear idea of the soul (*Réponse à la Dissertation*, OC 7:568).⁹

## IV. MAKING THE NOTIONS OF WILL AND FREEDOM MORE PRECISE AND DISTINCT AND FAMILIAR

Malebranche's first attempt to make our notions of will and freedom more precise, distinct, and familiar began with an explanation of "the customary distinction between intellect and will." To this end, he developed a comparison between the properties of minds and the properties of bodies: Intellect is like the capacity of bodies to receive different shapes, and will is like the capacity of bodies to receive motion. The difference that he stressed between intellect and will is that intellect is always passive, whereas will is sometimes active and sometimes passive.¹⁰ He also said that there is an important difference "between the impression or motion that the Author of nature produces in matter, and the impression or impulse toward the good in general that the same Author of nature constantly impresses in the mind." Matter is "entirely passive" and has "no force to arrest its motion or to direct it and turn it in one direction rather than another." Mind, by contrast, "in a sense can be said to be active, because our soul can direct in various ways the inclination or impression that God gives it" (*Search*, I.1, OC 1:46; LO 4).¹¹ He then provides an explanation of how he uses the terms "will" and "freedom":

I propose to designate by the word WILL, or capacity the soul has of loving different goods, *the impression or natural impulse that carries us toward general and undetermined good [vers le bien indéterminé et en général]*; and by FREEDOM [*LIBERTE*], I mean nothing else but *the power that the mind has of turning this impression toward the objects that please us so that our natural inclinations are made to settle upon [soient terminées] some particular object*, which inclinations were hitherto vaguely and indeterminately directed toward universal or general good [*le bien en général ou universel*], that is, toward God, who alone is the general good because He alone contains in Himself all goods. (*Search*, I.1, OC 1:46; LO 5)

He gave a slightly different definition of freedom in *TNG*:

Now this power of loving or not loving particular goods, the *non-invincibility* which is met with in the movement which brings minds to love that which does not seem to them in every sense to include all goods – this power, this *non-invincibility*, is what I call *liberty [liberté]*. So, putting the definition in place of what is defined, this expression, *our will is free*, means that the natural movement of the soul toward the good in general is not invincible with regard to the good in particular. (TNG, OC 5:118–9; R 170)

Both explanations turn on a distinction between the movement of the will toward the good in general, which is not free, and its movement toward determinate objects apprehended as good (or as he often says, toward determinate goods), which is free. Malebranche said that the inclination toward the good in general is an inclination toward God. However, this does not mean that the love of the good in general is the love of something thought of as God, or as a divine being. Rather it is the love of God only under the description "the good in general." Malebranche said that a person loves God in this sense even if he hates God.[12] Love of God, in this sense, is not free. By contrast, Malebranche held that if one loves God as a divine being, at least during this life here below, one does so freely.[13] His expression "to love that which does not seem to them in every sense to include all goods," must, therefore, be taken to mean "to love something in response to a cognition of it that does not make it clearly known to the lover that the object includes all goods," rather than "to love something under a description that does not imply that the object includes all goods." The love of God as a diving being, during this life here below, satisfies the first formula, but not the second.

In all of his discussions of volition and freedom, Malebranche identified the love of the good in general with the desire for happiness. Thus, in the first chapter of *The Search*, he says, "we do not love [the good in general] freely ... since it is not in the power of will not to wish to be happy" (OC 1:47; LO 5).[14] When he does so, he is using "happiness" to stand not for a state of a person who is happy, but rather for what makes a person happy. In this sense, Malebranche would be prepared to say that a miser thinks his happiness is money and a true Christian recognizes that his happiness is God. The word "good," according to Malebranche, is affected by a similar ambiguity:

The word good is equivocal: it can signify either the pleasure which makes one formally happy, or the cause of pleasure, real or apparent. In this discourse I shall always take the word good in the second sense; because pleasure indeed is impressed in the soul, in order that it love the cause that makes it happy, in order that it transport itself toward it through the motion of its love, and that it unite itself strictly [*étroitement*] with it to be continually happy. When the soul loves only its own pleasure, it in effect loves nothing distinct from itself; for pleasure is only a condition or modification of the soul which renders it presently happy and contented. Now since the soul cannot be, for itself, the cause of its happiness, it is unjust, it is ungrateful, it is blind, if it loves its pleasure, without offering the love and the respect that is due to the true cause which produces it in it. (*TNG*, OC 5:119; R 171)[15]

Malebranche goes on to say that because only God is a *true* cause of pleasure, only God is, strictly speaking, *good* in the sense at issue in this discussion, namely, *a cause of pleasure*. However, he said that he was prepared to speak of the *occasional* causes of pleasure as "good," in order not to depart unnecessarily from ordinary usage.

As the above passage makes clear, Malebranche thought of pleasure as an intentional state: To experience pleasure is to take pleasure in some object. Thus he says, "There is no perception without an object; every perception is relative to what one perceives. The pleasure, for example, that a drunkard takes in drinking, is related only to the wine, and is nothing but the pleasant perception of the wine" (*Conversations Chrétiennes*, OC 4:181). Furthermore, Malebranche held that one cannot love any object, including God, unless one takes pleasure in it.[16] The pleasure one takes in an object may be either an actual pleasure or an anticipation of pleasure, which Malebranche describes as a "foretaste" of an actual pleasure (*Prémotion*, OC 16:5).

Malebranche identified freedom, or the power of loving or not loving particular goods, with the power to give or withhold *consent*. This identification is made explicit in the "First Elucidation" to *The Search*, and repeated in all of Malebranche's subsequent treatments of human freedom, including *Prémotion*, where he said,

There are in the soul two different powers or activities. The first is properly only the action of God ... [who] continually creates the soul with the invincible desire to be happy, or continually moves it toward the good in general. But the second ... which is the essence of freedom, is ... very different from the first. It consists in a true power, not to produce, by its own efficacy, new modifications in itself, that is, new interesting perceptions or new movements in the will, but ... a true power of the soul to suspend or to give its consent to the movements that follow naturally upon interesting perceptions. (*Prémotion*, 16:46–7)

Unfortunately, Malebranche said very little about what he means by "consent." A text is cited above in which he said that his use of the term in his treatment of freedom was metaphorical, but he provided no explanation of the metaphor. In the second chapter of *The Search*, he distinguished "the will's consent to truth from its consent to goodness" (OC 1:49–53; LO 7–9). Consent to the true is assent to a proposition, and can be called "judgment." However, judgment has two components: On the part of the understanding, judging is apprehending a proposition. On the part of the will, judging is "assenting to, and voluntarily remaining with, what the understanding represents to it" (*Search*, I.2, OC 1:49–50; LO 7–8). Consent to the truth is free except when a proposition is apprehended with such evidence that there is no reason to doubt, and this occurs "often" even during this life here below.

Malebranche's notion of consent to goodness was that of an act whereby a desire or love, which at first is something that happens to us, and in which we are passive, becomes something that we actively acquiesce in and make our own. Suppose that a man experiences a desire to have sexual intercourse with a woman who is not his wife. Malebranche would say that, so far, no sin has occurred. However, if he then *consents* to the desire, he has sinned, whether or not he forms a plan to act on the desire. The desire is no longer something that has happened to him. It is now something he has actively acquiesced in and made his own. Malebranche stated that consent to the movement of the will toward a determinate object is always free during this life here below:

> In our present state, we often clearly perceive truths ... and hence the will is not at all indifferent in the consent it gives to these evident truths.... But it is not the same with goods, of which we know none without some reason to doubt that we ought to love it.

If one consents to a desire, then the desire continues. Sometimes Malebranche treated consent to the desire for an object, and the continuation of the love or desire, as a single act. For example, he said,

> The spiritual pleasure [of grace] is a sort of physical premotion, for it produces a necessary movement in the soul, which is a determination of the desire to be happy ... And when the will follows this movement and consents to it, the consenting is the free love [*l'amour libre*]. (*Prémotion*, OC 16:17)

It is not clear, however, that when one suspends consent to a desire, the desire necessarily ceases. Malebranche did say that the mind "can, through the movement which God imprints ceaselessly in it to carry it towards the good in general . . . halt its course towards any good that may be" (*TNG*, OC 5:121; R 173). However, the suspension of consent to a desire does not seem to constitute the cessation of the desire. Rather, the cessation of the desire seems to be something that occurs after, and as a result of, the suspension of consent.

The relation between consent to the true and consent to goodness is complicated. Malebranche's general account of will implies that assent to the truth of a proposition is derived from the natural movement of the will toward the good in general. Unfortunately, he did not provide any explicit account of how this derivation is to be understood. However, in a footnote appended to his explanation of the distinction between consent to the truth and consent to goodness he says, "Geometers do not love the truth, but knowledge of the truth, whatever might otherwise be said" (*Search*, I.2, OC 1:53; LO 9). I take the geometer's love of the knowledge of the truth, referred to in this footnote, to be the love of, and desire for, knowledge of the true answer to a question the geometer is interested in. This interpretation is borne out by Malebranche's explanation of why one is not free to suspend consent from a proposition that is entirely evident:

The things we consider appear entirely evident to us only when the understanding has examined them from all sides and has examined all the relations necessary to judge them. Whence it happens that the will, being unable to function without knowledge, can no longer act on the understanding, that is, the will cannot further desire that the understanding represent something new in its object because it has already considered all aspects related to *the question to be decided*. (*Search*, I.1, OC 1:51; LO 8; my italics)

These texts suggest that one way in which assent to the truth of a proposition can be derived from the desire for the good in general is that the assent arises from a desire to know the truth of the proposition. In such a case assent to the truth of a proposition is the outcome of a process that includes these steps: (a) I love the good in general; (b) I apprehend knowledge of the truth with respect to a proposition as a good; (c) I desire to know the truth with respect to the proposition; (d) I consent to the desire to know the truth with respect to the proposition; and (e) I assent to the proposition. This account fits best a case in which one is in a question-asking frame of mind, like a mathematician looking for the solution to a problem. However, it can be extended to other cases, assuming that the steps in the process can take place rapidly in a short period of time.

Malebranche also indicated that consent to the desire for, or more generally to the love of, a particular object presupposes consent to the truth of the proposition that the object of the desire or love is really good. Thus, in a reply to Arnauld, Malebranche said, "Although God leads me to love particular goods, as a result of the love of the good in general that He ceaselessly produces in me, this is not an invincible impression. I can suspend the judgment that rules the free determinations of my will." He goes on to describe this "free determination of the will" as "the consent of the will" *(Réponse à la Dissertation,* OC 7:566).[17] Here his position states that consent to a natural love is preceded by assent to a proposition about the object of the love. My consent to the desire for a glass of wine, for example, would be the outcome of the following process: (a′) I love the good in general; (b′) I apprehend a glass of wine as a good; (c′) I desire a glass of wine; (d′) I assent to the proposition that a glass of wine really is a good; and finally, (e′) I consent to the desire for a glass of wine. Step (d′) exemplifies a second way in which assent to the truth of a proposition can be derived from the love of the good in general. If I apprehend a glass of wine as a good, and naturally desire a glass of wine, I am already interested in whether it is true that a glass of wine really is a good, without needing a further desire to know whether that proposition is true and consent to such a further desire.

For Malebranche, then, consent to love or desire was not the same thing as consent (or assent) to the truth of a proposition, though the two are closely related. Consent to love or desire is an act whereby one makes one's own a love or desire that previously was something received in a passive way. However, what of *suspending* consent? While discussing what happens when one resists a temptation to sin, Malebranche said that to suspend consent to the natural desire for one object is to give consent to the natural desire for a different object. If I suspend consent to a temptation, he said,

. . . it is because I consent once again, or take my rest with regard to the true good. It is because I know, or sense, that if I stop at a particular good, I will deprive myself of the happiness that I would find in Him who includes all goods. (*Réponse à la Dissertation*, OC 7:566–68)

For Malebranche, sin always consists in freely "stopping at" a particular good other than God, that is, freely loving a particular good other than God absolutely and intrinsically. To be tempted is to desire or love a particular object absolutely and intrinsically, by a natural and nonfree movement of the will. When Malebranche stated that if I suspend consent to a temptation, it is because "I consent once again ... with regard to the true good," he was not referring to consent to the desire for happiness or the love of the good in general. He held that anyone who actually loves or desires any determinate object, always actually desires happiness and consents to that desire.[18] So if suspending consent to a temptation required no more than consenting to the desire for happiness, no one would ever give in to a temptation. Malebranche seemed rather to hold that when one is tempted and suspends consent to the temptation, the suspending of consent is preceded both by (i) the desire for a particular object, x, which constitutes the temptation, and (ii) a desire for a second-order good under the description "something greater than x." To suspend consent to (i) is to give consent to (ii). A person can also suspend consent, during this life here below, to the love of God. However, here again, to suspend consent with respect to God is to give consent to some other good.

But now a difficulty arises. For Malebranche says,

When two objects are presented to the human mind, and it determines itself with respect to them, I grant that it never fails to determine itself on the side wherein it finds the most reason and pleasure – on that side wherein, everything considered, it finds the most good. (*TNG*, OC 5:139; R 188)

He went on to say that "when sensible pleasures, or something of the sort, do not trouble the mind," that is, to the extent that one is free with respect to the attractive objects in question, "one can always suspend the judgment of one's love and not determine oneself ..." However, as we have just seen, to suspend consent with regard to one object is to give consent to another. Furthermore, one can consent with regard to an object only if one already desires or loves it, and hence only if it is already present to the mind. However, in that case, it looks as if one necessarily determines oneself with respect to whichever of the two objects is most attractive, or again, consents to whichever desire is stronger. So consent is free only if one has the power to determine which of two apparent goods is more attractive. Is this not something that is determined by causes outside one's control?

Malebranche's answer depended on his account of attention. Attention, he stated repeatedly, is an act of will whereby one desires that an object be present to the mind with greater clarity and vividness (*Search*, Eluc. 2, OC 3:40; LO 559). It is a "natural prayer" for a clearer and more vivid apprehension of an object that one already apprehends at least in an abstract way. This natural prayer is always answered, that is to say, it is the occasional cause of the desired apprehension. Malebranche said that this desire is itself a free act: It is up to us whether we attend to one or another of two attractive objects that are present to the mind, and the one we end up resting our attention upon is the one that will seem the more attractive. Thus, whether we consent or suspend consent with regard to a particular good is up to us to the extent that it is up to us to dwell attentively upon the particular good or upon other apparent goods that would provide a motive for suspending consent:

As we are able to love only by the love of the good, we always determine ourselves according to what appears best to us at the time we determine ourselves. Thus, were we in no way masters of our attention, or were our attention not the natural cause of our ideas, we would neither be free nor in a position to be worthy. For we would be unable even to suspend our consent, since we would not have the power to consider reasons capable of leading us to suspend it. (*Dialogues*, OC 12:289; JS 227)

Therefore, the power to give or suspend consent to a particular good includes the power to direct one's attention to that particular good or to some other good. Indeed there is reason to accept Jean Laporte's statement that, for Malebranche, "The act of resting one's attention upon one object and the act of consenting to that object are, in the end, one and the same act; and it is equally correct to locate freedom in the one or the other" ("La liberté selon Malebranche," p. 218). For if resting attention upon an object were followed by a distinct act of consent to desire, then one would necessarily consent to the desire for whichever object one rested one's attention upon.

Malebranche's account of attention also provides an explanation of why it is that when a person consents to a movement of the will toward one object, he *stops at* that object, and why it is that when a person suspends consent, he *goes farther on*. Because consenting with regard to an object involves focusing attention on that object, the attractions of other objects will not become present to one's mind. And because, on the other hand, suspending consent to the desire for one particular good is giving consent to the desire for something better, or at least different, and hence involves attending to another good, suspending consent always involves going farther on, and considering other goods. The only "reason capable of leading us to suspend" consent to a particular good that Malebranche mentioned is the general thought that something more than the particular good is needed to satisfy our desire for happiness. One may suspend consent to a particular good, $x$, then, by attending to an object under the general description, "something greater than $x$." Attending to this generically described object may then be the occasional cause of thoughts of particular goods other than $x$. A sequence of this sort is described in an example Malebranche gave of suspending consent: Suppose a person is attracted to "some honor he might hope for." The freedom of his mind with regard to the honor "consists in the fact that not being fully convinced that this honor contains all the good [his mind] is capable of loving, it can suspend its judgment and love, and then ... it can think about other things and consequently love other goods" (OC 1:48; LO 5). A more general description of such a sequence occurs in *TNG*:

When the good which is presented to the mind and to the senses ... is recognized under the idea ... of a good which does not enclose all goods ... [the mind] can still desire the sight and enjoyment of some other good; it can suspend the judgement of its love; it can refrain from resting in present enjoyment; it can, through its desires, seek out some new object. And since its desires are the occasional causes of its enlightenment, it can ... discover the true good, and in the true good many other particular goods different from that which it saw and relished before. (OC 5:120; R 172)[19]

## V. A QUALIFICATION OF MALEBRANCHE'S ACCOUNT OF HUMAN FREEDOM

The account of human freedom so far described can be summed up by saying that human freedom consists in the power to give or refuse consent to the natural desire for a particular apparent good. This account was presented by Malebranche, though not explicitly, in the first edition of *The Search*.²⁰ It was considerably developed in the First Elucidation to that work, in *TNG*, in Malebranche's responses to Arnauld, and in *Prémotion*. On the whole, the later works provide clarifications and defenses, but not substantial changes, to the original position – with one exception.²¹ In *The Search*, and in its First Elucidation, Malebranche claimed that we have freedom of indifference with respect to *any* desire for a particular good.²² However, in *TNG* he said that as a result of Adam's sin human freedom is diminished and human beings do not always have freedom of indifference with regard to particular goods.

According to *TNG*, freedom to suspend consent with regard to a particular good is a matter of degree and depends on the extent to which one's pleasures and passions are subject to voluntary control. For "a man who is perfectly free, such as we conceive Adam immediately after his creation," pleasures are in general "subjected to his volition," and hence "he does not let himself be intoxicated by them." For such a person, "the sole invincible pleasure is that of the blessed, or that which the first man would have found in God, if God had willed to anticipate and prevent his fall" (OC 5:123; R 174–5). However, in fact, for Adam and Eve, before the fall, no particular good was invincible. As a result of Adam's sin, however, Adam and Eve, and all their descendants lost the privilege of voluntary control over pleasure. Consequently, it is much more difficult for fallen man to suspend consent to a particular good with regard to which he has the "taste or foretaste" of pleasure (OC 5:131; R 181), and so his freedom is greatly diminished.²³ This diminishment of freedom in fallen man varies both from person to person and circumstance to circumstance.²⁴ However, "concupiscence has not entirely destroyed liberty in man ... one can defeat a sensible pleasure when it is weak: one can suspend the judgment of one's love, when one is not carried away by some pleasure which is too violent" (*TNG*, OC 5:134; R 183).²⁵

This qualification of Malebranche's position does not, however, affect his account of what human freedom is. He continued to hold that human freedom consists in the power to give or suspend consent to a natural desire for a particular good. The qualification has to do only with the scope of human freedom, and is consistent with Malebranche's treatment of human freedom in works written after

*TNG*. In these later works, Malebranche dropped the claim that human beings have freedom of indifference with regard to all particular goods. He does repeat the assertion, made in the First Elucidation (OC 3:18; LO 548), that "God does not lead us either necessarily or invincibly to the love of [particular goods]."[26] However, this is not in conflict with his position in *TNG*. There he said that particular goods are invincible for fallen man only because of concupiscence, and he argued in the First Elucidation to *The Search* that God is "not the author of our concupiscence," because concupiscence consists only in the loss of control over one's pleasures, and is no more real than sin (OC 3:34–5; LO 556–7). Therefore, even if some particular goods are invincible for fallen human beings, it is not God that leads us invincibly to love them.

## VI. MALEBRANCHE'S ARGUMENT FOR THE PROPOSITION THAT HUMAN BEINGS ARE CREATED FREE

As I have pointed out, Malebranche recognized that inner sensation can give at best knowledge of one's own case. How, then, did he claim to know that all human beings have free will? He argued in several places that human beings are free because without freedom there is no morality (*Search*, Eluc. 1, OC 3:29–30; LO 553–4; *Prémotion*, OC 16:27–8). The assumption of this argument, that human beings generally are subject to morality, was for Malebranche a datum of revelation. However, in the "First Elucidation" to *The Search*, he provided a more elaborate, and purely philosophical, argument. If this argument is sound, it established precisely that human beings are free in the determination of what they love absolutely and intrinsically:

Yet even if the inner sensation we have of ourselves were not enough to convince us that we are free, we could persuade ourselves of our freedom through reason. For, convinced as we are through the light of reason that God acts only for Himself and that He cannot give us an impulse that does not tend toward Himself, the impression toward the good in general might be invincible; but it is clear that the impression He gives us toward particular goods must necessarily be such that it is up to us whether to follow it or withhold our consent with regard to it. For if this impression were invincible, we would have no movement to lead us to [*jusqu'au*] God, although He gives us this impulse only for Himself; and we would be required to stop at [*de nous arrêter aux*] particular goods, although God, order, and reason prohibit us from doing so.

In the succeeding paragraph, he put the argument in slightly different terms:

Thus, even if we were not convinced of our freedom through the inner sensation we have of ourselves, we could discover through reason that man is necessarily created free – given that he is capable of desiring particular goods and that he can desire these goods only through the impression or impulse that God continuously gives him for loving Him, which can also be proved through reason. (*Search*, Eluc. 1, OC 3:28; LO 553)

In this argument "particular goods" refers specifically to created particular goods. The argument can be reformulated as follows:

1. Every human being is capable of loving particular created goods.
2. The love of particular created goods in the mind of a human being enables him to love God absolutely and intrinsically.

Therefore,

3. Every human being is capable of a love of particular created goods that enables him to love God absolutely and intrinsically. (from 1 and 2)
4. The love of particular created goods enables a human being to love God absolutely and intrinsically only if it is up to the human being to give or withhold consent with regard to the particular created goods.

Therefore,

5. Every human being is capable of a love of particular goods such that it is up to him to give or withhold consent with regard to the particular created goods. (from 3 and 4)

In other words, every human being is created free.

Malebranche understood it to be "evident" that "God can ... create minds only to know Him and to love Him" (*Search*, Preface, OC 1:10; LO xxxiv). From this he concluded that every created mind is constantly engaged in volition,[27] and that the natural volitions of human beings must, like those of the Creator, be directed toward

God: "Since the mind's natural inclinations are undoubtedly the constant impression of the Will of Him who has created and preserves them, it seems to me that these inclinations must be exactly like those of their Creator and Preserver. By their very nature, then, they can have no other principal end than His glory ..." (*Search*, IV.1, OC 2:11; LO 266). These are bedrock positions in Malebranche.

It is less clear why Malebranche held premise (4). In all of his treatments of human freedom, however, he assumed that the natural love of a particular object, which occurs when one apprehends it as good, is an absolute and intrinsic love of the object. Malebranche's thought seemed to be that when one apprehends an object as good, the natural movement of the mind is a love of that object and no other, and hence is not a love of the object in relation to another. Hence, one can love an object in relation to another only if one suspends consent to the initial, natural love, and then proceeds to consider other objects. If this is so, then one can love a particular created good without loving it absolutely and intrinsically (without stopping at it) only if one can suspend consent with regard to it.

Malebranche's formulation of the argument suggested that the human love of particular created goods is always able to lead us to God, and hence that it is always up to us to consent or not to consent to such a love. This is consistent with his position in the First Elucidation to *The Search*. However, the argument can be interpreted so as to make it also consistent with the position of *TNG*, that some particular goods are invincible for fallen human beings. In particular, the second premise can be taken to mean that the love of particular created goods, *as something caused by God*, necessarily enables one to love God absolutely and intrinsically. As pointed out above, Malebranche's position in *TNG* was that some particular goods are invincible after the fall because of concupiscence, and that concupiscence, being only the loss of a certain control over one's pleasures, is not caused by God. Therefore, if a particular good is invincible to someone on a given occasion, that is not because of the person's inclination toward the particular good, considered as something caused by God. Rather, it is because of the person's loss of control over his inclinations, and that is not something caused by God. Such an interpretation of the argument is, indeed, suggested by Malebranche's formulation of the conclusion in the First Elucidation to *The Search*: "Man is created free."

## VII. MALEBRANCHE'S ATTEMPT TO RECONCILE FREEDOM OF INDIFFERENCE WITH OCCASIONALISM

According to Malebranche's occasionalism, "it is God who does all in all things" (*TNG*, OC 5:148; R 196), and "the power of each [created] thing is nothing but the will of God" (*Search*, VI.2, OC 2:312; LO 448). This position seems clearly to be in conflict with the claim that human beings have the power to give or to withhold consent to desires for particular goods. Malebranche first addressed the difficulty in the First Elucidation to *The Search*.[28] He took it up again in his exchanges with Arnauld and in *Prémotion*.

Malebranche's solution depends on two closely related claims:

A. The act of consenting or suspending consent with regard to a particular good does not have "physical reality," that is, does not have real being.
B. A person's coming to consent or ceasing to consent with regard to a particular good is not a real change in the person.

For Malebranche, the two claims were equivalent, because an act has physical reality if and only if the onset or cessation of the act is a real change in the agent.

A good example of his use of both (A) and (B) is a passage in *Contre la Prévention*, his last reply to Arnauld, published in 1699, some five years after Arnauld's death: "[In my *Réponse a la Dissertation*] I proved that the soul is the real cause only of the act by which it gives, refuses, or suspends its consent, and that consent is only a *repos* and not a physical reality. So the immanent act of the will is truly an action, but an action that produces nothing physical" (OC 9:1129). In the earlier text to which he referred, he said, "If the power to follow or not follow the natural movement of the soul can indeed be said to be a real and true power, I agree that minds have that power. But I do not see that they produce in themselves a reality, or a modification that physically changes their substance" (OC 7:568). In the text from *Prévention*, he appeals to (A), and in the text from *Réponse à la Dissertation*, to (B).

In *Prémotion*, Malebranche relies mainly on (B). Thus, he says,

I agree that God is the sole author of all substances and of all their modes, that He the author of all beings: not only of all bodies but of all minds. But be careful: I understand by a *mode* of a substance only that which cannot change without there being some real or physical change in the substance of which it is the mode.... Once again, I agree that God is the sole efficacious cause of all the real changes that take place in the world ... (16:40).

Although God is the sole cause of all real changes, Malebranche added, the human soul is the true cause of its act of consenting or withholding consent:

I hold, then, that although the soul, as free and active, is the true cause of its acts, although it is the unique immediate cause of the consent it gives or refuses to give to the physical motives that anticipate and solicit the soul; nevertheless the soul is not the efficacious cause of any real changes that happen to it, just as it is not the real cause of what happens in its own body as a consequence of its volitions. (*Prémotion*, OC 16:43)

The assertion that the soul is the "true cause" or the "real cause" of its act of consent shows that in his later writings Malebranche recognized three types of cause: (1) true efficient causes, of which God is the only example; (2) occasional causes; and (3) a type of cause that might be called "agent causes," of which the main example is the mind or soul considered as the cause its act of giving or withholding consent. The difference between (1) and (3) is that for a true efficient cause, but not for an agent cause, what is caused is distinct from the causing of it.

At times, Malebranche spoke as if the metaphor comparing consent to bodily rest constitutes a defense of (A). However this would be a weak defense indeed. As Malebranche himself pointed out, the comparison limps. He maintained that rest in bodies is nothing but the absence of motion, and hence is a "pure privation."[29] However, he insisted, by contrast, that mental *repos* is an act. Hence, it is not a pure privation. Furthermore, Malebranche insisted that insofar as the will is active, it is unlike the power of bodies to be in motion or at rest.[30]

However, Malebranche had an argument for (A) that did not depend on the comparison of consent with bodily rest. It began with one explicit premise,

    1. God's creation of things is the same as His continual conservation of things together with all that is real in them.

and one implicit premise,

> 2. What God causes, no creature causes.[31]

From these, Malebranche concludes,

> 3. God "cannot ... give His creatures true power, or establish them as causes of any physical reality" (*Search*, Eluc. 1, OC 3:26; LO 551).[32]

Assuming

> 4. Human beings cause their acts of consenting or suspending consent.

it follows that

> 5. Human acts of consenting or suspending consent do not have physical reality. The claim that *repos* in bodies is a privation enters the argument at this point. Its role is to ward off the objection that no operation of the mind can lack physical reality: *Being at rest* is something bodies do, and yet lacks physical reality; therefore it is possible that consenting or withholding consent should be something minds do, and yet lack physical reality.

Malebranche also provided an argument for (B). The argument was presented most fully in *Prémotion* (16:42–4), and even there it is far from clear and distinct. However, it can be reconstructed as follows. There are three cases of change to consider: Either a person begins by consenting with regard to a particular good and (i) that consent is replaced by consent to another good, or (ii) it simply ceases; or (iii) a person begins without consenting to a particular good and then consents to a particular good. Malebranche held that everyone constantly consents to the desire for the good in general. So in every case, consent to the desire for one good (or set of goods) is replaced by consent to the desire for another good (or set of goods). This establishes the first premise of the argument,

> 6. A person's coming to consent or ceasing to consent to a particular good is a sequence in which consent with regard to

one good (more precisely, one set of goods) is replaced by consent with regard to another.

The next premise is

7. Acts of mind with different objects do not differ in their physical reality.

Assuming, with Malebranche, that a real change in a thing is always a sequence of states of the thing that differ in their physical reality, it follows from (6) and (7) that

8. A person's coming to consent or ceasing to consent to a particular object is not a real change in the person.

Malebranche held that the moral quality, the sinfulness or meritoriousness, of human action depends solely on the acts of consenting or suspending consent whereby the agent freely loves a good absolutely and intrinsically. Therefore, he sometimes puts (B) by saying that consent pertains to the moral order rather than the physical order:

The moral is not the physical.... The morality of acts ... depends uniquely on the variety of the objects in which the will takes its rest ... And although the soul is the true cause of the free acts that we can call moral, since they produce nothing physical by their own efficacy ... it is not the true cause of its own modes ... (*Prémotion*, OC 16:42).[33]

In the context of seventeenth-century philosophy and theology, the two most controversial premises in these arguments are (2) and (7), and both played a role in Malebranche's intellectual exchanges with Arnauld and others.[34] However, whatever one may think of these premises, Malebranche's reconciliation of his position on free will with his occasionalism is not defensible. For the following principle is clearly true:

9. Any change in a thing that is not a real change in that thing is a real change in something else.

Some examples may help to drive the point home. Aquinas says that if a pillar comes to be on the right of an animal (as the animal moves around it), this is not a real change in the pillar (*Summa The-ologiae*, I.13.7). However, of course, it is real change in the animal. Peter Geach offered these examples: If Theaetetus grows while Socrates does not, then Socrates's becoming shorter than Theaetetus is not a real change in Socrates, but it is a real change in Theaetetus. Again, if a school boy comes to admire Socrates, Socrates's coming to be admired by the school boy is not a real change in Socrates, but it is a real change in the boy.[35]

Now (P), together with Malebranche's (B), implies

10. The change from not consenting to consenting, or from consenting to not consenting, with regard to a particular good, is a real change in something other than the person who consents or ceases to consent.

However, given Malebranche's acceptance of the theological principle that God does not undergo real change, his occasionalism commited him to the rejection of (10). He did think that a person's act of consenting or suspending consent to a desire is the occasional cause of real changes in the person. However, these subsequent changes are not the same change as the onset or cessation of act of consenting or the onset or cessation of the act of suspending consent. Such an onset or cessation, he maintained, is a free-floating, nonreal change, a change that is not a real change in anything. Such changes cannot occur. I conclude that even if Malebranche's controversial premises, (2) and (7), can be defended, his attempt to reconcile occasionalism with the doctrine of human freedom of indifference is a failure.

The difficulty of reconciling Malebranche's position on human freedom with his occasionalism suggests the question: To which of the two is he more firmly committed? Or again, which of the two would he have abandoned if confronted with a proof that they cannot both be true? There is no obvious answer. He said that to deny occasionalism is idolatry. However, he also said that to deny freedom of indifference is a horrible heresy that implies that God is a cruel tyrant. No doubt he would resist the conclusion that the two positions are inconsistent, and continue, with his considerable ingenuity, to look for a way of reconciling them.[36]

NOTES

1 Laporte, "La liberté selon Malebranche," p. 247. Laporte also comments extensively on Malebranche's position in *La Doctrine de la grâce chez Arnauld*.

2 The relation of occasionalism to dualism is taken up in several of the essays in Nadler, *Causation in Early Modern Philosophy*.

3 Frankfurt, "The Importance of What We Care About," 80.

4 André Robinet, in *Systeme et Existence dans l'oeuvre de Malebranche*, showed that the introduction of full-blown occasionalism in the second volume of *The Search* was accompanied by a number of changes in the first volume that brought the text into line with the new doctrine.

5 Malebranche takes the commandment to "love God with all our strength and all things for God through the free choice of our will," to mean that we act unjustly when we direct our will "toward something other than Him and unrelated to Him [*en aimant ... autre chose que lui & sans rapport à lui*]" (*Search*, IV.1, OC 2:12–4; LO 266–8).

6 The crucial texts from the Council of Trent are the fourth and fifth cannons of the "Decree on Justification": (4) If anyone shall say that when the free decision of a man, moved and aroused by God, when he assents to God who excites and calls him, does not cooperate in such a way as to add anything to his disposition and preparation for obtaining the grace of justification, and that he cannot dissent if he wants, but that, like something inanimate, does nothing whatever and is merely passive, *let him be denounced*. (5) If anyone shall say that after Adam's sin man's free will is lost and destroyed, or that it is a thing in name only, indeed a name without a corresponding reality, a fiction introduced into the Church by Satan, *let him be denounced*.

7 McCracken takes this passage to indicate that Malebranche "was forced to concede that he could not solve the problem of our freedom, or explain clearly how to reconcile our impotence with our "power" to resist our inclinations" (*Malebranche and British Philosophy*, 110). However, Malebranche did not think that attempts to reconcile human freedom and creaturely impotence necessarily "distract us" or cause us to "lose sight of ourselves." As I show in section seven below, Malebranche claimed that in the First Elucidation to *The Search* he solved the problem that McCracken mentions.

8 Malebranche's position that inner consciousness gives only confused knowledge of the mind and its acts is the main topic of Schmaltz, *Malebranche's Theory of the Soul*.

9 See also *Search*, Eluc. 1, OC 3:30; LO 554; and *Réponse au livre des Vraies et des fausses idées*, OC 6:163–4.

10  "At the outset of this work, I distinguished, as it were, two parts in the simple and indivisible being of the soul, the one purely passive and the other both active and passive. The first is the mind or the understanding; the second is the will" (*Search*, "Conclusion of the First Three Books," OC 1:488; LO 261).

11  The fact that the will is said to be distinct both from the intellect and from bodily motion, because the will is active, suggests that Malebranche's comparison involved two different senses of "active" and "passive."

12  "The just, the impious, the blessed, and the damned all love God with this love. Given that this natural love we have for God is the same thing as the natural inclination that carries us toward the good in general ... it is clear that all minds love God with this love because He is the universal good ..." (*Search*, III.1.iv, OC 1:405; LO 211). Cf. the *First Elucidation* (OC 3:33; LO 556): "The sinner can hate God only by making an abominable use of the impulse He constantly gives him in order to lead him to His love."

13  When we apprehend God as a good, during this life, the "passions and inclinations make us cold and indifferent in our love ... and thus we sense our indifference, and are inwardly convinced that we make use of our freedom when we love God" (*Search*, I.2, OC 1:52; LO 8).

14  Similarly, *TNG*, OC 5:118; R 170; *Réponse à la Dissertation*, OC 7:565; *Prémotion*, OC 16:46.

15  This led to Arnauld's complaint that Malebranche is an Epicurean. See Jean-Luc Solère, "Tout plaisir rend-il heureux? Une querelle entre Arnauld, Malebranche et Bayle."

16  "In order for an object to be loved, it is necessary that it actually be pleasing or that one hope that it will be pleasing one day: it must be agreeable to us and agree with the natural desire for happiness" (*Prémotion*, OC 16:17).

17  "The judgment of the mind, which rules the consent of the will, is only a simple repose on our part."

18  "It cannot be said that consent to the desire to be happy is free: for inner sensation convinces us of the contrary" (*Prémotion*, OC 16:34).

19  An account of freedom given by Locke in the chapter "Of Power" in the *Essay Concerning Human Understanding* may well have been borrowed from Malebranche:

>  This is the hinge on which turns the liberty of intellectual beings, in their constant endeavors after, and a steady prosecution of true felicity, that they can *suspend* this prosecution in particular cases, til they have looked before them, and informed themselves whether that particular thing which is then proposed, or desired, lie in the way of their main end, and make a real part of that which is their greatest good ... they [human beings] can suspend their desires, and

> stop them from determining their wills to any action, till they have duly and fairly examined the good and evil of it … (Book II, Chapter 21, "Of Power," #52; Locke, *Essay*, 266–7)

20 It is implicit when Malebranche said that we have "freedom of indifference by which we can refrain from consenting," and that we make use of this freedom of indifference both when we sin and when we love God (OC 1:52–4; LO 8–9).

21 For a different interpretation, see Schmaltz, *Malebranche's Theory of the Soul*, p. 200, ff. Schmaltz argued that Malebranche's remarks in the opening chapters of *The Search* about consent and the "settling" of the will upon one object rather than another, are inconsistent, and that he changed his account in Eluc. 1 and the replies to Arnauld, and then again in *Prémotion*.

The development of Malebranche's thought about freedom is also a major theme in Book III of Robinet, *Système et Existence dans l'oeuvre de Malebranche*.

22 "This principle of our determinations is always free with regard to particular goods" (Eluc. 1, OC 3:20; LO 548).

23 "This power of suspending the judgment which actually governs love, this power which is the principle of our liberty … is very diminished since the advent of sin, though it is not annihilated" (*TNG*, OC 5:126; R 177).

24 It is this variation that Malebranche was especially interested in establishing in view of his overall project in *TNG*. (See OC 5:131; R 181.)

25 True enough, Malebranche also says, "The love of all these particular goods is not at all naturally invincible" (*TNG*, OC 5:118; R 170). However, the word "naturally" restricts the claim to what would be true were it not for original sin, as the next sentence makes clear: "Man, considered such as God made him, can keep himself from loving the goods which do not fill up his whole capacity for loving."

26 See *Réponse à la Dissertation*, OC 7:566, and *Prémotion*, OC 16:4–5.

27 *Search*, III.1.i, OC 1:382–3; LO 198–9; and IV.1, OC 2:10; LO 265.

28 He first formulates the difficulty explicitly in the *Fifteenth Elucidation*:

> The main proof adduced by philosophers for the efficacy of secondary causes is drawn from man's will and his freedom. Man wills, he determines himself by himself; and to determine oneself is to act. Certainly, it is man who commits sin. God is not author of sin any more than He is of concupiscence and error. Therefore man acts through his own efficacy. (3:224; LO 668)

However, he referred his reader back to the *First Elucidation*, where the core of his solution is presented as part of his answer to a request from "some persons" that he explain "what God brings about in us, and what we bring about ourselves, when we sin" (OC 3:17; LO, 547).

The identity of the "philosophers" and "persons" to whom Malebranche referred is not known. Malebranche's biographer, P. André, says that Malebranche wanted to gather objections to his work, as Descartes had to the *Meditations*, but that the only objections he received in writing were those of the unfortunate Foucher, whose weakness discouraged others from entering the fray. As a result, "The best that P. Malebranche could achieve was that his friends should report orally the difficulties raised against his principles in conversations in Paris and in learned lectures," and it was on this basis that he wrote the *Elucidations*. (P. André, *La Vie du R. P. Malebranche*, p. 35–6; cf. LO 537.)

29 This point is part of Malebranche's criticism of Descartes' physics. Malebranche argued against Descartes that God causes motion through a "positive volition," but that "it seems to suffice that God wills matter to exits, in order not only that it exist, but also that it exist at rest" (*Search*, VI.2.ix, OC 2:429; LO 515).

Malebranche's account of motion seems to straddle the divide between what Alan Gabbey calls "realism" with regard to motion, the view that motion "exists as a real entity in some sense independently of the mobile," and "nominalism," the view that motion "has no such independent existence, being merely a *form fluens* represented by the successive places occupied by the mobile" (Gabbey, "New Doctrines of Motion," p. 651; see also Ariew and Gabbey, "The Scholastic Background").

30 For matter [unlike mind] is entirely without action. It has no force to stop its movement ..." (*Search*, I.1, OC 1:46; LO 4).

31 (2) is suggested, though not strictly implied, by the formulation of the task Malebranche undertakes in the *First Elucidation*: "They [the objectors] would have me explain, if I can, what God does in us, and what we ourselves do when we sin" (OC 3:17; LO 547).

32 Lennon and Olscamp translate "quelque réalité physique" as "any material reality." This may mislead the reader. Malebranche was not making a point about bodily reality, but about concrete reality, or what a Scholastic might call "being of nature."

33 Robert C. Sleigh, Jr., acutely points out that Malebranche's position

> has its problems. There is a difference between consenting to an inclination as opposed to refusing to consent to it. By Malebranche's lights, the ultimate disposition of one's soul may turn on that difference. Yet, according to Malebranche, when the soul passes from a state of indecision to a state of consent (or a state of refusal) no real change has occurred, although, of course, a change has occurred ("Determinism and Human Freedom", 1243–4).

However, Sleigh overlooks Malebranche's argument from (6) and (7) to (B).

For another comment on the difficulties inherent in Malebranche's position, see McCracken, *Malebranche and British Philosophy*, 108–10.

34 Regarding (2), Arnauld said to Malebranche

> The source of this monstrous mixture of truth and error [in your account of grace and free will] is that you distinguish what is from God and grace and what is from free will, as if one and the same movement of love could not be ... both from God, who forms it efficaciously in us by the power of his grace ... and from free will, which loves and wills to love when it is moved by grace. But you would not have had that thought, which entirely overthrows what the Church believes about grace, if you had remembered wherein St. Thomas locates the source of one of the errors regarding predestination, namely, that some seem to have distinguished *inter id quod est ex gratia, et quod est ex libero arbitrio, quasi non possit idem esse ex utroque*, something that he treats as being self-refuting and manifestly false. (*Dissertation sur les miracles de l'ancienne Loi*, 113–4)

Pierre Bayle came to Malebranche's defense in *Nouvelles de la République des Lettres*, and in the process defended (7). Bayle says that Descartes' philosophy makes it plain that the materiality of sensible pleasures is not "a physical or *inherent* quality of the pleasures," because "if pleasures are considered only according to their physical reality, no one of them is any more spiritual than any other" (*Nouvelles ... Lettres*, December, 1685). In reply, Arnauld said that it is absurd "to suppose that the relation of different modifications – thoughts, loves, desires, pleasures – to their objects is not essential to each modification, and is merely an extrinsic denomination ... of which the modification could be deprived while remaining the same in its physical reality, as if my perception of a spider could become the perception of an elephant without there being any physical or real change in the perception" (*Dissertation sur le prétendu bonheur des plaisirs des sens*, 61–2).

35 Geach, "What Actually Exists," pp. 66 and 74, and "Praying for Things to Happen," p. 99.

36 I presented earlier versions of this paper at Yale University and the University of Western Ontario, and would like to thank those who attended for their questions. I would also like to thank Thomas Lennon, James C. Morrison, Denis Moreau, and Steven Nadler for their comments.

# 9 Malebranche's Moral Philosophy: Divine and Human Justice

## I. INTRODUCTION

Given the radical theocentrism of Malebranche's philosophy – in which God is the only "true" good and "true" cause, in which "we see all things in God," in which God "moves our arm" on the occasion of our willing it, in which existence is only "continual creation" by God, and in which nature is "nothing but the general laws which God has established" (*TNG*, 1st Illustration, iii, OC 5:148; R 196) – it is to be expected that a theodicy ("the justice of God"[1]) will be the central and governing moral-political notion, in an almost Leibnizian way, and that this quasi-*Theodicée* will then shape (say) the meaning of Christian love, the Pauline notion that "the greatest of these is charity" (I Corinthians xiii). This expectation is borne out: For Malebranche a "love of union" should be reserved for God alone (the true good, the true cause) while finite creatures should receive only a "love of benevolence." As he says in the *Traité de morale*,

The word love is equivocal, and therefore we must take care of it ... [we must] love none but God with a love of union or conjunction, because he alone is the cause of our happiness ... we must love our neighbor not as our good, or the cause of our happiness, but only as capable of enjoying the same happiness with us ...

We may join ourselves to other men; but we must never adore them within the motion of our love, either as our good, or as capable of procuring us any good; we must love and fear only the true cause of good and evil; we must love and fear one but God in the creatures ... The creatures are all particular beings, and therefore cannot be one general and common good. (*Morale* II, 6, vi, OC 11:195)

The God-centeredness of Malebranche's thought determined every-thing he said about morality and justice.[2]

Malebranche wrote an entire book on practical philosophy – on moral and political ideas, on divine and human justice, on virtue and duty, on "order" and "relations of perfection," on the various kinds of "love," which is the *Traité de morale*, from 1684. However, the *Treatise on Morality*, for the most part, simply draws out the practical implications of Malebranche's metaphysics, theology, and epistemology. It is well to begin with a preliminary sketch of these implications before turning to a fuller treatment of Malebranche's texts.

1. In what amounts to a theodicy or God-justification in works beginning with *Traité de la nature et de la grâce* (1680), Malebranche urged that just as God governs the universe, justly, through constant, simple, uniform "Cartesian" general laws and "general wills" (*volontés générales*) that are "worthy" of him, and not through an *ad hoc* patchwork of arbitrary particular wills (*volontés particulières*) and "miracles," so too wise statesmen should will and legislate generally – and even ordinary men should subordinate their "particular" passions and self-love to a general love or "order" (TNG I, xviii–xxxviii, OC 5:31–47; R 118–27). This is the radical side of Malebranchian practical thought – a *recherche de la généralité*, which leads finally to Rousseau's "the general will is always right,"[3] and even (in a transmogrified form) to Robespierre's claim to incarnate the *volonté générale* of the French nation.[4] In this part of Malebranche's moral-political thought, *theodicée=généralité*, and it is precisely the generality of God's willing that incidentally throws up particular evils (such as "monsters") – evils that are justifiable because God did not translate them into existence by a positive *volonté particulière*.

2. Because God is the "true" cause, and finite created beings are mere "occasional" causes, we should reserve a love of "union" for God (our true good), and practice toward others only a well-wishing love of "benevolence" (a limited love for those who enjoy God with us) (*Morale* II, 6, vii, OC 11:195). Hence, for Malebranche, the Pauline saying, "the greatest of these is charity" was (ironically) over-general, needs to be

nuanced, turned into what Augustine had called "regulated" or "ordered" love (in *De Doctrina Christiana*).[5] Indeed, Malebranche redefined charity *as* the love of order, much as his contemporary and friend Leibniz redefined justice as ordered *caritas sapientis*, "the charity of the wise,"[6] not as a flood of undifferentiated emotion.

3. Malebranche's "occasionalism" led, not surprisingly, to difficulties in his moral philosophy, inasmuch as human beings are not "true" causes but must nonetheless "suspend" their consent to "particular" motives arising out of self-love, while they seek out and will "order" and *le bien général*. (However, this "suspension" and "will" must involve "nothing *physical* [*rien de physic*]," as Malebranche insisted in the *Reflexions sur la prémotion physique* from 1715 [*Reflexions XII*, OC 16:49–50].)

Despite these difficulties the notion of "will" is central in Malebranche's conception of God and of man. Unless God has a will (*en général*), he cannot have a "general will" (*en particulier*) to rule the universe through simple, constant, uniform "Cartesian" natural laws that he creates (avoiding all *ad hoc* "particular wills" and lawless miraculous interventions in nature). Unless man has a will he cannot freely and meritoriously determine himself to embrace *le bien général*, "order," and "relations of perfection," while shunning deceptive *biens particuliers* (*Morale* I, 1, vi–xiv, OC 11:19–22). Both God and man must will the general and flee the particular in Malebranche: God does so "naturally" (as it were), because *généralité* is "worthy" of him; men must strive to do so, with the help of Christ-distributed grace (TNG II, i–xxviii, OC 5:65–96; R 138–44). This means that "will" was nearly as important to Malebranche as to more celebrated voluntarists such as Augustine or Kant (with their notions of *bona voluntas* and "good will");[7] and although Malebranche's occasionalism, which deprives finite creatures of true causality, is problematical for human free will and real self-determination, it remains true that *Malebranchisme* contains an important voluntarist strand. God simply has a *volonté générale*, and men ought to strive to have one.

4. The notion that "we see all things in God" is (*inter alia*) a quasi-Platonic view of the status of moral ideas that descends to Malebranche through Augustinianism. The notion is quasi-Platonic in two senses: (a) "absolute" ideas cannot be derived from the observation of mere natural phenomena ("I prefer being called a visionary … to agreeing that bodies might enlighten us" [*Search*, Eluc. X, OC 3:131; LO 613]); and (b) the moral idea of "relations of perfection" can only be "expressed" in mathematical "relations of size" (*Dialogues VIII*.13, OC 12:190–1; JS 142). (This "descent" from Plato to Malebranche comes mainly from the *Phaedo*, in which moral and mathematical "absolute" ideas – equally universal, necessary, and free of Heraclitan flux – are summoned up by reminiscence, not "seen" in observed phenomena.)[8] All of this demi-Platonism is finally aimed (in the *Réflexions sur la prémotion Physique*) against the English "empiricism" of Hobbes and Locke: Malebranche's view is that neither English philosopher can even account for the *conceivability* of "moral necessity" (*Réflexions*, XVIII, OC 16:84 ff.). (Here Leibniz, and then later Kant, would agree with Malebranche.)[9]

5. For Malebranche, "grace" is an integral and necessary part of moral philosophy and moral activity, given his view in the *Traité de morale* that "charity does not always operate in the just themselves," that "men cannot … persevere in justice, if they are not often aided by the particular grace of Jesus Christ, which produces, augments and sustains charity against the continual effects of concupiscence" (*Morale* I, 4, vii–xv, OC 11:53–7). This doctrine is just "late-Augustinian"; but without this (unmeritable) "particular" grace one can't be just or charitable. To doubt that incapacity constitutes Pelagian criminal pride – the illusion/delusion of self-sufficiency (in mere created beings), which *should* be ruled out by occasionalism, by God's being the only "true" cause, the only real wielder of power (Search VI, 2, iii, OC 2:318; LO 451). Even Leibniz, for all his ecumenical rationalism in the *Theodicée* and *Nouveaux essais*, couldn't dispense with grace entirely;[10] much less can Malebranche do so, because the Malebranchian cosmos is not populated by

autonomous Leibnizian monads, but rather by the dependent creatures described by St. Paul in the *Acts of the Apostles* (17:28): in God "we live, move, and have our being."

## II.  MALEBRANCHE ON GENERAL AND PARTICULAR WILL

In the "Premier Eclaircissement" of the *Traité de la nature et de la grâce*, one sees at once that Malebranche was not going to treat divine *volonté générale* as something confined to theology, to moral questions of grace and merit; one sees that he intends to treat general will as something that is manifested in *all* of God's operations – as much in the realm of nature as in that of grace. Malebranche argued that "God acts by *volontés générales* when he acts as a consequence of general laws which he has established." Nature, he added, "is nothing but the general laws which God has established in order to construct or to preserve his work by the simplest means, by an action [that is] always uniform, constant, perfectly worthy of an infinite wisdom and of a universal cause" (*TNG* 1st Illustration, i and iii, OC 5:147–9; R 195–6). God, on this view, does not act by *volontés particulières*, by lawless *ad hoc* volitions, as do "limited intelligences" whose thought is not "infinite." Thus, for Malebranche, "to establish general laws, and to choose the simplest ones that are at the same time the most fruitful, is a way of acting worthy of him whose wisdom has no limits." On the other hand, "to act by *volontés particulières* shows a limited intelligence that cannot judge the consequences or the effects of less fruitful causes" (TNG, 1st Illustration, xv, OC 5:166; R 211).

Even at this point, Malebranche's argument contained some points that could be read "legally," as elements of a theodicy: divine general will manifests itself in general laws that are "fruitful" and "worthy" of infinite wisdom, whereas particular will is "limited," comparatively unintelligent, and lawless. Indeed Malebranche himself occasionally "politicized" his argument, particularly in his effort to *justify* God's acting (exclusively) through *volontés générales*. If "rain falls on certain lands, and if the sun roasts others ... if a child comes into the world with a malformed and useless head ... this is not at all because God wanted to produce those effects by *volontés particulières*; it is because he has established [general] laws for the communication of motion, whose effects are necessary consequences." Thus, according to Malebranche, "one cannot say that God acts through caprice or ignorance" in permitting malformed children to be born or unripe fruit to fall. "He has not established the laws of the communication of motion for the purpose of producing monsters, or of making fruits fall before their maturity;" he has willed these laws "because of their fruitfulness, and not because of their sterility" (TNG, I, xviii–xix, OC 5:32; R 118–9). Those who claim that God *ought*, through special, *ad hoc volontés particulières*, to suspend natural laws if their operation will harm the virtuous or the innocent, or that he ought to confer grace only on those who will actually be saved by it, fail to understand that it is not worthy of an infinitely wise being to abandon general rules in order to find a suppositious perfect fit between the particular case of each finite being and a *volonté particuliére* suited to that case alone.

By this point, evidently, the theological (and physical) notion of *volonté générale* is becoming "legalized." *Volonté générale* originally manifested itself in general laws that were wise and fruitful; now that will, expressed in those laws, is *just* as well, and it is quite wrong to say that God ought to contrive a *volonté particulière* suited to each case, even though the generality of his will and of his laws will mean that grace will occasionally fall on a hardened heart incapable of receiving it (TNG I, xix ff., OC 5:32 ff.; R 118 ff). God, Malebranche urged, loves his wisdom more than he loves humankind ("c'est que Dieu aime davantage sa sagesse que son ouvrage" [TNG I, xxxix "addition," OC 5:47]). His wisdom is expressed in general laws, the operation of which may have consequences (monstrous children, unripened fruit) that are not *themselves* willed and that cannot therefore give rise to charges of divine injustice, caprice, or ignorance.

If Malebranche, in pleading the "cause" of God (to use Leibniz' legal phrase),[11] viewed divine *volonté générale* as issuing in wise and just laws, the *Traité de la nature et de la grâce* is further (and quite explicitly) politicized by an analogy that Malebranche himself drew between a well-governed earthly kingdom and a well-governed Creation. He began with an argument about enlightened and unenlightened will: "The more enlightened an agent is, the more extensive are his *volontés*. A very limited mind undertakes new schemes at every moment; and when he wants to execute one of them, he uses several means, of which some are always useless." However, a "broad and penetrating mind," he went on, "compares and weighs all things: he never forms plans except with the knowledge that he has the means to execute them." Malebranche then moved to his political analogy: "A great number of laws in a state" – presumably a mere concatenation of many *volontés particulières* – "often shows little penetration and breadth of mind in those who have established them: it is often the mere experience of need, rather than wise foresight, which has ordained them." God *qua* just legislator has none of these defects, Malebranche claimed: "He need not multiply his *volontés*, which are the executive laws of his plans, any further than necessity obliges." He must act through *volontés générales* "and thus establish a constant and regulated order" by "the simplest means." Those who want God to act, not through "les loix ou les volontés générales," but through *volontés particulières*, simply "imagine that God at every moment is performing miracles in their favor." This partisanship for the particular, Malebranche said, "flatters the self-love which relates everything to itself," and "accommodates itself quite well" to ignorance (TNG I, xxxviii-XL, OC 5:46, 63; R 126–7).

Malebranche certainly believed that those who imagine a God thick with *volontés particulières* will use that alleged divine particularism to rationalize their own failure to embrace general principles. Indeed, he appealed to the notion of *particularisme* in attempting to explain the lamentable diversity of the world's moral opinions and practices. In the *Traité de morale* (1684) Malebranche argued that although "universal reason is always the same" and "order is immutable," nonetheless "morality changes according to countries and according to the times." Germans think it virtuous to drink to excess; European nobles think it "generous" to fight duels in defense of their honor. Such people "even imagine that God approves their conduct," that, in the case of an aristocratic duel, he "presides at the judgment and ... awards the palm to him who is right" (*Morale* I, vii–x, OC 11:31–3). Of course, one can only imagine this if one thinks that God acts by *volontés particulières*. If even he is thought to operate particularly, why should not men as well? The man who imputes particular wills to God by "letting himself be led by imagination, his enemy," will also have his own *"Morale particulière*, his own devotion, his favorite virtue." What is essential is that one abandon *particularisme*, whether as something ascribed to God or as something merely derived from human "inclinations" and "humors." It is "immutable order" that must serve as our "inviolable and natural law," and "imagination" that must be suppressed (Ibid.), for order is general, while imagination is all too particular.

Malebranche's notion that those who believe that they are the beneficiaries of a miraculous *Providence particulière* are suffering from acute egomania – in effect a "love of union" with themselves – was strongly reinforced in the 1683 *Méditations chrétiennes*. In the eighth *méditation* Malebranche insisted that "the New Testament [*la nouvelle alliance*] is in perfect conformity with the simplicity of natural laws," even though those general laws "cause so many evils in the world." The New Testament promises *des biens éternels* to the just as compensation for their patience in enduring monstrous children and unripened fruit; therefore, it is "not at all necessary that God perform miracles often" in order to deliver the just from their "present evils." To be sure, Malebranche conceded, under the Old Testament, miracles – at least, "what are called miracles" – were more necessary; the ancient Jews, who lacked Christ's salvific grace and who were "un peu grossiers et charnels," asked for exceptions in their favor from general and simple laws. This, according to Malebranche, led God, "at least in appearance," to "trouble the simplicity of the laws" in Biblical times. However, Christians, Malebranche insisted, should know better, and must live with the simplicity of (occasionally ruinous) laws; Malebranche condemned those who, "failing to respect the order of nature," imagine that on all occasions God should "protect them in a particular way [*d'une manière particulière*]." Is some people's reliance on God, Malebranche asked rhetorically, a sign of "the greatness of their faith," or rather a mark of "a stupid and rash confidence" that makes them have contempt for human ways? Malebranche did not doubt that the piety of those who claim to be under "une protection de Dieu toute particulière" can often be sincere. That sincerity, however, is commonly "neither wise nor enlightened," but rather "filled with *amour-propre* and with secret pride." Some people, Malebranche added, fancy that God is only good insofar as he applies himself to making exceptions to the rules of wisdom; but it should be remembered that "God constantly follows the general laws which he has very wisely established." Here, then, *particularisme* is identified with self-love, rashness, stupidity, and making exceptions to just general laws (Méd. Chrét. VIII.5; OC 10:84).

So wise, constant, and just are God's *volontés générales*, in Malebranche's view, that it is often a moral wrong on one's part not to accept and respect these general wills and to make them the measure of human conduct. In one of his numerous defenses of *Nature et grâce*, Malebranche argued that "if God did not act in consequence of general laws which he has established, no one would ever make any effort. Instead of descending a staircase step by step, one would rather throw himself out of the windows, trusting himself to God." Why would it be sin as well as folly to hurl oneself from a window? "It would be sin," Malebranche answered, "because it would be tempting God: it would be claiming to obligate him to act in a manner unworthy of him, or through *volontés particulières*"; it would amount to telling God "that his work is going to perish, if he himself does not trouble the simplicity of his ways." In addition to sin, of course, hurling oneself would be folly, for one must be mad to imagine that "God must regulate his action by our particular needs, and groundlessly change, out of love for us, the uniformity of his conduct" (*Réponse au livre de M. Arnauld*, OC 6–7:43).

### III.  MALEBRANCHE'S RESPONSE TO HIS CRITICS

For Malebranche's orthodox and conservative critics (most notably Bossuet),[12] perhaps the most distressing aspect of Malebranche's theory of divine *volonté générale* was the much-diminished weight and value given to literally read Scripture. In *Nature et grâce*, Malebranche urged that "those who claim that God has particular plans and wills for all the particular effects which are produced in consequence of general laws" ordinarily rely not on philosophy but on the authority of Scripture to "shore up" their "feeling." (The verb and noun are sufficiently revealing.) However, Malebranche argued, "since Scripture was made for everybody, for the simple as well as for the learned, it is full of *anthropologies*." Scripture, continued Malebranche, endows God with "a body, a throne, a chariot, a retinue, the passions of joy, of sadness, of anger, of remorse, and the other movements of the soul;" it even goes beyond this and attributes to him "ordinary human ways of acting, in order to speak to the simple in a more sensible way." St. Paul, in order to accommodate himself to everyone, speaks of sanctification and predestination "as if God acted ceaselessly" through *volontés particulières* to produce those particular effects; even Christ himself "speaks of his Father as if he applied himself, through comparable *volontés*, to clothe the lilies of the field and to preserve the least hair on his disciples' heads." Despite all these "anthropologies" and "as ifs," introduced solely to make God lovable to "even the coarsest minds," Malebranche concluded, one must use the idea of God (qua perfect being), coupled with those nonanthropological scriptural passages that are in conformity to this idea, in order to correct the sense of some other passages that attribute "parts" to God, or "passions like our own" (TNG I.1.vii, OC 5:61–2; R 136–7).

The notion that Scripture represents God as a man who has "passions of the soul" and *volontés particulières* merely to acccommodate the weakness of "even the coarsest minds" leads to a difficulty that an Augustinian, and certainly a Jansenist, would find distressing. Pascal argued in his *Écrits sur la grâce* that God's prelapsarian *volonté générale* to save all people is replaced after the Fall by the election of a few for salvation through *miséricorde*, or "pity" (though none merited it).[13] Antoine Arnauld, in the preface to his translation of Augustine's *De correptione et gratia*, also stressed an undeserved divine *miséricorde*, which God might with perfect justice have withheld.[14] "Pity," of course, on a Malebranchian view, is a "passion of the soul," but it is only through weakness and anthropomorphism that we imagine these passions to animate God. If an *être parfait* does not "really" have these passions, it cannot be the case that – as in Pascal – a *volonté générale* to save all is replaced by a pitiful *volonté absolue* to save a few. Indeed, whereas in Pascal *volonté générale* comes first and gets "replaced" by *miséricorde*, in Malebranche divine general will justly governs the realms of nature and grace from the outset, once the world has been created by a *volonté particulière*.

Far from abandoning his position when he was accused of "ruining" Providence (in a work such as Jurieu's *Esprit de M. Arnauld*),[15] Malebranche maintained it stoutly in the "Dernier Eclaircissement" of *Nature et grâce*, provocatively entitled "The Frequent Miracles of the Old Testament Do Not Show at All that God Acts Often by Particular Wills," which he added to the fourth edition in 1684. The "proofs" that he has drawn from the idea of an infinitely perfect being, Malebranche insisted, make it clear that "God executes his designs by general laws." On the other hand, it is not easy to demonstrate that God operates ordinarily through *volontés partic-uliéres*, "though Holy Scripture, which accommodates itself to our weakness, sometimes represents God as a man, and often has him act as men act" (TNG, "Dernier Eclaircissement," OC 5:204). Here, as in the main text of *Nature et grâce*, the key notion is weakness, and any notion of divine *volonté particulière* simply accommodates that *faiblesse*. This was why Malebranche could maintain – this time in the "Troisiéme Eclaircissement" of 1683 – that "there are ways of acting [that are] simple, fruitful, general, uniform and constant," and that manifest "wisdom, goodness, steadiness [and] immutability in those who use them." On the other hand, there are also ways that are "complex, sterile, particular, lawless and inconstant," and that reveal "lack of intelligence, malignity, unsteadiness [and] levity in those who use them" (TNG, 3 ième Eclaircissement, vi, OC 5:180). Thus, a very effective heap of moral-legal execrations is mounded around any *volonté particuliére*, which turns out to be complex, sterile, lawless, inconstant, unintelligent, malignant, and frivolous.

Indeed, for Malebranche it was precisely *volonté particulière*, and not *volonté générale*, that "ruins" Providence and divine justice. In his *Réponse à une dissertation de M. Arnauld contre un éclaircissement de la nature et de la grâce* (1685), he argued that, if Arnauld's insistence on miracles and constant divine *volontés particulières* does not "overturn" Providence, it at least "degrades it, humanizes it, and makes it either blind, or perverse."

Is there wisdom in creating monsters by *volontés particulières*? In making crops grow by rainfall, in order to ravage them by hail? In giving to men a thousand impulses of grace which misfortunes render useless? In making rain fall equally on sand and on cultivated ground? But all this is nothing. Is there wisdom and goodness in making impious princes reign, in suffering so great a number of heresies, in letting so many nations perish? Let M. Arnauld raise his head and discover all the evils which happen in the world, and let him justify Providence, on the supposition that God acts and must act through *volontés particulières*. (*Réponse à une dissertation de Mr. Arnauld*, OC 6–7:591–2)

It was Malebranche's view, in fact, that the classical "theodicy problems" of reconciling a morally and physically imperfect world with God's "power," "goodness," and "wisdom" can *only* be solved by insisting that God wills generally. "God loves men, he wills to save them all," Malebranche asserted, "for order is his law." Nonetheless, God "does not will to *do* what is necessary in order that all [men] know him and love him infallibly," and this is simply because "order does not permit that he have practical *volontés* proper to the execution of this design.... He must not disturb the simplicity of his ways."[16]

In his final work, published in the year of his death (1715), Malebranche reformulated this argument in an even stronger way – a way that Leibniz, among others, found excessive.

Infinity in all sorts of perfections is an attribute of the divinity, indeed his essential attribute, that which encloses all the others. Now between the finite and the infinite, the distance is infinite; the relation is nothing. The most excellent of creatures, compared to the divinity, is nothing; and God counts it as nothing in relation to himself.... It seems to me evident, that God conducts himself according to what he is, in remaining immobile, [even while] seeing the demon tempt, and man succumb to the temptation.... His immobility bears the character of his infinity.... If God, in order to stop the Fall of Adam, had interrupted the ordinary course of his *providence générale*, that conduct would have expressed the false judgment that God had counted the worship that Adam rendered him as something, with respect to his infinite majesty. Now God must never trouble the simplicity of his ways, nor interrupt the wise, constant and majestic course of his ordinary providence, by a particular and miraculous providence.... God is infinitely wise, infinitely just, infinitely good, and he does men all the good he can–not absolutely, but acting according to what he is.... (*Réflexions* xix, OC 16:118)

After this, Malebranche's insistence that, nonetheless, "God sincerely wills to save all men" rings a little hollow. It is no wonder that Leibniz, for all his general agreement with Malebranche, complained that "I do not know whether one should have recourse to the expedient [of saying] that God, by remaining immobile during the Fall of man ... marks [in that way] that the most excellent creatures are nothing in relation to him." For Leibniz, that way of putting the matter can be abused, and can even lead to "the despotism of the supralapsarians."[17]

According to Malebranche, the theodicy problems that generality and simplicity of will are meant to solve *must* have a resolution, because the radical imperfection and evil in the universe are all too real, not merely apparent. "A monster," he declared, "is an imperfect work, whatever may have been God's purpose in creating it."

Some philosophers, perverted by an extravagant metaphysics, come and tell me that God wills evil as positively and directly as the good; that he truly only wills the beauty of the universe ... [and] ... that the world is a harmony in which monsters are a necessary dissonance; that God wants sinners as well as the just; and that, just as shadows in a painting make its subjects stand out, and give them relief, so too the impious are absolutely necessary in the work of God, to make virtue shine in men of good will.[18]

Those who reason along these lines, in Malebranche's view, are trying to resolve moral dilemmas and salvage divine justice by appealing to aesthetic similes; but the method will not serve. "Shadows are necessary in a painting and dissonances in music. Thus it is necessary that women abort and produce an infinity of monsters. What a conclusion!" He ends by insisting, "I do not agree that there is evil only in appearance."[19] Hence, *volonté générale* alone, which wills (positively) the good and only *permits* evil as the unavoidable consequence of general and simple laws, is the sole avenue of escape from theodicy problems if one calls evil "real."

## IV.  A POLITICIZATION OF DIVINE GOVERNANCE

Some of the contemporary opponents of Malebranche – particularly the orthodox Cartesian Pierre-Sylvain Régis – thought that the notion of a just and justifiable divine *volonté générale* was "political" in a wholly bad sense, that Malebranche had confused divine governance with ordinary human governance and hence had politicized theology. "I shall not say," Régis observed, "that God acts by *volontés générales*, or by *volontés particulières*, because these two kinds of will cannot be suitable to a perfect being." If God acted only through *volontés générales*, this would mean "that he willed things only in a general way, without descending to anything particular, as a king governs a kingdom through general laws, not having the power to guide each subject." A mere king falls back on general laws and *volonés générales* only because of political impotence, but "God cannot have *volontés générales* ... because these *volontés* suppose an impotence in God Which I cannot attribute to him." Because the notion that God operates through *volontés particulières* is no better, in Régis's view ("it would follow that the nature of God would be composed of as many different wills as there are particular things which God wills, which is repugnant to his simplicity"), it must be the case that "God acts by a simple, eternal and immutable will which embraces indivisibly and in a single act everything that is and will be."[20]

Malebranche, as it happens, had an answer to this kind of charge. In the seventh of his *Méditations chrétiennes et métaphysiques* (1683), he warned that when one says that God "permits certain natural disorders, such as the generation of monsters, the violent death of a good man, or something similar," one must not imagine that there is an autonomous "nature" to which God has given some of his power and that acts independently of God, "in the same way that a prince lets ministers act, and permits disorders which he cannot stop." God *could* stop all "disorders" (though a prince cannot) by acting through a multiplicity of *volontés particulières*, which would remedy all particular evils. Acting in this fashion, however, would derogate from the simplicity of his ways; God, Malebranche argued, "does good because he wants his work to be perfect," and he *permits* (rather than *does*) evil not because he "positively and directly" wills it but because "he wants his manner of acting to be simple, regular, uniform and constant, because he wants his conduct to be worthy of him and to wear visibly the character of his attributes" (Méd. Chrét. VII.19, OC 10:76–7). Thus, for Malebranche, to act by *volontés générales* and general laws does not manifest a quasi-human impotence at all: God can (of course) will anything, but acting through *volontés particulières* would not be worthy of him. What he can do is simply a question of power; what he actually wills is a question of wisdom and justice.

If there were critics of Malebranche who claimed that he had illegitimately thought of God as a mere earthly king, there were others who thought that political-legal analogies were, in themselves, perfectly acceptable, and that Malebranche had simply pitched upon false ones. In his *Réflexions sur le système de la nature et de la grâce* (1685), Antoine Arnauld argued that "there is no contradiction whatever [in the fact] that God wills by a *volonté absolue et particulière* the contrary of what he wills *en général* by an antecedent will, just as a good king wills by an antecedent will that all his subjects live contentedly, though by a consequent will he executes those who disturb public tranquility by murders and violence."[21] In Arnauld's view, Malebranche's theory of general justice suffered from the defect of virtually equating *volonté générale*, general law, wisdom, justice, and "the simplest means;" these terms, according to Arnauld, are not equivalent, and what "wisdom" requires (e.g., the remedying of particular evils) may not be attainable by "the simplest means," either for God or for a human ruler.

For Arnauld, Malebranche's fatal confusion was the conflation of general will and general law; in fact, the operation of a general law may contain a divine *volonté particulière*. In "proving" this, Arnauld had recourse to Scripture, which Malebranche had minimized. It is precisely the Old Testament, for Arnauld, that "recounts to us that a stone, falling high from a tower, smashed the head of Abimelech, son of Gideon, who had had all his brothers, save one, killed." One cannot reasonably doubt, Arnauld argued, that this stone "observed the general laws of the movement of heavy things," and that it crushed Abimelech's head "according to the laws of the communication of movement;" nevertheless, this generality of law does not *exclude* a divine particular will at all:

One can thus say that God acted, in injuring this wicked man, according to the general laws of nature, which he himself established. But does it follow from this that he acted only according to these laws, and that he had not the slightest *volonté particulière* in this matter? To judge of this, let us look farther back. This rock fell from this tower. Was it by itself? No. It was a woman who threw it. Now who can doubt that God led the will and the hand of this woman, if one considers that Scripture teaches us that this happened through a just vengeance of God, which had been predicted by the youngest of the children of Gideon, who had escaped the cruelty of his brother?[22]

If one could look back, one would often find a particular divine contribution to effects that *seem* to be "only consequences of the general laws of nature." Scripture teaches us where to find these hidden particular interventions. To deny these interventions is to deny that God can realize justice in this world, by punishing Abimelech, for example. Malebranchian generality thus undercuts justice and wisdom; it forbids God to do in particular what justice requires and makes him the "slave" of his own simplicity. In short, for Arnauld it was a Malebranchian confusion to identify general law with general will, for a *loi générale* can "carry out" a divine *volonté particulière*. Between Arnauld and Malebranche there was no middle ground that can be jointly occupied: for Arnauld, Scripture limits what philosophy can reveal about God; for Malebranche, it is philosophy that limits Scripture (and its "anthropologies").

Arnauld's criticisms, nonetheless, finally brought Malebranche to argue only that God "ordinarily" acts by *volontés générales* and "not often" by *volontés particulières* (*Réponse à une dissertation de M. Arnauld*, OC 6–7: 493ff.). This grudging admission opened the door, however narrowly, to Fénelon's point that "not often" is an indeterminate notion, that the frequency of *volontés particulières* must be relative to what "wisdom" requires.[23] This may be why Malebranche uses the notion of *volontés générales* somewhat sparingly in his later works.

## V. THE CRITIQUE OF DIVINE SOVEREIGNTY

In his last work, the *Réflexions sur la prémotion physique*, published in the year of his death (1715), Malebranche found an opportunity to show that his notions of *volonté générale* and general law have a general moral significance that can be used in refuting theories of justice that rely primarily on sovereign power, such as Hobbes'. The *Réflexions* were a commentary on Laurent Boursier's quasi-Jansenist *De l'action de Dieu sur les créatures* (1713)–a large section of which attempted to refute Malebranche's theory of the divine *modus operandi*. In *De l'action de Dieu*, Boursier treats God as a "sovereign" whose will is unrestricted by any necessity to act only through general laws ("God has willed [the world] thus, because he willed it") and argues that Malebranche's notion of divine wisdom renders God "impotent." "The sovereign who governs," Boursier claimed, whether God or a prince, "causes inferiors to act as he wills." He does this through "command": "He interposes his power in order to determine them." And "inferiors," for their part, act only "because they are excited and determined by the prince . . . they act in consequence of his determination."

Because God is a powerful sovereign who has willed the world to be what it is simply "because he has willed it," one cannot say that he prefers a Malebranchian generality or "the simplest means," or, indeed, that he prefers anything at all. The "greatness and majesty of the Supreme Being" must make us realize that "everything that he can will with respect to what is outside himself" is "equal" to him. Malebranche, Boursier complained, does not see that God can equally will whatever is in his power: "What an idea of God! He wishes, and he does not accomplish; he does not like monsters, but he makes them; he does not attain the perfection which he desires in his works: he cannot fashion a work without defects ... his wisdom limits his power. A strange idea of God! An impotent being, an unskillful workman, a wisdom based on constraint, a sovereign who does not do what he wills, an unhappy God."[24]

In his response to Boursier's theory of sovereignty based on will, command, and power, Malebranche actually abandoned the terms *volonté générale* and *volonté particulière* (conceivably because of the constant criticisms of Régis, Arnauld, Fénelon, and others), but he did not abandon the concepts for which the terms stood; thus, *volonté générale* and general law become "eternal law," while *volonté particulière* becomes *volonté absolue et bizarre* (which is more striking still). "My present design," Malebranche declared, "is to prove that God is essentially wise, just and good ... that his *volontés* are not at all purely arbitrary – that is to say that they are not wise and just simply because he is all-powerful ... but because they are regulated by the eternal law ... a law which can consist only in the necessary immutable relations which are among the attributes and perfections which God encloses in his essence." The ideas that we have of wisdom, justice, and goodness "are quite different from those that we have of omnipotence." To say that the *volontés* of God are "purely arbitrary," that "no reason can be given for his *volontés*, except his *volontés* themselves," and that everything that he wills and does is just, wise, and good because he is omnipotent and has a "sovereign domain" over his creatures – is "to leave the objections of libertines in all their force" (*Réflexions*, xviii–xix, OC 16:93–104).

The notion that God wills in virtue of eternal law, not simply through the bare possession of sovereign domain, led Malebranche to a criticism of Hobbes (and Locke) that is an interesting expansion of his notion of *volonté générale*. "If," Malebranche said, "God were only omnipotent, and if he were like princes who glory more in their power than in their nature," then "his sovereign domain, or his independence, would give him a right to everything, or he would not act as [an] all-powerful [being]." If this were true of God, then "Hobbes, Locke and several others would have discovered the true foundations of morality: authority and power giving, without reason, the right to do whatever one wills, when one has nothing to fear." This legal-positivist view of either human or divine justice Malebranche characterized as "mad," and he urged that those who "attribute this mode of operation to God" apparently "prefer force, the law of brutes (that which has granted to the lion an empire over the animals), to reason" (*Réflexions*, xviii, OC 16:93, 98).

However unfair this may be to Hobbes, and still more to Locke – though at least Hobbes did actually say, in chapter 31 of *Leviathan*, that "irresistible power" carries with it a natural right to "dominion"[25] – Malebranche's last work showed that he thought that rule through *volontés* that are *particulières* or *absolues* or (even) *bizarres* was wrong in either human or divine governance, and that rule through eternal laws that are of general validity is right. Of course, Malebranche was not alone in this; since Descartes' time a controversy had raged over the question of whether there *are* any eternal laws that God "finds" in his understanding and "follows" in his volitions. Leibniz (following Plato's *Euthyphro*) put forward a theory of general, nonarbitrary divine justice in his *Théodicée* (1710) that was very close to Malebranche's and criticized Hobbes along (roughly) Malebranchian lines in his *Opinion on the Principles of Pufendorf*.[26] Thus, arguments against Hobbism based on the notion that there are eternal laws of justice that keep divine will from being "willful" were certainly not scarce at the turn of the eighteenth century; and Malebranche was in perfect accord with Leibniz in disputing Hobbes (and Descartes) on this point.

In connection with his doctrine that God never operates through a *volonté* that is *absolue* or *bizarre*, but only through love of the eternal law, which is "co-eternal" with him, Malebranche designed one of the strikingly imaginative stage settings that even Voltaire found impressive:

If God were only all-powerful, or if he gloried only in his omnipotence, without the slightest regard for his other attributes – in a word, without consulting his consubstantial law, his lovable and inviolable law – how strange his plans would be! How could we be certain that, through his omnipotence, he would not, on the first day, place all of the demons in heaven, and all the saints in hell, and a moment after annihilate all that he had done! Cannot God, *qua* omnipotent, create each day a million planets, make new worlds, each more perfect than the last, and reduce them each year to a grain of sand? (*Réflexions* xviii, OC 16:100)

Fortunately, according to Malebranche, though God is in fact all-powerful and "does whatever he wills to do," nonetheless he does not will to do anything except "according to the immutable order of justice." This is why Malebranche insisted, in four or five separate passages of the *Réflexions sur la prémotion physique*, that St. Paul always said "O alitudo divitiarum Sapientiae et Scientiae Dei" and never "O altitudo voluntatis Dei." Will can be willful, if its only attribute is power, and that attribute is the one that Boursier (and Hobbes) wrongly endow with excessive weight.

Despite some disagreements with Malebranche, Leibniz could send a copy of the *Théodicée* to the Oratorian in the confident belief that most of it would prove congenial, and Malebranche's acknowledgment of Leibniz's present ("you prove quite well ... that God ... must choose the best") showed Leibniz to be right.[27] A shared Augustinian Platonism and love of eternal mathematical "order," a shared concern to "justify" God, formed the *rapport* between Malebranche and Leibniz; and, if Malebranche was a more nearly orthodox Cartesian than his Hannoverian correspondent, even the Oratorian shared Leibniz's distaste for the Cartesian notion that God wills to create mathematical, logical, and moral truth *ex nihilo*.

## VI.   ORDER, LIBERTY, AND "RELATIONS OF PERFECTION"

In treating Malebranche – particularly when *Nature et grâce* is the focus of attention – it is common enough to speak as if his whole philosophy confined itself to *elevating volonté générale* and execrating *volonté particuliére*. However, the notion of "general will" was not, for Malebranche, a complete or exhaustive doctrine; and even in *Nature et grâce* itself one finds, in addition to *généralité* and "Cartesian" simplicity, the notions of "order" (or "relations of perfection") and of "liberty," as well as the idea that men are merely the "occasional" casues of their own actions (while God the Father is *cause générale* of nature and grace), and the Jesus Christ *qua* man is the "occasional cause" of the distribution of grace to particular persons (TNG, II (passim), OC 5:65ff.; R 138ff.). Obviously, then, light needs to be thrown on those Malebranchian practical ideas which go beyond generality and simplicity; but one must also show the *rapport* between these "new" ideas and the *généralité* for which Malebranche was famous (or notorious). For this, one must consult not just *Nature et grâce*, but also – especially to gain a fuller idea of Malebranchian "order," and of liberty as the "suspension" of consent – the *Traité de morale*, the *Entretiens sur la métaphysique*, and the *Prémotion physique*.

The less-than-total importance of *volonté générale* in Malebranche became clear if one turns from the *Traité de la nature et de la grâce*, which is indeed mainly dominated by the notion of justifiable divine "general will," to a work such as the *Traité de morale*, where one finds different but equally characteristic Malebranchian practical ideas. In the opening chapter of the *"Premiére Partie"* of the *Traité de morale*, indeed, Malebranche began with the now familiar general – particular dichotomy, and only by a series of small steps arrives at the notion that there may be something of philosophical value *beyond* the "constancy" and "uniformity" of *volonté générale and loi générale*: and this something beyond he calls "order" or "relations of perfection" (*Morale* I, 1, OC 11:17–27).

"If," Malebranche began by observing, "God moved bodies by *volontés particuliéres*, it would be a crime to avoid by flight the ruins of a collapsing building; for one cannot, without injustice, refuse to return to God the life he has given us, if he demands it." If God positively willed everything in particular, "it would be an insult to God's wisdom, to correct the course of rivers, and turn them to places lacking water: one would have to follow nature and remain at rest." Because, however, God acts, not through *volontés particulieres* but through *des lois générales*, "one corrects his work, without injuring his wisdom; one resists his action, without resisting his will; because he does not will positively and directly everything that he does" (*Morale* I, 1, OC 11:25). He permits disorder, but he loves order.

The case is quite different, however, in Malebranche's view, if one "resists" or "corrects" the action of humans. "What is true of God is not so of men, of the general cause as of particular causes." When one resists the action of men, one "offends" them: "for, since they act only by *volontés particuliéres*, one cannot resist their acts without resisting their plans." However, in "resisting" God's general laws, manifested in something like the collapse of a building, one not only offends "not at all," one even favors God's plans. This is simply because the general laws that God follows do not always produce results which "conform" to order, or to "the best work"

(*Morale* I, 1, OC 11:26). (After all, as Malebranche remarks in *Nature et grâce*, "if one drops a rock on the head of passers-by, the rock will always fall at an equal speed, without discerning the piety, or the station, or the good or evil dispositions of those who pass by" (TNG I, 1, vii, OC 5:63; R 137). He gave this same thought a complacent cast in the *Méditations chrétiennes*, where he urged that God, by permitting general laws to operate, lets "the ruins of a house fall on a just person who is going to the aid of an unfortunate, as well as on a villain who is going to cut the throat of an *homme de bien*" [*Méd. Chrét.* VII, 19, OC 10:77].) Hence, there is no moral obligation, in Malebranche's opinion, to allow *les lois générales* to "cause death," or even to let their operation "inconvenience" or "displease" us. Our duty, Malebranche concluded, "consists then in submitting ourselves to God's law, and to following order;" and we can know this order only through "union" with "the eternal Word, with universal reason" – the one thing all humans share, whatever their "particular" dispositions (*Morale* I, 1, OC 11:26–7).

What did Malebranche mean in calling this "order" – something that transcends the *généralité* of *Nature et grâce* – a "relation of perfection?" "In supposing that man is reasonable," the *Traité de Morale* argues, and even that he belongs to a *société spirituelle* with God, which "nourishes" all "minds," one cannot deny that man "knows something of what God thinks, and of the way in which god acts." For "in contemplating the intelligible substance of the Word, which alone makes me reasonable," Malebranche continued, "I can clearly see the relations of size [*rapports de grandeur*] which exist between the intelligible ideas which it [the Word] encloses;" and these relations are "the same eternal truths that God sees," for God sees, as does a man, that "two times two makes four." A man can also discover, Malebranche insisted, "at least confusedly," the existence of "relations of perfection [*rapports de perfection*]" which constitute the "immutable order that God consults when he acts – an order which ought also to regulate the esteem and love of all intelligent beings" (*Morale*, I, 1, vi, OC 11:19).

This is, perhaps, more eloquent than clear; but in a succeeding passage Malebranche fleshed out the notion of "relations of perfection." The reason that it is true that "a beast is more estimable than a stone, and less estimable than a man" is that "there is a greater relation of perfection from the beast to the stone, than from the stone to the beast," and that there is "a greater *rapport de perfection* between the beast compared to the man, than between the man compared to the beast." Or, in simpler language, humans enjoy a greater measure, a greater degree, of "perfection," than beasts, and beasts more perfection than stones. Plainly, Malebranche envisioned a hierarchy of more or less "perfect" beings – their "perfection" defined in terms of their capacity for "union" with "the Word" or "universal reason" – and held that one should "regulate his esteem" in view of degrees of perfection. Thus, for Malebranche, whoever "esteems his horse more than his coachman" does not really "see" the *rapport de perfection* "which he perhaps thinks he sees." Linking this up with his familiar general-particular distinction, Malebranche added that the unreasonable horse-lover fails to see *la raison universelle*, that he takes his own *raison particulière* for his rule. However, Malebranche went on, to abandon *la raison universelle* and "order" for *la raison particulière* is to manifest *amour-propre*, "error," and "lawlessness": thus the language of *Nature et grâce* reappears, and begins to color "order" and "relations of perfection" themselves (*Morale* I, 1, xiii–xiv, OC 11:21–2).

From all of this, Malebranche concluded – following St. Augustine's following of Plato – that "it is evident that there is a true and a false, a just and an unjust," and that this holds "with respect to all intelligences." Just as what is true for God is true for angels and humans, so too "that which is true for God is true for angels and men," and so too "that which is injustice or disorder with respect to man is also such with respect to God himself." Just as "all minds" discover the same mathematical *rapports de grandeur*, so those same minds discover "the same truths of practice, the same laws, the same order," when they see and love the *rapports de perfection* enclosed in the Word (*Morale*, I, 1, v–vii, OC 11:18–9). (It is Platonic, but also especially Augustinian, to "relate" mathematics and morality: as Augustine says in *De Doctrina Christiana* XXVII, 28, "He lives in justice and sanctity ... who has an ordinate love ... He neither loves more what should be loved less, loves equally what should be loved less or more, nor loves less or more what should be loved equally." Here love and mathematical order fuse in a Malebranche-anticipating way.)[28]

The "love of order," then, according to Malebranche, is "our principal duty": it is "mother virtue, universal virtue, fundamental virtue." (This order, these "related" perfections, actually *exist* only in God; hence the love of God, of perfection, and of order are equivalent, together constitute Malebranche's rather unorthodox version of "charity" – a charity that extends to humans [in the limited form of "love of benevolence"] as citizens of God's *société spirituelle*.) "Speculative truths" or *rapports de grandeur* do not "regulate" our duties; "it is principally the knowledge and the love of relations of perfection, or of practical truths, which constitute our perfection." Hence, Malebranche's closing perroration: "Let us then apply ourselves to know, to love and to follow order; let us work for our perfection" (*Morale* I, 1, xix, OC 11:p. 24).

Is there a "relation" between *rapports de grandeur* and *rapports de perfection*? In Malebranche's great contemporary and correspondent Leibniz, the answer is plainly "yes," for Leibniz argued (in a 1696 letter) that "order and harmony are ... something mathematical and which consist in certain proportion;" and he added in *Opinion on the Principles of Pufendorf* (1706) that "justice follows certain rules of equality and of proportion which are no less founded in the immutable nature of things, and in the ideas of the divine understanding, than the principles of arithmetic and geometry."[29] In Malebranche himself, the initial answer appears to be "no," for he called *rapports de grandeur* "quite pure, abstract, metaphysical," while *rapports de perfection* are "practical" and serve as "laws." However, one might object that the notion of *rapports de perfection* and of "order" are also "quite abstract": as Jeremy Bentham later observed, "the worst order is as truly order as the best."[30]

In fact, Malebranche finally abandoned the abstractness of "order," and his less than concrete characterization of "relations of perfection"; and, in the work commonly accounted his masterpiece – the *Entretiens sur la métaphysique* – he moved in the direction of Leibniz's (virtual) identification of "proportion" or "equality" in mathematics and in notions of rightness. Malebranche began the thirteenth section of *Entretien VIII* by calling *rapports de grandeur* "speculative" and *rapports de perfection* "practical" (as in *Traité de morale*), but then went on to say that "relations of perfection cannot be known clearly unless they are *expressed* in relations of size." That two times two equals four, Malebranche continued, "is a relation of equality in size, is a speculative truth which excites no movement in the soul – neither love nor hate, neither esteem nor contempt."

However, the notion that man is "of greater value than the beast," he goes on, is "a relation of inequality in perfection, which demands not merely that the soul should accept it, but that love and esteem be regulated but the knowledge of this relation or of this truth." Because, for Malebranche, we ought to love perfection, we ought to love beings closer to divinity in the scale of being, in preference to "lower" beings and things – without, however, falling into the "idolatry" of loving finite creatures as if they constitute our "true" good (*Dialogues* VIII.13, OC 12–13:190–1; JS 142). In this way, the unfamiliar notion of *rapports de perfection* is assimilated to the much more familiar idea of a "great chain of being";[31] if this makes Malebranchism more ordinary, it also makes it more concrete and intelligible.

To be sure, this concreteness had already been intimated in the tenth "Éclaircissement" of *Recherche de la vérité*, where Malebranche argued that "if it is true, then, that God ... encloses in himself all beings in an intelligible manner, and that all of these intelligible beings ... are not in every sense equally perfect, it is evident that there will be an immutable and necessary order between them." Further, he adds that "just as there are necessary and eternal truths, because there are *rapports de grandeur* between intelligible beings," so too "there must be an immutable and necessary order, because of the *rapports de perfection* which exist between these same beings." It is thus in virtue of "an immutable order that minds are nobler than bodies, as it is a necessary truth that two times two makes four" (*Search*, Eluc. X, OC 3:126; LO 618). "Order," then, requires respect (or love of "benevolence") for the degree of perfection attained by every created being in the great chain of being. This is at its clearest in the *Traité de morale*, where "order" gives new meaning to traditional Pauline Christian "charity":

The charity which justifies [men], or the virtue which renders just and virtuous those who possess it, is properly a ruling love of the immutable order ... The immutable order consists of nothing else than the relations of perfection which exist between the intelligible ideas that are enclosed in the substance of the eternal Word. Now one ought to esteem and love nothing but perfection. And therefore our esteem and love should be conformable to order ... From this it is evident that charity or the love of God is a consequence of the love of order, and that we ought to esteem and love God, not only more than all things....

Now there are two principal kinds of love, a love of benevolence, and a love which may be called a love of union.... One loves persons of merit through a love of benevolence, for one loves them even though they are not in a condition to do us any good.... Now God alone is [truly] good, he alone has the power to act in us ... thus all love of union ought to incline towards God. (*Morale* I, 3, vi–viii, OC 11:41–2)

Even in these passages that stress the notions of love, charity, order, and perfection, and that seem to have left the general-particular dichotomy far behind, Malebranche found an occasion for animadversions against *particularisme*. Just as everyone can see that twice two is four, Malebranche urged, so too everyone can see that "one ought to prefer one's friend to one's dog"; the mathematical *rapport de grandeur* and the moral *rapport de perfection* both rest in "a universal reason that enlightens me and all intelligences whatever." This "universal" reason, which is "coeternal" and "consubstantial" with God, and which all intelligences "see" (in God), is to be strictly distinguished from "particular reasons," the not very reasonable reasons that "a passionate man follows." The passionate man turns out to be the familiar horse lover:

When a man prefers the life of his horse to that of his coachman, he has his reasons, but they are particular reasons that every reasonable man abhors. They are reasons that fundamentally are not reasonable, because they are not in conformity with the sovereign reason, or the universal reason, that all men consult. (*Search*, Eluc. X, OC 3:131; LO 613)

Malebranche, then, will not countenance any *raisons que la raison ne connaît point*.[32] If in this passage he appeals to what is "universal" and not merely "general," he still found time to lump des raisons particulières with "passion" and the "abhorrent." And toward the end of the tenth *"Éclaircissement,"* even the notion of the "universal" yields, and *le général* makes its way back in: one can finally see, Malebranche urged, "what the immutable order of justice is, and how this order has the force of law through the necessary love that God has for himself." Because humans ought to love the order that God loves, "one sees how this law is general for all minds, and for God himself"; one sees that to abandon the idea of "eternal" and "immutable" order, common to all intelligences, is to "establish *pyrrhonisme* and to leave room for the belief that the just and the unjust are not at all necessarily such" (*Search*, Eluc. X, OC 3:140;

LO 620). Thus, even the treatment of "relations of perfection" manages to hold on to Malebranche's antiparticularism, and to reflect his equation of generality with justice in *Nature et grâce.*

However, what, finally, is the "relation" between these relations of size and perfection – the latter constituting "order" – and the rule of divine "general will" in the realms of nature and grace? One cannot simply say that "nature" is to *rapports de grandeur* as grace is to *rapports de perfection,* because the created world is not "orderly": It contains monsters and hardened hearts. "The present world is a neglected work," Malebranche insisted. "Man ... inhabits ruins, and the world which he cultivates is only the *débris* of a more pefect world" (*Méd. Chrét.* VII, xii, OC 10:73). The main passage in which Malebranche tried to "relate" moral relations to the "general will" is to be found in the *Méditations chrétiennes et métaphysiques* in *Méditation* VII:

> God has two kinds of laws which rule him in his conduct. The one is eternal and necessary, and this is order; the others are arbitrary, and these are the general laws of nature and of grace. But God established the latter only because order required that he act in that way. (*Méd. Chrét.* V, xviii, OC 10:76)

This "works," of course, only if order entails the simplicity (of divine action) that makes general laws better than a multiplicity of particular ones. In any case, the formulation of *Méditation* VII contains a great tension: "order" or "perfection" is "eternal" and "necessary," while the *volontés générales* that govern nature and grace are "arbitrary." However, the burden of *Nature et grâce* is to show that *volonté générales* are, unlike *volontés particulières,* precisely not "arbitrary," instead, that they are wise, constant, and just (TNG, I (passim), OC 5:11 ff.; R 112 ff.). "Arbitrary," perhaps unfortunately, calls to mind Malebranche's characterization of the *volonté particulière* of some earthly sovereigns: "une volonté aveugle, bizarre et impérieuse." However, "arbitrary" may simply mean "not necessary" and "not eternal"; after all, the world itself is neither necessary nor eternal (this would be a "Spinozistic" denial of creation, in Malebranche's view), and therefore the "general wills" that govern the world's realms, nature, and grace cannot be necessary or eternal either.

Even if, however, the "arbitrariness" of *volonté générale* simply means noneternity and nonnecessity, one can still ask: why, if

*volonté générale* and *lois générales* are inferior to "order" and to
*rapports de perfection* – as must necessarily be the case – should God
have "realized" a world that can have nothing more than a shadow
of a "relation" to order and perfection (or perhaps *no* intelligible relation, unless order generates simplicity and simplicity then yields
generality)? Malebranche himself, of course, asked this radical question at the very beginning of *Nature et grâce*; and he concluded that
there is no "relation" between God and the world, between infinity and finitude (TNG I, 1, 1st "Addition," OC 5:11–2). He realized
throughout *Nature et grâce* that he must show that it is in some
sense "better" that a sin-disordered world, now governed by *volontés
générales* that permit monsters and grace falling uselessly on hardened hearts, should exist rather than never have been. His "solution"
is of course Christian, indeed drastically Christocentric: The ruined
world as *redeemed* by Christ is of greater worth than the nonexistence (or never-existence) of that world. Because the Incarnation
constitutes philosophical "salvation" for Malebranche, quite literally "saves" his system, and gives a perfect being a motive for creating a "ruined" world, a great deal – everything – turns on the advent
of Christ; for Malebranche, *culpa* is not simply *felix*, but essential.
"The world as saved by Jesus Christ," Malebranche insisted in the
*Entretiens sur la métaphysique*, "is of greater worth than the same
universe as at first constructed, otherwise God would never have
allowed his work to become corrupted."

Man ... is a sinner, he is not such as God made him. God, then, has allowed
his work to become corrupt. Harmonize this with his wisdom, and his power,
save yourself from the difficulty without the aid of the man-God, without
admitting a mediator, without granting that God has had mainly in view the
incarnation of his son. I defy you to do it even with the principles of the best
philosophy. (*Dialogues*, IX, vii, OC 12–13:207; JS 156–7)

It is in view of this that Malebranche can insist that while it is true
that "everything is in disorder," this is the consequence of "sin":
"order itself requires disorder to punish the sinner" (*Méd. Chrét.* IV,
8, OC 10:39). This, then, would be the "relation" between *rapports
de perfection* and a very imperfect (thought still generally governed)
world: Order necessitates disorder, and so *mere* "general will" is
justifiable. Even so, one can ask: is "disorder" the unintended, un-
wanted, unwilled upshot of God's "simplicity" and "generality" of

operation (as *Nature et grâce* insists), or is the intended, wanted, and willed divine punishment of human sin? Or is it precisely human sin – divinely previewed – which justifies God in creating a disordered world which can be no *more* than "simple" and "general"? This final version – in which "Cartesian" generality is fused with something much more specifically Christian – might seem to be the most comprehensive and adequate; for, particularly in the *Méditations chrétiennes*, Malebranche suggested that the (generally governed but) "ruined" world expresses or symbolizes human depravity. He made this suggestion in a wonderfully imaginative descriptive passage:

The present world is a neglected work. It is the abode of sinners, and it was necessary that disorder appear in it. Man is not such as God made him: thus he has to inhabit ruins, and the earth he cultivates can be nothing more than the debris of a more perfect world. . . . . It was necessary that the irregularity of the seasons shorten the life of those who no longer think of anything but evil, and that the earth be ruined and submerged by the waters, that it bear until the end of all centuries visible marks of divine vengeance. (VII, xii, OC 10:73)

Though divine wisdom does not appear in the ruined world "in itself," Malebranche added, none-the-less in "relation" to both "simplicity" *and* the punishment of "sinners," the world is such that only an "infinite wisdom" could comprehend all its "beauties."

At least this argument, whatever its implausibilities, is more successful than Leibniz's demi-Christian one: demi-Christian in the sense that Leibniz insisted that "universal justice" – for God and men alike – consists in the "charity of the wise" (*caritas sapientis*),[33] but then is hard-pressed to explain why a "charitable" God would create an imperfect world that can be (at best) "best" (the "best of all possible worlds"), though not good (absolutely). In explaining God's decision to create, Leibniz stressed God's glory and the notion that the world "mirrors" that glory;[34] here, however, charity has vanished altogether. At least Malebranche's deployment of Christ as redeemer – of both men and Malebranchism – does not attempt, *per impossibile*, to combine "charity" and "glory."

One can still ask, of course, why an *être parfait* would see, as a sufficient manifestation of "order," an historical drama in which fallen and corrupt beings are redeemed through the sacrifice of Christ *qua* "perfect victim"; but this would be to question Christianity more closely than Malebranche was ever prepared to do. As early as 1687,

Fénelon complained that, whether one considers Malebranche's version of the Incarnation theologically or scripturally, it is radically problematical. From a theologian's perspective, Fénelon argued that "if one examines exactly what glory is truly added by the Incarnation" to the "infinite and essential glory" of God, one finds that it "only adds an accidental and limited glory;" what Christ suffered, though "infinite in price," is "not at all something infinitely perfect, which can be really distinguished from the perfection of the divine person." Scripturally, for Fénelon, Malebranche is no better off: Malebranche argued that "it would be unworthy of God to love the world, if this work were not inseparable from his son," Fénelon suggested, but "Jesus Christ teaches us, on the contrary,that "God so loved the world, that he gave it his only son."[35]

Malebranchism, indeed, seems to suffer from a great difficulty: Malebranche wanted to operate only with an *être parfait*, and imagine what such a perfect being *would* justly do – leaving out all scriptural "anthropology." Yet, the idea of an *être parfait* acting uniformly through general laws leads to deism, not to Christianity. The concept of a perfect being does not yield a "son" of God who, *qua* "perfect victim," redeems and justifies a ruined and sin-disordered world. "Anthropological" scripture does indeed yield Christ and his earthly works; but anthropology is a concession to "weakness" and "anthropomorphism." Only Christ "saves" Malebranche's system, and gives the Father a motive for creating a world unworthy of him; but Christ is not (and cannot be) spun out of the bare idea of "perfection." Malebranche thus needed historical Christianity, even as he claimed to rely solely on the concept of *l'être parfait*. It is this need that drives him to the astonishing claim – in the *Traité de morale* – that God the Father "never had a more agreeable sight than that of his only son fastened to the cross to re-establish order in the universe" (*Morale* I, 3, v, OC 11:41).

If, finally, "order" and "relations of perfection" seem to have toppled more "general will" from the high place it occupies in *Nature et grâce*, one can still recall that God, who "encloses" all perfection and order, is called by Malebranche *le bien général*, while mere earthly goods are styled *les biens particuliers*. So even here "generality" recovers some of its lost lustre; it is preserved even as it is canceled. As Malebranche has "the Word" itself say to a *dévot* in the *Méditations chrétiennes*, "God inclines you invincibly to love *le bien en général,* but he does not incline you invincibly to love *les biens particuliers" (Méd. Chrét.* VI, xvii, OC 10:65). If *généralité* does not shape the whole of what is right in Malebranche, at least *particularisme* is constantly and uniformly condemned – as it had been in *Nature et grâce.*

## VII.   GENERAL WILL AND OCCASIONALISM

Even if what Malebranche said about "order" and *rapports de perfection* deprives "general will" of some of the importance it seemed to have in *Nature et grâce,* that *volonté générale* is still the regulator of the realms of nature and grace, and thus remains quite significant. However, what is the relation between the "general will" of God and the "occasionalism" for which Malebranche is celebrated? Originally (that is, in the Cartesian tradition) occasionalism was only a theory of perception and of will. If the essence of body is extension and the essence of mind is thought, then mind and body cannot "modify" each other, because thought is not a modification of extension and extension is not a modification of thought.[36] Given a strict mind-body dualism, the obvious question is, How can minds "perceive," if perception is viewed as a physical modification of the eye or the ear, as motion "in" a sense organ, and how can minds "move" bodies – through "volition" – if thought cannot modify extended substances? The obvious answer for an occasionalist must be that so-called "perception" is not *really* a modification of mind by sensed matter, and that volition is not *really* efficacious. Instead, God presents to the mind the *idea* of the thing "seen" on the *occasion* of its being "seen," just as he moves bodies (for us, as it were) on the occasion of our "willing." This occasionalism does not, of course, require a constantly intervening *Deus ex machina* who scurries about the universe giving efficacy to occasional causes. Indeed, for Malebranche, whenever one wills to move his arm, it moves, thanks to a constant, general (though nonnatural) conjunction between mind and body, which God has established by a general will. "It is only God," he insisted in the *Conversations chrétiennes,* "who can act in the [human] soul ... through his general will which makes the natural order" (*Conv. Chrét.* III, OC 4:83).

It was not simply in order to be a "Cartesian" that Malebranche was an occasionalist; indeed, his motivation was as much religious as philosophical, as much moral as speculative. Malebranche's view was that the attribution of independent causal efficacy to nondivine beings is literally *impious*; to make that clear, he employed the political idea of "sovereignty." "The idea of a sovereign power is the idea of a sovereign divinity," Malebranche urged in *De la recherche de la vérité*, "and the idea of a subordinate power is the idea of an inferior divinity.... Thus one admits something divine in all the bodies that surround us, when one admits ... real beings capable of producing certain effects by the [causal] force of their nature; and one thus enters insensibly into the sentiment of the pagans." It is true, he added, that "faith corrects us" by reminding us of the Pauline notion that *in God* we "move" and "have our being"; nonetheless, if one reads too much Aristotle, "the mind is pagan" even if "the heart is Christian." This is why one must prefer St. Augustine, "this great saint [who] recognized that the body cannot act upon the soul, and that nothing can be above the soul, except God" (*Search* VI, 2, iii, OC 2:310; LO 446–7). It is no wonder that Malebranche read Descartes as an Augustinian, and the Aristotle-loving Scholastics as thinly veiled pagans. (No doubt Malebranche's reservation of "sovereignty" for God alone leads also to his quasi-Pascalian politics in *Traité de morale* II, viii, which urges that citizens owe princes only "external and relative submission," following "the customs and the laws of the state" (*Morale* II, 8, xvi, OC 11:219). Here Bossuet's notion of the prince as a sovereign demi-God in *Politics drawn from the Very Words of Holy Scripture* is rejected.[37] Bossuet was court preacher to Louis XIV; it is impossible to imagine Malebranche in that role.)

One can begin Malebranchian "occasionalism," as does Malebranche himself, with knowledge and perception. The most important passage in which he treated the moral significance of the notion that "we see all things in God" is a remarkable commentary on St. Augustine in the *Trois Lettres* of 1685. Malebranche began by allowing that St. Augustine himself did not claim to find *all* things in God: "I realized," he granted, "that this Father spoke only of truths and of eternal laws, of the objects of the sciences, such as arithmetic, geometry, morality; and that he did not urge that one saw in God things which are corruptible and subject to change, as are all the things that surround us." Malebranche himself did not claim that one sees corruptible and changing things in God; "to speak exactly, one sees in God only the essences" of things, and those essences or ideas of things alone are "immutable, necessary and eternal." One sees in God only "that which represents these things to the mind, ... that which renders them intelligible" (*Trois Lettres*, OC 6–7:199–200). (As Malebranche put the matter in his correspondence of 1714 with Dortous de Mairan, "I see immediately [in God] only the idea, and not the *ideatum*, and I am persuaded that the idea has been for an eternity, without [any] *ideatum*" [*Correspondence*, OC 19:910].) Corruptible things are problematical because they change, though their essence does not, but incorruptible, unchanging things one sees *simply* in God. "One can see only in an immutable nature, and in eternal wisdom, all the truths which, by their nature, are immutable and eternal." It would not be difficult to prove, "as St. Augustine did," that "there would no longer be any certain science, any demonstrated truths, any assured difference between the just and the unjust – in a word, truths and laws that are necessary and common to all minds – if that which all intelligences contemplate were not ... by its nature absolutely immutable, eternal and necessary" (*Trois Lettres*, OC 6–7:199). All of this, of course, simply reinforces the view that God and men "see" the same speculative and practical truths.

Malebranche maintained this view of the moral importance of a "vision" in which nothing is seen, which is not a modification of mind by body, to the end of his philosophical career. In the fragmentary remains of a letter of 1713 to Fénelon, he argued that "if the mind forms its ideas by a vital act," and if "our ideas as distinguished from our perceptions are only chimeras," then Pyrrhonism will be established. If *all* ideas are simply mind modified by matter, then "Hobbes and Locke, authors greatly esteemed by many men, will be right." If they *are* right, "there will be no more true, nor false, immutably such; neither just, nor unjust, neither science nor morality." If "empirical" notions of perception and knowledge carry the day, "St. Augustine will pass for a fanatical Platonist" who taught his "subtle atheism" to Malebranche himself. In Malebranche's view, Hobbes and Locke simply extend the theory of Aristotle (and of his "impious commentator" Averroës) that "seeing objects is accomplished by means of impressed species ... by the power of an active intellect which presents [ideas] to a passive intellect." However, this, Malebranche insisted, is a "fiction of men who wanted to discuss what they did not understand" (*Correspondance*, OC 19:842–3).

Locke thought Malebranche's "vision in God" just as impious as Malebranche thought Locke's "sense perception." In his "Examination of Père Malebranche's Opinion of Seeing All Things in God" Locke argued that, "God has given me an understanding of my own; and I should think it presumptuous in me to suppose I apprehended anything by God's understanding, saw with his eyes, or shared of his knowledge." He went on to ask, "In which of the perfections of God does a man see the essence of a horse or an ass, of a serpent or a dove, of hemlock or parsley?" Locke confessed that he himself cannot see the essence of any of these things "in any of the perfections of God." It is perfectly true, he went on, that "the perfections that are in God are necessary and unchangeable." However, it is not true that "the ideas that are ... in the understanding of God ... can be seen by us"; it is still less true that "the perfections that are in God represent to us the essences of things that are out of God."[38]

In another criticism of Malebranche, Locke added that the Malebranchian notion that God cannot communicate to creatures the powers of real perception and real volition sets "very narrow bounds to the power of God, and, by pretending to extend it, takes it away." He concludes his assault on occasionalism with a moral objection:

The creatures cannot produce any idea, any thought in man. How then comes he to perceive or think? God upon the occasion of some motion in the optic nerve, exhibits the colour of a marygold or a rose to his mind. How came that motion in his optic nerve? On occassion of the motion of some particles of light striking on the retina, God producing it, and so on. And so whatever a man thinks, God produces the thought: let it be infidelity, murmuring or blasphemy.[39]

For Locke, then, *tout en Dieu* is a moral enormity; for Malebranche it is a moral necessity. For Malebranche, as for Kant a century later, mere sense perception of a natural world can never explain the possibility of the idea of moral necessity, because that idea does not arise in perception. Kant argued in his *Critique of Pure Reason* that "'ought' expresses a kind of necessity ... which is found nowhere in the whole of nature,"[40] and Malebranche would have wholly agreed with that.

Before leaving *tout en Dieu* behind, it should be pointed out that Malebranche sometimes drew moral consequences *directly* from his occasionalism. For example, in his *Défense de l'auteur de la recherche de la vérité* (1684) he asserted that "to love even one's father, one's protector, one's friend, as if they were capable of doing us good" is to "render them an honor due only to God." According to Malebranche, this mistake follows from the false supposition that "the bodies which surround us can act as true causes in us." According to the occasionalist doctrine, this must be false; therefore, one "should love his brothers, not as capable of doing us [any] good, but as capable of enjoying with us the true good" (*Défense*, "2d Preuve," OC 17-1:518). (The whole *Traité de morale*, indeed, is an enormous elaboration of this basic thought.)

On occasion, Malebranche made occasionalism yield slightly different social consequences. In the relatively late *Entretien d'un philosophe chrétien et d'un philosophe chinois* (1708), he first argued for divine *volonté générale*, then went on to insist that "it is absolutely necessary for the preservation of the human race and the establishment of societies" that God "act ceaselessly" in terms of the "general laws of the union of the soul and the body" – that, if God did not *constantly* give men the same perceptions through the operation of these general laws, this alone "would destroy society.... A father would fail to recognize his child, a friend his friend ... take away the generality of natural laws [for example, of perception, which permits recognition] and everything collapses in chaos" (*Philosophe chinois*, OC 15:31). Here occasionalism and *généralité* fuse to generate a *social* doctrine; even occasionalism, then, leans heavily on the ideas of *Nature et grâce*.

## VIII.   HUMAN WILL AND THE "SUSPENSION OF CONSENT"

For Malebranche, just as there is no "empirical" perception in the Hobbesian or Lockean sense, so too there is little notion of human will – "little" rather than "no" because of an obvious problem. If humans are merely the occasional causes of their own actions, in what sense are they free agents who are accountable for good action, for choosing order or *le bien général* in preference to *amour-propre* and *les biens particuliers*? (As Malebranche himself says in *Recherche de la vérité*, "without liberty there are neither good nor bad actions" [*Search*, OC 3:225; LO 669].)

According to Malebranche, people are free and hence possibly responsible in the sense that they must "consent" to a "motive"; God
inclines people through Augustinian *délectation* toward *le bien* or
order *en général*, and one must feel this delight before consent is
possible. (Or, as Malebranche put it in an untranslatable passage, "il
faut sentir ... avant que de consentir" [*Réflexions* vi, OC 16:18].)
Nevertheless, one can suspend one's consent, can be motivated by
a *délectation* without being irresistibly or "invincibly" determined
by it. Hence, Malebranche's most adequate definition of will, at least
in his later work, is "consenting to a motive." The essence of liberty, he argued in *Réflexions sur la prémotion physique*, "consists
in a true power ... which the soul has, to suspend or to give its
consent to motives, which naturally follow interesting perceptions"
(*Réflexions* xii, OC 16:47). In suspending one's consent to an interesting or even delectable motive, however, one does not actually *cause*
anything to happen – as Malebranche was careful to make clear in
the first "Eclaircissement" of the *Recherche de la vérité*. If we allow
a *délectation* that is *déreglé* (such as self-love or "concupiscence") to
overwhelm us, and if we fail to suspend our consent to this motive
in favor of order or *rapports de perfection*, what do we actually *do*?

Nothing. We love a false good, which God does not make us love by an invincible impression. We cease to look for the true good.... The only thing
we do is stop ourselves, put ourselves at rest. It is through an act, no doubt,
but through an immanent act which produces nothing physical in our substance ... that is, in a word, through an act which does nothing and which
makes the general cause [God] do nothing ... for the repose of the soul, like
that of the body, has no force or physical efficacy. (*Search*, Eluc. 1, OC 3:24–5;
LO 551)

This peculiar doctrine, in which human willing is "an act, no
doubt," but one that "produces nothing physical," is necessitated by
Malebranche's view that God alone is the *true* cause, but that, at the
same time, humans must in *some* way be accountable for their volitions. In his last work, the *Réflexions sur la prémotion physique*,
Malebranche tried especially hard to make this doctrine plausible
by drawing a fine distinction between two different "powers" or activities in the human soul. He began by asserting that "the *willing*
power of the soul, so to speak, its desire to be happy, its movement
toward the good in general" is the first power or activity; but it is a

power that is "certainly the effect of the Creator's will." This power, then, is "only the action of God" *in* the soul; it is therefore "like that of created bodies in motion ... whose moving force ... depends on the action of God." It is a power *in* us, indeed, but it is not "ours"; it is, to recall a favorite Malebranchism, *en nous sans nous* (*Réflexions* xii, OC 16:46–7).

For Malebranche, it is the second power of the soul that was more interesting with regard to human moral responsibility, because it is really ours: "The second power or activity of the soul ... which constitutes the essence of liberty ... consists in a true power, not to produce in itself, through its own efficacity, any new modifications; but it consists in a true power which the soul has, to suspend or give its consent to motives, which naturally follow interesting perceptions" (Ibid.). Therefore, will, understood as "consent to a motive," consists in passively permitting that motive to operate.

Even if one can perhaps characterize this passive consent as involving "rien de physic," can one say the same of "suspending" a motive (such as concupiscence) while one searches for order and *rapports de perfection*? Do "suspending" and "searching" involve *rien de physic*? Malebranche seemed to be caught between God as the only true cause and the wish to avoid a "Spinozistic" determinism in which men are unfree "modes" of the divine substance, and will is therefore an illusion; hence his account of will as both passive and active. However, Malebranche thought that he was avoiding one of the chief errors of Jansenism – namely, viewing the *délectation* of "efficacious" grace as irresistible.[41] An irresistible motive, which one cannot suspend or resist without contradiction, truly destroys the possibility of freely loving order and *le bien général* and of meritoriously abandoning *les biens particuliers*, such as the pleasures of the body, which has no natural *rapport* with the mind.

Locke thought Malebranche's attenuated notion of "will" even more impious, if possible, than the notion of "vision in God": "A man cannot move his arm or his tongue; he has no power; only upon occasion, the man willing it, God moves it.... This is the hypothesis that clears doubts, and brings us at last to the religion of Hobbes and Spinoza, by resolving all, even the thoughts and will of men, into an irresistible fatal necessity."[42] It is ironic, of course, that in the second edition (1694) of his *Essay Concerning Human Understanding* Locke himself defines human liberty as the capacity to "suspend" any "particular" desire while one searches for happiness "in general," for the true good. Here there is a strong Locke-Malebranche "relation," and this *rapport* is at its clearest in the account of the alterations to the 1694 edition of the *Essay* that Locke provided in a letter to his friend Molyneux, the Dublin *savant*, in August 1693: "All that we desire is only to be happy. But though this general desire of happiness operates constantly and invariably in us, yet the satisfaction of any particular desire can be suspended from determining the will to any subservient action, till we have maturely examined whether the particular apparent good we then desire make a part of our real happiness."[43]

Like Malebranche, Locke spoke of a "general" desire happiness; this general desire operates "constantly and invariably" (like all Malebranchian general laws). Moreover, all "particular" desires can be "suspended" (Malebranche's very terms), and "particular" goods may be merely "apparent" and not part of "real" or "general" happiness. In book 2 chapter 28 of the *Essay*, entitled "Of Other Relations," Locke argued that "there is another kind of relation, which is the conformity or disagreement men's voluntary actions have to a rule to which they are referred ... which, I think, may be called *moral relation*"; he goes on to call three "sorts" of moral relation *laws* (divine, civil and "of reputation").[44] Despite a seemingly strong relation between the two thinkers, Locke's final view may well be that Malebranche had no grounds for insisting on the real existence of human "will" and hence is not entitled to speak of "suspension," even as an "immanent" act that "does nothing," produces *rien de physic*.

## IX.  CHRIST AS THE "OCCASIONAL CAUSE" OF GRACE

Unusual as are Malebranche's notions of knowledge, perception, and will–from a Lockean perspective not only unusual but impious–perhaps the most peculiar part of his occasionalism is his view that the "human soul" of Jesus Christ is the occasional cause of the distribution of grace. Malebranche began his treatment of Christ as "distributor" of grace by arguing that, "since it is Jesus Christ alone who can merit grace for us, it is also him alone who can furnish occasions for the general laws, according to which it is given to men." The human soul of Jesus Christ

thus having different thoughts successively in relation to the different dispositions of which [men's] souls in general are capable, these different thoughts
[in Christ] are accompanied by certain desires in relation to the sanctification
of those souls. Now these desires being the occasional causes of grace, they
must diffuse it in some persons *en particulier*, whose dispositions are like
those which the soul of Jesus presently thinks. (TNG II, xiv, OC 5:73; R 143)

Because the "different movements of the [human] soul of Jesus
Christ" are the occasional causes of grace, one should not be aston-
ished if grace is sometimes given by Christ to "great sinners" or to
"persons who will not make the slightest use of it." The reason for
this is (again) a physicalist one, resembling Malebranche's treatment
of grace as a variety of rain in *Nature et grâce*: just as the mind of
an architect thinks "in general of square stones" when "those sorts
of stones are actually necessary to his building," so too the soul of
Jesus Christ needs "minds of a certain character" to serve as building blocks of his church – a "temple of vast extent and of an infinite
beauty" – and hence "diffuses in them the grace that sanctifies them"
(TNG II, xvii, OC 5:75; R 144).

Malebranche's reasoning here seems a little odd. One can see why
Christ would will *particularly* the gracious sanctification of a former great sinner whom he wants to use as a stone in his temple,
but why would he will particularly the attempted sanctification of
"persons who will not make the slightest use" of grace? God the
Father allows grace to fall "uselessly" because his operation is *general*, and the generality excuses and justifies the uselessness; but if
God the Son confers useless grace particularly, through a desire of his
human soul, does this not lead to the possibility of charging Christ
with "acceptation of persons" and arbitrariness, even as the Father
escapes this charge with his simplicity and uniformity? Certainly,
it was Malebranche's view that Christ wills many things particularly: "We have," he urged, "reason to believe, that the vocation of
St. Paul was the effect of the efficacity of a particular desire of Jesus
Christ" (TNG II, xviii, OC 5:76; R 145). Not everyone, of course,
will be given such a vocation, for the "different desires of the soul
of Jesus" do not diffuse grace equally upon all. Finally, however,
perhaps recalling what he had said about the "levity" and inconstancy of *volonté particulière*, Malebranche attempted to distinguish

between the particular wills of Christ and what is permanent in his volitions.

It is by present, passing and particular desires of the soul of Jesus, that grace is diffused to persons who are not prepared for it, and in a way which has something singular and extraordinary about it. But it is by permanent desires that it is given regularly to those who receive the sacraments with the necessary disposition. For the grace which we receive through the sacraments is not at all given to us precisely because of the merit of our action ... it is because of the merits of Jesus Christ, which are liberally applied to us as a consequence of his permanent desires. (TNG II, xxii, OC 5:91; R 147)

In this passage one notices, apart from the Augustinian effort to preserve the gratuity of grace, that Malebranche tried to bring the human soul of Christ as *near* to the Father as possible by speaking of *désirs permanens*; these are not quite *volontés générales*, of course, but they are an advance on *des désires actuels, passagers et particuliers*. This keeps Christ from being charged with any more *particularisme* than is required to explain something as particular as the vocation of St. Paul. Nonetheless, those who say that in Malebranche, generality saves the Father and brings down upon Christ reasonable complaints of "inequity" in distributing grace unequally through mere desires of his "human soul" seem to have a point.[45]

One can hardly say that Malebranche was unaware of this difficulty. In a manuscript from c. 1680–1683 entitled *De la prédestination*, he insisted that, while some people imagine that "all desires of Jesus Christ with respect to the distribution of grace are commanded of him in detail and through *volontés particulières* [of the Father]," such a view makes it impossible to "justify divine providence." He ends the manuscript with the unequivocal assertion that "it is thus in Jesus Christ as man that one must seek the reason for the distribution of grace, if one wants to justify the conduct of God in this matter; and this is what I have tried to do in the *Traité de la nature et de la grâce*" (*Prédestination*, OC 17-1:560). If the blame for all people not being saved thus falls on Christ's human "particularism," *ainsi* (apparently) *soit il*.

The problem, finally, is this: if humans *ought* to incline toward God, order, and perfection – toward *le bien général*, and away from *les biens particuliers* – they need grace; to deny this would be a "Pelagian" assertion of perfect human independence. However, because grace is given on the Father's part only by a *loi* or *volonté générale*, and not particularly, is there any *rapport* between those who need grace (in order to love order) and those who get it? The Father cannot attend to this difficulty, because that would turn him into a Calvinist who elects a few and damns all others. Yet Christ's particularism does not always pick out just those persons who need grace; as Malebranche stated, Christ may choose "great sinners" for his temple, and not those who want to love order, who want a "love of union" with God. At the same time, Malebranche wanted to avoid the Jansenist "heresy" that "some commandments are not possible for the just."[46] One wonders how completely he escapes this difficulty.

## X. CONCLUSION

Given the radical theocentrism of Malebranche's philosophy, God must be "sovereign," and all finite, created beings must be dependent "occasional causes" who ought to receive only a limited "love of benevolence"; but it is essential that divine sovereignty not be "Hobbesian" sovereignty, in which natural dominion flows from "irresistible power" alone.[47] If a "ruined" universe, which has deviated from "order" and perfection is to be justifiable, in a proto-*Theodicée*, then God must have a general "will," but not be high-handedly willful: like Leibniz in the *Discourse on Metaphysics*, Malebranche wanted to say that *stat pro ratione voluntas* is "properly the motto of a tyrant."[48] This nonwillful voluntarism is at its clearest in Malebranche's very last work, the *Prémotion physique*, in which

moral relations are not simple *truths*, but ... also have the force of *laws*; for one must esteem all things in proportion as they are estimable and lovable; in proportion as they participate in the divine perfections. And since the nature of God is immutable and necessary, and since God can neither see nor will that two times two be equal to five, how can it fail to be perceived that God can neither see nor will that the idea of man which he has participate less in his perfections than that of the beast? As a consequence, he can neither see nor will that it be just to prefer, or rather will to prefer, one's horse to one's coachman, simply because one can or wants to? Power or will adds nothing to the eternal law, to the relations of perfection which subsist between the eternal and immutable ideas. (*Réflexions* XVIII, OC 16:99)

At the end of his life, Malebranche's Augustine-conveyed Platonism was almost as pure as Leibniz'; both have taken the *Euthyphro* to heart. For Malebranche, in the end, will is necessary, but not sufficient: *volonté* is naturally *générale* in God, and that generality should remain an object of constant human striving – at least when "order" is fully realized neither in the actual world nor in human moral effort. Why there should be a merely "general" world of "ruins" and *débris* that deviates so widely *from* "order" and "perfection" remains a central Malebranchian problem: to the Leibnizian question, "Why is there something rather than nothing?"[49] Malebranche returns an answer that is not as persuasive as it is pious.

### NOTES

1 "Theodicée ou apologie de la justice de Dieu," in Leibniz 1948, vol. 2, 495.
2 JS, vii–xii.
3 See Riley 1986, passim.
4 Ibid., pp. 9–12.
5 Augustine, *De Doctrina Christiana* xxvii, 28: "He lives in justice ... who has an ordinate love."
6 *Codex iuris gentium*, in Leibniz 1768, xi–xiii.
7 Augustine, *De Libera Arbitrio* I, xii; Kant 1949, 12ff. See also Riley 1983, ch. 2.
8 Plato, *Phaedo*, esp. 75d; cf. *Meno*, 826ff.
9 See Riley 1996, 52–3; cf. "What is independent of sensation," in Leibniz 1875–90, vol. 6, 70ff.
10 See Riley 1996, 118–24.
11 Leibniz 1952, "Preliminary Dissertation" (passim).
12 Letter to the Marquis d'Allemans, in Bossuet 1909–25, vol. 8, 163.
13 *Écrits sur la grâce*, in Pascal 1914, vol. 11, 133–40.
14 Arnauld 1644, 4–7.
15 Jurieu 1687, 80 ff.
16 Cited in Dreyfus 1958, 114.
17 Leibniz, letter to Malebranche, in Robinet 1955, 408.
18 Cited in Robinet 1965, 104.
19 Ibid, p. 105.
20 Régis 1691, vol. 1, 92.
21 Arnauld, *Réflexions sur le système de la nature et de la grâce*, OA 39:174ff.
22 Ibid., p. 177.

23 *Réfutation du système du Père Malebranche*, in Fénelon 1835, vol. 2, 256ff.
24 Boursier 1713, 36ff.
25 Hobbes 1946, ch. 31.
26 *Opinion on the Principles of Pufendorf*, in Leibniz 1972, 68–72.
27 Malebranche, letter to Leibniz, cited in Robinet 1955, 407.
28 *Augustine, De Doctrina Christiana*, XXVII, 28.
29 *Opinion on ... Pufendorf*, Leibniz 1972, 71.
30 *Handbook of Fallacies*, in Bentham 1834–8, vol. 2, 441.
31 Lovejoy 1936, ch. 3.
32 *Pensées*, no. 231.
33 *Codex iuris gentium*, xi–xiii, in Leibniz 1875–90.
34 *Radical Origination of Things*, in Leibniz 1998, 962.
35 *Réfutation du système du Père Malebranche*, in Fénelon 1835, vol. 2, ch. 36.
36 Alquié 1974, passim.
37 *Politics Drawn From the Very Words of Holy Scripture*, in Bossuet 1990, Book 5.
38 "An Examination of P. Malebranche's Opinion," in Locke 1813, vol. 9, 211–55.
39 "Remarks Upon Some of Mr. Norris's Books," in Locke 1813, vol. 10, 255.
40 Kant, *Critique of Pure Reason*, A547/B575.
41 R 60–1.
42 "Remarks upon some of Mr. Norris' Books," in Locke 1813, vol. 10, 255–6.
43 Locke 1962–, vol. 4, 722.
44 Locke, *Essay*, Bk. II, ch. 21.
45 Saint-Beuve 1908, vol. 6, 501.
46 Paquier 1962, 162.
47 Hobbes 1946, 232ff.
48 Leibniz, "Discourse on Metaphysics," section 26.
49 "Principles of Nature and Grace," section 7, in Leibniz 1978, 415. See also Gaudemar 1998.

## 10 The Critical Reception of Malebranche, from His Own Time to the End of the Eighteenth Century

Malebranche was the master of an elegant and accessible style of writing. As well as writing treatises, he popularized his philosophy by presenting it in dialogue form. Moreover, he also taught what many thinking people wished to believe, that the "modern" philosophy of Descartes could, after all, be reconciled with traditional Christian beliefs. As a result, he had a considerable following[1] among lay people of the leisured classes, at the Academy of Sciences in Paris, as well as among those, like some of the clergy, who made philosophy part of their profession.[2] His aristocratic admirers included the Palatine Princess Elizabeth – noted as a correspondent of Descartes – and Mlle. Nicole-Geneviève de Vailly, who assembled a company of *Malebranchistes* in her salon each week.[3] His disciples included some other Oratorians,[4] such as Bernard Lamy,[5] whose influence helped to mediate Malebranche to the *philosophes* of the French Enlightenment.[6] One of his most faithful followers was the Jesuit priest Yves-Marie André, who wrote the first biography.[7] His admirers also included the mathematicians Pierre Rémond de Montmort and the Marquis de l'Hôpital.[8] He also found a significant following in Italy, where his influence was felt by Vico and other philosophers right into the nineteenth century.[9] A considerable upsurge of interest in Malebranche occurred in England in the 1690s and early 1700s, when a number of his major works were translated.[10] Malebranche's popularity declined in both England and France as Locke came to be regarded as the philosopher of the age. However, there was a revival of support in mid-eighteenth century France and a corresponding upsurge of criticism of Locke.[11]

If the importance of a philosopher were to be measured by the number of disciples they acquired, Malebranche would certainly be a more important philosopher than, say, Leibniz or Spinoza. Indeed, if having disciples were what counted, then some philosophers, such as Berkeley or Hume, would hardly be of any importance. However, the importance of a philosopher is not measured in this way. A great philosopher may arrive at conclusions that, despite the strength of the arguments that lead to them, are found so outrageous that others are more concerned to refute or dismiss them than defend them. This was true, it would generally be agreed, of Spinoza, Berkeley, and Hume. It was also true of Malebranche. Some of most important doctrines: his occasionalism, his doctrine that we see all things in God, and his claim that there are laws of grace as well as laws of nature, as we will see, were found outrageous and immediately unacceptable by many of his contemporaries. Such was the charm and the earnest piety of his writing, however, that his disciples often found ways of glossing over its problematic implications. Thus, for instance, the vision in God was often represented blandly and inaccurately as if it was a traditional doctrine[12] originating from Augustine and hardly modified by Malebranche. In fact, however, Malebranche had transformed the doctrine and placed it in the context of contemporary philosophical problems.

Philosophers are of interest, of course, not only for the doctrines that they espouse officially but also for doctrines they seem to be committed to or to which their views seem readily to lead. Malebranche seemed closer to Spinozism than he ever admitted. Moreover, his thought was taken, as we will see, as tending to deism as well as to idealism. The fact that his arguments seemed to point in directions that he himself was not tempted to take is one reason why his writings continued to exercise an influence on subsequent philosophy. Thus, as well as looking at the critical reception by some other philosophers of some of Malebranche's main doctrines, it is appropriate to consider some of the directions in which his philosophy has been thought to lead.

I. OCCASIONALISM

If there is a single part of Malebranche's philosophy that ought to secure for him a place in the history of philosophy, it is his defense of occasionalism. He offered strong and clear arguments for this doctrine and, even though it was commonly thought to be unacceptable or to have unacceptable consequences, those who thought the matter through often retained a residual occasionalism even while appearing to have dissociated themselves from it. The view that the only "true cause" is God, and that what are commonly called "causes" are no more than occasions of God's acting, has the air of a paradox because, at least prephilosophically, people not only believe that they are the causes of their actions (if they freely choose to do them) but also that material bodies can be the causes of change. Many of those who responded to Malebranche took him up on the implications of his occasionalism for human free will. Locke, for instance, objected that if we suppose that a man "cannot move his arm or his tongue; he has no power; only upon occasion, the man willing it, God moves it," then this "brings us at last to the religion of Hobbes and Spinoza, by resolving all, even the thoughts and will of men, into an irresistible fatal necessity."[13] Yet, Locke seems to have been influenced by the occasionalists in coming to his view that the clearest notion of power is to obtained by reflecting on our notion of spirits.[14]

For Leibniz, like Locke, the problem of human agency in Malebranche was a point of departure.[15] This is the point of his oft-repeated criticism that occasionalism requires God constantly to perform "miracles" because "properly speaking, God performs a miracle when He does anything that surpasses the powers He has given to and conserved in created things."[16] Leibniz wanted to allow that miracles could happen sometimes but the occasionalist, according to him, has to say they are happening all the time. He advocated the view that all substances possess the power to act and, in the case of rational substances, act freely. At the same time, he agreed with Malebranche and the occasionalists[17] that finite substances cannot act on one another and, to that extent, there is an important residue of occasionalism in Leibniz's own philosophy.

One of those who defended the view that bodies can be "true causes" of effects on other bodies was Bernard Le Bovier de Fontenelle (1657–1757). Fontenelle claimed that it was inappropriate to appeal to divine intervention in physics, which ought to make the universe intelligible in mechanistic terms.[18] This objection is similar to one made by Leibniz, that in "philosophy" we should try to explain things in their own terms and, therefore, natural things should be explained in terms of secondary causes.[19]

Berkeley was, of all the important philosophers of the eighteenth century, perhaps the one to have been most influenced by Malebranche's occasionalism.[20] To be sure, his comments on Malebranche were usually critical, and his early notes make it clear why he could not accept occasionalism in full: "We move our legs ourselves. Tis we that will their movement. Herein I differ from Malebranche."[21] However, Berkeley seemed to have derived from Malebranche the thought that it is from the will of a spirit that we derive our notion of a cause. In relation to nature, Berkeley was an out-and-out Malebranchean occasionalist. God, he insisted, is the sole author of "all those effects, which some heathens and philosophers are wont to ascribe to Nature...."[22] Nature as an entity apart from God and with powers of its own is, he claimed, a *chimera.*"[23] Berkeley intended this in an even more radical sense than Malebranche.[24] However, like him, he took the laws of nature to be constituted by God's will and their uniform working to be evidence of God's goodness and wisdom.[25] Otherwise, on Berkeley's account, there is nothing more to these laws than the fact that certain ideas of sense are "constantly followed" by certain others.

David Hume was another philosopher who was profoundly influenced by Malebranche's occasionalism.[26] Hume rejected the theocentric dimension of full-blown Malebranchism. In his *Treatise of Human Nature*, he claimed that "the Cartesians" were inconsistent in concluding that matter cannot contain any "efficacious principle" (because they cannot discover one in it) while at the same time they allowed such a principle in God.[27] It is equally impossible, Hume claimed, "to discover or even imagine any such principle in the deity." The truth is, Hume concluded, philosophers "have no adequate idea of power or efficacy in any object." In arriving at this conclusion Hume was, in some measure, using Malebranche's arguments against himself. He seemed to have taken over Malebranche's definition of a "true cause" as "one such that the mind perceives a necessary connection between it and its effect" (*Search* VI. 2. iii, OC 2: 316, LO 450). According to the common interpretation of Hume as a skeptic about causality, it might be said that he extended Malebranche's skepticism about the existence of necessary connections between events in the world one stage further, denying that we had any better idea of power or necessary connection in the deity and so concluding that there is nothing more to a causal connection between events than the fact that they are constantly conjoined.[28] The necessary connection is something subjective that we feel as a result of seeing two objects constantly conjoined with one another and which we project onto the world. Thus Hume, if this is not a contradiction in terms, seems like an occasionalist, only without God.

In recent years, this common interpretation of Hume has been challenged. However, the challenge may only add to the importance of Malebranche for Hume's thought. According to an alternative interpretation,[29] Hume really did believe in necessary connections in nature and so rejected occasionalism entirely. However, Hume's "realism" about causality is founded upon a theory of *natural judgment* according to which we should believe what we would believe if we followed our natural judgment. Thus, our belief in necessary connections is not to be taken as merely subjective and therefore illusory but as a belief properly arrived at according to the ways in which our beliefs are naturally formed. If this was Hume's true view, then he (still) took a thoroughly Malebranchean notion[30] and used it to arrive at an un-Malebranchean conclusion.

Malebranche's notion of natural judgment was also to influence another important Scottish philosopher, Thomas Reid.[31] It is a measure of the fertility of Malebranche's philosophy that it contains notions like that of natural judgment, which, even now, seem worth exploring further and could influence philosophers who were, in many respects, very different. However, whatever the correct interpretation of Hume, the potential of the notion of natural judgment was played down by those who thought that Malebranche's philosophy led to idealism. Malebranche's occasionalism was important as a precursor of theories of causality: specifically Berkeley's curious "agency" theory and what came to be known as the "constant conjunction" theory of causation.

## II.    SEEING ALL THINGS IN GOD

The doctrine of seeing all things in God, unlike occasionalism, is in some respects peculiar to Malebranche. None of his contemporaries, even those who thought some version of the doctrine was defensible, was associated more closely with it than he was. In some ways, of course, it was a quite traditional doctrine. Malebranche consciously[32] drew on the Augustinian doctrine of the divine illumination according to which knowledge of eternal truths is knowledge of incorruptible things that exist in God alone. This aspect of Malebranche's thought was attractive to many admirers, especially others in the broad Christian Platonist tradition, such as Leibniz and John Norris (1657–1712).

Leibniz, as early as 1676, sought to defend the view that ("as Plato and Malebranche think") an "idea" could be "the immediate object of perception." If, as he (though not Malebranche) supposed, ideas are to be identified with the attributes of God, then, to the extent that what we see are ideas we do in some sense "see all things in God."[33] Leibniz was, however, thinking only of certain simple ideas (such as "being" and "duration") and failed at this stage to acknowledge that Malebranche's doctrine involved a very considerable extension and modification of what he derived from Augustine. Some years later, however, he made use of the recognizably Malebranchean argument that, unless we suppose that we see all things in God, we cannot explain our perception of the world:

God is the sole immediate object of the mind, outside of itself . . . it is only through the medium of God our ideas represent to us what passes in the world; for on no other supposition can it be conceived how the body can act on the soul, or how different created substances can communicate with one another. . . .[34]

Leibniz was soon to move beyond this view to one he claimed was quite different from that of the author of the *Recherche*: namely, that all the perceptions of the soul arise "spontaneously out of its own nature" and that they correspond to what happens in the universe in virtue of a preestablished harmony.[35] He seemed, therefore, to be committed to defending either the second or the third of the four views Malebranche rejected as false accounts of how the soul sees external objects.[36] Leibniz seemed to have wanted to retain as much as possible of the doctrine of seeing all things in God without the occasionalism that is integral to Malebranche's version of it. Thus, he was able to say, in a draft of the *Discourse on Metaphysics*, that

. . . it is only in virtue of the continual action of God on us that we have in our souls the ideas of everything, i.e., because every effect expresses its cause and hence the essence of our souls is a particular expression, imitation, or image of the essence, thought and will of God and of all the ideas included in Him. Hence it can be said that God alone is our immediate object outside us, and that it is **in** Him that we see all things.... [37]

Leibniz later changed the "in" to "by" thus transforming the doctrine very considerably. Indeed, here agreeing with Arnauld against Malebranche, he rejected the view that our ideas are strictly *in* God at all and was thus committed to denying that we see ideas *in* God on any plain interpretation of that phrase. Leibniz held, along with Malebranche, that God is the only true cause acting on us and (in agreement with him and Augustine) that He is the source of any truth in our ideas. He sometimes suggested that is tantamount to holding that we see all things in God.[38] It seems, in conclusion, that although he believed that the Malebranchean view was only partially true, the part that was true was important enough to Leibniz to justify exaggerating the extent to which he agreed that we see all things in God.

Another philosopher in whom Malebranche's doctrine found a ready response was the Anglican divine, John Norris. Norris claims to have first arrived at the belief that everything we know we perceive in God by his own reflections. He found confirmation of some such doctrine in the writings of Platonic philosophers, including Plotinus, Proclus, Augustine, and Ficino. However, it was, in his view, Malebranche who "established the truth of it beyond all cavil or exception."[39] Norris sometimes took over Malebranche's arguments but he developed a theory of the "ideal" or "eternal" world as the archetype for the natural world, which relies more on traditional sources.

In the 1690s, there was a remarkable upsurge of interest in Malebranche in England,[40] which was partly due to Norris's influence and was reflected in a flurry of translations unprecedented and unsurpassed until our own time. Partly because of this attention to Malebranche, John Locke undertook to write a refutation of the account given in the *Recherche* of the origin and nature of ideas. His own *Essay Concerning Human Understanding*, published in 1690, defended an empiricist view of the origin and nature of ideas. He at first intended, and was encouraged, to include his refutation in a later edition of the *Essay*. However, Locke had no taste for controversies and even professed a "personal kindness" for the author of the *Recherche*.[41] Furthermore, he seems by 1704 to have come to the view that Malebranche's opinion that we see all things in God was one "that spreads not and is like to die of itself; or at least do no great harm."[42] Locke's *Examination of Père Malebranche's Opinion of Seeing All Things in God* was not published until after his death.[43]

Malebranche's argument was, in effect, that the vision in God was the only remotely plausible explanation of how the soul sees external objects.[44] Locke objected to this argument that a theory is not confirmed by objections to its rivals and that it loses its force once we recognize the limitations to human understanding.[45] He also objected that the vision in God does not really explain anything. It tells us that "we have ideas because God is pleased to discover them to us" but fails to tell us by what means God's will that we have ideas of things is realized. Because I come by my ideas, according to Malebranche, "by ways that I know not," then, Locke claimed, "I ... am not got one jot further."[46]

Locke's *Examination* received no response from Malebranche himself. Leibniz, however, wrote some remarks[47] on it and, some years later, it received a full reply from the Savoyard priest, Giacinto Gerdil.[48] Both accepted that Malebranche's argument, as it stood, was unsound. Leibniz, for his part, contented himself with pointing out that, in principle, such an argument is good "if one can completely enumerate the means and exclude all but one."[49] If it could be shown that logically there are only certain possibilities and that all but one of them is to be rejected then this would constitute a demonstration of the possibility that remained. Gerdil went further and proposed a restatement of Malebranche's argument, which would make it formally rigorous. Locke would not have accepted some of his assumptions, however, and his enumeration was less than complete.[50]

As to the second of Locke's objections, Leibniz seemed to have accepted it, agreeing that Malebranche's theory does not explain what we want to understand. The objection can indeed be taken to be similar to Leibniz's objection to occasionalism generally that, in "philosophy," we should not have recourse to the first cause but explain the phenomena of nature in natural terms (i.e., in terms of secondary causes).[51] Gerdil, for his part, sought to defend Malebranche by arguing that, even if we cannot entirely understand how God, who is an active spirit, acts on our minds so as to cause us to see external objects, this notion is not so difficult to understand as what Locke himself proposes, namely, that matter, despite being passive, somehow acts on our minds.[52]

Malebranche's theory of the vision in God continued, thanks to Gerdil, to have adherents in Italy into the nineteenth century, when it was taken up by Antonio Rosmini among others.[53] However, in the eighteenth century, metaphysical "systems" of that kind, partly because of the influence of Locke's *Essay*, came to be regarded as pretentious, unintelligible, and unhelpful.[54]

### III.  LAWS OF GRACE

Malebranche's emphasis on God's general laws, on His *volontés generales*, and on His being a universal cause who has established a general order gives a distinctive character to his philosophy. It was taken up with enthusiasm by a few, some of whom wanted to take it even further. However, it was unhesitatingly condemned by many, especially those who professed to speak on behalf of Christian orthodoxy. Malebranche himself partly provoked this by adopting a polemical stance against much popular and, as it seemed, traditional religion in the view he took of providence and "laws of grace." One might even call his a "generalist" view of providence to clarify the contrast with the view of providence to which Malebranche was opposed – which is usually called "*particularism.*" He objected to "particularism" because it involved a superstitious and inadequate idea of God. Religious superstition assumes that God's will can be affected by what humans do, for good or ill, and that He will intervene on particular occasions to benefit those whom He favors and punish those of whom He disapproves. Malebranche gives the example of European nobility who think it "generous" to fight duels in defense of their honor. They "have even imagined that God approved their conduct," that he "presided at the judgment and gave victory to the one who was in the right" (*Traité de morale* I. 2. vii, OC 11:32; TE 55). Those who think of God like this have an inadequate notion of God's wisdom. Their religion is also a false one. Particularism, according to Malebranche, "flatters the self-love which relates everything to itself" and is a view of providence characteristic of ignorant people (TNG 1: lix, OC 5: 63; R 137). It is unworthy of God's wisdom to act by such "particular wills." God loves his wisdom more than his own creation and his wisdom requires him to act by general wills and in the simplest possible way. The simplicity and fecundity of God's decrees are the hallmarks of His wisdom, according to Malebranche. "God," he explained, "is always bound to act in a way that is worthy of him, by ways that are simple, general, constant and uniform – in a word, conforming to the idea we have of a general cause..." (TNG 1: xliii, OC 5:49; R 128f.).

Malebranche's account had attractions for those to whom the received view of the deity made Him appear indefensibly petty in intervening sometimes in response to the prayers of those in favor. Even more, perhaps, it appealed to some for whom the received view of the deity made Him seem inconsistently cruel in arbitrarily imposing evil on those who had done little or nothing to deserve it. Among those who welcomed Malebranche's philosophy for its contribution to solving the problem of evil was the Anglican clergyman, Thomas Taylor. Taylor is best known as one of the first English translators of Malebranche.[55] However, he was also a religious apologist who took up and defended the doctrine that there are laws of grace just as there are laws of nature.[56] Like Malebranche, he thought that God's perfection expresses itself in the simplicity, regularity, and richness of the natural world and that the operations of divine providence are also by the same criteria of perfection. Nothing God does, according to this Malebranchean view, can be arbitrary or *ad hoc*. It is "not conceivable" that a particular shower of rain should have been designed from all eternity to fall on the field of a particular "Husbandman" because of his merit or his petitionary prayer. The rain falls on the just as well as the unjust because God can only act in accordance with His perfection and this means always in the most simple and orderly way, in accordance with laws.

Though Taylor was not alone in thinking that Malebranche's "laws of grace" provided the basis on which it would be possible to resolve the problem of evil, others thought that there was something far wrong with a god who was too concerned with his perfection to care about the happiness of his creation. Pierre Bayle came to think that Malebranche's god was rather like a prince who preferred to build a city with grandiose architecture to one designed with the convenience of its inhabitants in mind.[57]

Whatever the merits of the doctrine of laws of grace as a solution to problems about the nature of providence and evil, it seemed to many to be inconsistent with belief in God's freedom.[58] Boursier complained that, as represented by Malebranche, God is an "impotent" being who cannot prevent evils that He abhors.[59] Others, like Arnauld, objected to the view of wisdom that requires God only to act by *volontés générales*.[60] Malebranche's laws of grace seemed to leave no room for grace as traditionally understood and no room for miracles or a particular providence either. One of his most formidable opponents was the powerful Bishop of Meaux, Jacques Benigne Bossuet,[61] who made a thinly veiled attack on Malebranche at a public funeral:

What contempt I have for those philosophers who, measuring the counsels of God by their own thoughts, make him the author of nothing more than a certain general order, out of which the rest may develop as it may! As if he had, after our fashion, only general and confused views, and as if the sovereign intelligence could not include in his plans particular things, which alone truly exist.[62]

Bossuet is reputed to have written on his personal copy of the *Traité de la Nature et de la Grâce* the words: "*pulchra, nova, falsa.*"[63] "Beautiful, novel, false" does, at any rate, summarize the reaction of many conservative divines. For the latter part of his life, the Oratorian was involved in controversies and his *Treatise of Nature and of Grace*, like most of his other books, was placed on the Catholic Church's Index of Prohibited Books.[64] Contrary to his intentions, this aspect of Malebranche's thought was to influence philosophers whose interest in having a more adequate notion of the deity was not curbed by concerns about orthodoxy and whose tendency was to what is called "deism."

### IV.  DEISM

Malebranche's rejection of "particularism" led him to reject miracles as commonly understood, viz. as events that violate all order and are produced by a special intervention of the deity on a particular occasion. Whatever God wills must, of course, happen. However, his wills are general, not particular. Hence, Malebranche wrote that "God never performs miracles. He never acts against His own laws by means of particular volitions, unless order either requires or permits it" (*Dialogues* IV. 10.v, OC 12:95; JS 59).

Malebranche denied miracles insofar as they are conceived as interruptions of the general order. On the other hand, the Bible is full of miracles and a seventeenth-century Oratorian would hardly have been a skeptic about whether such events as Jesus walking on water actually occurred. Malebranche would never have gone so far as to deny miracles in every sense, only in the common, superstitious, sense.

What he does is to postulate an underlying order beyond the naturally known order. Miracles do not conform to the order humans know about. However, they do conform to an underlying order. Thus, having acknowledged the infinity of miracles among the Jews, he adds a footnote: "By *miracles* I understand effects depending upon general laws which are not naturally known to us" (*Dialogues* XII.14.xiii, note, OC 12:295; JS 231).

Malebranche's *Treatise of Nature and of Grace* had a lasting impact on Leibniz's thinking on related subjects. Leibniz, in common with Malebranche, emphasized that God always acted for a reason, that His will was always an expression of His wisdom. Moreover, Malebranche seemed to have inspired in Leibniz the thought that God, if He is perfect, must be utterly simple and uniform in His ways. Leibniz was more thorough-going than Malebranche in rejecting the idea that God ever acts by particular wills or is prepared to interrupt the general order for something more important to Him.[65] In extending Malebranche's thought in this direction, Leibniz took it a step closer to what is commonly referred to as "deism," in which miracles and a particular providence is denied outright.

In this respect, Malebranche had an unintended influence on some still more radical thinkers, who took his notion of laws of grace to what seemed to them to be its logical conclusion. Thus, Voltaire criticizes the theologians (Malebranche, presumably, being the honorable exception) because they all reason on a principle that is "evidently false," namely, that "God operates in particular ways."[66] This is false because "the eternal being never acts by particular laws like vile humans, but by his general laws, eternal like him."[67] It would likewise be absurd to imagine that such a God would "invert the eternal play of the immense engines which move the entire universe" in order to favor "three or four hundred ants." Miracles are also inconsistent with a proper notion of the infinite God.[68]

The tendencies in Malebranche that others have seen as tendencies to deism are also ones that link Malebranche's thought with that of Spinoza, particularly with the author of the *Tractatus Theologico-Politicus*.[69] However, while Malebranche was more or less thoughtfully linked with Spinoza in his own time, it was on other grounds, linking him to the author of the *Ethics*.

## V.  SPINOZISM

Malebranche was not a Spinozist, but a number of his contemporaries thought they detected a Spinozistic direction in his thought. If God is indeed the only true cause and we suppose, further, that any true substance is "active," then it follows very quickly that God is the only substance.[70] If, on the other hand, a substance does not need to be active, as Cartesian material substances are not, then it is not clear on what basis one is considered separate from the others and not clear, once again, why there is thought to be more than one substance. Leibniz thought this latter problem was a difficulty with occasionalism that could only be resolved by supposing, as he did, that there was more to material substance than mere extension (i.e., by abandoning a cardinal Cartesian doctrine).[71] He was too diplomatic and too well-intentioned toward Malebranche to accuse him of Spinozism. However, it is clear that he thought that Cartesian occasionalism had a tendency in that direction.

Locke also thought that Malebranche's arguments took him in a Spinozistic direction. He thought that occasionalism led to fatalism.[72] More significantly, he thought that Malebranche's claim that intelligible extension exists in God is very near to saying that material things are God or at least a part of him.[73] A similar criticism was put to Malebranche by his correspondent Jean-Jacques Dortous de Mairan: "If intelligible extension is in God, every body is the modification of the divine essence, or the divine essence is the substance of all bodies."[74] Malebranche rejected the affinity with Spinoza, however, insisting on a distinction (which he alleged Spinoza failed to make) between created extension (the world) and the idea of that extension, which was what he was calling "intelligible extension."[75] Dortous de Mairan replied, nonetheless, that there was not the equivocation in Spinoza that Malebranche alleged and that "You only have to open his book to see that the extension that he calls substance is the same infinite extension the idea of which is present to the mind."[76] On the other hand, it was not clear what Malebranche could mean by "infinite extension," because it could be neither the substance of the world (which he, unlike Spinoza, held to be finite), nor could it be intelligible extension if that was only an idea. It seems as if there is no reality corresponding to God's idea and that Malebranche must deny the existence of bodies, which are no more than modifications of infinite extension.[77] Malebranche, in his rather short reply, conceded that the idea of extension might have no *ideatum* and that I would still see and feel as I do even if I had no body and God "had created nothing but my mind."[78] Though the correspondence is inconclusive,[79] Malebranche seems to have been willing, under pressure, to consider embracing idealism rather than to concede an infinite extension.

## VI.  IDEALISM

Malebranche was not an idealist. Yet his philosophy seemed to many of his early commentators to lead in that direction. If, as followed from his doctrine of seeing all things in God, material bodies are not needed as causes of our sense perceptions, it is not clear why they are needed at all. Malebranche did not accept the argument of Descartes, which purported to demonstrate the existence of material bodies. However, he thought it highly probable that there were material bodies and indeed, because he took it to be a Biblical teaching, held that a Christian should accept that there are bodies as a matter of faith. This suggestion was taken up by Bayle as a concession to skepticism.[80] Locke and other critics objected that Malebranche had no good reason to suppose that there were material bodies at all:

... since God does all things by the most compendious ways, what need is there that God should make a sun that we might see its idea in him when he pleased to exhibit it, when this might as well be done without any real sun at all?[81]

One reason why Malebranche was so often seen in this light is that hardly anyone was convinced by Descartes' attempt to demonstrate the existence of material bodies. Malebranche's first critic, the skeptic Simon Foucher, objected that he was no more entitled to assume the existence of things outside us that are represented by

our ideas than was Descartes.[82] Further, when Leibniz presented his
"New System" as a development from Malebranche's occasionalism,
Foucher accused him of encumbering himself unnecessarily with the
problems of the Cartesians. Foucher claimed that Leibniz was also
open to the objection that, in his system, matter and material bodies
were "useless."[83]

Malebranche's most distinguished English follower, John Norris
(1657–1711), was led by such considerations to the brink of idealism.
However, he also but held back from doubting the existence of bodies
altogether – at least partly because he did not wish to be suspected
of "indulging a Skeptical humor."[84] Norris elsewhere seemed,
like Malebranche, to make some appeal to the notion of "natural
judgement,"[85] but his position did not seem plausible to his own
follower, Arthur Collier (1680–1732), who took Norris's view one
final stage to a denial of the existence of an external material world.

Scholars have found it hard to believe that Collier could independently have arrived at such a similar theory around the same
time as his now more famous contemporary, George Berkeley (1685–
1753). However, the convergence of their thought becomes much
less surprising once it is recognized how far they were influenced
by Malebranche.[86] All three were much attracted by a highly philosophical quotation from the Bible in which some Greek philosophers
are referred to the God "in whom we live, and move, and have our
being."[87] Malebranche had already appealed to it in defending his
doctrine that we see all things in God.[88] It became a favorite Biblical
quotation for both Berkeley and Collier.[89] As with Malebranche,
their philosophies were motivated partly by a concern to produce
a theological outcome – to defend belief in the omnipresence of God
and the total dependence upon Him of the whole creation.

Both Berkeley and Collier were preoccupied with the dangers of
materialism, which they sought to combat in service of a Christian
apologetic. Collier sought to resist the Aristotelian view of matter
as eternal and wished to defend a view of the Creation as resulting
from a Spirit on which everything depended. This led him to hold
that particulars, as such, have no distinct substances of their own, but
only "different forms or similitudes to the one true substance, which
one substance is the common substratum to all particulars."[90] If that
is so, then there is no "independent," "absolute" matter. So far from
matter supplanting God, as is partly threatened in the Aristotelian

view, God supplants (absolute) matter. Thus, Collier, by dropping matter, was able to embrace the spiritualistic panentheism[91] he read into the Biblical, saying that in God "we live, and move, and have our being."

Berkeley was also anxious about matter and extension being elevated to the status of a deity, as is clear from his early remark:

The great danger of making extension exist without the mind. In that if it was it must be acknowledged infinite immutable eternal etc. which will be to make either God extended (which I think dangerous) or an eternal, immutable, infinite, being beside God.[92]

Berkeley noted the difficulty of conceiving matter as produced out of nothing and remarked that this was the reason why "the most celebrated among the ancient philosophers, even of those who maintained the being of a God, have thought Matter to be uncreated and co-eternal with Him."[93] This seems to be the reason for his remark: "matter once allowed. I defy any man to prove that God is not matter...."[94] Berkeley's concerns were more addressed to Locke and Hobbes than to Aristotle. Like Collier, however, he opposed the acceptance of such absolute uncreated beings other than God by affirming a spiritualistic panentheism. This he expressed early in the *Principles* in the statement that "... all the choir of heaven and the furniture of the earth ... subsist in the mind of some Eternal Spirit...."[95]

Like Collier, Berkeley was familiar with Malebranche's thought. He seemed also to have been aware of some of the standard objections. He made use of the stock argument, of which Collier showed no awareness, that material substances are redundant in systems of philosophers who introduce them.[96] Indeed, most of his references to Malebranche were critical.[97] However, Berkeley's idealism as stated becomes incredible once the Malebranchean framework is removed, which allows him to infer that God is the cause of all those ideas we do not produce ourselves. Particularly important for him were the negative aspects of occasionalism, that rule out any true causes but God, and his qualification of occasionalism, which insists that human spirits can be true causes as well. He was thus able to distinguish between those ideas that are dependent on his will and those that are not, which are then inferred to be dependent on the will of some other spirit. That this spirit is God is something Berkeley concluded by an argument based on the "steddiness, order and coherence" of the ideas of sense which, he claims, "sufficiently testifies the wisdom and benevolence of its author."[98] Thus, it appears, from both Berkeley's and Collier's perspective, that Malebranche was not thorough-going enough in embracing the teaching that in God "we live, and move, and have our being." He cited this quotation from Acts 17:40 in support only of saying that "God is the intelligible world or the place of minds, as the material world is the place of bodies." However, because Malebranche cannot allow that matter is part of God, he is, on the face of it, embrassed by seeming to make it into a principle alongside God. It is a short step to cutting the Gordian knot and to attempt, as Berkeley and Collier did in different ways,[99] to articulate a metaphysics in which matter was dropped out.


VII.  OTHER TOPICS

There are other topics of significance to the critical reception of Malebranche than those that fall conveniently under the headings adopted here. One of these is our knowledge of our own minds. Malebranche had held, as against Descartes, that we do not have an idea of the soul but that, nonetheless, we do know some things about the soul and hence, *pace* Descartes, we can have knowledge of some matters even where we do not have ideas. In this matter, Locke followed Descartes and, initially, Berkeley seemed to followed Locke. He soon[100] came around to Malebranche's position, however, and later developed it in his own way, arguing that we have no idea of mind, self, soul or spirit even though we do know certain things about them, such as that they are active substances and are the cause of our ideas. Like Malebranche, he thought we knew our own existence through "inward feeling."[101]

Among the other topics largely neglected here is Malebranche's ethics. Malebranche held what has seemed a paradoxical position about the nature of self-love. On one hand, he held that if we were to take away from a person all self-love and let nothing give pleasure to a person then "here doubtless you will have a person incapable of any love."[102] On the other hand, the saints in heaven have forgotten themselves "and happily lose themselves in divinity." Self-love seems to be a psychological fact. Yet we are enjoined by Malebranche to love God "not only more than the present life, but more than our own being."[103] Malebranche held that it is the gift of God's love that makes this transformation possible so that souls are able to transcend the basic motivation of self-love. The suggestion that souls will, by the grace of God, "happily lose themselves in divinity" brought down on Malebranche the charge of Quietism from some theologians. However, his moral psychology of souls (in the Fallen state) was received more positively by some of the Scottish moral philosophers of the eighteenth century.[104] The state of research into the critical reception of Malebranche is, however, still far from complete. It seems reasonable to expect that the fertile writings of this author on ethics[105] and other topics will be discovered to have had influences and critical responses not yet suspected in the century or so after their publication.

## NOTES

1 Accounts of the *Malebranchistes* are given, for instance, in Ollé-laprune, *La Philosophie de Malebranche*, Vol. II, Ch. II and Rodis-Lewis, *Nicolas Malebranche*, pp. 329–37.

2 Those who taught philosophy in universities at this time were variously discouraged and, in France, forbidden to teach Cartesian doctrines. Some account of this is given by Nicholas Jolley in his "The Reception of Descartes' Philosophy."

3 A few years before she died, Princess Elizabeth began a correspondence with Malebranche. (See OC 18:130–3.) On Mlle. de Vaille's salon, see OC 20:199–201.

4 See André Robinet's "Le groupe malebranchiste de l'Oratoire" in OC 20: 137–40.

5 On Bernard Lamy, see Girbal, "A propos de Malebranche et de Bernard Lamy."

6 Lamy's *Entretiens sur les sciences* was later to be read over and over again by Jean-Jacques Rousseau. Rousseau's introduction to philosophy was through books that mixed devotion and the sciences, especially those from the Oratory and the Port Royal. It seems plausible that he was subject to some Malebranchist influences at this time. Montesquieu was a pupil at the Oratory and this seems to be the explanation for the Malebranchism traceable in his work. See Riley, *The General Will before Rousseau*, Ch. IV.

7 *La Vie du R. P. Malebranche . . .*, written around 1720. André's support for Malebranche was much opposed by his order, who were responsible for many attacks on Malebranche's orthodoxy. On Malebranche and André, see Robinet, "Malebranche et les Jésuits," OC 20:209–24.

8 On these and other admirers at the Academy of Sciences see Robinet, "Les Académiciens des Sciences Malebranchistes," OC 20:162–76.

9 See, for instance, Lantrua, "Malebranche et il pensiero italiano dal Vico al Rosmini." Antonio Banfi's "Malebranche et l'Italie" gives particular attention to Fardella, Gerdil, and Giovenale.

10 There were two separate English editions of the *Search* (1694 and 1694–95) and the *Treatise of Nature and Grace* (both in 1695) as well as editions of *Christian Conferences* (1695) and *A Treatise of Morality* (1699). By far the best account of the reception of Malebranche in the English-speaking world (including colonial North America) is McCracken, *Malebranche and British Philosophy*. McCracken devotes a chapter to the English Malebrancheans, focusing on John Norris, Thomas Taylor, and Arthur Collier.

11 This is discussed by John Yolton in his *Locke and French Materialism*.

12 The English Malebranchean, Arthur Collier, for instance, could write: "Everyone, I suppose, has heard of the doctrine of seeing the divine ideas, or (as Mr Malebranche expresses it), seeing all things in God. By this every mode of pure or intellective perception is accounted for...." (*Clavis Universalis*, p. 38f.)

13 Locke, "Remarks on Some of Mr. Norris's Books ...," p. 255f.

14 Locke's debt, as McCracken points out (*Malebranche and British Philosophy*, p. 153 ff.), was not specifically to Malebranche. He was probably also familiar with the views of Cordemoy, La Forge, and Clauberg. It has been suggested, however, that Locke's moral psychology was indebted to Malebranche. See Vienne, "Malebranche and Locke: The Theory of Moral Choice, a Neglected Theme."

15 In his *Discourse on Metaphysics* (1686), he notes the difficulty of distinguishing the actions of God from those of creatures and sets himself, as one of his tasks, to show how far those are right who think that "God does everything." (§8) He concludes that "every substance has a perfect spontaneity (which in intelligent substances becomes liberty)" in relation to itself but that, apart from God (on whom all finite substances depend), individual substances can be no more than "occasional causes" of what happens to one another. (§32)

16 Letter to Arnauld, April, 1687, *Philosophische Schriften* II.93. Leibniz's objection that occasionalism involves supposing God to perform perpetual miracles has often been taken to mean that God is constantly having to intervene, whereas, with his own preestablished harmony, all the adjustments are made at the beginning. Anyone who made such an objection would show a basic misunderstanding of Malebranche, whose God showed His perfection by the simplicity and orderliness of his laws. Leibniz, so far from making this mistake, particularly valued this aspect of Malebranche's thought. See my "Malebranche's Occasionalism and

Leibniz's Pre-established Harmony: an 'Easy Crossing' or an Unbridge-able Gap?"

17  Though Leibniz credits Malebranche with making occasionalism "fash-ionable," he writes that "*they* have gone a long way with this problem in telling us what cannot happen." ('New System . . .', §13, emphasis added.) Leibniz wrote to Malebranche in 1679 that he heartily approved of the Frenchman's proposition that "bodies do not strictly act on us" but implied that he had arrived at this conclusion himself in a different way (*Philosophische Schriften* I.339, *G. W. Leibniz: Philosophical Pa-pers and Letters*, p. 210). For an account of Leibniz's early occasionalism, see Wilson's *Leibniz's Metaphysics*.

18  *Oevres de Fontenelle*, vol. 9.

19  "New System . . .," §13.

20  This was not appreciated by Berkeley scholars until Luce's important *Berkeley and Malebranche* was published in 1934. For a recent treat-ment, see McCracken, *Malebranche and British Philosophy*, Ch. 6.

21  *Philosophical Commentaries*, §548. The misspelling of Malebranche's name is Berkeley's own.

22  *Three Dialogues between Hylas and Philonous*, in *Berkeley: Works* II 236.

23  *Principles of Human Knowledge*, §150. Whether consciously or not, Berkeley echoed Malebranche's language. See, for instance, TNG Eluc. 3, OC 5:19, R 196.

24  His idealism, which Malebranche did not share, is discussed below.

25  *Principles of Human Knowledge*, §32.

26  He suggested, in a letter to Michael Ramsay of 1737, that as preparation for reading his own *Treatise of Human Nature* he should read the *Search after Truth*. Hume urged his friend also to read Berkeley's *Principles*, some of the articles in Bayle's *Dictionary* and Descartes' *Meditations*. "These books," he assured Ramsay, "will make you easily comprehend the Metaphysical Parts of my Reasoning. . . ." (Quoted from Popkin, "So, Hume Did Read Berkeley," p. 775.)

27  ". . . the same course of reasoning shou'd determine them to exclude it from the supreme being." (*Treatise* I.iii.14, Selby-Bigge edition, p. 160)

28  See his *Treatise* I.iii.14.

29  I have in mind here the one offered by John P. Wright. See his *The Skepti-cal Realism of David Hume* and his "Hume's Criticism of Malebranche's Theory of Causation: A Lesson in the Historiography of Philosophy."

30  See, for instance, *Search*, Eluc. 6, OC 3:62; LO 573.

31  See McCracken, *Malebranche and British Philosophy*, p. 301f.

32  See, for instance, *Search* III. 2. vi, OC 1:445; LO 234). Nicholas Jolley has argued that Malebranche uses Cartesian innovations to extend Au-gustine's theory of divine illumination (*The Light of the Soul*, Ch. 5).

33  Leibniz's Notes on Foucher's *Réponse pour la critique á la préface du second volume de la recherche de la verité (sic) sur la philosophie des académiciens* (Paris, 1676). The argument is in the notes relating to p. 39 of Foucher's book. See *Sämtliche Schriften und Briefe* VI.iii 316: *Leibniz: Philosophical Papers and Letters*, p. 155. At the end of his later (c. 1708) "Remarks on the Opinion of Malebranche that *We See All Things in God* ..." Leibniz writes in the same vein, taking Malebranche's view to be that "we see the essences of things in the perfections of God." (*Sämtliche Schriften und Briefe* VI.vi.558: *Leibniz Selections*, p. 503.)

34  *System of Theology*, p. 73.

35  See his letter to Foucher of 1686, *Philosophische Schriften* I.381-2: Martin & Brown, *G. W. Leibniz: Discourse on Metaphysics and Related Writings*, pp. 129-31 as well as *Discourse on Metaphysics* §33.

36  See *Search* II. 2, chapters 4 and 5.

37  Section 28 draft, Lestienne, Henri (ed.), *Discours de Métaphysique*, Paris: Vrin, 1952, p. 76: Martin & Brown, *G. W. Leibniz: Discourse on Metaphysics and Related Writings*, p. 72.

38  See, for instance, *Philosophische Schriften* VI.578: *Leibniz Selections*, p. 503; *Leibniz; Philosophical Essays*, p. 268: *Philosophische Schriften* VI.593f.; and *Philosophische Schriften* I.659.

39  *Reason and Religion*, p. 185f. It was only in the late 1680s, after he had been a Fellow of All Souls in Oxford for some years, that Norris made a study of Malebranche. But his *Theory and Regulation of Love* of 1688 and his *Reason and Religion* of 1689 are full of acknowledgments to Malebranche and in his later writings Norris became the leading advocate of Malebranchism in England.

40  McCracken, in his Introduction to *Malebranche and British Philosophy*, has given the best available account of the growing interest in this period.

41  In a letter to William Molyneux of 1695. See *The Correspondence of John Locke* V: 352f.

42  Letter to Peter King, 2 and 25 October, 1704. *The Correspondence of John Locke* VIII: 413.

43  In *Posthumous Works of Mr John Locke* (ed. P. King), London, 1706.

44  As he puts it: "In the preceding chapters we have examined four different ways in which the soul might see external objects, all of which seem to us very unlikely. There remains only the fifth, which alone seems to conform to reason ..." (*Search* III. 2. vi, OC 1:437; LO 230).

45  We should "have humility enough to allow, that there may be many things which we cannot fully comprehend." *Examination*, §2. Locke accused Malebranche of an *argumentum ad ignorantiam*.

46  *Examination*, §25.

47 "Remarques sur l'écrit de Locke: *Examination of Malebranche's Opinion of seeing all Things in God," Sämtliche Schriften und Briefe* VI.vi 553–8. A translation is to be found in Wiener (ed.), *Leibniz Selections,* pp. 497–503.

48 *Défense du sentiment du P. Malebranche sur la nature, & l'origine des Idées, contre l'Examen de M. Locke,* Turin: 1748. Gerdil was a Cardinal and indeed his election as Pope in 1800 was vetoed by the Austrians on political grounds and not on account of his Malebranchism.

49 Leibniz, *Sämtliche Schriften und Briefe* VI.vi 553f: Wiener (ed.), *Leibniz Selections,* p. 498. Leibniz referred to the use of "this method of exclusion" in mathematics.

50 As is explained by McCracken in *Malebranche and British Philosophy,* pp. 128–31.

51 For instance, in his "New System ...," Leibniz wrote that "...to solve problems it is not enough to make use of a general cause and to introduce what is called a *deus ex machina.* For to do this, without giving any other explanation in terms of the order of secondary causes, is really to have recourse to a miracle." (§13, quoted from Woolhouse & Francks (eds.) *Leibniz's "New System" and Associated Contemporary Texts,* p. 17.

52 *Défense,* p. 23.

53 See McCracken, *Malebranche and British Philosophy,* p. 312f. and Lantrua, "Malebranche et il pensiero italiano dal Vico al Rosmini."

54 Condillac, in his *Traité des systèmes,* Ch. 7, is an example of a Lockean *philosophe* who attacked philosophers like Malebranche and Leibniz.

55 There were two English translations of the *Recherche de la Vérité* in preparation in 1694. (See Brown, "Malebranche's First English Translators.") Taylor included a translation of Malebranche's much shorter *Traité de la Nature et de la Grâce* and his edition was the one that made Malebranche available to Berkeley, among others.

56 Especially in his *Two Covenants of God with Mankind.* For a fuller account, see McCracken, *Malebranche and British Philosophy,* pp. 179–91.

57 *Réponse aux questions d'un provincial, Oevres diverses de M. Bayle* iii 826, quoted from Patrick Riley's Introduction to his edition of the *Treatise of Nature and of Grace,* p. 85f.

58 Pierre Bayle took Malebranche's thought to confine God's goodness and power "within more or less restricted limits" leaving Him "no freedom of action" (*Réponse aux questions d'un provincial,* Vol. III, Ch. 151).

59 *De l'action de Dieu sur les créatures,* p. 79.

60 *Réflections philosophiques et théologiques,* in OA 39:174ff.

61 Bossuet (1627–1704) exercised a huge influence in court and ecclesiastical circles in France. As well as being a court preacher he was tutor

to the Dauphin. In addition to his own attacks he encouraged others to write against Malebranche.

62 From his *Oraison funèbre de Marie-Thérèse*, delivered in September, 1683. Quoted from the Introduction to the Treatise, R 70.

63 To understand the force of the word "*nova,*" in this context, we need to remember that the Church regarded itself as the custodian of the divine revelation and that an innovation in religious matters would be seen as a departure from the Church's teaching. For a fuller account of Bossuet's reaction, see the editorial introduction to the *Treatise of Nature and Grace*, R 67–77.

64 These controversies passed over, however, and one of Malebranche's most noted followers in the mid-eighteenth century was Giacinto Gerdil, who became a Cardinal and would have been made Pope but for his nationality. Gerdil did not, however, defend Malebranche's view of grace.

65 "I agree with Father Malebranche that God does things in the way most worthy of him. However, I go a little further than he, with regard to 'general and particular acts of will.' As God can do nothing without reasons, even when he acts miraculously, it follows that he has no will about individual events but what results from some general truth or will. Thus I would say that God never has a particular will such as this Father implies, that is to say, 'a particular primitive will.' (*Theodicy,* §206)

66 Quoted from Alquié's *Malebranche et le rationalisme chrétien*, p. 84. Alquié ascribes the quoted words to Voltaire's article "Sur la Grâce" in the *Dictionnaire Philosophique*, but they are not there in the editions referred to here. The unintended influence of Malebranche on the *philosophes*, including Helvétius, Montesquieu, Rousseau and d'Holbach, as well as Voltaire, is referred to in this book and argued more fully in his *Le Cartésianisme de Malebranche*. Alquié's work has been taken up and developed by Riley in his *The General Will before Rousseau*.

67 Article on "Grace," *Dictionnaire Philosophique*, Complete Works 36: p. 180; Philosophical Dictionary, p. 229.

68 *Complete Works* 36: p. 375; *Philosophical Dictionary*, p. 312. The entry on "Miracles" also shows the influence of Malebranche.

69 Spinoza seems to have been attacking much the same superstition as Malebranche's "particularism." Arguments based on miracles, he claimed, would serve only to promote atheism and not belief in the true, unchanging, God. People imagine differently, he argued, because they picture God as some kind of "royal potentate" who idles much of the time, leaving Nature to her own devices, but intervenes on the side

of his "favourites" and overrides the powers of Nature. Of such people Spinoza exclaimed: "They have no single sound conception either of God or of Nature, they confuse God's decisions with human decisions, and they imagine Nature to be so limited that they believe man to be its chief part" (*Tractatus Theologico-Politicus*, p. 125).

70 Leibniz, for instance, took it to be part of the definition of a substance to be "active."

71 Leibniz claimed that Spinoza's arguments for his conclusion that the universe is a single substance did not contain "even the shadow of a proof." His argument is directed to the Cartesian Burcher de Volder (*Philosophische Schriften* II.257f.: Loemker, *Philosophical Papers and Letters*, p. 532).

72 See above, note 13, and the quotation in text to which it relates.

73 *Remarks on Some of Mr. Norris's Books*, §16.

74 Third Letter (6 May, 1714). OC 19:878; *Malebranche's First and Last Critics*, intro. & trans. Watson and Grene, p. 83.

75 Third reply (12 June, 1714). OC 19:882; *Malebranche's First and Last Critics*, p. 85.

76 Fourth Letter (26 August, 1714). OC 19:896; *Malebranche's First and Last Critics* p. 93.

77 *Ibid.* OC 19:905; *Malebranche's First and Last Critics*, p. 100.

78 Fourth reply. (6 September, 1714). OC 19:910; *Malebranche's First and Last Critics*, p. 104.

79 There has, nonetheless, been a considerable controversy over who was winning. Joseph Moreau prefaced his edition of the correspondence with a vigorous defence of Malebranche against the charge of Spinozism. Bréhier, in his *History of Philosophy*, took the opposite view, claiming that "Nothing penetrates more deeply into the system of Malebranche than Mairan's criticism" (*The Seventeenth Century*, p. 218).

80 Bayle, in his famous article on Zeno of Elea, treated Malebranche as a fellow skeptic: "It is useful to know that a Father of the Oratory, as illustrious for his piety as for his philosophical knowledge, maintained that faith alone can truly convince us of the existence of bodies." (*Dictionnaire historique et critique*, edn. 1820–4 Paris, Vol. XV, p. 52: *Historical and Critical Dictionary: Selections*, p. 377 f).

81 Locke, "An Examination of Père Malebranche's Opinion of Seeing All Things in God," §20.

82 *Critique de la recherche de la verité*, section 5; *Malebranche's First and Last Critics*, pp. 29–31.

83 "In truth, it seems to me, this system has no advantage over that of the Cartesians ... you should be asked why God is not content to produce all the thoughts and modifications of the soul ... without useless

bodies (*corps inutiles*) that the mind can never either move or know" (*Philosophische Schriften* IV.489).

84 *An Essay Towards the Theory of the Ideal or Intelligible World* I 191.

85 *Ibid.* I 207.

86 I have dealt with the issue of Collier's alleged plagiarism more fully in my "Platonic Idealism from Malebranche to Berkeley."

87 Acts 17:18. As Stoic philosophers were listed among Paul's audience, the author of Acts of the Apostles may be presumed to have intended the phrase to be taken in a Stoic way. But Berkeley clearly interpreted the phrase in a Platonic way, assuming God to be a pure Spirit.

88 See, for instance, *Search* III. ii. 6, OC I 447; LO 235. Malebranche cannot allow that matter is part of God and holds that "God is the intelligible world or the place of minds, as the material world is the place of bodies."

89 The Berkeley citations include *Philosophical Commentaries* §827, *Principles of Human Knowledge* I §§66 and 149, and the title page of the *Theory of Vision Vindicated*. For citations in the *Three Dialogues*, see *Works* II 214 & 236. In the case of Collier, some of the evidence is probably lost, but according to Robert Benson, who had access to the lost manuscripts, this was one of Collier's "favourite maxims" (*Memoirs of the Reverend Arthur Collier*, pp. 54f.). One citation, from an abstract of Collier's *Logology*, is quoted by Benson (*ibid.*, p. 76). Collier seems to have interpreted the "Platonic" passages of the Bible in the light of one another and took the early verses of John 1 to mean that God made all things by, through and in the Son. (Clavis, p. 104). He may have used Acts 17:18 to support his unusual view that the whole creation existed not only by and through but in the Son of God.

90 According to an abstract of his now extinct *Logology*, quoted in Benson, *Memoirs of the Life and Writings of the Rev. Arthur Collier*, p. 192.

91 "Panentheism" is the view that all things are *part* of the divine reality and is to be distinguished from "pantheism," according to which all things are *identical* with God. Both views deny that there is any reality apart from God but the pantheist can allow, as Malebranche, Berkeley, and Collier certainly wanted to do, that God transcends and is more than the creation.

92 *Philosophical Commentaries*, §290.

93 *Principles of Human Knowledge* I §92.

94 *Philosophical Commentaries*, §625.

95 *Principles* I §6.

96 *Principles* I §19. It seems reasonable to infer that Berkeley had Malebranche as well as Locke in mind in making this criticism.

97 Nonetheless, he was aware of the accusation that he was a Malebranchean and inserted an interchange in the second of his *Three Dialogues* in which his spokesman is given the opportunity to explain why he regarded himself as "remote from ... the enthusiasm of Malebranche." See *Works* II 213ff.

98 *Principles* I §30.

99 The convergence between Berkeley and Collier becomes even less remarkable when we reflect that idealism as a problem was a legacy of Descartes. It was hardly difficult to think of it as an option in the context of that legacy (shared with Malebranche). The real difficulty was to defend idealism against the obvious objections and here Berkeley is much more credible than Collier.

100 In his *Philosophical Commentaries*, §730, he wrote: "We may have certainty & knowledge without Ideas."

101 *Principles* I §89. Malebranche uses the phrase "sentiment intérieur" in this connection (*Search* III.2.vii.4, OC I:451, LO 237).

102 *Traité de Morale* I.8, §15, OC 11:192, *Treatise on Ethics*, p. 105.

103 *Traité de Morale* I.8, §16, OC 11:103; *Walton*, p. 105.

104 Lord Alexander Forbes of Pitsligo studied the differences between Mandeville and Malebranche on self-love in his Essays (1734). See the entry on him by Walton in the *Dictionary of Eighteenth Century British Philosophers*.

105 Some suggestions as to areas of research are made in *Walton* 30f.

# 11 Malebranche's Life and Legacy

The twentieth century has done much in the way of transforming the life and work of Malebranche into a cultural legacy. The effects of this transformation are first making themselves felt only now, at the end of the century. At the very least, the century that begins with the year 2000 will have at its disposal all it needs to study and explain his *oeuvre*, if not to grasp it in full. The history of philosophy is now fully equipped and ready to take possession of that *oeuvre* and thereby procure for itself entirely new opportunities. The publication of the *Oeuvres complètes* provides us with all the available texts attributable to Malebranche; in the past fifty years only a single new letter has been found! The method used in compiling this monumental collection gathered together the variations of all the recorded editions. I am not speaking of handwritten manuscripts; for as much as we can avail ourselves of interesting paleographic approaches in the case of Leibniz and Descartes, in the case of Malebranche we cannot return to the primordial state of the texts' composition.

However, in fact, Malebranche considered the previous editions of his books to be the rough drafts – so much so that the work published during his lifetime is only one long rough draft worth all the unpublished writings at Hanover. Evidence for this is found in the fact that there is no permanent dogmatism in any of these writings. The author's retrospection, as well as his conflicts with other philosophers, led him to take account of the objections that were made to him in a way quite different from that in which Descartes responded to the objections that he received. Descartes' thought remained subservient to the necessity of what he was demonstrating; it progresses in an involuted way. He held back the publication of certain fundamental elements, elements that appear only very deliberately and about which one never knows whether they express the totality of Cartesian thought. Malebranche was less rigid; he is more accepting of difference, quick to introduce innovations. We can see in Malebranche a crisis provoked by the publication of the "Elucidations" in 1678, a crisis that opened the century of the enlightenment even before the century of the enlightened was at issue. We can also spot it in Leibniz, when in 1670, he used his work on the *jurismodalia* to build the first instance of his *mathesis divina*. However, nothing like this appears in Descartes, where, with the exception of a few theses concerning theological actuality, it is very difficult to observe any structural evolution after the dialectical logic of the *Regulae*.

If I have entitled the two volumes of the *Oeuvres complètes* devoted to correspondence and biographical pieces "Malebranche vivant," it was not in order to confine the biographical to a place where it would have nothing to do with the philosophical. For in fact, there is no biography of Malebranche other than the intellectual. Neither his college notes nor his sole journey in the southwest of France could take its place. His biography is found squarely between both sides of the street on the rue du Louvre, extending about 200 meters from the Maison de l'Oratoire where he lived for 50 years toward the Pont-Neuf.

Contact with libraries and Dutch life played a large part in the life and work of Descartes. As for Leibniz, he was a great traveler for a citizen of the Republic of Letters: he even went all the way to the foot of Vesuvius to experimentally justify his theory of the volcanic development of the Earth. Malebranche made use of just a small personal library of well-chosen books, the sole decoration in his room aside from a few scientific instruments. He had the Oratory's library close at hand and, on the other side of the street, the library of the King. He was more a thinker than a reader; Leibniz did nothing but read, writing as he read, while Descartes only reluctantly admitted his own readings, which were more significant than is commonly thought.

The edition of the *Oeuvres* and the works that ensued also helped reveal the important role of Academy of Sciences in Malebranche's life. The Academy was at that time seated at the Palace of the Louvre, and Malebranche could frequent just by crossing the street. The number of his visits, the variety of academicians and subjects with which he was familiar, the role of these scientific facts in the development of his work – all these transform what is known about the man. His philosophy demanded a relationship with and among the sciences, and this relationship involved a constant back and forth. The work bears remarkable traces of this movement. It is true that, as with Descartes and Leibniz, Malebranche left experimental matters to others. He consigned the concept of experience to an ancillary role that stems precisely from the primacy of logical evidence over the results of experience or experimentation. The experience that proves the theory is good; that which conflicts with it, bad. However respected Bacon, Galileo, Mersenne, and Huygens were, theory remained for them a conclusion, whereas, for Malebranche, it had become an unsurpassable point of departure.

Why did Malebranche choose the Oratory and, notably, the Maison de Paris? The families who belonged to the Parlements de justice or held administrative functions in the royal court chose to send their children to the colleges of the Oratory, where they received a totally new education in the French language, one in which scientific culture was by and large integrated into the curriculum. The religious tone of what was taught was dominated by the work of Bérulle, however, other Oratorians, such as Condren or Gibieuf, had a substantial following. The creed was more christo-centric than trinitarian, more incarnationist than redemptionist. The Oratorian teachers were, from the beginning, on good terms with the tenets of Cartesian dualism, recovering the Augustinian inspiration in it, shared equally by the Jansenists. This means that the pedagogical rivalry with the Jesuits, who remained focused on the Scholastic Aristotelian-Thomist tradition, was heartily encouraged in the midst of Parlement. Malebranche's family included members who facilitated his entrance and residence at the Oratory. About 1665, the young Malebranche joined a congregation that was in league with the Jansenists in seeking to purify and rejuvenate the morals of the French Church. In such an environment, Cartesian philosophy was widely admitted, even though it ran up against the interdictions enacted by the teaching of the Jesuit colleges. It is not surprising that Malebranche discovered with great admiration Descartes' treatise *On Man*, which had just been published.

However, he did not line up docilely behind Descartes, even less than Rohault or Cordemoy did. The original Augustinian context led him into his own theoretical choices, to an Augustinianism within which he never failed to evolve and distinguish himself. There is surely something surprising in seeing a *Search After Truth* (the writing of Descartes which bears this name was not yet known) open with a Preface that refers each chapter – chapters that could be considered as inspired by Descartes – to some biblical or patristic citation! Descartes was very careful to stand at a distance from arguments based on authority or tradition and took cautions against mixing rational proofs and the articles of faith. This was one of the first winds that blew Cartesianism down the path of the disparate hermeneutics, which have seized it for three centuries now.

This Augustinian basis of Malebranche's thought is not negligible. It possesses its own lines of orientation, making it by and large compatible with the Arnauldian group at Port-Royal. Malebranche became the young metaphysician on whom the author of the *Fourth Objections* can count – the same author who will become, in the name of the Cartesian thesis of representational modes, the most ferocious adversary of the theory of vision in God.

However, the doctrine of vision in God is affirmed as early as the first edition of the *Search*, and this affirmation is made against both Descartes and Arnauld. Why did Arnauld not react immediately? Because those other, more important questions – the ones that became problematic – had not yet been raised. On issues within the theory of knowledge, it is legitimate to tolerate some deviation on the part of a young author. On questions pertaining to the distribution of grace, however, it is much more difficult for a militant follower of Jansenism to support, *de facto* and *de jure*, such unorthodoxies.

Up until the "Elucidations" of 1678, Malebranche remained reserved on these questions, which do not have to be touched on when dealing with the problem of knowledge. In point of fact, the passages where the theory of grace or of creation and redemption appear are still composed in a manner that even the most rational of the Jansenists could admit. If the theory of knowledge stands directly beneath the sign of universal Reason governed by an unchangeable Order shared by all humans, the theory of grace is still found under the absolutist government of divine decrees and particular acts of will concerning the salvation of the elect few.

However, how could a system develop around such an extreme opposition between two types of creative and salvific governance – one that depends on general and legal acts of will in which all finite intelligences participate, and another that is carried out by particular private acts of will that concern the salvation of each? It is not possible to controvert the generality of the laws of nature, largely admitted by Arnauld's geometric and creationist Cartesianism, and Malebranche tended to go this way in all regions of physical, psychophysical, and psychic being. However, it was not clear that, in this landscape of knowledge, the Arnauldians could be in agreement with the occasionalism that appeared with the publication of the six books of the *Search*. What was the principle of physical and psychic action?

We have not sufficiently shown how the *Search* contradicted the *Port-Royal Logic*. It was contrary to it in the sense that it did not admit any of the Aristotelian furnishings the *Logic*; it bore as an epigraph the proof of all truth by recourse to evidence, which to be sure was the dominant drift of the *Logic*. There was agreement as to the end, but there was none about the necessity of dragging the Porphyrian and analytic ball and chain through the methodic procedures of thought.

It quickly became obvious that, within the landscape of the *Logic* of Port-Royal, the gulf between the evidence of the laws of nature and the probability of human acts was creating an antinomy. How did it happen that the last chapter of the *Logic* began by integrating a "mathesis universalis" of the probable – worked out for the most part by Pascal, notably in his correspondence with Fermat – and concluded with its inadequacy to the problems of eternity and salvation. If probabilistic mathematics must yield to a wager of the Pascalian type that leads to the impossibility of setting up an appreciable connection between infinity and nothing, then one shifts the playing field; one abandons all "mathesis universalis" for risks without measure. Pascal and the *Logic* abandoned the Cartesian term *indefinite*, which was too conciliatory in the matter of infinity and nothing. By contrast, Malebranche made use of it and does not hesitate to follow Leibniz in his judgment of the infinites and the infinity of infinites – God in his mature philosophy became the concept of the "infinitely infinite infinity." If its comprehension was still far from adequate or complete, its understanding and explanation became accessible to the human understanding.

If the major polemic of Malebranche's work is laid out under the sign of the hidden God, the concessions made to Port-Royal are not to the taste of all the Cartesians. An author such as Desgabets revolts against Malebranche's demonstration of the immortality of the soul, which the *Search* made too abstract in its relation with the body. The substantial union of the soul and the body is not the effect of divine will, but depends on the very nature of the two substances. Substance offers a better guarantee than acts of will for what Desgabets calls "the indefectability of creatures," which makes the soul inseparable from the body for its cognitive operations. That is to say, as early as the publication of the first three books of the *Search*, the theory of vision in God gave rise to difficulties in the Cartesian and Arnaldian contexts.

It also gave rise to difficulties for the defenders of Pyrrhonism, who had not given up denouncing the discovery of truth by evidence. They took as little account of the critiques of *Meditation I* as they did of those of the *Search*, which set up a theory of truth and of the relations between ideas that have a warrant outside the decisions of the divine power. One soon begins to realize that Malebranche's philosophy reintroduced what, in Descartes' work, could have been a sign of pyrrhonianism: the critique of finality, recovered by Malebranche; upholding one sole efficient cause, destroyed by occasionalism, and so forth.

However, it goes without saying that the signals given to the Arnauldian group earned Malebranche the gift of an advance copy of Pascal's *Pensées*, the 1670 edition made by Port-Royal, which Malebranche signed off on for the good of the Jansenists and appeared as the metaphysician of the group.

It was therefore clear, as early as the creation of the *Oeuvres complètes*, that all the critical apparatuses in the volumes published before the *Elucidations (Éelaircissements)* retained the trace of an archeology of the Malebranchian architecture.

One was still far away from generalized occasionalism and governance of the domain of grace by the general acts of God's will. Computerized lexicographical review lends the details necessary to confirm the presence in the texts of a highly oppositional structure between general will for the laws of nature and particular acts of will for the incitements to grace. A first general act of God's will conveys creation and conservation, according to laws in which human reason can participate. A second act of will must intervene in this universe where the order of the first laws was reversed by the effect of sin. It must, in effect, help reestablish the threatened preeminence of the mind over the body. However, humankind is no longer capable of such control except by the efficacious grace of election. The corrupted nature can be healed only through the intervention of a restorative and redemptive will. These textual fragments are where the particular miracles that appear in time and reestablish the threatened order of creation come up. It could be said that we exist in a broken world whose origin had been foreseen as directly inspired with a soteriological finality but in which the Fall brought about a dysfunction. Omnipotence, which is submitted to Wisdom in the context of natural laws, takes no account of it when it is a question of choosing the elect.

We also observe in the texts of this *haute époque* another strictly oppositional structure between the vision in God, which is effected without the mind's modes, and the sensibility that "touches" the depths of the soul's capacity. We therefore cannot expect anything from hedonistic motives, and all desire to be happy is suspect of subjugating the mind to the body. Only a powerful grace of feeling can block pleasure from getting carried away, and the best the mind could hope for is a certain aridity that leads to the deserts of Port-Royal. Certainly, not all of the senses are corrupted, and the theory of natural judgment begins to come to light in the form of dominant sensations. However, they are not yet submitted to a universal order and are therefore reparable only through the intervention of one particular act of will.

In such a context, the Cartesian anthropology is disavowed as much in what concerns the effects of the Fall as in what pertains to vision in God. The concept of *occasion*, which begins to manifest itself from the beginning of the work, can be seen in the treatise *On Man* and in the use that the first occasionalists made of it. Descartes was already compelled to use the term *occasion*, without theorizing it. Malebranche set off from here and built a whole architectonic around it.

The principle of occasionalism leads to the recognition that there is only a single God because there is only one cause, that every cause is deprived of any philosophical meaning and depends on entities, what Descartes called metaphysical beings. If there is only one true cause, the cause of knowledge can no longer be found in as many "storehouses of ideas" as there are human beings. The new principle of the economy of ways, which takes root with the great combinatory metaphysics of the end of the century, reduces this lot of ideas to unity in the one and only eternal Word. Reasons, which have no principle of independence, neither substantial nor entitative, are directly related to the divine Wisdom that all share. There is therefore no more than a single "storehouse of ideas" from which knowledge spreads as soon as humans consult it. This central point is named *logos*, which Malebranche translates with "*la Raison.*" By contrast, no centralization is imagined for the government of grace, which continues to be carried out according to the good pleasure of the election of the fortunate, without anything in it falling within the reach of human reason.

It seems to me today, in the wake of recent work concerned with the young Leibniz and his time in Paris, that it is appropriate to pose the question of his possible role in the revision Malebranche brought about in 1678. During their first correspondence of 1671, then after his arrival in Paris, Leibniz offered Arnauld a detailed explanation of this "science of life," which Descartes had left on the margins of his project. In 1670, while wondering about the significance of his juridical works during his university days, Leibniz began to feel the need for a concept of prudence that was no longer defined within the framework of "mediocritas," but in that of a "harmonia universalis." Through Arnauld and through the Académie des sciences, it was easy for the two authors to meet one another, which they certainly did during the time between the publication of the first two volumes of the *Search*. The discussion was dense and proves that Leibniz made a frontal assault on the Cartesian theory of extension to which Malebranche continued to reduce matter. However, it also opened onto the intelligibility of the concepts of the void and movement, coming eventually to the question of a "real distinction." What is the simple idea of an absolute being? The discussion was deliberately directed toward the question of the divine attributes and toward the insufficiency of a definition of the reality of bodies in terms of the evidence of the simple notion of extension. Now, Leibniz himself had had the same problems to resolve, and the innovations he brought about in 1670 established the necessity of rethinking the concept of substance more along the lines of Aristotle than as Port-Royal had defined it in its *Logic*. If, moreover, the substance that implies the collection of its attributes was part of a universal harmony, then it is through a calculation of the finite perfections of each substance that the "panespistemonicon Dei" is seen to be the optimal source of the perfections of the world. The discussion with Arnauld had been in full swing since 1671; it concerned this new problematic and did so in a scope never before reached. Had the "mathesis universalis" run its course, and was it necessary to open a new architectural concept centering on a "mathesis divina," which would explain precisely the calculation of optimum perfections within-the-world, of which the "mathesis universalis" would be a particular case, applicable to mutually expressive phenomena represented by substance? To be sure, Malebranche kept, until 1715, the dualism of substances defined in the Cartesian way; to be sure, he did not progress toward a phenomenal conception of bodies as representations of a mind. However, this does not preclude the Leibnizian idea of a logical machine reparable by human reason in virtue of its created origin from striking Malebranche, seeing as he will agree with such positions when he generalizes occasionalism.

The five periods of the Malebranche-Leibniz correspondence will prove this mutual esteem and interest in one another. This is all the more true in matters of mathematics and physics. Malebranche, an Académicien des sciences, became the spokesperson for the Leibnizian innovations concerning the theory of the laws of motion and the introduction of infinitesimal calculus in France. Now these two theoretical positions joined both the dynamism to which Leibniz was leaning during the first Parisian correspondence and a conceptual grasp of the infinite and the infinites that animated the writings of Malebranche after 1700.

June 30, 1678, marked the publication of the third volume of the *Search*, entitled *Elucidations*. It is immediately clear from this volume that the theory of vision in God was confirmed in all respects and, above all, that the analysis of the free act and the gracious act were subsumed beneath the general laws of divine Wisdom, which had been extended to include all that the Port-Royal *Logic* abandoned to particular acts of will under determination by general acts of will: eternity and salvation. Is it then June 30, 1678, which marks the origin of the century of enlightened thinkers, *les lumières*? Numerous works support such a view. The plural of the term (*lumières*) is frequent in Malebranche's work: what is certain is that the century of the Enlightenment ascends to the throne there and then. The Ramist dialectic, the Port-Royal *Logic*, and the architectonic of the *Regulae* had made the concept "natural light" into something other than a metaphor: it became a dominant concept in which the ambition of thinking humanity was condensed, a humanity desirous of assuming its destiny through reason. The doctrine of vision in God brings this to its consummation in and through the application of light and laws to all the kingdoms of the universe, from physics to soteriology. It might seem that Malebranche broke definitively with the traces of Jansenism discernible in his early writings. He must have been aware that he also broke with Arnauld, who had nevertheless offered a very warm welcome to the first *Search*. However, the Oratory was compelled, in order to save its constituents, to sign in September 1678 an "order" banishing Jansenism from the congregation. The Oratory, however, kept Augustine as a norm beside Thomas Aquinas. It was necessary to avoid making the efficacy of grace act on the will with necessity, and teach instead that there is always a sufficient grace giving the power to accomplish the divine commandments. By contrast, none of the properly philosophical recommendations of these pamphlets will be applied in Malebranche's work, and notably not the reservations that condemn Cartesianism.

It seems clear that mutual friends tried to bring about a reconciliation between Arnauld and Malebranche, but nothing came of it. The discussion within the framework of Augustinian hermeneutics did not reach a conclusion, and Leibniz was the first to be stunned by the break between Arnauld and Malebranche, both of whom he had known as friends. Leibniz had just settled in Hanover on his return from Paris, and there he would soon lay the principles for a disjunctive architecture where the phenomenal theory of bodies existing for the thought of a mind was joined with an explanation centering on the hylomorphic principle of matter and form, a path that Malebranche would refuse to take.

The publication of the *Treatise on Nature and Grace*, which Arnauld had examined in manuscript form, brought with it a definitive break between followers of Arnauld and those of Malebranche. That the government of grace falls under the laws of a Wisdom, which supplants every particular intervention of omnipotence, that this government is handed over to Jesus Christ considered as occasional cause of grace, that deliberation concerning salvation falls under general laws that depend on an order that will be designated "ordinatism" – all this was intolerable to Port-Royal. What the *Elucidations* let be divined, the *Treatise* explained in detail.

It could be said now that the tragic structures engendered by the function P > S yield to the optimizing structures following S > P. The division of the doctrines of seventeenth century between an omnipotence that has sway over wisdom and a wisdom that has sway over omnipotence here reaches its limit: nothing that concerns the act of the omnipotence internal to the concept of God or else "ad extra" is foreign to the deliberation with which wisdom calculates in an effort to realize the optimal ordering of the world. Descartes had espoused the positions of Grégoire of Valence more than those of Suarez and endowed divine omnipotence with an absolute power of which the divine understanding and the divine will were only immediate effects. Arnauld agreed with such a position for reasons dependant on the Augustinian interpretation of Jansenius. By reversing the relation P > S, Malebranche confirmed the opening of the century of enlightened thinkers. From now on, attention will have to be given to the law, as well as to laws, the order among the laws, the general Order among all the laws of the different fields of creation, with the term Order taking a capital "O" to indicate that the method has passed from research applied to order-commandment to a reason bearing on order-organization. It could be said then that the old saying "credo ut intelligam" is used as fully as possible and that the end of History must be read in this principle of sufficient reason, which appears at each level of Being as a function of the concept of a law which concerns it.

If this becomes the general formula that affects and explains the whole of the book, all its thematic details had to have been arranged according to it; for at the outset, it was difficult to imagine such an upheaval. Malebranche therefore reconsiders each of his early writings with the intention of correcting them. To take account of these modifications, we needed all five-hundred pages of *Système et existence dans l'oeuvre de Malebranche*, as well as the four-hundred page companion volume, *Malebranche de l'Académie des sciences*.

Generalized occasionalism leaves the field open for a "mathesis divina," which makes of the method and the "mathesis universalis" merely means. During this first period, the image of God-the-craftsman was sufficient to account for the rules arranging corporeal substances, because the spiritual substances escaped the jurisdiction of law and escaped themselves. In the name of the four kinds of knowledge, the individual mind was not known by a clear idea, but only in and through feeling, inner consciousness. The variety of nature is that of the rare and the marvelous, and the divine glory is recognized by the magnificence of creation. However, that is no longer possible as soon as it is the arrangement between the totality of created beings that makes the divine act worthy of interest. One is on the road to God-the-architect, which the philosophy of the enlightened will keep and which is glorified in the simplicity of the ways that combine the finite perfections of each detail of the universe. Nothing rules out the possibility that Leibniz announced to Malebranche his work on both the *De Arte combinatoria* and the limits of Lulle's interpretation of a combination of circular perfections. The simplicity of the law is more worthy of admiration than the material enacted into law. In the domain of nature as in that of grace, it is no more the selection of this material than the choice of the diverse concatenations that textures the relations between matter and form, movement, and shape. The thesis of infinite intelligible extension will provide the unifying concept among the types of bodies, between bodies and minds, and between the knowledge that minds have of bodies and that with which the Word deals with them. From now on, individuation can happen only through the law, and a corporeal substance is neither an entelechy nor a substantial form, but a function that depends on the parameters of extension, movement, and position – which saves the Cartesian definition. As for the individuation of minds, it remains all the more unsolvable as the *cogito* no longer has a clear and distinct idea of itself and is known only in and through feeling. We will see that this does not mean that there is no idea of the individual soul, but that we have no access to it during the time of the soul's presence in a body – this idea being accessible to each of us in the future state of the glorified body.

For what the mature work attests is an anthropology that dominates a work that makes the "science of man" the most important of the "human sciences." If it is too early for the term anthropology to emerge in Malebranche's lexicon, it is no less obvious that this science of man rests on a comparative arrangement of three states of humanity, which permit the comparison of man's actual state, which is his state in a "society of commerce," with what this state could be in an original "society of innocence" or in a final "society of minds." This range of distinctions, which go so far as to introduce differences in the respective conditioning of the corporeal elements of man in their relation with his mind, permits us to establish a primary comparison concerning the metaphysics of morals where the uchronic and utopic intervene in moral and political judgment.

This notion of humanity evolving from a state of nature to a restored state makes present society not the sequel to the state of nature, but a break with this state. This is to say that the representation of the primal Adam grounds a differential method that definitively ruins the representation of man limited to present duties and rights, to the definition of merit by created goods or of virtue by accomplished tasks. Whatever the calling, prince or bishop, his behavior must be "in conformity" with the universal order, understanding by that a disposition of consciousness that renders it free from all contingency so as to apply the imperative of the general law. Thus, it stands apart from the Jansenist attitude in which human's nature had been so corrupted that it was forgotten. This delivers society to self-love rather than letting it direct itself according to the precepts of mechanical subordination of forces. The finalities, origins, and ends that run through humanity disconnect man from every physiological observation and arrange his conduct in conformity with that of the general law and universality of reasons. In this way, Malebranchian theory is inscribed in the growing ranks of the *déludovicisation* of consciousness – all power being submitted to the law of the order, every divine act included.

This did not forbid the spontaneous exercise of a sort of natural grace, which in man is the desire to be happy. Malebranche can be criticized for a hedonism in which he certainly did not partake. The desire to be happy was the key to his resisting the doctrines of pure love, which according to Lamy and Fénelon had to be purely disinterested. Nothing stops consciousness from conforming to the order, if it does so not through love of concupiscence or benevolent love, but according to the requirement of unitive love. There too the primacy of love for this other, known as little as our own consciousness is because it is grasped "in conjecture," brings up the jurisprudential modalities that the young Leibniz could have put forward in Paris. To love is to find felicity in the pleasure of others. This perspective is coherent with the Adamic creation of a state of man that depends directly on the overabundant activity of divine power, something that happens all the more in creation as it does not have a second home in the occasionalist context. Divine jurisprudence like human jurisprudence rests on this act of loving alterity and variety. That the fall clouded the origins is obvious, but that is not the original state of human beings; and, in contrast to Hobbes and Locke, it is not at all fitting to make self-love the driving force in a science of humans, which entirely exceeds its reach.

Nevertheless, the architecture of the work continues to exert its influence over itself, notably because a motivation by feeling can either belong to the clarity of reason or else remain entirely foreign to the idea. What I called "the renewal of 1695" puts a number of concepts back on the table. The difference between the early redactions and the final versions is so great that one arrives at a series of aporias if one considers them generally, without modifying one's structures with diachronic indices that serve as parameters.

First of all, the introduction of differential and integral calculus into the Malebranchian group of the Académie des sciences entailed a radical revision as much of the bibliography conveyed by the *Search* as of the different concepts. The break Descartes imposed between mechanical and transcendental graphs fell beneath the blow of Leibniz's discoveries, communicated to Malebranche early on and never forgotten. Being familiar with the mathematical infinite had the effect of effacing the taboos that resulted from it in the Cartesian corpus. The exercises pertaining to the calculus of proportions in the differential and integral field upset the dominant concepts in Cartesian philosophy. Equality becomes a transition, every zero is a passage, a number falls within an infinite process, a point contains an infinity of angles, an arc is equivalent to a cord. The criteria of methodic evidence, adequate to these givens of "mathesis universalis," collapse and yield their place to continuity and movement. Under the influence of the Leibnizian speciousness that L'Hospital and especially Varignon will help to enrich and apply, the rules of equipollence replace those of equality. If one were to integrate the mathematics of the infinite and the laws of dynamics in Malebranche's work, it would be evident that innovations and ruptures occur. The two major testimonies to this historicity of Malebranche's system are found in the analysis of the concept "order" and in that of the efficacy of ideas.

For one really had to possess as many general laws as there were domains of creation: in physics, in psychology, in knowledge, in the will through unity with the Word and Omnipotence, one did not, for all that, find the law of laws. The system's ultimate thrust toward a concept of Order that was sufficiently all-encompassing to agree with all the laws, and sufficiently intense to refresh discourse, can be seen in the conception of the Trinity by that of extended bodies. If on the one hand, there is an infinite God who is the creator of a world with finite perfections, how can a world with finite perfections be so pleasing to this God with infinite perfections as to incite his loving overabundance to create it?

It is only when the infinitist procedures of Leibniz were admitted that concepts could be applied to such subjects. For a finite world to be the object of such a loving desire, it had to bear in itself the sign of some infinity. If the first writings were gladly redemptionist, the final writings moved the Incarnation to the forefront of the dogma – first by creatorial justification, next as salvific justification. For the "fiat" to answer some necessity, it had to be inspired by the immanent trinitarian act in which the procession of Persons without any qualitative difference gives birth to the eternal Word. The eternal Word became, with the theory of ideas, the model of the universe, and it sufficed to have it figure in the constitution of creation. The Incarnation of the Word, in the occasional cause Jesus Christ, brings to the universe the value infinity that nourishes the collection of laws and materials, notably spiritual matter. The connection that the God-Man brings about is represented by this dash. The world is created only because it bears not only the image but the trinitarian reality of omnipotence. It is at the same time, the key according to which the act of omnipotence must be read in order to take on meaning. The Incarnation is absolutely necessary to give the world a weight worthy of the divine *fiat*: It would have happened, even in other worlds where man had not sinned! That is, the break with Port-Royal generated two cultural universes so different that nothing could bring them together. The infinitely infinite is present in the world: it is no longer the impassive spectator, but becomes, in and through Jesus-Christ, the immanent actor. What is called the "necessity of being" finds its reason in the participation of the Persons and in the presence in the world of the incarnation of one of the eternals. Everything in the universe, the ways, the laws, the materials, enters into a combinatory order of compensations, which confer its grandeur on it.

As for the theory, which sets up an opposition between what was an idea "that does not touch" and a feeling "which touches," it is subject to serious emendations. I can say today that there too the philosophical structures experience pressure from the infinitist structures deployed by the Malebranchian group. Before the mass of objections deployed by Arnauld, reiterated by Régis against the theory of ideas "which do not touch" and which contradict the Cartesian theory of the representative modalities of the mind, Malebranche is led to reconsider his position. Consequently, from 1695 on, a new structure is set up, one which moves from the structure opposing idea and feeling to a structure opposing "pure perception" and "sensible perception." In both cases, the soul is affected, but either gently (in the case of the idea) or strongly (in the case of sensation). How could the mind register in its own way the presence of an idea if it is not inwardly modified by it? The idea therefore will be qualified as "efficacious," and intelligible extension is endowed with this efficacy because the Word whose reason it partakes of keeps something of the power that is not differentiated from it. Without this efficacy, the idea could not affect the mind. Thus, vision in God is no longer what is peculiar to knowledge in and through the idea, but it also includes an effective and affective power that can be infinitely small, as in the case of the idea of God. The infinitist mathematical symbolism invades the later work, at the same time rehabilitating the cognitive value of sensibility. This order of justice reigns as much between the infinite perfections in the act within God as in the finite perfections resulting from the act ad extra. As for Leibniz, a philosophy of the possible is deployed with the concept of wisdom as well as that of an optimal calculation between these possibilities. All things are "ordinatissimes." Knowledge is referred to relations of truth, action should be in conformity with relations of perfection. A fruitful signification invades the final work, supplanting the more austere remarks of the first editions.

This fruitful tone agrees with the harmony of this creationist and soteriological optimum, thus joining up with the utopia of Fénelon's *Télémaque*, of Castel de Saint Pierre's *Polysynodie*, Leibniz's reorientation of the Counsels of the Empire along the lines of the English Parliament. The Regency is inspired by these conciliar philosophies where universal reason speaks in the most humble of subjects as well as in the authority of the prince or bishop. This search for conformity of the internal act of conscience to the order-organization whose clarity and enjoyment each has in himself signals the undoing of the order-commandment, which is founded in pure, absolute power, rule by whim and unsharable. The great philosophical combinative analyses of the end of the century teach one how to think the totality and the law within the totalization. Every authority is submitted to the same rule of universal reason. The *Traité de morale*, founded on the rights and duties of the person, had safeguarded the duties of reciprocal esteem and respect, attaining the first two laws of natural right, but the duty of obedience, by virtue of its required conformity of all – subjects, princes, bishops, and even God – to the law of the Order, is contested by a series of dispositions that submitted its validity to a right of resistance that Malebranche had both practiced and theorized. Malebranche's legacy was in this way ensured, and numerous authors have shown its immediate importance through the eighteenth century, and even its importance to a categorical imperative that knows its only referent to be the law.

# BIBLIOGRAPHY

Acworth, Richard, "Malebranche and His Heirs," *Journal of the History of Ideas* 38 (1977), 673–6.

Acworth, Richard, *The Philosophy of John Norris of Bemerton (1657–1712)* (Hildesheim and New York: Olms, 1979).

Adam, M., *Malebranche et le problème moral* (Bordeaux: Bière, 1995).

Adams, R. M., "Flavors, Colors and God," in *The Virtues of Faith and Other Essays in Philosophical Theology* (Oxford: Oxford University Press, 1987).

Alquié, Ferdinand, *Le Cartésianisme de Malebranche* (Paris: J. Vrin, 1974).

Alquié, Ferdinand, *Malebranche et le rationalisme chrètien* (Paris: Seghers, 1977).

André, Y. M., *La vie du R. P. Malebranche, prêtre de l'Oratoire, avec l'histoire de ses ouvrages* (Paris: Poussielgue/Geneva: Slatkine, 1886/ reprinted 1970).

Anon, trans., *Christian Conferences: Demonstrating the Truth of the Christian Religion and Morality. By F. Malebranche. To which is added, his Meditations on Humility and Repentance* (London, 1695a).

Anon., trans., *A Treatise of Nature and Grace. [By Malebranche] To which is added the author's idea of Providence; and his answers to several objections against the foregoing discourse* (London, 1695b).

Aquinas, Thomas, *Summa Theologiae*, 60 volumes, ed. and trans. Blackfriars (New York: McGraw Hill, 1964).

Ariew, Roger, "The Infinite in Descartes's Conversation with Burman," *Archiv für Geschichte der Philosophie* 69 (1987), 140–63.

Ariew, Roger, and Alan Gabbey, "The Scholastic Background," in Daniel Garber and Michael Ayers (eds.), *The Cambridge History of Seventeenth-Century Philosophy*, 2 volumes, volume 1 (Cambridge: Cambridge University Press, 1998), 425–53.

Arnauld, Antoine, "Introduction" to translation of Augustine's *De Correptione et Gratia* (Paris, 1644).

Arnauld, Antoine, *Réflexions philosophiques et théologiques sur le nouveau système de la nature & de la grace* (Cologne, 1686).

Arnauld, Antoine, *Oeuvres de Messire Antoine Arnauld*, 43 volumes (Paris: Sigismond d'Arnay; reprinted in Brussells, 1780/reprinted 1967).

Arnauld, Antoine, *On True and False Ideas, New Objections to Descartes's Meditations and Descartes's Replies*, trans. E. J. Kremer (Lewiston: The Edwin Mellon Press, 1990).

Arnauld, Antoine, and Pierre Nicole, *Logic, or the Art of Thinking*, trans. Jill Vance Buroker (Cambridge: Cambridge University Press, 1996).

Balz, G. A., "Clauberg and the Development of Occasionalism," in G. A. Balz (ed.), *Cartesian Studies* (New York: Columbia University Press, 1951).

Banfi, Antonio, "Malebranche et l'Italie," *Revue philosophique de la France et de l'étranger* 125 (1938), 253–74.

Bardout, Jean-Christophe, *Malebranche et la métaphysique* (Paris: Presses Universitaires de France, 1999).

Bastide, G. (ed.), *Malebranche: L'Homme et l'oeuvre, 1638–1715* (Paris: J. Vrin. 1967).

Battail, Jean-François, *L'Avocat philosophe Géraud de Cordemoy* (The Hague: Martinus Nijhoff, 1973).

Bayle, Pierre, *Pensées diverses sur la comète* (Paris, 1682).

Bayle, Pierre, *Nouvelles de la République des Lettres* (Paris, 1685).

Bayle, Pierre, *Oeuvres diverses*, 4 volumes (The Hague, 1727).

Bayle, Pierre, *Dictionnaire historique et critique*, A. J. Q. Beuchot (ed.) (Paris, 1820–24/reprinted Geneva: Slatkine, 1969).

Bayle, Pierre, *Historical and Critical Dictionary: Selections*, ed. and trans. Richard H. Popkin (Indianapolis: Hackett, 1965).

Belaval, Yvon, *Leibniz: Critique de Descartes* (Paris: Gallimard, 1960).

Benson, Robert, *Memoirs of the Life and Writings of the Rev. Arthur Collier* (London, 1837).

Bentham, Jeremy, *Works*, R. Tait (ed.) (Edinburgh, 1834–38).

Berkeley, George, *A Treatise Concerning the Principles of Human Knowledge, Part I. Wherein the chief Causes of Error and Difficulty in the Sciences, with the Grounds of Scepticism, Atheism, and Irreligion, are inquir'd into* (Dublin, 1710).

Berkeley, George, *Three Dialogues between Hylas and Philonous* (London, 1713).

Berkeley, George, *The Works of George Berkeley, Bishop of Cloyne*, A. A. Luce and T. E. Jessop (eds.) (London: Nelson, 1949).

Bonno, G., *Les Relations intellectuelles de Locke avec la France* (Berkeley: University of California Press, 1955).

Bossuet, Jacques-Bénigne, *Oraison Funèbre de Marie-Thérèse d'Autriche* (Paris, 1683).

Bossuet, Jacques-Bénigne, *Correspondance*, C. Urbain and J. Levesque (eds.) (Paris: Hachette, 1905–25).

Bossuet, Jacques-Bénigne, *Politics drawn from the Very Words of Holy Scripture*, trans. Patrick Riley (Cambridge: Cambridge University Press, 1990).

Bouillier, Francisque, *Histoire de la philosophie Cartésienne*, 2 volumes (Paris: Durand, 1954).

Boursier, Laurent, *De l'action de Dieu sur les créatures* (Paris: Babuty, 1713).

Bracken, Harry M., "The Malebranche-Arnauld Debate: Philosophical or Ideological?" in Stuart Brown (ed.), *Nicolas Malebranche: His Philosophical Critics and Successors* (Assen: Van Gorcum, 1991).

Bréhier, Émile, *Histoire de la Philosophie: La Philosophie Moderne I: Le dix-septième siècle* (Paris: Presses Universitaires de France, 1938).

Bréhier, Émile, "Les lectures malebranchistes de J.-J. Rousseau," *Revue internationale de philosophie*, 1 (1938–39), 113–42.

Bridet, L., *La Théorie de la connaissance dans la philosophie de Malebranche* (Paris: M. Rivière, 1929).

Brown, Stuart (ed.), *Nicolas Malebranche: His Philosophical Critics and Successors* (Assen: Van Gorcum, 1991a).

Brown, Stuart, "Malebranche's Occasionalism and Leibniz's Pre-established Harmony: an 'Easy Crossing' or an Unbridgeable Gap?" in Staurt Brown (ed.), *Nicolas Malebranche: His Philosophical Critics and Successors* (Assen: Van Gorcum, 1991b).

Brown, Stuart, "Malebranche's First English Translators," *British Society for the History of Philosophy Newsletter*, New Series 1.2 (1996), 19–23.

Brown, Stuart, "Platonic Idealism in Modern Philosophy from Malebranche to Berkeley," in G. A. J. Rogers et al. (eds.), *The Cambridge Platonists in Philosophical Context* (Dordrecht: Kluwer, 1997).

Carr, Jr., T. M., *Descartes and the Resilience of Rhetoric: Varieties of Cartesian Rhetorical Theory* (Carbondale, IL: Southern Illinois University Press, 1990).

Church, Ralph W., "Malebranche and Hume," *Revue internationale de Philosophie* 1 (1938), 143–61.

Clair, Pierre, "Louis de la Forge et les origines de l'occasionalisme," *Recherches sur le dix-septième siècle* 1 (1976), 63–72.

Collier, Arthur, *Clavis Universalis: or, a New inquiry after truth. Being a demonstration of the nonexistence, or the impossibility of an external world* (London: Robert Gosling, 1713).

Condillac, Étienne Bonot de, *Traité des systèmes, où l'on en démêle les inconvenients et les advantages* (Amsterdam & Leipzig, 1946).

Connell, Desmond, *The Vision in God: Malebranche's Scholastic Sources* (Paris and Louvain: Nauwelaerts, 1967).

Cook, Monte, "Malebranche versus Arnauld," *Journal of the History of Philosophy* 29 (1991), 183–91.

Cook, Monte, "The Ontological Status of Malebranchean Ideas," *Journal of the History of Philosophy* 36 (1998), 525–44.

Dear, Peter, "Method and the Study of Nature," in Daniel Garber and Michael Ayers (eds.), *The Cambridge History of Seventeenth-Century Philosophy* (Cambridge: Cambridge University Press, 1998).

Delbos, Victor, *Etude de la philosophie de Malebranche* (Paris: Bloud et Gay, 1958).

Descartes, René, *Oeuvres de Descartes*, 12 volumes, C. Adam and P. Tannery (eds.) (Paris: J. Vrin. 1897–1913).

Descartes, René, *The Philosophical Writings of Descartes*, 2 volumes, trans. J. Cottingham, R. Stoothoff, and D. Murdoch (Cambridge: Cambridge University Press, 1984).

Dreyfus, Ginette, *La Volonté selon Malebranche* (Paris: J. Vrin, 1958).

Elengu, P.-E., *Etendue et connaissance dans la philosophie de Malebranche* (Paris: J. Vrin, 1973).

Fénelon, François de, *Oeuvres de Fénelon*, 3 volumes (Paris: Didot Frères, 1835).

Fontenelle, Bernard le Bovier de, *Doutes sur le système physique des causes occasionelles* (Paris, 1686).

Fontenelle, Bernard le Bovier de, *Oeuvres de Fontenelle*, 2 volumes, G.-B. Depping (ed.) (Paris/Geneva: Slatkine Reprints, 1818/reprint 1968).

Foucher, Simon, *Critique de la Recherche de la verité où l'on examine en même-tems une partie des Principes de Mr Descartes. Lettre, par un Academicien* (Paris. Reprinted with an introduction by R. A. Watson, New York: Johnson Reprint, 1675/1969).

Foucher, Simon, *Réponse pour la critique á la préface du second volume de la recherche de la verité (sic) sur la philosophie des académiciens* (Paris, 1676).

Frankfurt, Harry, "The Importance of What We Care About," in *The Importance of What We Care About, Philosophical Essays* (Cambridge: Cambridge University Press, 1988), 80–95.

Gabbey, Alan, "New Doctrines of Motion," in Daniel Garber and Michael Ayers (eds.), *The Cambridge History of Seventeenth-Century Philosophy*, Volume I (Cambridge: Cambridge University Press, 1998), 649–79.

Ganault, J., "Les Contraintes métaphysiques de la polémique d'Arnauld et de Malebranche," *Revue des sciences philosophique et théologiques* 42 (1992), 101–6.

Garber, Daniel, and Michael Ayers (eds.), *The Cambridge History of Seventeenth-Century Philosophy*, 2 volumes (Cambridge: Cambridge University Press, 1998).

Gaudemar, Martine de, "Malebranche et Leibniz," in Bruno Pinchard (ed.), *La légèreté de l'être: Études sur Malebranche* (Paris: J. Vrin, 1998).

Gaukroger, Stephen, *Descartes: An Intellectual Biography* (Oxford: Clarendon Press, 1995).

Geach, Peter, "Praying for Things to Happen," in *God and the Soul* (Bristol: Thoemmes Press, 1994).

Geach, Peter, "What Actually Exists," in *God and the Soul* (Bristol: Thoemmes Press, 1994).

Gerdil, Giacinto, *Defense du sentiment du P. Malebranche sur la nature, & l'origin des Idées, contre l'Examen de M. Locke* (Turin, 1748).

Getchev, G. S., "Some of Malebranche's reactions to Spinoza as revealed in his correspondence with Dortous de Mairan," *The Philosophical Review* 41 (1932), 385–94.

Geulincx, Arnold, *Arnoldi Geulincx Antverpiensis Opera Philosophica*, 2 volumes, J. P. N. Land (ed.) (The Hague, 1892).

Gibson, J., *Locke's Theory of Knowledge and its Historical Relation* (Cambridge: Cambridge University Press, 1917).

Girbal, François, "A propos de Malebranche et de Bernard Lamy," *Revue internationale de philosophie* 9 (1955), 288–90.

Glauser, R., "Arnauld critique de Malebranche: le statut des idées," *Revue de théologie et de philosophie* 38 (1988), 389–410.

Gouhier, Henri, *La Vocation de Malebranche* (Paris: J. Vrin, 1926).

Gouhier, Henri, "La première polemique de Malebranche," *Revue d'histoire de la philosophie* 1 (1927), 23–48, 168–91.

Gouhier, Henri, *La Pensée métaphysique de Descartes*, 4th ed. (Paris: J. Vrin, 1964).

Gouhier, Henri, *La Philosophie de Malebranche et son expérience religieuse*, 2nd ed. (Paris: J. Vrin, 1978).

Groethuysen, B., *Origines de l'esprit bourgeois en France* (Paris: Gallimard, 1927).

Gueroult, Martial, *Malebranche* (Paris: Aubier, 1955–59).

Gueroult, Martial, *Etendue et psychologie chez Malebranche*, 2nd ed. (Paris: J. Vrin, 1987).

Harrison, J., and Peter Laslett, *The Library of John Locke* (Oxford: Clarendon Press, 1971).

Hatfield, Gary, "Force (God) in Descartes's Physics," *Studies in the History and Philosophy of Science* 10 (1979), 113–40.

Hatfield, Gary, "The Cognitive Faculties," in Daniel Garber and Michael Ayers (eds.), *The Cambridge History of Seventeenth-Century Philosophy* (Cambridge: Cambridge University Press, 1998).

Hausman, David, and Alan Hausman, *Descartes's Legacy* (Toronto: University of Toronto Press, 1997).

Hintikka, Jaako, "A Discourse on Descartes's Method," in Michael Hooker (ed.), *Descartes: Critical and Interpretive Essays* (Baltimore: Johns Hopkins University Press, 1978).

Hobbes, Thomas, *Leviathan*, Michael Oakeshott (ed.) (Oxford: Basil Blackwell, 1946).

Hume, David, *Enquiries Concerning Human Understanding and Concerning the Principles of Morality*, L. A. Selby-Bigge and P. H. Nidditch (eds.) (Oxford: Clarendon Press, 1975).

Hume, David, *A Treatise of Human Nature*, L. A. Selby-Bigge and P. H. Nidditch (eds.) (Oxford: Clarendon Press, 1978).

Jacques, Emile, *Les Années d'exil d'Antoine Arnauld* (Louvain: Nauwelaerts, 1976).

Johnston, Charlotte, "Locke's Examination of Malebranche and John Norris," *Journal of the History of Ideas* 19 (1958), 553–4.

Jolley, Nicholas, *The Light of the Soul: Theories of Ideas in Leibniz, Malebranche and Descartes* (Oxford: Clarendon Press, 1990).

Jolley, Nicholas, "The Reception of Descartes' Philosophy," in John Cottingham (ed.), *The Cambridge Companion to Descartes* (Cambridge: Cambridge University Press, 1992).

Jolley, Nicholas, "Intellect and Illumination in Malebranche," *Journal of the History of Philosophy* 32 (1994), 209–24.

Jones, Howard, *Pierre Gassendi's "Institutio logica": 1658* (Assen: Van Gorcum, 1981).

Jurieu, Pierre, *L'Esprit de M. Arnauld* (Paris, 1687).

Kant, Immanuel, *Groundwork for the Metaphysics of Morals*, trans. T. K. Abbott (Indianapolis: Library of Liberal Arts, 1949).

Kremer, Elmar, "Arnauld's Philosophical Notion of an Idea," in E. Kremer (ed.), *The Great Arnauld and Some of his Philosophical Correspondents* (Toronto: University of Toronto Press, 1994).

Laird, John, *A Study in Realism* (Cambridge: Cambridge University Press, 1920).

Laird, John, "The Legend of Arnauld's Realism," *Mind* 33 (1924), 176–9.

Lantrua, Antonio, "Malebranche et il pensiero italiano dal Vico al Rosmini," in A. Gemelli (ed.), *Malebranche nel terzo centenario della nascita* (Milano: Vite e pensiero, 1938).

Laporte, Jean, *La Doctrine de la grace chez Arnauld* (Paris: Presses Universitaires de France, 1922).

Laporte, Jean, *La Doctrine de Port-Royal: Les vérités sur la grâce* (Paris: J. Vrin, 1923).

Laporte, Jean, "La liberté selon Malebranche," in Jean Laporte (ed.), *Études d'Histoire de la philosophie française au XVII^e siècle* (Paris: Vrin, 1951), 193–248.

Leibniz, G. W., *Opera Omnia*, 6 volumes, L. Dutens (ed.) (Geneva, 1768).

Leibniz, G. W., *Die Philosophischen Schriften von Gottfried Wilhelm Leibniz*, 7 volumes, C. I. Gerhardt (ed.) (Berlin: Weidmann, 1875–90).

Leibniz, G. W., *Sämtliche Schriften und Briefe* (Darmstadt and Leipzig: Deutsche Akademie der Wissenschaften, 1923– ).

Leibniz, G. W., *Textes inédits d'après les manuscrits de la Bibliothèque provinciale de Hanovre*, G. Grua (ed.) (Paris, 1948).

Leibniz, G. W., *Leibniz Selections*, P. P. Wiener (ed.) (New York: Charles Scribner's Sons, 1951).

Leibniz, G. W., *Theodicy*, trans. J. Huggard (New Haven: Yale University Press, 1952).

Leibniz, G. W., *Philosophical Papers and Letters*, 2nd ed., ed. and trans. L. Loemker (Dordrecht: Reidel, 1969).

Leibniz, G. W., *Political Writings*, trans. Patrick Riley (Cambridge: Cambridge University Press, 1972).

Leibniz, G. W., *G. W. Leibniz: Discourse on Metaphysics and Related Writings*, ed. and trans. R. Niall, D. Martin, and Stuart Brown (Manchester: Manchester University Press, 1988).

Leibniz, G. W., *Philosophical Essays*, Roger Ariew and Daniel Garber (eds.) (Indianapolis & Cambridge: Hackett, 1989).

Leibniz, G. W., *Leibniz's 'New System' and Associated Contemporary Texts*, R. S. Woolhouse and Richard Francks (eds.) (Oxford: Clarendon Press, 1997).

Leibniz, G. W., *Monadology*, R. Latta (ed.) (Oxford: Oxford University Press, 1998).

Lennon, Thomas, "Philosophical Commentary," in LO (1980).

Lennon, Thomas, *The Battle of the Gods and Giants: The Legacies of Descartes and Gassendi, 1655–1715* (Princeton: Princeton University Press, 1993).

Lennon, Thomas, "Pandora; or, Essence and Reference: Gassendi's Nominalist Objection and Descartes's Realist Reply," in Roger Ariew and Marjorie Grene (eds.), *Descartes and His Contemporaries* (Chicago: University of Chicago Press, 1995).

Locke, John, "An Examination of P. Malebranche's Opinion of Our Seeing All Things in God," in P. King (ed.), *Posthumous Works of Mr John Locke* (London, 1706).

Locke, John, "Remarks on Some of Mr. Norris's Books wherein he asserts Père Malebranche's Opinion, of our Seeing All Things in God" (1694), in P. DesMaixeaux (ed.), *A Collection of Several Pieces of Mr. John Locke, never before published* (London, 1720).

Locke, John, *An Essay Concerning Human Understanding*, Peter H. Nidditch (ed.) (Oxford: Clarendon Press, 1975).

Locke, John, *The Correspondence of John Locke*, 9 volumes, E. S. de Beer (ed.) (Oxford: Clarendon Press, 1976– ).

Locke, John, *The Works of John Locke*, 10 volumes (London: Routledge/ Thoemes Press, 1997).

Lovejoy, A. O., "Representative Ideas in Malebranche and Arnauld," *Mind* 32 (1923), 449–61.

Lovejoy, A. O., "Reply to Professor Laird," *Mind* 33 (1924), 180–1.

Lovejoy, A. O., *The Great Chain of Being* (Cambridge, MA: Harvard University Press, 1936).

Luce, A. A., *Berkeley and Malebranche: A Study in the Origin of Berkeley's Thought* (London: Oxford University Press, 1934).

MacKenna, Antony, "Pascal et Epicure. L'intervention de Bayle dans la controverse entre Antoine Arnauld et le P. Malebranche," *XVIIe siècle*, (1982), 421–8.

Mairan, Dortous de, "Correspondance de Malebranche et de Mairan" (1713–14), V. Cousin (ed.), *Fragments de philosophie cartésienne* (Paris: Charpentier, 1845).

Malebranche, Nicolas, *Dialogues on Metaphysics*, trans. Morris Ginsberg (New York: Macmillan, 1923).

Malebranche, Nicolas, *Oeuvres complètes de Malebranche*, 20 volumes, dir. André Robinet (Paris: J. Vrin, 1958–67).

Malebranche, Nicolas, *Treatise on Nature and Grace*, trans. Patrick Riley (Oxford: Oxford University Press, 1992).

Malebranche, Nicolas, *Treatise on Ethics*, trans. Craig Walton (Dordrecht: Kluwer Academic Publishers, 1993).

Malebranche, Nicolas, *The Search After Truth*, trans. T. M. Lennon and P. J. Olscamp (Cambridge: Cambridge University Press, 1997a).

Malebranche, Nicolas, *Dialogues on Metaphysics and on Religion*, ed. N. Jolley, trans. D. Scott (Cambridge: Cambridge University Press, 1997b).

McCracken, Charles J., *Malebranche and British Philosophy* (Oxford: The Clarendon Press, 1983).

Montcheuil, Yves de, *Malebranche et le quiétisme* (Paris: Aubier, 1946).

Moreau, Denis, "Malebranche et le désordre et le mal physique. Et noluit consolari," in B. Pinchard (ed.), *La légèreté de l'être* (Paris: J. Vrin, 1998).

Moreau, Denis, *Deux cartésiens. La polémique entre Antoine Arnauld et Nicolas Malebranche* (Paris: J. Vrin, 1999).

Moreau, Joseph, "Malebranche et le spinozisme," in J. Moreau (ed.), *Correspondance avec J.-J. Dortuous de Mairan* (Paris: J. Vrin, 1947).

Mouy, Pierre, *Le Développement de la physique cartésienne: 1646–1712* (Paris: J. Vrin, 1934).

Nadler, Steven, "Reid, Arnauld and the Objects of Perception," *History of Philosophy Quarterly* 3 (1986), 165–74.

Nadler, Steven, *Arnauld and the Cartesian Philosophy of Ideas* (Princeton: Princeton University Press, 1989).

Nadler, Steven, "Malebranche and the Vision in God: A Note on *The Search After Truth* III.2.iii," *Journal of the History of Ideas* 52 (1991), 309–14.

Nadler, Steven, *Malebranche and Ideas* (New York: Oxford University Press, 1992).

Nadler, Steven (ed.), *Causation in Early Modern Philosophy* (University Park, Pennsylvania: The Pennsylvania State University Press, 1993a).

Nadler, Steven, "Occasionalism and General Will in Malebranche," *Journal of the History of Philosophy* 31 (1993b), 31–47.

Nadler, Steven, "Choosing a Theodicy: The Leibniz-Malebranche-Arnauld Connection," *Journal of the History of Ideas* 55 (1994), 573–89.

Nadler, Steven, "'No Necessary Connection': The Medieval Roots of the Occasionalist Roots of Hume," *The Monist* 79 (1996), 448–66.

Nadler, Steven, "Occasionalism and the Mind-Body Problem," in M. A. Stewart (ed.), *Studies in Seventeenth-Century European Philosophy* (Oxford: Clarendon Press, 1997).

Nadler, Steven, "Louis de la Forge and the Development of Occasionalism," *Journal of the History of Philosophy* 36 (1998), 215–31.

Nadler, Steven, "Connaissance et causalité chez Malebranche et Geulincx," *XVIIième Siècle* 203 (1999), 335–45.

Ndiaye, Aloise-Raymond, *La philosophie d'Antoine Arnauld* (Paris: J. Vrin, 1991).

Norris, John, *Reason and Religion: or the grounds and measures of devotion consider'd from the nature of God* (London, 1689).

Norris, John, *An Essay Towards the Theory of the Ideal or Intelligible World* (London, 1701–4).

Ollé-Laprune, L., *La Philosophie de Malebranche* (Paris: Ladrange, 1890).

Paquier, R., *Le Jansénisme* (Paris: J. Vrin, 1962).

Pascal, Blaise, *Oeuvres de Pascal*, 13 volumes (Paris: Les Grands Ecrivains, 1914).

Pinchard, Bruno, (ed.), *La légèreté de l'être: Études sur Malebranche* (Paris: J. Vrin, 1998).

Popkin, Richard H., *The History of Skepticism from Erasmus to Spinoza* (Berkeley: University of California Press, 1979).

Prost, J., *Essai sur l'atomisme et l'occasionalisme dans la philosophie Cartésienne* (Paris: Paulin, 1907).

Radner, Daisie, *Malebranche: A Study of a Cartesian System* (Assen: Van Gorcum, 1978).

Radner, Daisie, Review of LO, *International Studies in Philosophy* 14 (1982), 106–8.

Radner, Daisie, and Michael Radner, *Animal Consciousness* (Buffalo: Prometheus Books, 1989).

Régis, Pierre-Sylvain, *Cours entier de philosophie, ou système general selon les principes de M. Descartes*, 3 volumes (New York: Johnson Reprint, 1691/reprint 1970).

Reid, Thomas, *The Works of Thomas Reid*, 2 volumes W. Hamilton (ed.) (Edinburgh: Machlachlan and Stewart, 1863).

Riley, Patrick, *Kant's Political Philosophy* (Totowa, NJ: Rowman and Littlefield, 1983).

Riley, Patrick, *The General Will before Rousseau* (Princeton: Princeton University Press, 1986).

Riley, Patrick. *Leibniz' Universal Jurisprudence: Justice as the Charity of the Wise* (Cambridge: Harvard University Press, 1996).

Robinet, André, *Malebranche et Leibniz: Relations personnelles* (Paris: J. Vrin, 1955).

Robinet, André, *Système et Existence dans l'oeuvre de Malebranche* (Paris: J. Vrin, 1965).

Robinet, André, *Malebranche de l'Académie des Sciences: L'oeuvre scientifique, 1674–1715* (Paris: J. Vrin, 1970).

Robinet, André, "Aux sources jansénistes de la première oeuvre de Malebranche," *Les études philosophiques*, 29 (1974), 465–79.

Rodis-Lewis, Geneviève, *Nicholas Malebranche* (Paris: Presses Universitaires de France, 1963).

Rodis-Lewis, Geneviève, "La Connaissance par idée chez Malebranche," in G. Bastide (ed.), *Malebranche: L'Homme et l'oeuvre, 1638–1715* (Paris: J. Vrin, 1967).

Rousseau, Jean-Jacques, *Religious Writings*, R. Grimsley (ed.) (Oxford: Clarendon Press, 1970).

Rutherford, Donald, "Natures, Laws and Miracles: The Roots of Leibniz's Critique of Occasionalism," in S. Nadler (ed.), *Causation in Early Modern Philosophy* (University Park, PA: Penn State Press, 1993).

Rutherford, Donald, *Leibniz and the Rational Order of Nature* (New York: Cambridge University Press, 1995).

Sainte-Beuve, C.A., *Port-Royal*, 7 volumes, (Paris, La Connaissance, 1908).

Sault, Richard (trans.), *Malebranche's Search after Truth ... To which is added the Author's defence against the accusations of Monsieur de la Ville. Also the life of ... Malebranche ... with particulars of his controversies ... Arnauld ... and Regis. Written by ... Le Vasseur ...*, 2 volumes (London, 1694–5).

Schmaltz, Tad, "Malebranche's Cartesianism and Lockean Colors," *History of Philosophy Quarterly* 12 (1995), 387–403.

Schmaltz, Tad, *Malebranche's Theory of the Soul: A Cartesian Interpretation* (New York: Oxford University Press, 1996).

Schulthess, Daniel, "Antoine Arnauld et Thomas Reid, défenseurs des certitudes perceptives communes et critiques des entités représentatives," *Revue internationale de philosophie*, 158 (1986), 278–91.

Senofonte, C., *Ragione moderna e teologia. L'uomo di Arnauld* (Naples: Guida, 1989).

Shipton, James (trans.), *A Treatise of Morality ... written in French by F. Malebranch*, 2 volumes (London: J. Knapton, 1699).

Shklar, Judith N., "General Will," in P. Wiener (ed.), *Dictionary of the History of Ideas*, volume 2 (New York: Scribner's, 1973).

Sleigh, Jr., Robert C., *Leibniz and Arnauld: A Commentary on their Correspondence* (New Haven: Yale University Press, 1990).

Sleigh, Jr., Robert C., Vere Chappell, and Michael Della Rocca, "Determinism and Human Freedom," in Daniel Garber and Michael Ayers (eds.), *The Cambridge History of Seventeenth-Century Philosophy*, Volume 2 (Cambridge: Cambridge University Press, 1998), 1195–1278.

Solère, Jean-Luc, "Tout plaisir rend-il heureux? Une querelle entre Arnauld, Malebranche et Bayle," in *Antoine Arnauld (1612–94), Chroniques de Port-Royal*, No. 44 (Paris: Bibliothèque Mazarine, 1995), 351–79.

Sorrell, Tom, *The Rise of Modern Philosophy* (Oxford: Clarendon Press, 1993).

Spinoza, Baruch, *Tractatus Theologico-Politicus*, trans. Samuel Shirley (Leiden: Brill, 1991).

Suarez, Francisco, *Opera Omnia*, 28 volumes (Paris: Vives, 1856).

Taylor, Thomas, *Father Malebranch's treatise concerning the Search after Truth. The whole work compleat. To which is added the author's treatise of Nature and Grace ... together with his answer to the animadversions upon the first volume: his defence against the accusations of Mr De la Ville, etc., relating to the same subject*, 2 volumes (Oxford, 1694).

Taylor, Thomas, *Father Malebranche his treatise concerning the Search after Truth ... To which is added the author's treatise of Nature and Grace ... The second edition, corrected ... With the addition of a Short Discourse upon Light and Colours, etc.* (London: Bennet, Leigh and Midwinter, 1700).

Taylor, Thomas, *Two Covenants of God with Mankind ... in an Essay designed to shew the Use and Advantage of some of Mr. Malebranch's Principles in the Theories of Providence and Grace* (London, 1704).

Tertre, Rodolphe de, *Réfutation d'un nouveau système de métaphysique proposé par le Père Malebranche* (Paris, 1715).

Verga, L., *Il Pensiero filosofico e scientifico di Antoine Arnauld* (Milan: Catholic University of Milan Press, 1972).

Vienne, Jean Michel, "Malebranche and Locke: The Theory of Moral Choice, a Neglected Theme," in *Malebranche: His Philosophical Critics and Successors* Stuart Brown (ed.) (Assen: Van Gorcum, 1991).

Voltaire, François-Marie de, *Oeuvres de Voltaire*, 45 volumes (Garnier, 1908).

Wahl, R., "The Arnauld-Malebranche Controversy and Descartes's Ideas," *The Monist* 71 (1988), 560–72.

Walton, Craig, *De la recherche du Bien: A Study of Malebranche's Science of Ethics* (The Hague: Martinus Nijhoff, 1972).

Watson, Richard A., *The Downfall of Cartesianism: 1673–1712* (The Hague: Martinus Nijhoff, 1966).

Watson, Richard A., and Marjorie Grene (eds.), *Malebranche's First and Last Critics* (Carbondale and Edwardsville: Southern Illinois University Press, 1995).

Weir, W., "Der Okasionalismus des Johannes Clauberg und sein Verhaltnis zu Descartes, Geulincx, Malebranche," *Studia Cartesiana*, 2 (1981), 43–62.

Wilson, Catherine, "Leibnizian Optimism," *Journal of Philosophy* 80 (1983), 765–83.

Wilson, Catherine, *Leibniz's Metaphysics: A Historical and Comparative Study* (Manchester: Manchester University Press, 1989).

Wright, John, *The Skeptical Realism of David Hume* (Minneapolis: University of Minnesota Press, 1983).

Wright, John, "Hume's Criticism of Malebranche's Theory of Causation," in Stuart Brown (ed.), *Nicolas Malebranche: His Philosophical Critics and Successors* (Assen: Van Gorcum, 1991).

Yolton, John, *Perceptual Acquaintance from Descartes to Reid* (Oxford: Blackwell, 1984).

Yolton, John, *Locke and French Materialism* (Oxford: Clarendon Press, 1991).

Yolton, John, and Vladimir Price (eds.), *Dictionary of Eighteenth Century British Philosophers* (Bristol: Thoemmes, 1999).

# INDEX

Académie Royal des Sciences, 6, 25, 262, 289
al-Ghazali, Abu Hamid, 114
animal spirits, 122
André, Father Yves-Marie, 3, 21, 262
Aquinas, St. Thomas, 213
Aristotle, 25, 37, 276
Arnauld, Antoine, 5, 12–14, 19–20, 47–50, 51, 59, 61–4, 68–9, 73–6, 87–108, 166, 177, 219n34, 229, 233–5, 290–3, 296, 298
Augustine, 3, 4, 32, 64, 166, 222, 250, 266

Bacon, Francis, 11
Bayle, Pierre, 89, 91, 219n34, 271, 275
Berkeley, George, 27n18, 265, 276–8
Berrand, Pierre, 140
Bérulle, Cardinal, 3, 290
body
    as cause, 115–25
    essence of, 119
    idea of, 69, 72, 117
    knowledge of, 150–2, 275–8
    motion of, 115–33
    perception of, 70
Bossuet, Jacques Benigne, 89, 90, 228, 250, 272
Boursier, Laurent, 235, 236, 272

Carre, L., 25
Cartesianism, 3, 4, 288–9
causation, 112–36, 190, 211
certainty, 5, *see also* method
Christianity, 31, 159, 165–7, 169,

177–85, 193, 195, 198, 227, 228, 243–4, 246–8, 275, 276
Clauberg, Johannes, 113
Collège de la Marche, 3
Collier, Arthur, 276–8
Connell, Desmond, 70
Cordemoy, Géraud de, 113
creation, 126–9, 167–71

deism, 262, 272–4
Descartes, René, 10, 12, 15–19, 32–6, 37–42, 43–4, 56–7, 65–8, 72, 81, 142, 143–4
Desgabets, Dom Robert, 293
divine concurrence, 129, 212
Duns Scotus, Joannes, 104

Elizabeth, Palatine Princess, 262
error, 20–6, 117
evil, 117, 165, 171, 173–4, 220–1, 230–2, 271
extension
    idea of, 46–8, 54–7, 74, 76, 78, 120
    intelligible, 24, 69, 71, 74–7, 79, 150–2, 274–5
    essence of, 65–8

Fénelon, F., 89, 90, 235, 248
Fontenelle, Bernard Le Bovier de, 89, 90, 118, 262
force, 119
Foucher, Simon, 6, 275–6
Frankfurt, Harry, 190
freedom
    divine, 98, 102–4, 107, 167
    human, 15, 190–214, 249–56

318     INDEX